COMMENTARIES

ON THE

EPISTLES TO THE PHILIPPIANS, COLOSSIANS, AND THESSALONIANS:

WITH

FOUR HOMILIES OR SERMONS
ON IDOLATRY, &c.

AND AN

EXPOSITION OF PSALM LXXXVII.

THE CALVIN TRANSLATION SOCIETY,

INSTITUTED IN MAY M.DCCC.XLIII.

FOR THE PUBLICATION OF TRANSLATIONS OF THE WORKS OF
JOHN CALVIN.

Acting and Editorial Secretary, Robert Pitcairn, F.S.A. Scot.
Calvin Office, 9, Northumberland Street, Edinburgh.

ON

THE EPISTLES OF PAUL THE APOSTLE

TO

THE PHILIPPIANS, COLOSSIANS, AND THESSALONIANS.

BY JOHN CALVIN.

TRANSLATED AND EDITED FROM THE ORIGINAL LATIN, AND COLLATED WITH THE FRENCH VERSION,

BY THE REV. JOHN PRINGLE.

WIPF & STOCK · Eugene, Oregon

" VERE MAGNI ILLIUS ET NUNQUAM SATIS LAUDATAE MEMORIAE VIRI, D. JOANNIS CALVINI."—*Beza.*

" IT IS IMPOSSIBLE TO REFUSE HIM (CALVIN) THE PRAISE OF VAST KNOWLEDGE, EXQUISITE JUDGMENT, A PENETRATION WHICH IS UNCOMMON, A PRODIGIOUS MEMORY, AND ADMIRABLE TEMPERANCE AND SOBRIETY."—*Annotators on Spon's History of Geneva.*

Wipf and Stock Publishers
199 W 8th Ave, Suite 3
Eugene, OR 97401

Commentaries on the Epistles of Paul the Apostle
to the Philippians, Colossians, and Thessalonians
By Calvin, John
ISBN 13: 978-1-55635-313-0
ISBN 10: 1-55635-313-8
Publication date 2/28/2007
Previously published by Calvin Translation Society, 1851

" IN WHICH TWO THINGS, (THE INSTITUTES AND EXPOSITIONS,) WHOSOEVER THEY WERE THAT AFTER HIM (CALVIN) BESTOWED THEIR LABOUR, HE GAINED THE ADVANTAGE OF PREJUDICE AGAINST THEM IF THEY GAINSAYED, AND OF GLORY ABOVE THEM IF THEY CONSENTED."—*Hooker.*

TRANSLATOR'S PREFACE.

THE COMMENTARIES OF CALVIN on the EPISTLES OF PAUL are generally considered to be among the most successful of his Expositions of Scripture. In the writings, indeed, of one whose vast powers have been applied to the exposition of nearly the whole of the Inspired Volume, and whose rare endowments, as an interpreter of Scripture, have drawn forth expressions of the profoundest admiration even from the most inveterate adversaries of the system of doctrine maintained by him, there is room for some diversity of opinion as to the particular portions of Divine truth which he has most successfully expounded. It is mentioned by *M. Teissier*, in his extracts from *M. de Thou's* History,[1] that "although all the works of CALVIN have merited the esteem of persons of good taste, he has in the opinion of some succeeded best in unfolding the doctrine of Providence," while, according to *Joseph Scaliger*, who "reckoned CALVIN to have had a divine genius, and to have excelled in the explication of Scripture, so that no one among the ancients could be compared" to him, "the best of his theological treatises was his Commentary on DANIEL."

While, however, there may be some difference of opinion among the many admirers of CALVIN as to the particular portion of his expository writings, in which his vast powers shine forth to most advantage, there can be no question that his expositions of the Epistles of PAUL are singularly felici-

---

[1] "*Les Eloges des Hommes Savans.*"—Tom. i. p. 240.

mentaries on the New Testament, " those on the Epistles of PAUL are by far the best," and that " in the Pauline Epistles, he merges himself in the spirit of the Apostle, and becoming one with him, as every one clearly feels, he deduces everywhere the explanation of that which is particular from that which is general."[1] A similar view of the peculiar excellence of CALVIN'S expositions of the Epistles of PAUL is given by *Böhmer*, of Berlin, in his introduction to the Epistle to the Colossians, (as quoted by the late *Dr. Pye Smith*, in his encomium on the writings of CALVIN.) "JOHN CALVIN well merited the epithet, often given to him, of THE GREAT DIVINE. Independent, in the highest degree, of other men, he most often discerns, with piercing eye, the spiritual mind of PAUL, and with his masterly command of language, makes it so clear, that both the most learned student of theology, and the plain affectionate believer, are equally benefited and satisfied."[2]

That the Expository Treatises of CALVIN on PAUL'S Epistles should be considered by the most eminent critics to be peculiarly successful is the more remarkable, when we take into view the disadvantageous circumstances under which most, if not all, of them were prepared. His Commentaries on six of PAUL'S Epistles were written by him (as we are informed by *Beza*, in his Life of CALVIN[3]) in 1548, a year of most harassing conflict with the enemies of the truth. His Correspondence, however, at this period, clearly shews that his devout mind found tranquillity in an assurance of Divine support. In writing to *Brentius*, who was then living in exile at Basle, he says: " Amidst all these calamities one consideration supports and refreshes my mind: I assure myself that God, in commencing the wonderful restoration of his Church, which we have witnessed, has not held out a vain and transient hope to us, but has begun a work that he will not fail to accomplish in spite of the malice of men and the opposition of Satan. In the meantime let us patiently un-

[1] " Merits of CALVIN," pp. 6, 31.   [2] *Ibid.*, pp. 65, 66.
[3] CALVIN'S Tracts, vol. i. p. liii.

Commentaries on four of Paul's Epistles, addressed to Christopher, Duke of Wirtemberg, that he had found the Epistles of Paul peculiarly consoling to his mind amidst outward troubles. Calvin is thought, indeed, to have had a marked resemblance in disposition and character to the great Apostle of the Gentiles, so that he has been termed by an eloquent writer,[2] "the Paul of the Reformation,"—a circumstance which is thought to have contributed to render him more successful in the exposition of Paul's Epistles, while, as is justly observed by the Translator of Calvin on Galatians and Ephesians in the *Biblical Cabinet*, (vol. xxx.) "the chief cause unquestionably lay in his singularly clear perception of that system of doctrine which Paul was honoured to declare."

THE EPISTLE TO THE PHILIPPIANS stands associated with a most interesting event in the history of the progress of Christianity. While the charge given to the Apostles as to the universal promulgation of the Gospel was most explicit, it was in a gradual manner, and for the most part under the guidance of circumstances seemingly fortuitous, that their sphere of labour was extended. "Beginning at Jerusalem," (Luke xxiv. 47,) as expressly instructed by their Master, they would, to all appearance, have continued to pursue their labours in and around that city, had not occurrences taken place from time to time, and these, too, of an untoward nature, considered in themselves, which led them to extend the benefits of the Gospel to countries more and more remote from their original sphere of labour.

Philippi was the first place in Europe in which the Gospel of Christ was proclaimed, and it is sufficiently manifest from Luke's narrative, that the introduction of the Gospel at that time into Europe was not the result of any preconcerted plan on the part of the Apostles themselves. Had they been left

---

[1] "Calvin and the Swiss Reformation," p. 350.
[2] Dr. Mason of New York.

Asia Minor; but, instead of this, they were specially directed by the Spirit of God to "come over into Macedonia," (Acts xvi. 9,) by which means the Gospel was for the first time introduced into Europe. And when we consider the important place which Europe has held during so many ages in connection with the progress of Christianity, and more especially the high honour assigned to European Christians, as being chiefly instrumental in its diffusion throughout the world, we cannot fail to mark with deep interest the circumstances connected with the first preaching of the Gospel at Philippi. "The little rill," says *Foster*, "near the source of one of the great American rivers, is an interesting object to the traveller, who is apprized, as he steps across it, or walks a few miles along its bank, that this is the stream which runs so far, and which gradually swells into so immense a flood."[1] For a similar reason, the preaching of the Gospel by PAUL in the hearing of a few women by a river's side near Philippi, trivial as the circumstance may appear in itself, becomes invested with the deepest interest, when viewed in connection with the state and prospects of Christianity at the present day.

While LUKE makes mention only of two individuals—Lydia and the Jailer—with their respective households, as the fruits of the first preaching of the Gospel at Philippi, it clearly appears, from the Epistle to the Philippians, that from these small beginnings a flourishing Christian Church had sprung up, which, at the time when the Epistle was written, was in so prosperous a state, that the Apostle, who reproves so sharply the Churches of CORINTH and GALATIA, finds no occasion for censuring the PHILIPPIANS, but commends in the highest terms their exemplary deportment.

Philippi was originally called *Crenides*, from the numerous *fountains* of water in its neighbourhood, and afterwards *Dathos*, or *Datos*, from its gold and silver mines. The city received the name of Philippi from Philip, father of Alex-

---

[1] Foster's Essays, (Lond. 1819,) p. 5.

CALVIN in the Argument on the Epistle to the Philippians, for a signal victory which was gained by Octavius, afterwards Augustus Cæsar, and Antony over Brutus and Cassius; and it is not a little remarkable, that a city which was the scene of a victory that decided the fate of the Roman Empire, should have been afterwards illustrious as the scene of a nobler victory, intimately connected with the signal triumph of the Gospel in Europe.

The Epistle bears evidence of having been written by PAUL when a prisoner for the sake of Christ; and there seems every reason to believe that it was written by him during his first imprisonment at Rome. *Dr. Paley,* in his Horæ Paulinæ, adduces a variety of arguments, founded on incidental notices in the Epistle itself, to prove that it was written " near the conclusion of St. PAUL's imprisonment at Rome, and after a residence in that city of considerable duration." It is generally believed to have been written about A.D. 62. The Epistle " breathes," says *Barnes,* " the spirit of a ripe Christian, whose piety was mellowing for the harvest; of one who felt that he was not far from heaven, and might soon be with Christ. . . . At the mercy of such a man as Nero; a prisoner; among strangers, and with death staring him in the face, it is natural to suppose that there would be a peculiar solemnity, tenderness, pathos, and ardour of affection breathing through the entire Epistle. Such is the fact; and in none of the writings of Paul are these qualities more apparent than in this letter to the Philippians."

THE EPISTLE TO THE COLOSSIANS is generally supposed to have been written by PAUL about A.D. 62, in the ninth year of the reign of the Emperor NERO. It bears evidence of having been written during PAUL's first imprisonment at Rome. The Apostle, in the course of the Epistle, makes repeated allusions to the circumstance of his being at the time in "bonds" (Col. iv. 18) for the sake of Christ. COLOSSE

ing city in the south of Phrygia, situated most picturesquely under the immense range of Mount Cadmus, and near the confluence of the rivers Lycus and Meander; but, about a year after PAUL'S Epistle was written, was, along with the neighbouring cities of Laodicea and Hierapolis, destroyed by an earthquake, as is noticed by CALVIN in the Argument of the Epistle. The site of the ancient city, the only remaining vestiges of which consist of arches, vaults, squared stones, and broken pottery, is now occupied by the village of Khonas, in which, as stated by the General Assembly's Deputation to Palestine in 1839, " a band of about thirty Greek Christians are found."[1]

It has been matter of controversy by whom the CHURCH OF COLOSSE was planted. *Dr. Lardner* adduces a variety of considerations tending to shew that it was founded by PAUL, chiefly the following:—That as PAUL was twice in Phrygia, as stated by LUKE, (Acts xvi. 6, and xviii. 23,) it is extremely probable, that on one or other of those occasions he was at Colosse, and planted a Church there; that he expresses himself toward the close of the first chapter in such terms as seem to imply that he had himself dispensed the Gospel to the Colossians, and that the general tenor of the Epistle seems to indicate that he is not writing to strangers, but to persons with whom he had been personally conversant, and to whom he had been, under God, the instrument of conversion. On the other hand, many distinguished commentators are of opinion that the Church of Colosse was not founded by PAUL. CALVIN, in the Argument of the Epistle, speaks of the Colossians as having been instructed in the Gospel, *not* by PAUL, but by EPAPHRAS and other Ministers. *Hug* and *Koppe* are decidedly of opinion that PAUL did not plant the Church of Colosse, and had no personal acquaintance with the Christians there. *Davenant* is of opinion that the Church of Colosse was planted by EPAPHRAS. *Byfield*, in his Exposition of the Colossians, thinks it probable that the

[1] " Narrative of a Mission of Inquiry to the Jews," p. 339.

argument from whence it can certainly be inferred that he" (PAUL) " was personally acquainted with the Colossians." *Scott*, in his Preface to the Epistle, gives it as his " decided *opinion*, that the evidence against the Apostle's having been at Colosse is far stronger than any that has been adduced on the affirmative side of the question." In short, there is no inconsiderable force in the arguments adduced on both sides, and "uncertainty still lies on the dispute whether PAUL was ever at Colosse."[1]

While, however, there is so much uncertainty as to the person by whom the Church of Colosse was planted, that uncertainty, it is to be noticed, does not by any means arise from any indication of comparative indifference on the part of the Apostle PAUL to the welfare of the Colossian converts in the Epistle which he addresses to them. While a prisoner at Rome for the sake of the Gospel, he had heard with deep concern of the insidious attempts which had been made by certain false teachers to draw off the Colossian Christians from the doctrine in which they had been instructed. It is not certain what were the precise tenets, that were attempted to be disseminated among them. There seems to have been a strange blending of the doctrines of the Essenes with the subtleties of Platonism, and the asceticism of Oriental Philosophy.

The general scope of the Epistle is briefly stated by *Davenant* as follows—that the hope of man's salvation is placed entirely in Christ alone, and that consequently we must rest satisfied with faith in Christ, and live according to the rule laid down in the Gospel, to the rejection of Mosaic ceremonies and philosophical speculations. The attentive reader of the New Testament cannot fail to observe a striking similarity between the Epistle to the Colossians and that addressed to the Ephesians, not merely in their general structure, but also in the subjects treated of, and even in the order and connection in which they are introduced—a closeness of

---

[1] *Eadie's* Biblical Cyclopædia, Art. *Colossians*.

same time, but also that the Churches to whom they were addressed, were in many respects similarly situated.

Among the expository treatises on the Epistle to the Colossians, there is, apart from that of CALVIN, no one that better deserves, or will more amply repay attentive perusal, than that of *Bishop Davenant*, as a sound, judicious, and eminently practical exposition of a portion of the New Testament, in which the distinctive doctrines and principles of Christianity are so largely brought into view. It deserves also to be mentioned in connection with this, that *Mr. Howe*, in his funeral sermon on the death of his intimate friend, the Rev. Richard Adams of Oxford, afterwards of London, speaks with high commendation of his "judicious and dilucid expositions of the Epistles to the Philippians and the Colossians—which was the part he bore in the supplement to that useful work—the English Annotations on the Bible, by the Rev. Mr. Matthew Pool."[1]

THE FIRST EPISTLE TO THE THESSALONIANS is generally believed to have been the first Epistle written by PAUL to any of the Churches of Christ. It appears to have been written towards the close of A.D. 52, about two years subsequently to the introduction of the Gospel into Thessalonica by the instrumentality of PAUL and SILAS. THESSALONICA was a large and populous city, situated on the Thermean Bay. The city was originally called Thermæ, but came to receive the name of Thessalonica from Philip, King of Macedon, by whom it was rebuilt and enlarged, in memory of the *victory* which he there gained over the *Thessalians*. Its present name is Saloniki—manifestly a corruption of Thessalonica. It contains a population of 70,000, and is a city of great commercial importance.

In the account which LUKE gives of the introduction of the Gospel into Thessalonica, mention is made of PAUL'S

---

[1] *Howe's* Works, (Lond. 1822,) vol. iii. p. 435.

This was the means of converting to the Christian faith some of his Jewish hearers; but, as is manifest from PAUL's First Epistle to the Thessalonians, the converts gained were chiefly from among the idolatrous Gentiles. Thessalonica "adored many gods, but principally Jupiter, as the father of Hercules, the alleged founder of its ancient royal family."[1] A violent tumult which had been raised against PAUL and SILAS by the unbelieving Jews constrained them to quit THESSALONICA on a sudden, and escape to Berea, and afterwards to Athens; and the abrupt manner in which the Apostle's labours at Thessalonica were broken off, seems to have led him to feel the more solicitous as to the prosperity of the Gospel in that city, and to have given occasion for the Church of the Thessalonians being favoured to receive the earliest of PAUL's Epistles.

The First Epistle to the Thessalonians concludes with a special direction that we do not find to be given in connection with any other of PAUL's Epistles: "I charge you by the Lord, that this Epistle be read unto all the holy brethren." (1 Thess. v. 27.) The strict charge thus given as to the public reading of the Epistle is justly adduced by *Paley*, in his Horæ Paulinæ, as a most convincing evidence of the authenticity of the Epistle. "Either the Epistle was publicly read in the Church of Thessalonica during St. PAUL's lifetime, or it was not. If it was, no publication could be more authentic, no species of notoriety more unquestionable, no method of preserving the integrity of the copy more secure. If it was not, the clause we produce would remain a standing condemnation of the forgery, and, one would suppose, an invincible impediment to its success."

It is an interesting circumstance, that the first Epistle written by PAUL to any Christian Church affords a most pleasing view of the fruits of the Gospel among the Christians to whom it is addressed; while it presents a most attractive picture of zeal and devotedness on the part of the

---

[1] *Illustrated Commentary*, vol. v. p. 297.

study the second chapter of this Epistle" (1st Thessalonians); "and if I wished to see a pattern of a Christian people, I know not where I could look better than to the Church of the Thessalonians."[1] The general design of the Epistle is to express the high satisfaction afforded to the mind of the writer by the favourable accounts which had been brought him by Timothy respecting the Christians at Thessalonica, as well as to encourage them to stedfast adherence to the truth amidst more than ordinary temptations to apostasy. " Imagine," says *Benson*, in his Preface to the Epistle, "the GREAT APOSTLE OF THE GENTILES to be full of a just resentment and generous indignation against his countrymen, the unbelieving Jews, who had lately treated him and them so maliciously; and at the same time having the most tender and parental care and affection for the young converts at Thessalonica, and you will have the very posture of his mind during the writing of this Epistle, for these two things appear everywhere throughout the Epistle."

THE SECOND EPISTLE TO THE THESSALONIANS appears to have been written a short time after PAUL's former Epistle to that Church. The Apostle had learned, that some expressions in his former Epistle in reference to the hopes of Christians beyond the grave had been misapprehended by the Thessalonian converts, as though he had intended to intimate that Christ's second advent was near at hand. In correcting this mistaken idea, he takes occasion to predict a great apostasy that was to overspread to a large extent the Christian Church, and when we consider how directly opposed "THE MYSTERY OF INIQUITY" (2 Thess. ii. 7) here predicted is to the nature of Christianity, and how unlikely the breaking out of such a system of error must have appeared at the time when the prediction was given forth, this portion of the Apostolical Writings must be regarded as affording un-

---

[1] *Fuller's* Works, vol. iv. p. 513.

of his Epistles, and when writing to a Church that was in a most flourishing condition, foretells with the utmost distinctness and minuteness, the rise and progress of a system of delusive error, which was not to be fully developed until several centuries subsequently to the time when the prediction was committed to writing; while it manifests itself even at the present day so strikingly in accordance with PAUL's prediction, that no historian of recent times could have furnished a more accurate delineation of the appalling system in all its leading features, than was thus presented to the mind of PAUL eighteen hundred years ago by the Spirit of Inspiration. Thus the Second Epistle to the Thessalonians, while it is the shortest of PAUL's Epistles to the Churches, is invested with more than ordinary interest, as predicting the rise, progress, and final destinies of the Papal system.

" The Epistle naturally divides itself," as is remarked by *Dr. Adam Clarke*, " into three parts, and each is contained in a separate chapter:

" PART I., CHAP. I., contains the Address, and Motives of Consolation in their afflicted and persecuted state.

" PART II., CHAP. II., is partly Prophetical, and partly Didactic. It contains the doctrine concerning Christ's Coming to Judgment, and a Prophecy concerning some future but great Apostasy from the Christian Faith.

" PART III., CHAP. III., is wholly Hortatory, and contains a number of important Advices relative to Christian Virtues and a proper behaviour in those situations in life in which it had pleased God to call them."

The Reader will find prefixed to the present translation of CALVIN's Commentary on the COLOSSIANS, a copy of the Translator's "Epistle Dedicatorie" to the old English translation of Calvin's Commentary on that Epistle, published in black letter in 1581. The Translator, who gives merely his initials, (R. V.,) appears to have been Robert Vahne, or

follows:—"A Commentarie of M. Iohn Caluine, vpon the Epistle to the Colossians. And translated into English by R. V.

> Pray for the peace of Hierusalem, they shall prosper that loue thee. Psal. 121. 6.

AT LONDON, Printed by Thomas Purfoote, and are to be sold at his shop ouer against S. Sepulchers Church."

He is also the author of "A Dialogue defensyue for women agaynst malicyous detractoures," published in 1542; and of a translation published in 1582, of "Examination of the Councell of Trent, touching the Decree of Traditions, by Mart. Kemnicious."

It will be observed, that there is no separate Dedication by CALVIN of his Commentaries on the PHILIPPIANS and COLOSSIANS—his Commentaries on these Epistles having been dedicated by him, along with those on GALATIANS and EPHESIANS, to CHRISTOPHER, Duke of Wirtemberg. The Dedication will be inserted in a future volume of THE CALVIN TRANSLATIONS, which will contain the Translation of the Commentaries on GALATIANS and EPHESIANS.

MATURINUS CORDERIUS, (*Mathurin Cordier,*) to whom CALVIN dedicates his Commentary on the First Epistle to the THESSALONIANS, was, as stated by *Beza*, in his Life of Calvin,[1] "a man of great worth and erudition, and in the highest repute in almost all the schools of France as a teacher of youth." He taught at Paris, Nevers, Bordeaux, Neufchatel, Lausanne, and Geneva. He was the author of the "Colloquies," so much used in the education of youth throughout Europe. CALVIN was his pupil at the *College de la Marche*. He died at Geneva, where he taught till within a few days of his death, in 1564, at the age of eighty-five.

BENEDICT TEXTOR, to whom CALVIN dedicates his Commentary on the *Second* Epistle to the THESSALONIANS, appears to have been the son or nephew of Jean Tixier de Ravisi, or Ravisius Textor (Lord of Ravisi,) who was Rector of the

---

[1] CALVIN's Tracts, vol. i. p. xxi.

extant containing "Epistles" (to the number of 149,) which appears to have been written by a relative of Benedict Textor. It bears date 1602, and is entitled " Epistolæ Joannis Ravisii Textoris (Nivernensis)—non vulgaris eruditionis."

While THE COMMENTARIES OF CALVIN everywhere abound with important statements in reference to POPERY, so that the reader will find able and successful refutations of the errors of that corrupt and delusive system brought forward in connection with the interpretation of passages of the Word of God, which might have seemed to have no particular bearing on the Papal system, and introduced by him for the most part with less abruptness than is to be observed in the writings of some of his contemporaries, the present Volume of his Commentaries is rendered the more interesting, and will, we trust, under the Divine blessing, be productive of the greater utility, in the present eventful times, from its containing CALVIN'S exposition of a portion of THE NEW TESTAMENT that presents the minutest and most comprehensive view that is to be found in any part of the Sacred Writings, of the rise, progress, and ultimate overthrow of Antichrist.

J. P.

ELGIN, *March* 1851.

TO THE WORSHIPFVL
and reuerende fathers maister Noel,
Deane of Poules, M. Mullins Archdeacon of London, maister D. Walker, Archdeacon of Essex, & maister Towers professor of diuinity, his singuler good frlendes and Patrons, R. V. wisheth all health.

Many in the dedications of their trauails are accustomed to set forth the praises of such persons as they do dedicate the same vnto. And surely I thinke it not amisse if flattery be absent. For who is ignorant that virtus laudata crescit, *praise virtue, and it shall encrease. I speake not this, right worshipful and reuerende fathers, to the ende that I meane to do the like to you, although no man that knoweth you but he will say you worthelye deserue the same: for if I shoulde either praise your learning or diligence in your vocation which euery where is knowen, or your godly conuersation which vnto your nighest frendes is well tried, or your liberality which all those that haue neede, but spetially the Godly poore haue found and daily do fynde, who might iustly reprehend me: but letting passe these things to the consideration of vpright iudges, I purpose to shew and that very brieflye what hath moued me to dedicate this present booke vnto your worshippes. You knowe that I receaued at your handes (that worthye man maister D. Watts beynge then aliue, whom with reuerence I remember) that liuinge which I haue: and althoughe you sell not your benefices (as manye in these dayes do) yet reason woulde that I should not remaine vnthankefull for the same, though it were a greate deale lesse then it is. And wheras want of abilitye vvould not suffer me to recompence othervvyse your good will, yet rather then still I should continue vnthankeful, I chose this litle commentary of that worthye father M. Caluine to supply that which els might be left vndon: vvherin I vvish that my hart lay open to be vievved: then vvould you not more regard the thinge it selfe, vvhich no doubt is vvorthy the accepting, then the good vvil of him that presenteth the same vnto you. Fare you vvel. At high Easter the first of Nouember.*

Yours to commaund
R. V.

COMMENTARY

ON

THE EPISTLE TO THE PHILIPPIANS.

THE ARGUMENT

ON

THE EPISTLE OF PAUL TO THE PHILIPPIANS.

It is generally known that PHILIPPI was a city of Macedonia, situated on the confines of Thrace, on the plains of which *Pompey* was conquered by *Cesar;*[1] and *Brutus* and *Cassius* were afterwards conquered by *Antony* and *Octavius.*[2] Thus Roman insurrections rendered this place illustrious by two memorable engagements. When PAUL was called into Macedonia by an express revelation,[3] he first founded a Church in that city, (as is related by LUKE in Acts xvi. 12,) which did not merely persevere steadfastly in the faith, but was also, in process of time, as this Epistle bears evidence, enlarged both in the number of individuals, and in their proficiency in respect of attainments.

The occasion of PAUL'S writing to the PHILIPPIANS was this,—As they had sent to him by EPAPHRODITUS, their pastor, such things as were needed by him when in prison, for sustaining life, and for other more than ordinary expenses, there can be no doubt that EPAPHRODITUS explained to him at the same time the entire con-

---

[1] Cesar's celebrated victory over Pompey took place on the plains of Pharsalia, in Thessaly, with which Philippi in Macedonia is sometimes confounded by the poets. (See Virg. G. I. 490, Juvenal, viii. 242.) Their being sometimes confounded with each other appears to have arisen from the circumstance that there was near Pharsalos, in Thessaly, a town named Philippi, the original name of which was Thebae, distinguished from Thebae in Bœotia by its being called Thebae *Thessaliae,* or *Phthioticae,* but having fallen under the power of Philip, King of Macedon, was in honour of the conqueror called *Philippi,* or *Philippopolis.—Ed.*

[2] The decisive engagement referred to was, as Dio Cassius observes, the most important of all that were fought during the civil wars, as it determined the fate of Roman liberty, so that the contest thenceforward was not for freedom, but—what master the Romans should serve. From its having been fought on the plains of Philippi, it is called by Suetonius *Philippense bellum,* (*the battle of Philippi,*) Suet. Aug. 13; and by Pliny, *Philippense praelium,* (*the engagement at Philippi.*)—*Ed*

[3] " Vne vision enuoyee de Dieu;"—" A vision sent from God."

appears, however, that attempts had been made upon them by false apostles,[1] who wandered hither and thither, with the view of spreading corruptions of sound doctrine; but as they had remained steadfast in the truth, the Apostle commends their steadfastness. Keeping, however, in mind human frailty, and having, perhaps, been instructed by EPAPHRODITUS that they required to be seasonably confirmed, lest they should in process of time fall away, he subjoins such admonitions as he knew to be suitable to them.

And having, first of all, with the view of securing their confidence, declared the pious attachment of his mind towards them, he proceeds to treat of himself and of his bonds, lest they should feel dismayed on seeing him a prisoner, and in danger of his life. He shews them, accordingly, that the glory of the gospel is so far from being lessened by this means, that it is rather an argument in confirmation of its truth, and he at the same time stirs them up by his own example to be prepared for every event.[2] He at length concludes the *First Chapter* with a short exhortation to unity and patience.

As, however, ambition is almost invariably the mother of dissensions, and comes, on this account, to open a door for new and strange doctrines, he, in the commencement of the *Second Chapter*, entreats them, with great earnestness, to hold nothing more highly in esteem than humility and modesty. With this view he makes use of various arguments. And that he may the better retain them,[3] he promises to send Timothy to them shortly, nay more, he expresses a hope of being able to visit them himself. He afterwards assigns a reason for delay on the part of EPAPHRODITUS.[4]

In the *Third Chapter* he inveighs against the false apostles, and sets aside both their empty boastings and the doctrine of circumcision, which they eagerly maintained.[5] To all their contrivances

---

[1] " Auoyent essayer les esbranler ;"—" Had attempted to shake them."

[2] " De s'apprestre a tout ce qu'il plaira a Dieu leur enuoyer ;"—" To be prepared for everything that it shall please God to send upon them."

[3] " Et pour leur donner courage, afin qu'ils ne se laissent cependant abuser ;"—" And with the view of encouraging them, that they may not allow themselves in the meantime to go astray."

[4] " Il excuse Epaphrodite de ce qu'il auoit tant demeuré sans retourner vers eux ;"—" He excuses Epaphroditus for having remained so long, instead of returning to them."

[5] " Pour laquelle ils debatoyent, voulans qu'elle fust obseruee ;"—" For which they contended, being desirous that it should be observed."

true image of Christian piety shone forth. He shews, also, that the summit of perfection, at which we must aim during our whole life, is this—to have fellowship with Christ in his death and resurrection; and this he establishes by his own example.

He begins the *Fourth Chapter* with particular admonitions, but proceeds afterwards to those of a general nature. He concludes the Epistle with a declaration of his gratitude to the PHILIPPIANS, that they may not think that what they had laid out for relieving his necessities had been ill bestowed.

COMMENTARY

ON

THE EPISTLE OF PAUL TO THE PHILIPPIANS.

CHAPTER I.

1. Paul and Timotheus, the servants of Jesus Christ, to all the saints in Christ Jesus which are at Philippi, with the bishops and deacons:

2. Grace *be* unto you, and peace, from God our Father, and *from* the Lord Jesus Christ.

3. I thank my God upon every remembrance of you,

4. Always in every prayer of mine for you all, making request with joy,

5. For your fellowship in the gospel from the first day until now;

6. Being confident of this very thing, that he which hath begun a good work in you, will perform *it* until the day of Jesus Christ.

1. Paulus et Timotheus, servi Iesu Christi, omnibus sanctis in Christo Iesu, qui sunt Philippis, cum Episcopis et Diaconis:

2. Gratia vobis et pax a Deo Patre nostro, et Domino Iesu Christo.

3. Gratias ago Deo meo in omni memoria vestri.[2]

4. Semper in omni precatione mea pro vobis omnibus cum gaudio precationem faciens,

5. Super communicatione vestra in Evangelium, a primo die hucusque;

6. Hoc ipsum persuasus, quod qui cœpit in vobis opus bonum, perficiet usque in diem Iesu Christi.

[1] " Arrogance et vanterie ;"—" Arrogance and boasting."

[2] " Toutes les fois que i'ay souuenance de vous, *ou*, auec entiere souuenance de vous ;"—" Every time that I have remembrance of you, *or*, with constant remembrance of you."

employ titles of distinction, with the view of procuring credit for himself and his ministry, there was no need of lengthened commendations in writing to the Philippians, who had known him by experience as a true Apostle of Christ, and still acknowledged him as such beyond all controversy. For they had persevered in the calling of God steadfastly, and in an even tenor.[1]

Bishops. He names the *pastors* separately, for the sake of honour. We may, however, infer from this, that the name of *bishop* is common to all the ministers of the Word, inasmuch as he assigns several *bishops* to one Church. The titles, therefore, of *bishop* and *pastor*, are synonymous. And this is one of the passages which Jerome quotes for proving this in his epistle to Evagrius,[2] and in his exposition of the Epistle to Titus.[3] Afterwards[4] there crept in the custom of applying the name of *bishop* exclusively to the person whom the presbyters in each church appointed over their company.[5] It originated, however, in a human custom, and rests on no Scripture authority. I acknowledge, indeed, that, as the minds and manners of men are, there cannot be order maintained among the ministers of the word, without one presiding over the others. I speak of particular bodies,[6] not of whole provinces, much less of the whole world. Now, although we must not contend for words, it were at the same time better for us in speaking to follow the Holy Spirit, the author of tongues, than to change for the worse forms of speech which are dictated to us by Him. For from the corrupted

---

[1] " Sans se desbaucher;"—" Without corrupting themselves."

[2] " *Evagrius*, a native of Antioch, and a presbyter apparently of the Church of Antioch. He travelled into the west of Europe, and was acquainted with Jerome, who describes him as a man *acris ac ferventis ingenii, (of a keen and warm temper.)*"—*Smith's* Dictionary of Greek Biography and Mythology.—*Ed.*

[3] The reader will find both of the passages referred to quoted at full length in the *Institutes*, vol. iii. pp. 75, 76.—*Ed.*

[4] " Depuis les temps de l'Apostre;"—" After the times of the Apostle."

[5] " Ordonnoyent conducteur de leur congregation;"—" Appointed leader of their congregation."

[6] " De chacun corps d'Eglise en particulier;"—" Of each body of the Church in particular."

one of them, under the pretext of a new appellation, usurped dominion over the others.

Deacons. This term may be taken in two ways—either as meaning administrators, and curators of the poor, or for elders, who were appointed for the regulation of morals. As, however, it is more generally made use of by Paul in the former sense, I understand it rather as meaning stewards, who superintended the distributing and receiving of alms. On the other points consult the preceding commentaries.

3. *I give thanks.* He begins with thanksgiving[2] on two accounts—*first,* that he may by this token shew his love to the Philippians; and secondly, that, by commending them as to the past, he may exhort them, also, to perseverance in time to come. He adduces, also, another evidence of his love—the anxiety which he exercised in supplications. It is to be observed, however, that, whenever he makes mention of things that are joyful, he immediately breaks forth into thanksgiving—a practice with which we ought also to be familiar. We must, also, take notice, what things they are for which he gives thanks to God,—the fellowship of the Philippians in the gospel of Christ; for it follows from this, that it ought to be ascribed to the grace of God. When he says, *upon every remembrance of you,* he means, " As often as I remember you."

4. *Always in every prayer.* Connect the words in this manner: "*Always presenting prayer for you all in every prayer of mine.*" For as he had said before, that the remembrance of them was an occasion of joy to him, so he now subjoins, that they come into his mind as often as he prays. He afterwards adds, that it is *with joy* that he presents prayer in their behalf. *Joy* refers to the past; *prayer* to the future. For he rejoiced in their auspicious beginnings, and was desirous of their perfection. Thus it becomes us always to rejoice in the blessings received from God in

---

[1] " Tous prestres et pasteurs;"—" All priests and pastors."
[2] " Vne protestation, qu'il est ioyeux de leur bien;"—" A protestation, that he is delighted on account of their welfare."

5. *For your fellowship.* He now, passing over the other clause, states the ground of his joy—that they had come into the *fellowship of the gospel,* that is, had become partakers of the gospel, which, as is well known, is accomplished by means of faith; for the gospel appears as nothing to us, in respect of any enjoyment of it, until we have received it by faith. At the same time the term *fellowship* may be viewed as referring to the common society of the saints, as though he had said that they had been associated with all the children of God in the faith of the gospel. When he says, *from the first day,* he commends their promptitude in having shewn themselves teachable immediately upon the doctrine being set before them. The phrase *until now* denotes their perseverance. Now we know how rare an excellence it is, to follow God immediately upon his calling us, and also to persevere steadfastly unto the end. For many are slow and backward to obey, while there are still more that fall short through fickleness and inconstancy.[1]

6. *Persuaded of this very thing.* An additional ground of joy is furnished in his confidence in them for the time to come.[2] But some one will say, why should men dare to assure themselves for to-morrow amidst so great an infirmity of nature, amidst so many impediments, ruggednesses, and precipices?[3] Paul, assuredly, did not derive this confidence from the steadfastness or excellence of men, but simply from the fact, that God had manifested his love to the Philippians. And undoubtedly this is the true manner of acknowledging God's benefits—when we derive from them occasion of hoping well as to the future.[4] For as they are tokens at once of

---

[1] " Qui se reuoltent ou defaillent en chemin par legerete;"—" Who revolt or fall back in the way through fickleness."

[2] " Qu'il se confioit d'eux qu'ils perseuereroyent de reste de leur vie;"— " That he had confidence in them that they would persevere during the remainder of their life."

[3] " Entre tant d'empeschemens, mauuais passages et fascheuses rencontres, voire mesme des dangers de tomber tout a plat en perdition;"— " Amidst so many impediments, hard passes, and disagreeable collisions, nay, even so many hazards of falling headlong into perdition."

[4] See CALVIN on the Corinthians, vol. ii. p. 121.

of hope and good courage! In addition to this, God is not like men, so as to be wearied out or exhausted by conferring kindness.[1] Let, therefore, believers exercise themselves in constant meditation upon the favours which God confers, that they may encourage and confirm hope as to the time to come, and always ponder in their mind this syllogism: God does not forsake the work which his own hands have begun, as the Prophet bears witness, (Psalm cxxxviii. 8; Isaiah lxiv. 8;) we are the work of his hands; therefore he will complete what he has begun in us. When I say that we are the work of his hands, I do not refer to mere creation, but to the calling by which we are adopted into the number of his sons. For it is a token to us of our election, that the Lord has called us effectually to himself by his Spirit.

It is asked, however, whether any one can be certain as to the salvation of others, for Paul here is not speaking of himself but of the Philippians. I answer, that the assurance which an individual has respecting his own salvation, is very different from what he has as to that of another. For the Spirit of God is a witness to me of my calling, as he is to each of the elect. As to others, we have no testimony, except from the outward efficacy of the Spirit; that is, in so far as the grace of God shews itself in them, so that we come to know it. There is, therefore, a great difference, because the assurance of faith remains inwardly shut up, and does not extend itself to others. But wherever we see any such tokens of Divine election as can be perceived by us, we ought immediately to be stirred up to entertain good hope, both in order that we may not be envious[2] towards our neighbours, and withhold from them an equitable and kind judgment of charity; and also, that we may be grateful to God.[3] This, however, is a general rule both as to ourselves

---

[1] "Il ne se lasse point en bien faisant, et son thresor ne diminue point;"—"He does not weary himself in doing good, and does not diminish his treasure."

[2] "Enuieux et desdaigneux;"—"Envious and disdainful."

[3] "Pour recognoistre le bien que Dieu leur a fait, et n'estre point ingrats

Until the day of Jesus Christ. The chief thing, indeed, to be understood here is—until the termination of the conflict. Now the conflict is terminated by death. As, however, the Spirit is accustomed to speak in this manner in reference to the last coming of Christ, it were better to extend the advancement of the grace of Christ to the resurrection of the flesh. For although those who have been freed from the mortal body do no longer contend with the lusts of the flesh, and are, as the expression is, beyond the reach of a single dart,[1] yet there will be no absurdity in speaking of them as in the way of advancement,[2] inasmuch as they have not yet reached the point at which they aspire,— they do not yet enjoy the felicity and glory which they have hoped for; and in fine, the day has not yet shone which is to discover the treasures which lie hid in hope. And in truth, when hope is treated of, our eyes must always be directed forward to a blessed resurrection, as the grand object in view.

7. Even as it is meet for me to think this of you all, because I have you in my heart; inasmuch as both in my bonds, and in the defence and confirmation of the gospel, ye all are partakers of my grace.

8. For God is my record, how greatly I long after you all in the bowels of Jesus Christ.

9. And this I pray, that your love may abound yet more and more in knowledge and *in* all judgment;

7. Sicuti iustum est mihi hoc de vobis omnibus sentire, propterea quod in corde vos habeam, esse omnes participes gratiæ meæ, et in vinculis meis, et in defensione, et confirmatione Evangelii.

8. Testis enim mihi est Deus, ut desiderem vos omnes in visceribus[3] Iesu Christi.

9. Et hoc precor, ut caritas vestra adhuc magis ac magis abundet cum agnitione, omnique intelligentia:

enuers luy;"—" That we may acknowledge the kindness which God has shewn them, and may not be ungrateful to him."

[1] " Extra teli jactum"—Virgil makes use of a corresponding phrase— " intra jactum teli;"—" Within the reach of a dart." Virg. Æn. xi. 608. —*Ed.*

[2] " En voye de proufiter, ou auancer;"—" In the way of making progress, or advancement."

[3] " Aux entrailles de Jesus Christ, *ou,* Es cordiale affection de Jesus Christ;"—" In the bowels of Jesus Christ, *or,* In the cordial affection of Jesus Christ."

day of Christ;

11. Being filled with the fruits of righteousness, which are by Jesus Christ, unto the glory and praise of God.	11. Impleti fructibus iustitiæ, qui sunt per Iesum Christum, in gloriam et laudem Dei.

7. *As it is reasonable.* For we are envious[1] valuators of the gifts of God if we do not reckon as children of God those in whom there shine forth those true tokens of piety, which are the marks by which the Spirit of adoption manifests himself. Paul accordingly says, that equity itself dictates to him,[2] that he should hope well of the Philippians in all time to come, inasmuch as he sees them to be associated with himself in participation of grace. It is not without due consideration that I have given a different rendering of this passage from that of Erasmus, as the judicious reader will easily perceive. For he states what opinion he has of the Philippians, which was the ground of his hoping well respecting them. He says, then, that they are *partakers with him of the same grace* in his *bonds,* and in the *defence of the gospel.*

To *have them in his heart* is to reckon them as such in the inmost affection of his heart. For the Philippians had always assisted Paul according to their ability, so as to connect themselves with him as associates for maintaining the cause of the gospel, so far as was in their power. Thus, although they were absent in body, yet, on account of the pious disposition which they shewed by every service in their power, he recognises them as in bonds along with him. "*I have you,* therefore, *in my heart;*" that is, sincerely and without any pretence, assuredly, and with no slight or doubtful opinion—as what? as *partakers of grace*—in what? *in my bonds,* by which the gospel is defended. As he acknowledged them to be such, it was reasonable that he should hope well respecting them.

Of my grace and in the bonds. It were a ludicrous thing

---

[1] " Maigres et desdaigneux;"—" Miserable and disdainful."

[2] " Raison mesme et equite luy disent;"—" Even reason and equity tell him."

common honour that God confers upon us, when we suffer persecution for the sake of his truth. For it was not in vain that it was said, (Matt. v. 11,) *Blessed shall ye be, when men shall afflict and harass you with all kinds of reproaches for my name's sake.* Let us therefore bear in remembrance also, that we must with readiness and alacrity embrace the fellowship of the cross of Christ as a special favour from God. In addition to *bonds* he subjoins the *defence and confirmation of the gospel*, that he may express so much the better the honourableness of the service which God has enjoined upon us in placing us in opposition to his enemies, so as to bear testimony to his gospel. For it is as though he had entrusted us with the defence of his gospel. And truly it was when armed with this consideration, that the martyrs were prepared to contemn all the rage of the wicked, and to rise superior to every kind of torture. And would that there were present to the mind of all that are called to make a confession of their faith, that they have been chosen by Christ to be as advocates to plead his cause! For were they sustained by such consolation they would be more courageous than to be so easily turned aside into a perfidious revolt.[1]

Here, however, some one will inquire, whether the *confirmation of the gospel* depends on the steadfastness of men. I answer, that the truth of God is in itself too firm to require that it should have support from any other quarter; for though we should all of us be found liars, God, nevertheless, remains true. (Rom. iii. 4.) There is, however, no absurdity in saying, that weak consciences are confirmed in it by such helps. That kind of confirmation, therefore, of which Paul makes mention, has a relation to men, as we learn from our own experience that the slaughter of so many martyrs has been attended at least with this advantage, that they have been as it were so many seals, by which the gospel

[1] " Ils seroyent si constans et fermes, qu'ils ne pourroyent estre aiseement induits a se reuolter laschement et desloyaument ;"—" They would be so steadfast and firm, that they could not be easily induced to revolt in a cowardly and disloyal manner."

Church,"—which I have imitated in a certain poem : " But that sacred blood,[1] the maintainer of God's honour, will be like seed for producing offspring."[2]

8. *For God is my witness.* He now declares more explicitly his affection for them, and, with the view of giving proof of it, he makes use of an oath, and that on good grounds, because we know how dear in the sight of God is the edification of his Church. It was, too, more especially of advantage, that Paul's affection should be thoroughly made known to the Philippians. For it tends in no small degree to secure credit for the doctrine, when the people are persuaded that they are beloved by the teacher. He calls God as a witness to the truth, inasmuch as he alone is the Truth, and as a witness of his affection, inasmuch as he alone is the searcher of hearts. In the word rendered *long after*, a particular term is made use of instead of a general, and it is a token of affection, inasmuch as we *long after* those things which are dear to us.

In the bowels. He places the *bowels of Christ* in opposition to carnal affection, to intimate that his affection is holy and pious. For the man that loves according to the flesh has respect to his own advantage, and may from time to time change his mind according to the variety of circumstances and seasons. In the meantime he instructs us by what rule the affections of believers ought to be regulated,

---

[1] Sanctus at ille cruor, divini assertor honoris,
Gignendam ad sobolem seminis instar erit.

[2] " A l'imitation duquel au chant de victoire composé par moy en Latin en l'honneur de Jesus Christ, 1541, et lequel depuis a este reduit en rime Francois, i'ay dit :—
' Or le sang precieux par martyre espandu
Pour auoir a son Dieu tesmoignage rendu,
A l'Eglise de Dieu seruira de semence
Dont enfans sorteront remplis d'intelligence.'"

" In imitation of which, in the song of victory composed by me in Latin in honour of Jesus Christ, in 1541, and which has since that time been rendered into French rhyme, I have said :—
' But the precious blood shed by martyrs
That it might be as a testimony rendered to its God,
Will in the Church of God serve as seed
From which children shall come forth, filled with understanding.'"

from no other source than from the *bowels of Crhist*, and this, like a goad, ought to affect us not a little—that Christ in a manner opens his *bowels*, that by them he may cherish mutual affection between us.¹

9. *This I pray that your love.* He returns to the prayer, which he had simply touched upon in one word in passing. He states, accordingly, the sum of those things which he asked from God in their behalf, that they also may learn to pray after his example, and may aspire at proficiency in those gifts. The view taken by some, as though the *love of the Philippians* denoted the Philippians themselves, as illiterate persons are accustomed very commonly to say, " Your reverence,"— " Your paternity," is absurd. For no instance of such an expression occurs in the writings of Paul, nor had such fooleries come into use. Besides, the statement would be less complete, and, independently of this, the simple and natural meaning of the words suits admirably well. For the true attainments of Christians are when they make progress in *knowledge*, and *understanding*, and afterwards in *love*. Accordingly the particle *in*, according to the idiom of the Hebrew tongue, is taken here to mean *with*, as I have also rendered it, unless perhaps one should prefer to explain it as meaning *by*, so as to denote the instrument or formal cause. For, the greater proficiency we make in *knowledge*, so much the more ought our *love* to increase. The meaning in that case would be, " That your love may increase according to the measure of knowledge." *All knowledge*, means what is full and complete—not a knowledge of all things.²

¹ *Beza*, when commenting on the expression, *in the bowels of Jesus Christ*, observes, " Alibi solet dicere, *In Christo*. Ut autem significet ex quo fonte promanet affectus iste, et quo etiam feratur, additum *visceribus* nomen magnum pondus addit sententiæ, ut intimus amor significetur. Solent enim Hebraei רחמים, *rachamim*, id est, *viscera* omnes teneros ac veluti maternos affectus vocare ;"—" He is accustomed in other cases to say, *In Christ*. But to intimate from what fountain that affection flows, and in what direction also it tends, the addition of the term *bowels* adds great weight to the statement, so as to express intimate affection. For the Hebrews are accustomed to employ the term רחמים *rachamim*, that is, *bowels*, to denote all tender and as it were motherly affections."—*Ed.*

² " The word rendered *judgment* is capable of being rendered *sense* (πάση

vantageous or expedient—not to torture the mind with empty subtleties and speculations. For the Lord does not wish that his believing people should employ themselves fruitlessly in learning what is of no profit: From this you may gather in what estimation the Sorbonnic theology ought to be held, in which you may spend your whole life, and yet not derive more of edification from it in connection with the hope of a heavenly life, or more of spiritual advantage, than from the demonstrations of Euclid. Unquestionably, although it taught nothing false, it well deserves to be execrable, on the ground that it is a pernicious profanation of spiritual doctrine. For *Scripture is useful*, as Paul says, in 2 Tim. iii. 16, but *there* you will find nothing but cold subtleties of words.

That ye may be sincere. This is the advantage which we derive from *knowledge*—not that every one may artfully consult his own interests, but that we may live in pure conscience in the sight of God.

It is added—*and without offence.* The Greek word ἀπρόσκοποι is ambiguous. Chrysostom explains it in an *active* sense—that as he had desired that they should be pure and upright in the sight of God, so he now desires that they should lead an honourable life in the sight of men, that they may not injure their neighbours by any evil examples. This exposition I do not reject: the *passive* signification, however, is better suited to the context, in my opinion. For he desires wisdom for them, with this view—that they may with unwavering step go forward in their calling until the *day of Christ*, as on the other hand it happens through ignorance,[1] that we frequently slip our foot, stumble, and turn aside. And how many stumblingblocks Satan from time to time throws in our way, with the view of either stopping our

---

αἰσθήσει) *in all sense.* ' I pray that you may have your spiritual senses in exercise—that you may have a judicious distinguishing sense.' For what? Why, ' that ye may approve things that are excellent,'—so it follows, or, as the words there may be read, to ' distinguish things that differ.' "—*Howe's* Works, (Lond. 1822,) vol. v. p. 145.—*Ed.*

[1] " Par ignorance et faute de prudence ;"—" Through ignorance and want of prudence."

11. *Filled with the fruits of righteousness.* This now belongs to the outward life, for a good conscience produces its fruits by means of works. Hence he desires that they may be fruitful in good works for the glory of God. Such fruits, he says, are by Christ, because they flow from the grace of Christ. For the beginning of our well-doing is, when we are sanctified by his Spirit, for he rested upon him, that we might all receive of his fulness. (John i. 16.) And as Paul here derives a similitude from trees, we are *wild olive-trees*, (Rom. xi. 24,) and unproductive, until we are ingrafted into Christ, who by his living root makes us fruitbearing trees, in accordance with that saying, (John xv. 1,) *I am the vine, ye are the branches.* He at the same time shews the end—that we may promote the glory of God. For no life is so excellent in appearance as not to be corrupted and become offensive in the view of God, if it is not directed towards this object.

Paul's speaking here of works under the term *righteousness*, is not at all inconsistent with the gratuitous righteousness of faith. For it does not immediately follow that there is righteousness wherever there are the fruits of righteousness, inasmuch as there is no righteousness in the sight of God, unless there be a full and complete obedience to the law, which is not found in any one of the saints, though, nevertheless, they bring forth, according to their measure, the good and pleasant[1] fruits of righteousness, and for this reason, that, as God begins righteousness in us, through the regeneration of the Spirit, so what is wanting is amply supplied through the remission of sins, in such a way that all righteousness, nevertheless, depends upon faith.

12. But I would ye should understand, brethren, that the things *which happened* unto me have fallen out rather unto the furtherance of the gospel;

13. So that my bonds in Christ are manifest in all the palace, and in all other *places*;

14. And many of the brethren in the Lord waxing confident by my

12. Scire autem vos volo, fratres, quod, quae mihi acciderunt, magis in profectum cesserunt Evangelii,

13. Ut vincula mea in Christo illustria fuerint in toto praetorio, et reliquis omnibus locis:

14. Et multi ex fratribus in Domino, vinculis meis confisi, uberius

---

[1] " Bons et aimables;"—" Good and amiable."

even of envy and strife; and some also of good will.	et contentionem, alii autem etiam per benevolentiam, Christum praedicant.
16. The one preach Christ of contention, not sincerely, supposing to add affliction to my bonds;	16. Alii, inquam, ex contentione Christum annuntiant, non pure, existimantes afflictionem se suscitare meis vinculis:
17. But the other of love, knowing that I am set for the defence of the gospel.	17. Alii autem ex caritate, scientes quod in defensionem Evangelii positus sim.

12. *But I wish you to know.* We all know from our own experience, how much the flesh is wont to be offended by the abasement of the cross. We allow, indeed, Christ crucified to be preached to us; but when he appears in connection with his cross, then, as though we were thunderstruck at the novelty of it,[1] we either avoid him or hold him in abhorrence, and that not merely in our own persons, but also in the persons of those who deliver to us the gospel. It may have happened to the Philippians, that they were in some degree discouraged in consequence of the persecution of their Apostle. We may also very readily believe, that those bad workmen[2] who eagerly watched every occasion, however small, of doing injury, did not refrain from triumphing over the calamity of this holy man, and by this means making his gospel contemptible. If, however, they were not successful in this attempt, they might very readily calumniate him by representing him as hated by the whole world; and at the same time leading the Philippians to dread, lest, by an unfortunate association with him,[3] they should needlessly incur great dislike among all; for such are the usual artifices of Satan. The Apostle provides against this danger, when he states that the gospel had been promoted by means of his bonds. The design, accordingly, of this detail is, to encourage the Philippians, that they may not feel deterred[4] by the persecution endured by him.

[1] " Estans estonnez comme d'vne chose nouuelle et non ouye;"—" Being astonished as at a thing new and unheard of."

[2] " Et faux apostres;"—" And false apostles."

[3] " En prenant ceste dangereuse accointance de S. Paul;"—" By contracting this dangerous acquaintance with St. Paul."

[4] " Afin qu'ils ne soyent point destournez;"—" That they may not be turned aside."

for he intimates that his bonds had become illustrious, so as to promote the honour of Christ.[1] The rendering given by some—*through Christ*, seems forced. I have also employed the word *illustria* (*illustrious*) in preference to *manifesta*, (*manifest*,)—as having ennobled the gospel by their fame.[2] " Satan, indeed, has attempted it, and the wicked have thought that it would turn out so, that the gospel would be destroyed ; but God has frustrated both the attempts of the former and the expectations of the latter,[3] and that in two ways, for while the gospel was previously obscure and unknown, it has come to be well known, and not only so, but has even been rendered honourable in the *Praetorium*, no less than in the rest of the city."

By the *praetorium* I understand the hall and palace of Nero, which Fabius[4] and writers of that age call *Augustale*, (*the Augustal.*) For as the name praetor was at first a general term, and denoted all magistrates who held the chief sway, (hence it came that the dictator was called the sovereign praetor,[5]) it, consequently, became customary to employ the term *praetorium* in war to mean the tent, either of the consul,[6] or of the person who *presided*,[7] while in the city

[1] " Ses liens ont este rendus celebres, et ont excellement serui a auancer la gloire de Christ;"—" His bonds had become celebrated, and had admirably contributed to advance the glory of Christ."

[2] " Pource qu'il entend que le bruit qui auoit este de ses liens, auoit donné grand bruit a l'Euangile ;"—" Because he means that the fame, which had arisen from his bonds, had given great fame to the gospel."

[3] " Dieu a aneanti les efforts malicieux de Satan, et a frustré les meschans de leur attente;"—" God has made void the malicious efforts of Satan, and has disappointed the wicked of their expectation."

[4] Our author has most probably in view an expression which occurs in the writings of *Quinctilian*, (Instit. Orator., lib. 8, 2, 8,)—" tabernaculum ducis Augustale;"—(" a general's tent is called the Augustal.") In the best editions of Quinctilian, however, the reading is *Augurale*, as synonymous with *auguraculum*, or *auguratorium;*—(*an apartment for the augur's taking omens.*)—*Ed.*

[5] The dictator is called by *Livy*, " praetor maximus;"—" the highest praetor."—(*Liv.* vii. 3.)—*Ed.*

[6] " La tente ou du consul, ou de celuy qui estoit chef de l'armee, quelque nom qu'on luy donast ;"—" The tent of the consul, or of the person who was head of the army, whatever name was applied to him."

[7] " *Praeibat.*"—There is manifestly an allusion here to the etymology of praetor, as being derived from *praeire*, to *go before*, or *preside.*—*Ed.*

the bench of praetor is also called the *praetorium*.³

14. *Many of the brethren.* By this instance we are taught that the tortures of the saints, endured by them in behalf of the gospel, are a ground of confidence⁴ to us. It were indeed a dreadful spectacle, and such as might tend rather to dishearten us, did we see nothing but the cruelty and rage of the persecutors. When, however, we see at the same time the hand of the Lord, which makes his people unconquerable,⁵ under the infirmity of the Cross, and causes them to triumph, relying upon this,⁶ we ought to venture farther than we had been accustomed, having now a pledge of our victory in the persons of our brethren. The knowledge of this ought to overcome our fears, that we may speak boldly in the midst of dangers.

15. *Some indeed.* Here is another fruit of Paul's bonds, that not only were the brethren stirred up to confidence by his example—some by maintaining their position, others by becoming more eager to teach—but even those who wished him evil were on another account stirred up to publish the gospel.

16. *Some, I say, from contention.* Here we have a lengthened detail, in which he explains more fully the foregoing statement; for he repeats that there are two classes of men

---

¹ "At Rome it" (the term *praetorium*) "signified the public hall where causes were tried by the praetor; but more usually it denoted the camp or quarters of the praetorian cohorts without the city. . . . The name of *praetorium* was, in the provinces, given to the palace of the governors, both because they administered justice, and had their guards stationed in their residence. Hence it is inferred that, although the Apostle was at Rome when he wrote this, and although the circumstances to which he refers occurred in that city, yet, writing to persons residing in the provinces, he uses the word *praetorium* in the provincial sense, and means by it the *emperor's palace.*"—*Illustrated Commentary.*—*Ed.*

² "Depuis que les empereurs usurperent la monarchie;"—"From the time that the emperors usurped the monarchy."

³ "Pretoire signifioit aussi le lieu ou le preteur tenoit la cour, et exerçoit sa iurisdiction;"—"The praetorium signified also the place where the praetor held his court, and exercised jurisdiction."

⁴ "Confiance et asseurance;"—"Confidence and assurance."

⁵ "Courageux et inuincibles;"—"Courageous and unconquerable."

⁶ "Estans asseurez sur ceste main et puissance du Seigneur;"—"Confidently relying upon this hand and power of the Lord."

the other by pious zeal, as being desirous to maintain along with him the defence of the gospel. The former, he says, do not *preach Christ purely*, because it was not a right zeal.[1] For the term does not apply to doctrine, because it is possible that the man who teaches most purely, may, nevertheless, not be of a sincere mind.[2] Now, that this impurity was in the mind, and did not shew itself in doctrine, may be inferred from the context. Paul assuredly would have felt no pleasure in seeing the gospel corrupted; yet he declares that he rejoices in the preaching of those persons, while it was not simple or sincere.

It is asked, however, how such preaching could be injurious to him? I answer, that many occasions are unknown to us, inasmuch as we are not acquainted with the circumstances of the times. It is asked farther, " Since the gospel cannot be preached but by those that understand it, what motive induced those persons to persecute the doctrine of which they approved?" I answer, that ambition is blind, nay, it is a furious beast. Hence it is not to be wondered if false brethren snatch a weapon from the gospel for harassing good and pious pastors.[3] Paul, assuredly, says nothing here[4] of which I have not myself had experience. For there are living at this very day those who have preached the gospel with no other design, than that they might gratify the rage of the wicked by persecuting pious pastors. As to Paul's enemies, it is of importance to observe, if they were Jews, how mad their hatred was, so as even to forget on

---

[1] " Pource que leur zele n'estoit pas pur;"—" Because their zeal was not pure."

[2] " Il se peut bien faire, que celuy qui enseignera vne doctrine pure et saine, aura toutesfois vne mauvaise affection;"—" It may quite well happen, that the man who teaches pure and sound doctrine, will have, nevertheless, an evil disposition."

[3] " Il ne se faut esbahir si les faux-freres prenent occasion de l'evangile, et s'ils s'en forgent des bastons.pour tormenter les bons et fideles pasteurs;"—" It ought not to appear surprising, if false brethren take occasion from the gospel, and contrive weapons for themselves for torturing good and faithful pastors."

[4] " Certes le sainct Apostre ne dit rien yci;"—" Certainly the holy Apostle says nothing here."

gospel, on account of which they were hostile to him; but they imagined, no doubt, that the cause of Christ would stand or fall¹ in the person of one individual. If, however, there were envious persons,² who were thus hurried away by ambition, we ought to acknowledge the wonderful goodness of God, who, notwithstanding, gave such a prosperous issue to their depraved affections.

17. *That for the defence.* Those who truly loved Christ reckoned that it would be a disgrace to them if they did not associate themselves with Paul as his companions, when maintaining the cause of the gospel; and we must act in such a manner, as to give a helping hand, as far as possible, to the servants of Christ when in difficulty.³ Observe, again, this expression—*for the defence of the gospel.* For since Christ confers upon us so great an honour, what excuse shall we have, if we shall be traitors to his cause,⁴ or what may we expect, if we betray it by our silence, but that *he* shall in return desert our cause, who is our sole *Advocate*, or Patron, *with the Father?*⁵ (1 John ii. 1.)

18. What then? notwithstanding, every way, whether in pretence, or in truth, Christ is preached; and I therein do rejoice, yea, and will rejoice.	18. Quid enim? caeterum quovis modo, sive per occasionem, sive per veritatem, Christus annuntiatur: atque in hoc gaudeo, quin etiam gaudebo.
19. For I know that this shall turn to my salvation through your prayer, and the supply of the Spirit of Jesus Christ,	19. Novi enim quod hoc mihi cedet in salutem per vestram precationem, et subministrationem Spiritus Iesu Christi,
20. According to my earnest expectation and *my* hope, that in nothing I shall be ashamed, but *that*	20. Secundum expectationem et spem meam, quod in nullo re pudefiam, sed cum omni fiducia, quem-

¹ "*Mais voyla: il leur sembloit que la doctrine consistoit ou tomboit bas;*"—" But mark! it seemed to them that doctrine stood or fell."

² "*Que si 'c'estoit d'autres que Juifs, ascauoir quelques enuieux de Sainct Paul;*"—" But if there were other than Jews—some that were envious of St. Paul."

³ "*Estans en quelque necessite;*"—" When they are in any emergency."

⁴ "*Praevaricatores.*" The term is employed by classical writers in the sense of betraying the cause of one's client, and by neglect or collusion assisting his opponent. See Quinct. ix. 2.—*Ed.*

⁵ "*Si nous nous entendons auec la partie aduerse d'iceluy;*"—" If we should connect ourselves with the party opposed to him."

death.

21. For to me to live *is* Christ, and to die *is* gain.

21. Mihi enim vivendo Christus est, et moriendo lucrum.

18. *But in every way.* As the wicked disposition of those of whom he has spoken might detract from the acceptableness of the doctrine,[1] he says that this ought to be reckoned of great importance, that they nevertheless promoted the cause of the gospel, whatever their disposition might be. For God sometimes accomplishes an admirable work by means of wicked and depraved instruments. Accordingly, he says that he rejoices in a happy result of this nature; because this one thing contented him—if he saw the kingdom of Christ increasing—just as we, on hearing that that impure dog Carolus[2] was scattering the seeds of pure doctrine at Avignon and elsewhere, we gave thanks to God because he had made use of that most profligate and worthless villain for his glory: and at this day we rejoice that the progress of the gospel is advanced by many who, nevertheless, had another design in view. But though Paul rejoiced in the advancement of the gospel, yet, had the matter been in his hand, he would never have ordained such persons as ministers. We ought, therefore, to rejoice if God accomplishes anything that is good by means of wicked persons; but they ought not on that account to be either placed by us in the ministry, or looked upon as Christ's lawful ministers.

19. *For I know that.* As some published the gospel with the view of rendering Paul odious, in order that they might kindle up against him the more the rage of his enemies, he tells them beforehand that their wicked attempts will do him no harm, because the Lord will turn them to a contrary design. "Though they plot my destruction, yet I trust that all their attempts will have no other effect but that Christ

[1] "Pouuoit diminuer l'authorite de la doctrine;"—"Might diminish the authority of the doctrine."

[2] Our Author appears to refer here to Peter Carolus, of whom the reader will find particular mention made by Beza in his Life of CALVIN.—CALVIN'S *Tracts*, vol. i. pp. xxx. xxxi.—*Ed.*

speaking of the safety of the body. But whence this confidence on the part of Paul? It is from what he teaches elsewhere, (Rom. viii. 28,)—that all things contribute to the advantage of God's true worshippers, even though the whole world, with the devil, its prince, should conspire together for their ruin.

Through your prayer. That he may stir them up to pray more ardently, he declares that he is confident that the Lord will give them an answer to their prayers. Nor does he use dissimulation: for he who depends for help on the prayers of the saints relies on the promise of God. In the mean time, nothing is detracted from the unmerited goodness of God, on which depend our prayers, and what is obtained by means of them.

And the supply. Let us not suppose, that because he joins these two things in one connection, they are consequently alike. The statement must, therefore, be explained in this manner:—" I know that all this will turn out to my advantage, through the administration of the Spirit, you also helping by prayer,"—so that the supply of the Spirit is the efficient cause, while prayer is a subordinate help. We must also observe the propriety of the Greek term, for ἐπιχορηγία is employed to mean the furnishing of what is wanting,[1] just as the Spirit of God pours into us everything of which we are destitute.

He calls him, too, the *Spirit of Jesus Christ,* to intimate, that if we are Christians, he is common to all of us, inasmuch as he was poured upon him with all fulness, that, according to the measure of his grace, he might give out, so far as is expedient, to each of his members.

20. *According to my expectation.* Should any one object, " From what do you derive that knowledge?" he answers, " From hope." For as it is certain that God does not by any means design to frustrate our hope, hope itself ought not to be wavering. Let then the pious reader carefully

---

[1] " The word ἐπιχορηγία, which we translate *supply,* signifies also *furnishing whatever is necessary.*"—*Dr. A. Clarke.*—*Ed.*

that the Lord will fulfil our expectation, inasmuch as it is founded on his own word. Now, he has promised that he will never be wanting to us even in the midst of all tortures, if we are at any time called to make confession of his name. Let, therefore, all the pious entertain hope after Paul's example, and they will not be put to shame.

With all confidence. We see that, in cherishing hope, he does not give indulgence to carnal desires, but places his hope in subjection to the promise of God. "*Christ,*" says he, "*will be magnified in my body, whether by life or by death.*" By making express mention, however, of the body, he intimates that, amongst the conflicts of the present life, he is in no degree doubtful as to the issue, for we are assured as to this by God. If, accordingly, giving ourselves up to the good pleasure of God, and having in our life the same object in view as Paul had, we expect, in whatever way it may be, a prosperous issue, we shall no longer have occasion to fear lest any adversity should befall us; for if we live and die to him, we are his in life and in death. (Rom. xiv. 8.) He expresses the way in which *Christ will be magnified*—by full assurance. Hence it follows, that through our fault he is cast down and lowered, so far as it is in our power to do so, when we give way through fear. Do not those then feel ashamed who reckon it a light offence to tremble,[1] when called to make confession of the truth? But how much ashamed ought those to feel, who are so shamelessly impudent as to have the hardihood even to excuse renunciation?

He adds, *as always,* that they may confirm their faith from past experience of the grace of God. Thus, in Romans v. 4, he says, *Experience begets hope.*

21. *For to me to live.* Interpreters have hitherto, in my opinion, given a wrong rendering and exposition to this passage; for they make this distinction, that Christ was life to Paul, and death was gain. I, on the other hand, make Christ the subject of discourse in both clauses, so that he is declared to be gain to him both in life and in death; for

[1] "De varier et chanceler;"—"To shift and waver."

also corresponds better with the foregoing statement, and contains more complete doctrine. He declares that it is indifferent to him, and is all one, whether he lives or dies, because, having Christ, he reckons both to be *gain*. And assuredly it is Christ alone that makes us happy both in death and in life; otherwise, if death is miserable, life is in no degree happier; so that it is difficult to determine whether it is more advantageous to live or to die *out of Christ*. On the other hand, let Christ be with us, and he will bless our life as well as our death, so that both will be happy and desirable for us.

22. But if I live in the flesh, this *is* the fruit of my labour: yet what I shall choose I wot not.	22. Quodsi vivere in carne operae pretium mihi est, etiam quid eligam ignoro.[1]
23. For I am in a strait betwixt two, having a desire to depart, and to be with Christ; which is far better:	23. Coarctor enim ex duobus cupiens dissolvi et esse cum Christo: multo enim hoc melius.
24. Nevertheless to abide in the flesh *is* more needful for you.	24. Manere vero in carne, magis necessarium propter vos.
25. And having this confidence, I know that I shall abide and continue with you all, for your furtherance and joy of faith;	25. Atque hoc confisus novi, quod manebo et permanebo cum omnibus vobis, in vestrum profectum et gaudium fidei,
26. That your rejoicing may be more abundant in Jesus Christ for me, by my coming to you again.	26. Ut gloriatio vestra exsuperet in Christo Iesu de me, per meum rursus adventum ad vos.

22. *But if to live in the flesh.* As persons in despair feel in perplexity as to whether they ought to prolong their life any farther in miseries, or to terminate their troubles by death, so Paul, on the other hand, says that he is, in a spirit of contentment, so well prepared for death or for life, because the condition of believers, both in the one case and in the other, is blessed, so that he is at a loss which to choose. *If it is worth while;* that is, "If I have reason to believe that there will be greater advantage from my life than from my death, I do not see which of them I ought to prefer." To

---

[1] " Or encore que viure en chair me fust proufitable, ie ne scay lequel ie doy eslire, *ou*, Or si viure en chair me est proufitable, et que c'est qu' ie doy eslire, ie ne scay rien;"—" But although to live in the flesh would not be profitable to me, I know not what I ought to choose; *or*, But if to live in the flesh is profitable to me, and that it is what I ought to choose, I know not."

23. *For I am in a strait.* Paul did not desire to live with any other object in view than that of promoting the glory of Christ, and doing good to the brethren. Hence he does not reckon that he has any other advantage from living than the welfare of the brethren. But so far as concerns himself personally, it were, he acknowledges, better for him to die soon, because he would be *with Christ.* By his choice, however, he shews what ardent love glowed in his breast. There is nothing said here as to earthly advantages, but as to spiritual benefit, which is on good grounds supremely desirable in the view of the pious. Paul, however, as if forgetful of himself, does not merely hold himself undetermined, lest he should be swayed by a regard to his own benefit rather than that of the Philippians, but at length concludes that a regard to them preponderates in his mind. And assuredly this is in reality to live and die to Christ, when, with indifference as to ourselves, we allow ourselves to be carried and borne away whithersoever Christ calls us.

Having a desire to be set free and to be with Christ. These two things must be read in connection. For death of itself will never be desired, because such a desire is at variance with natural feeling, but is desired for some particular reason, or with a view to some other end. Persons in despair have recourse to it from having become weary of life; believers, on the other hand, willingly hasten forward to it, because it is a deliverance from the bondage of sin, and an introduction into the kingdom of heaven. What Paul now says is this; "I desire to die, because I will, by this means, come into immediate connection with Christ." In the mean time, believers do not cease to regard death with horror, but when they turn their eyes to that life which follows death, they easily overcome all dread by means of that consolation. Unquestionably, every one that believes in Christ ought to be so courageous as to *lift up his head* on mention being made of death, delighted to have intimation of his *redemption.* (Luke xxi. 28.) From this we see how many are Christians only in name, since the greater part, on hearing mention made

word respecting Christ. O the worth and value of a good conscience! Now faith is the foundation of a good conscience; nay more, it is itself goodness of conscience.

To be set free. This form of expression is to be observed. Profane persons speak of death as the destruction of man, as if he altogether perished. Paul here reminds us, that death is the separation of the soul from the body. And this he expresses more fully immediately afterwards, explaining as to what condition awaits believers after death—that of *dwelling with Christ.* We are *with Christ* even in this life, inasmuch as the *kingdom of God is within us,* (Luke xvii. 21,) and *Christ dwells in us by faith,* (Eph. iii. 17,) and has promised that he *will be with us even unto the end of the world,* (Matt. xxviii. 20,) but that presence we enjoy only in hope. Hence as to our feeling, we are said to be at present at a *distance* from him. See 2 Cor. v. 6. This passage is of use for setting aside the mad fancy of those who dream that souls sleep when separated from the body, for Paul openly declares that we enjoy Christ's presence on being set free from the body.

25. *And having this confidence.* Some, reckoning it an inconsistent thing that the Apostle[1] should acknowledge himself to have been disappointed of his expectation, are of opinion that he was afterwards freed from bonds, and went over many countries of the world. Their fears, however, as to this are groundless, for the saints are accustomed to regulate their expectations according to the word of God, so as not to promise themselves more than God has promised. Thus, when they have a sure token of God's will, they in that case place their reliance also upon a sure persuasion, which admits of no hesitation. Of this nature is a persuasion respecting a perpetual remission of sins, respecting the aid of the Spirit for the grace of final perseverance, (as it is called,) and respecting the resurrection of the flesh. Of this nature, also, was the assurance of the Prophets respecting their prophecies. As to other things, they expect nothing except conditionally, and hence they subject all events to the pro-

[1] " Vn tel sainct Apostre;"—" So holy an Apostle."

continue, means, to remain for a long time.

26. *That your glorying.* The expression which he employs, ἐν ἐμοί, I have rendered *de me* (*as to me*,) because the preposition is made use of twice, but in different senses. No one assuredly will deny that I have faithfully brought out Paul's mind. The rendering given by some—*per Christum,* (*through Christ*,) I do not approve of. For *in Christ* is employed in place of *Secundum Christum*, (*According to Christ*,) or *Christiane,* (*Christianly*,) to intimate that it was a holy kind of *glorying.* For otherwise we are commanded to *glory in God alone.* (1 Cor. i. 31.) Hence malevolent persons might meet Paul with the objection, How is it allowable for the Philippians to glory as to thee? He anticipates this calumny by saying that they will do this *according to Christ*—glorying in a servant of Christ, with a view to the glory of his Lord, and that with an eye to the doctrine rather than to the individual, and in opposition to the false apostles, just as David, by comparing himself with hypocrites, boasts of his righteousnesses. (Psalm vii. 8.)

27. Only let your conversation be as it becometh the gospel of Christ: that whether I come and see you, or else be absent, I may hear of your affairs, that ye stand fast in one spirit, with one mind striving together for the faith of the gospel;
28. And in nothing terrified by your adversaries: which is to them an evident token of perdition, but to you of salvation, and that of God.
29. For unto you it is given in the behalf of Christ, not only to believe on him, but also to suffer for his sake;
30. Having the same conflict which ye saw in me, *and* now hear *to be* in me.

27. Tantum digne Evangelio Christi conversamini : ut sive veniens videam vos, sive absens, audiam de vobis, quod stetis in uno spiritu, una anima, concertantes fide Evangelii.
28. Nec ulla in re terreamini ab adversariis, quae illis est demonstratio exitii: vobis autem salutis, idque a Deo.
29. Quia vobis donatum est pro Christo, non tantum ut in illum credatis, sed etiam ut pro ipso patiamini:'
30. Idem habentes certamen, quale vidistis in me, et nunc auditis de me.

27. *Only in a manner worthy of the gospel.* We make use of this form of expression, when we are inclined to pass on to a new subject. Thus it is as though he had said, "But as for me, the Lord will provide, but as for you, &c., whatever

and honourable conversation as being worthy of the gospel, he intimates, on the other hand, that those who live otherwise do injustice to the gospel.

That whether I come. As the Greek phrase made use of by Paul is elliptical, I have made use of *videam*, (*I see*,) instead of *videns* (*seeing*.) If this does not appear satisfactory, you may supply the principal verb *Intelligam*, (*I may learn*,) in this sense: "Whether, when I shall come and see you, or whether I shall, when absent, hear respecting your condition, I may learn in both ways, both by being present and by receiving intelligence, that ye *stand in one spirit.*" We need not, however, feel anxiety as to particular terms, when the meaning is evident.

Stand in one spirit. This, certainly, is one of the main excellences of the Church, and hence this is one means of preserving it in a sound state, inasmuch as it is torn to pieces by dissensions. But although Paul was desirous by means of this antidote to provide against novel and strange doctrines, yet he requires a twofold unity—of *spirit* and *soul.* The *first* is, that we have like views; the *second*, that we be united in heart. For when these two terms are connected together, *spiritus* (*spirit*) denotes the *understanding*, while *anima* (*soul*) denotes the *will.* Farther, agreement of views comes first in order; and then from it springs union of inclination.

Striving together for the faith. This is the strongest bond of concord, when we have to fight together under the same banner, for this has often been the occasion of reconciling even the greatest enemies. Hence, in order that he may confirm the more the unity that existed among the Philippians, he calls them to notice that they are fellow-soldiers, who, having a common enemy and a common warfare, ought to have their minds united together in a holy agreement. The expression which Paul has made use of in the Greek (συναθλοῦντες τῇ πίστει) is ambiguous. The old interpreter renders it *Collaborantes fidei*, (*labouring together with the faith.*)[1] Erasmus

---

[1] In accordance with the Vulgate, Wiclif (1380) renders as follows: " traueilynge to gidre to the feith of the gospel."—*Ed.*

As, however, the dative in Greek is made use of instead of the ablative of instrumentality, (that language having no ablative,) I have no doubt that the Apostle's meaning is this: "Let the faith of the gospel unite you together, more especially as that is a common armory against one and the same enemy." In this way the particle σύν, which others refer to *faith*, I take as referring to the Philippians, and with greater propriety, if I am not mistaken. In the first place, every one is aware how effectual an inducement it is to concord, when we have to maintain a conflict together; and farther, we know that in the spiritual warfare we are armed with the *shield of faith*, (Eph. vi. 16,) for repelling the enemy; nay, more, faith is both our panoply and our victory. Hence he added this clause, that he might shew what is the end of a pious connection. The wicked, too, conspire together for evil, but their agreement is accursed: let us, therefore, contend with one mind under the banner of faith.

28. *And in nothing terrified.* The second thing which he recommends to the Philippians is fortitude of mind,[1] that they may not be thrown into confusion by the rage of their adversaries. At that time the most cruel persecutions raged almost everywhere, because Satan strove with all his might to impede the commencement of the gospel, and was the more enraged in proportion as Christ put forth powerfully the grace of his Spirit. He exhorts, therefore, the Philippians to stand forward undaunted, and not be thrown into alarm.

Which is to them a manifest proof. This is the proper meaning of the Greek word, and there was no consideration that made it necessary for others to render it *cause*. For the wicked, when they wage war against the Lord, do already by a trial-fight, as it were, give a token of their ruin, and the more fiercely they insult over the pious, the more do they prepare themselves for ruin. The Scripture, assuredly,

[1] "La force et constance de courage;"—"Strength and constancy of courage."

in another instance, too, speaks of them as a *manifest token* or *proof,* (2 Thess. i. 5,) and instead of ἔνδειξιν, which we have here, he in that passage makes use of the term ἔνδειγμα.[1] This, therefore, is a choice consolation, that when we are assailed and harassed by our enemies, we have an evidence of our salvation.[2] For persecutions are in a manner seals of adoption to the children of God, if they endure them with fortitude and patience: the wicked give a token of their condemnation, because they stumble against a stone by which they shall be bruised to pieces. (Matt. xxi. 44.)

And that from God. This is restricted to the last clause, that a taste of the grace of God may allay the bitterness of the cross. No one will naturally perceive the cross a token or evidence of salvation, for they are things that are contrary in appearance. Hence Paul calls the attention of the Philippians to another consideration—that God by his blessing turns into an occasion of welfare things that might otherwise seem to render us miserable. He proves it from this, that the endurance of the cross is the gift of God. Now it is certain, that all the gifts of God are salutary to us. *To you,* says he, *it is given, not only to believe in Christ, but also to suffer for him.* Hence even the sufferings themselves are evidences of the grace of God; and, since it is so, you have from this source a token of salvation. Oh, if this persuasion were effectually inwrought in our minds—that persecutions[3] are to be reckoned among God's benefits, what progress would be made in the doctrine of piety![4] And yet, what is more certain, than that it is the highest honour that is conferred upon us by Divine grace, that we suffer for his name either reproach, or imprisonment, or miseries, or tortures, or even death, for in that case he adorns us with his marks of

[1] " Là où il vse d'vn mot qui descend d'vn mesme verbe que celuy dont il vse yci;"—" Where he makes use of a word which comes from the same verb as that which he employs here."

[2] " Cela nous est vne demonstrance et tesmoignage de nostre salut;"— " This is to us a clear proof and token of our salvation."

[3] " Les afflictions et persecutions;"—" Afflictions and persecutions."

[4] " Combien aurions—nous proufité en la doctrine de vraye religion;"— " How much progress we would make in the doctrine of true religion."

alacrity the cross when it is presented to them. Alas, then, for our stupidity![2]

29. *To believe.* He wisely conjoins faith with the cross by an inseparable connection, that the Philippians may know that they have been called to the faith of Christ on this condition—that they endure persecutions on his account, as though he had said that their adoption can no more be separated from the cross, than Christ can be torn asunder from himself. Here Paul clearly testifies, that faith, as well as constancy in enduring persecutions,[3] is an unmerited gift of God. And certainly the knowledge of God is a wisdom that is too high for our attaining it by our own acuteness, and our weakness shews itself in daily instances in our own experience, when God withdraws his hand for a little while. That he may intimate the more distinctly that both are unmerited, he says expressly—for Christ's sake, or at least that they are given to us on the ground of Christ's grace; by which he excludes every idea of merit.

This passage is also at variance with the doctrine of the schoolmen, in maintaining that gifts of grace latterly conferred are rewards of our merit, on the ground of our having made a right use of those which had been previously bestowed. I do not deny, indeed, that God rewards the right use of his gifts of grace by bestowing grace more largely upon us, provided only you do not place merit, as they do, in opposition to his unmerited liberality and the merit of Christ.

30. *Having the same conflict.* He confirms, also, by his own example what he had said, and this adds no little authority to his doctrine. By the same means, too, he shews them, that there is no reason why they should feel troubled on account of his bonds, when they behold the issue of the conflict.

---

[1] " Il nous vest de sa liuree ;"—" He arrays us in his livery."
[2] " Maudite donc soit nostre stupidite ;"—" Accursed, then, be our stupidity."
[3] " Les afflictions et persecutions ;"—" Afflictions and persecutions."

1. If *there be* therefore any consolation in Christ, if any comfort of love, if any fellowship of the Spirit, if any bowels and mercies,

2. Fulfil ye my joy, that ye be like-minded, having the same love, *being* of one accord, of one mind.

3. *Let* nothing *be done* through strife or vain-glory; but in lowliness of mind let each esteem other better than themselves.

4. Look not every man on his own things, but every man also on the things of others.

1. Si qua igitur consolatio (*vel, exhortatio*) in Christo, si quod solatium dilectionis, si qua communicatio Spiritus, si qua viscera et misericordiae.[1]

2. Implete gaudium meum ut idem sentiatis, eandem habentes caritatem, unanimes, unum sentientes.

3. Nihil per contentionem, aut inanem gloriam, sed per humilitatem alii alios existiment se ipsis excellentiores.

4. Non considerans quisque quod suum est, sed quisque quod est aliorum.

1. *If there is therefore any consolation.* There is an extraordinary tenderness in this exhortation,[2] in which he entreats by all means the Philippians mutually to cherish harmony among themselves, lest, in the event of their being torn asunder by intestine contentions, they should expose themselves to the impostures of the false apostles. For when there are disagreements, there is invariably a door opened for Satan to disseminate impious doctrines, while agreement is the best bulwark for repelling them.

As the term παρακλήσεως is often taken to mean *exhortation,* the commencement of the passage might be explained in this manner: "If an exhortation which is delivered in the name and by the authority of Christ, has any weight with you." The other meaning, however, corresponds better with the context: "If there is among you *any consolation of Christ,*" by means of which you may alleviate my griefs, and if you would afford me *any consolation* and relief, which you assuredly owe me in the exercise of love; if you take into view that *fellowship of the Spirit,* which ought to make us all one; if any feeling of humanity and mercy resides in you, which might stir you up to alleviate my miseries, *fulfil ye my joy,* &c. From this we may infer, how

[1] " Entrailles et misericordes, *ou,* cordiales affections et misericordes;"—" Bowels and mercies, *or,* cordial affections and mercies."

[2] " Ceste exhortation est plene d'affections vehementes;"—" This exhortation is full of intense affections."

at the same time take notice, how he humbles himself by beseechingly imploring their pity, while he might have availed himself of his paternal authority, so as to demand respect from them as his sons.² He knew how to exercise authority when it was necessary, but at present he prefers to use entreaties, because he knew that these would be better fitted to gain an entrance into their affections,³ and because he was aware that he had to do with persons who were docile and compliant. In this manner the pastor must have no hesitation to assume different aspects for the sake of the Church.⁴

2. *Fulfil ye my joy.* Here again we may say, how little anxiety he had as to himself, provided only it went well with the Church of Christ. He was kept shut up in prison, and bound with chains; he was reckoned worthy of capital punishment—before his view were tortures—near at hand was the executioner; yet all these things do not prevent his experiencing unmingled joy, provided he sees that the Churches are in a good condition. Now what he reckons the chief indication of a prosperous condition of the Church is—when mutual agreement prevails in it, and brotherly harmony. Thus the 137th Psalm teaches us in like manner, that our crowning joy is the remembrance of Jerusalem. (Ps. cxxxvii. 6.) But if this were the completion of Paul's joy, the Philippians would have been worse than cruel if they had tortured the mind of this holy man with a twofold anguish by disagreement among themselves.

---

¹ "Et que les pasteurs le doyuent procurer d'vne affection vehemente et zele ardent;"—"And that pastors should endeavour to procure it with intense desire and ardent zeal."

² "Il peust vser d'authorite paternelle, et demander que pour la reuerence qu'ils luy deuoyent comme ses enfans, ils feissent ce qu'il enseigne yci;"—"He might have exercised paternal authority, and have demanded that in consideration of the respect which they owed him as his children, they should do what he here inculcates."

³ "Pour entrer dedans leurs cœurs, et es mouuoir leurs affections;"—"For entering into their hearts, and moving their affections."

⁴ "Ne doit faire difficulte de se transformer selon qu'il cognoistra que ce sera la proufit de l'Eglise;"—"Should have no hesitation in transforming himself according as he may perceive that this will be for the advantage of the Church."

mention of agreement in doctrine and mutual love; and afterwards, repeating the same thing, (in my opinion,) he exhorts them to be of one mind, and to have the same views. The expression τὸ αὐτὸ, (*the same thing,*) implies that they must accommodate themselves to each other. Hence the beginning of love is harmony of views, but that is not sufficient, unless men's hearts are at the same time joined together in mutual affection. At the same time there were no inconsistency in rendering it thus :—" that ye may be of the same mind—so as to have mutual love, to be one in mind and one in views ;" for participles are not unfrequently made use of instead of infinitives. I have adopted, however, the view which seemed to me less forced.

3. *Nothing through strife or vain-glory.* These are two most dangerous pests for disturbing the peace of the Church. *Strife* is awakened when every one is prepared to maintain pertinaciously his own opinion; and when it has once begun to rage it rushes headlong[1] in the direction from which it has entered. *Vain-glory*[2] tickles men's minds, so that every one is delighted with his own inventions. Hence the only way of guarding against dissensions is—when we avoid strifes by deliberating and acting peacefully, especially if we are not actuated by ambition. For ambition is a means of fanning all strifes.[3] *Vain-glory* means any glorying in the flesh; for what ground of glorying have men in themselves that is not vanity?

But by humility. For both diseases he brings forward one remedy—*humility,* and with good reason, for it is the mother of moderation, the effect of which is that, yielding up our

[1] " Sans pouuoir estre arrestee ;"—" Without being capable of being arrested."

[2] " Κινοδόξοι, persons whose object is to acquire power, and who, if they see others superior to themselves, are offended. (Gal. v. 26.) This κινοδοξία, vain-glory, produces contentions of all kinds; and it produces this evil besides, that persons who have gone wrong, and who might have been restored to truth and virtue by humble, friendly admonition, are often, by the interference of *vain-glorious,* ostentatious instructors, confirmed in error and vice."—*Storr.* See *Biblical Cabinet,* vol. xl. p. 132, *note.*—*Ed.*

[3] " Est le sufflet qui allume toutes contentions ;"—" Is the bellows that kindles up all strifes."

humility—when every one esteems himself less than others. Now, if anything in our whole life is difficult, this above everything else is so. Hence it is not to be wondered if humility is so rare a virtue. For, as one says,[1] "Every one has in himself the mind of a king, by claiming everything for himself." See! here is pride. Afterwards from a foolish admiration of ourselves arises contempt of the brethren. And so far are we from what Paul here enjoins, that one can hardly endure that others should be on a level with him, for there is no one that is not eager to have superiority.

But it is asked, how it is possible that one who is in reality distinguished above others can reckon those to be superior to him who he knows are greatly beneath him? I answer, that this altogether depends on a right estimate of God's gifts, and our own infirmities. For however any one may be distinguished by illustrious endowments, he ought to consider with himself that they have not been conferred upon him that he might be self-complacent, that he might exalt himself, or even that he might hold himself in esteem. Let him, instead of this, employ himself in correcting and detecting his faults, and he will have abundant occasion for humility. In others, on the other hand, he will regard with honour whatever there is of excellences, and will by means of love bury their faults. The man who will observe this rule, will feel no difficulty in preferring others before himself. And this, too, Paul meant when he added, that they ought not to have every one a regard to themselves, but to their neighbours, or that they ought not to be devoted to themselves. Hence it is quite possible that a pious man, even though he should be aware that he is superior, may nevertheless hold others in greater esteem.

| 5. Let this mind be in you, which was also in Christ Jesus: | 5. Hoc enim sentiatur in vobis quod et in Christo Iesu: |
| 6. Who, being in the form of God, thought it not robbery to be equal with God; | 6. Qui quum in forma Dei esset, non rapinam arbitratus esset, Deo aequalem se esse: |

[1] "Comme quelqu'vn a dit anciennement;"—"As some one has said anciently."

likeness of men:	ut homo.
8. And being found in fashion as a man, he humbled himself, and became obedient unto death, even the death of the cross.	8. Humiliavit, inquam, se ipsum, factus obediens usque ad mortem, mortem vero crucis.
9. Wherefore God also hath highly exalted him, and given him a name which is above every name:	9. Quamobrem et Deus illum superexaltavit, et dedit illi nomen quod esset super omne nomen,
10. That at the name of Jesus every knee should bow, of *things* in heaven, and *things* in earth, and *things* under the earth;	10. Ut in nomine Iesu omne genu flectatur, cælestium, terrestrium, et infernorum,
11. And *that* every tongue should confess that Jesus Christ *is* Lord, to the glory of God the Father.	11. Et omnis lingua confiteatur, quod Dominus Iesus in gloriam est Dei Patris.

5. He now recommends, from the example of Christ, the exercise of humility, to which he had exhorted them in words. There are, however, two departments, in the *first* of which he invites us to imitate Christ, because this is the rule of life:[1] in the *second*, he allures us to it, because this is the road by which we attain true glory. Hence he exhorts every one to have the same disposition that was in Christ. He afterwards shews what a pattern of humility has been presented before us in Christ. I have retained the passive form of the verb, though I do not disapprove of the rendering given it by others, because there is no difference as to meaning. I merely wished that the reader should be in possession of the very form of expression which Paul has employed.

6. *Inasmuch as he was in the form of God.* This is not a comparison between things similar, but in the way of greater and less. *Christ's* humility consisted in his abasing himself from the highest pinnacle of glory to the lowest ignominy: *our* humility consists in refraining from exalting ourselves by a false estimation. *He* gave up his right: all that is required of *us* is, that we do not assume to ourselves more than we ought. Hence he sets out with this—that, *inasmuch as he was in the form of God, he reckoned it not an*

---

[1] "Pourceque l'imitation d' iceluy est la regle de bien viure;"—"Because imitation of him is the rule of right living."

from so great a height, how unreasonable that we, who are nothing, should be lifted up with pride!

The *form of God* means here his majesty. For as a man is known by the appearance of his *form*, so the majesty, which shines forth in God, is his figure.[1] Or if you would prefer a more apt similitude, the *form* of a *king* is his equipage and magnificence, shewing him to be a king—his sceptre, his crown, his mantle,[2] his attendants,[3] his judgment-throne, and other emblems of royalty; the *form* of a *consul* was—his long robe, bordered with purple, his ivory seat, his lictors with rods and hatchets. Christ, then, before the creation of the world, was in the form of God, because from the beginning he had his glory with the Father, as he says in John xvii. 5. For in the wisdom of God, prior to his assuming our flesh, there was nothing mean or contemptible, but on the contrary a magnificence worthy of God. Being such as he was, he could, without doing wrong to any one, *shew himself equal with God;* but he did not manifest himself to be what he really was, nor did he openly assume in the view of men what belonged to him by right.

Thought it not robbery. There would have been no wrong done though he had shewn himself to be *equal with God.* For when he says, *he would not have thought,* it is as though he had said, "He knew, indeed, that this was lawful and right for him," that we might know that his abasement was voluntary, not of necessity. Hitherto it has been rendered in the indicative—*he thought*, but the connection requires the subjunctive. It is also quite a customary thing for Paul to employ the past indicative in the place of the subjunctive, by leaving the potential particle ἄν, as it is called, to be supplied—as, for example, in Romans ix. 3, ηὐχόμην, for *I would have wished;* and in 1 Cor. ii. 8, εἰ γὰρ ἔγνωσαν, *if*

---

[1] "Car tout ainsi qu'vn homme est cognu quand on contemple la forme de son visage et sa personne, aussi la maieste, qui reluit en Dieu, est la forme ou figure d'iceluy;"—" For just as a man is known, when we mark the form of his appearance and his person, so the majesty, which shines forth in God, is his form or figure."

[2] "Le manteau royal;"—"His royal mantle."

[3] "La garde a l'entour;"—"The guard in attendance."

his abasement. Accordingly he mentions, not what Christ did, but what it was allowable for him to do.

Farther, that man is utterly blind who does not perceive that his eternal divinity is clearly set forth in these words. Nor does Erasmus act with sufficient modesty in attempting, by his cavils, to explain away this passage, as well as other similar passages.[1] He acknowledges, indeed, everywhere that Christ is God; but what am I the better for his orthodox confession, if my faith is not supported by any Scripture authority? I acknowledge, certainly, that Paul does not make mention here of Christ's divine essence; but it does not follow from this, that the passage is not sufficient for repelling the impiety of the Arians, who pretended that Christ was a created God, and inferior to the Father, and denied that he was consubstantial.[2] For where can there be *equality with God* without *robbery*, excepting only where there is the essence of God; for God always remains the same, who cries by Isaiah, *I live; I will not* give my glory to another. (Isaiah xlviii. 11.) *Form* means figure or appearance, as they commonly speak. This, too, I readily grant; but will there be found, apart from God, such a *form*, so as to be neither false nor forged? As, then, God is known by means of his excellences, and his works are evidences of his eternal Godhead, (Rom. i. 20,) so Christ's divine essence is rightly proved from Christ's majesty, which he possessed equally with the Father before he humbled himself. As to myself, at least, not even all devils would wrest this passage from me—inasmuch as there is in God a most solid argument, from his glory to his essence, which are two things that are inseparable.

7. *Emptied himself.* This *emptying* is the same as the abasement, as to which we shall see afterwards. The expression, however, is used, ἐμφατικοτέρως, (*more emphatically*,) to mean,—being brought to nothing. Christ, indeed, could

[1] " Comme s'ils ne faisoyent rien a ce propos-la ;"—" As if they had no bearing on that point."

[2] " C'est à dire d'vne mesme substance auec le Pere;"—" That is to say, of the same substance as the Father."

flesh. Hence he laid aside his glory in the view of men, not by lessening it, but by concealing it.

It is asked, whether he did this as man? Erasmus answers in the affirmative. But where was the *form of God* before he became man? Hence we must reply, that Paul speaks of Christ wholly, as he was *God manifested in the flesh,* (1 Tim. iii. 16;) but, nevertheless, this *emptying* is applicable exclusively to his humanity, as if I should say of man, "Man being mortal, he is exceedingly senseless if he thinks of nothing but the world," I refer indeed to man wholly; but at the same time I ascribe mortality only to a part of him, namely, to the body. As, then, Christ has one person, consisting of two natures, it is with propriety that Paul says, that he who was the Son of God,—in reality equal to God, did nevertheless lay aside his glory, when he in the flesh manifested himself in the appearance of a servant.

It is also asked, secondly, how he can be said to be *emptied,* while he, nevertheless, invariably proved himself, by miracles and excellences, to be the Son of God, and in whom, as John testifies, there was always to be seen a glory worthy of the Son of God? (John i. 14.) I answer, that the abasement of the flesh was, notwithstanding, like a vail, by which his divine majesty was concealed. On this account he did not wish that his transfiguration should be made public until after his resurrection; and when he perceives that the hour of his death is approaching, he then says, *Father, glorify thy Son.* (John xvii. 1.) Hence, too, Paul teaches elsewhere, that he was *declared to be the Son of God* by means of his resurrection. (Rom. i. 4.) He also declares in another place, (2 Cor. xiii. 4,) that he *suffered through the weakness of the flesh.* In fine, the image of God shone forth in Christ in such a manner, that he was, at the same time, abased in his outward appearance, and brought down to nothing in the estimation of men; for he carried about with him the *form of a servant,* and had assumed our nature, expressly with the view of his being a servant of the Father, nay, even of men. Paul, too, calls him the Minister of the

had long before been foretold by Isaiah—*Behold my servant,* &c.

In the likeness of men. Γενόμενος is equivalent here to *constitutus*—(*having been appointed*.) For Paul means that he had been brought down to the level of mankind, so that there was in appearance nothing that differed from the common condition of mankind. The Marcionites perverted this declaration for the purpose of establishing the phantasm of which they dreamed. They can, however, be refuted without any great difficulty, inasmuch as Paul is treating here simply of the manner in which Christ manifested himself, and the condition with which he was conversant when in the world. Let one be truly man, he will nevertheless be reckoned unlike others, if he conducts himself as if he were exempt from the condition of others. Paul declares that it was not so as to Christ, but that he lived in such a manner, that he seemed as though he were on a level with mankind, and yet he was very different from a mere man, although he was truly man. The Marcionites therefore shewed excessive childishness, in drawing an argument from similarity of condition for the purpose of denying reality of nature.[1]

Found means here, *known* or *seen*. For he treats, as has been observed, of estimation. In other words, as he had affirmed previously that he was truly God, the equal of the Father, so he here states, that he was reckoned, as it were, abject, and in the common condition of mankind. We must always keep in view what I said a little ago, that such abasement was voluntary.

8. *He became obedient.* Even this was great humility—that from being Lord he became a servant; but he says that he went farther than this, because, while he was not only immortal, but the Lord of life and death, he nevertheless became obedient to his Father, even so far as to endure death. This was extreme abasement, especially when we take into view the kind of death, which he immediately adds, with the view of enhancing it.[2] For by dying in this manner he

[1] See CALVIN'S *Institutes*, vol. ii. 13-15.
[2] "Pour amplifier et exaggerer la chose;"—"For the sake of amplifying and enhancing the thing."

a pattern of humility as ought to absorb the attention of all mankind; so far is it from being possible to unfold it in words in a manner suitable to its dignity.

9. *Therefore God hath highly exalted.* By adding consolation, he shews that abasement, to which the human mind is averse, is in the highest degree desirable. There is no one, it is true, but will acknowledge that it is a reasonable thing that is required from us, when we are exhorted to imitate Christ. This consideration, however, stirs us up to imitate him the more cheerfully, when we learn that nothing is more advantageous for us than to be conformed to his image. Now, that all are happy who, along with Christ, voluntarily abase themselves, he shews by his example; for from the most abject condition he was exalted to the highest elevation. Every one therefore that humbles himself will in like manner be exalted. Who would now be reluctant to exercise humility, by means of which the glory of the heavenly kingdom is attained?

This passage has given occasion to sophists, or rather they have seized hold of it, to allege that Christ merited first for himself, and afterwards for others. Now, in the first place, even though there were nothing false alleged, it would nevertheless be proper to avoid such profane speculations as obscure the grace of Christ—in imagining that he came for any other reason than with a view to our salvation. Who does not see that this is a suggestion of Satan—that Christ suffered upon the cross, that he might acquire for himself, by the merit of his work, what he did not possess? For it is the design of the Holy Spirit, that we should, in the death of Christ, see, and taste, and ponder, and feel, and recognise nothing but God's unmixed goodness, and the love of Christ toward us, which was great and inestimable, that, regardless of himself, he devoted himself and his life for our sakes. In every instance in which the Scriptures speak of the death of Christ, they assign to us its advantage and price;—that by means of it we are redeemed—reconciled to God—restored to righteousness—cleansed from our pollutions—life is pro-

persons referred to maintain, on the other hand, that the chief part of the advantage is in Christ himself—that a regard to himself had the precedence of that which he had to us—that he merited glory for himself before he merited salvation for us?

Farther, I deny the truth of what they allege, and I maintain that Paul's words are impiously perverted to the establishment of their falsehood; for that the expression, *for this cause,* denotes here a consequence rather than a reason, is manifest from this, that it would otherwise follow, that a man could merit Divine honours, and acquire the very throne of God—which is not merely absurd, but even dreadful to make mention of. For of what exaltation of Christ does the Apostle here speak? It is, that everything may be accomplished in him that God, by the prophet Isaiah, exclusively claims to himself. Hence the glory of God, and the majesty, which is so peculiar to him, that it cannot be transferred to any other, will be the reward of man's work!

Again, if they should urge the mode of expression, without any regard to the absurdity that will follow, the reply will be easy—that he has been given us by the Father in such a manner, that his whole life is as a mirror that is set before us. As, then, a mirror, though it has splendour, has it not for itself, but with the view of its being advantageous and profitable to others, so Christ did not seek or receive anything for himself, but everything for us. For what need, I ask, had he, who was the equal of the Father, of a new exaltation? Let, then, pious readers learn to detest the Sorbonnic sophists with their perverted speculations.

Hath given him a name. Name here is employed to mean dignity—a manner of expression which is abundantly common in all languages—" Jacet *sine nomine* truncus; He lies a headless *nameless* carcass."[1] The mode of expression, however, is more especially common in Scripture. The meaning therefore is, that supreme power was given to Christ,

[1] *Virg. Æn.* ii. 557, 558.

that is equal to his. Hence it follows that it is a Divine name.[1] This, too, he explains by quoting the words of Isaiah, where the Prophet, when treating of the propagation of the worship of God throughout the whole world, introduces God as speaking thus:—"I live: every knee will bow to me, and every tongue will swear to me," &c. (Isaiah xlv. 23.) Now, it is certain that adoration is here meant, which belongs peculiarly to God alone. I am aware that some philosophise with subtlety as to the name *Jesus*, as though it were derived from the ineffable name Jehovah.[2] In the reason, however, which they advance, I find no solidity. As for me, I feel no pleasure in empty subtleties;[3] and it is dangerous to trifle in a matter of such importance. Besides, who does not see that it is a forced, and anything rather than a genuine, exposition, when Paul speaks of Christ's whole dignity, to restrict his meaning to two syllables, as if any one were to examine attentively the letters of the word *Alexander*, in order to find in them the greatness of the name that Alexander acquired for himself. Their subtlety, therefore, is not solid, and the contrivance is foreign to Paul's intention. But worse than ridiculous is the conduct of the Sorbonnic sophists, who infer from the passage before us that we ought to bow the knee whenever the name of *Jesus* is pronounced, as though it were a magic word which had all virtue included in the sound of it.[4] Paul, on the other hand, speaks of the honour that is to be rendered to the Son of God—not to mere syllables.

10. *Every knee might bow.* Though respect is shewn to men also by means of this rite, there can nevertheless be no

---

[1] "Et de cela il s'en ensuit, que c'est vn nom ou dignite propre a Dieu seul;"—"And from this it follows, that it is a name or dignity that belongs to God alone."

[2] "Comme s'il estoit deduit du nom Jehouah, lequel les Juifs par superstition disent qu'il n'est licite de proferer;"—"As if it were derived from the name Jehovah, which the Jews superstitiously say that it is not lawful to utter."

[3] "En ces subtilitez vaines et frivoles;"—"In these empty and frivolous subtleties."

[4] "Duquel toute la vertu consistast au son et en la prononciation;"—"The whole virtue of which consisted in the sound and the pronunciation."

is a token.[1] As to this, it is proper to notice, that God is to be worshipped, not merely with the inward affection of the heart, but also by outward profession, if we would render to him what is his due. Hence, on the other hand, when he would describe his genuine worshippers, he says that they *have not bowed the knee to the image of Baal.* (1 Kings xix. 18.)

But here a question arises—whether this relates to the divinity of Christ or to his humanity, for either of the two is not without some inconsistency, inasmuch as nothing new could be given to his divinity; and his humanity in itself, viewed separately, has by no means such exaltation belonging to it that it should be adored as God? I answer, that this, like many things else, is affirmed in reference to Christ's entire person, viewed as *God manifested in the flesh.* (1 Tim. iii. 16.) For he did not abase himself either as to his humanity alone, or as to his divinity alone, but inasmuch as, clothed in our flesh, he concealed himself under its infirmity. So again God exalted his own Son in the same flesh, in which he had lived in the world abject and despised, to the highest rank of honour, that he may sit at his right hand.

Paul, however, appears to be inconsistent with himself; for in Rom. xiv. 11, he quotes this same passage, when he has it in view to prove that Christ will one day be the judge of the living and the dead. Now, it would not be applicable to that subject, if it were already accomplished, as he here declares. I answer, that the kingdom of Christ is on such a footing, that it is every day growing and making improvement, while at the same time perfection is not yet attained, nor will be until the final day of reckoning. Thus both things hold true—that all things are now subject to Christ, and that this subjection will, nevertheless, not be complete until the day of the resurrection, because that which is now only begun will then be completed. Hence, it is not without reason that this prophecy is applied in different ways at different times, as also all the other prophecies, which speak

[1] " Vn signe et ceremonie externe ;"—" An outward sign and rite."

ever, we infer that Christ is that eternal God who spoke by Isaiah.

Things in heaven, things on earth, things under the earth. Since Paul represents all things from heaven to hell as subject to Christ, Papists trifle childishly when they draw purgatory from his words. Their reasoning, however, is this—that devils are so far from bowing the knee to Christ, that they are in every way rebellious against him, and stir up others to rebellion, as if it were not at the same time written that they *tremble* at the simple mention of God. (James ii. 19.) How will it be, then, when they shall come before the tribunal of Christ? I confess, indeed, that they are not, and never will be, subject of their own accord and by cheerful submission; but Paul is not speaking here of voluntary obedience; nay more, we may, on the contrary, turn back upon them an argument, by way of *retortion*, (αντιστρέφον,) in this manner:—" The fire of purgatory, according to them, is temporary, and will be done away at the day of judgment: hence this passage cannot be understood as to purgatory, because Paul elsewhere declares that this prophecy will not be fulfilled until Christ shall manifest himself for judgment." Who does not see that they are twice children in respect of these disgusting frivolities?[1]

11. *Is Lord, to the glory of God the Father.* It might also be read, IN *the glory,* because the particle εἰς (*to*) is often used in place of ἐν, (*in.*) I prefer, however, to retain its proper signification, as meaning, that as the majesty of God has been manifested to men through Christ, so it shines forth in Christ, and the Father is glorified in the Son. See John v. 17, and you will find an exposition of this passage.

12. Wherefore, my beloved, as ye have always obeyed, not as in my presence only, but now much more in my absence, work out your own salvation with fear and trembling:	12. Itaque amici mei, quemadmodum semper obedistis, ne quasi in praesentia mea solum, sed nunc multo magis in absentia mea, cum timore et tremore vestram salutem operamini:

[1] " Qui ne voit qu'ils sont plus qu' enfans en telles subtilitez friuoles et niaiseries qu'ils affectent ?"—" Who does not see that they are worse than children in such frivolous subtleties and fooleries which they affect ?"

14. Do all things without murmurings and disputings;	14. Omnia facite absque murmurationibus et disceptationibus,
15. That ye may be blameless and harmless, the sons of God, without rebuke, in the midst of a crooked and perverse nation, among whom ye shine as lights in the world:	15. Ut sitis tales, de quibus nemo conqueratur, et sinceri filii Dei irreprehensibiles, in medio generationis pravae et tortuosae, inter quos lucete, tanquam luminaria in mundo:
16. Holding forth the word of life; that I may rejoice in the day of Christ, that I have not run in vain, neither laboured in vain.	16. Sermonem vitae sustinentes, in gloriam meam, in diem Christi, quod non frustra cucurrerim, nec frustra laboraverim.

12. *Therefore, &c.* He concludes the whole of the preceding exhortation with a general statement—that they should humble themselves under the Lord's hand, for that will very readily secure, that, laying aside all arrogance, they will be gentle and indulgent to each other. This is the only befitting way in which the mind of man may learn gentleness, when one who, while viewing himself apart, pleased himself in his hiding-places, comes to examine himself as compared with God.

As ye have always obeyed. He commends their previous obedience, that he may encourage them the more to persevere. As, however, it is the part of hypocrites to approve themselves before others, but so soon as they have withdrawn from public view, to indulge themselves more freely, as if every occasion of reverence and fear were removed, he admonishes them not to shew themselves *obedient in his presence merely*, but also, and even *much more, in his absence.* For if he were present, he could stimulate and urge them on by continued admonitions. Now, therefore, when their monitor is at a distance from them,[1] there is need that they should stir up themselves.

With fear and trembling. In this way he would have the Philippians testify and approve their obedience—by being submissive and humble. Now the source of humility is this —acknowledging how miserable we are, and devoid of all

---

[1] " Maintenant donc qu'il est loin d'eux, et qu'il ne les peut plus admonester en presence;"—" Now, therefore, when he is at a distance from them, and can no longer admonish them when present."

produces, when we please ourselves, and are more puffed up with confidence in our own virtue, than prepared to rest upon the grace of God. In contrast with this vice is that *fear* to which he exhorts. Now, although exhortation comes before doctrine, in the connection of the passage, it is in reality after it, in point of arrangement, inasmuch as it is derived from it. I shall begin, accordingly, with doctrine.

13. *It is God that worketh.* This is the true engine for bringing down all haughtiness—this the sword for putting an end to all pride, when we are taught that we are utterly nothing, and can do nothing, except through the grace of God alone. I mean supernatural grace, which comes forth from the spirit of regeneration. For, considered as men, we already *are, and live and move in God.* (Acts xvii. 28.) But Paul reasons here as to a kind of *movement* different from that universal one. Let us now observe how much he ascribes to God, and how much he leaves to us.

There are, in any action, two principal departments—the inclination, and the power to carry it into effect. Both of these he ascribes wholly to God; what more remains to us as a ground of glorying? Nor is there any reason to doubt that this division has the same force as if Paul had expressed the whole in a single word; for the inclination is the groundwork; the accomplishment of it is the summit of the building brought to a completion. He has also expressed much more than if he had said that God is the Author of the beginning and of the end. For in that case sophists would have alleged, by way of cavil, that something between the two was left to men. But as it is, what will they find that is in any degree peculiar to us? They toil hard in their schools to reconcile with the grace of God free-will—of such a nature, I mean, as they conceive of—which might be capable of turning itself by its own movement, and might have a peculiar and separate power, by which it might co-operate with the grace of God. I do not dispute as to the name, but as to the thing itself. In order, therefore, that free-will may harmonize with grace, they divide in such a manner,

have received from God the power of willing aright, but assign to man a good inclination. Paul, however, declares this to be a work of God, without any reservation. For he does not say that our hearts are simply turned or stirred up, or that the infirmity of a good will is helped, but that a good inclination is wholly the work of God.[1]

Now, in the calumny brought forward by them against us —that we make men to be like stones, when we teach that they have nothing good, except from pure grace, they act a shameless part. For we acknowledge that we have from nature an inclination, but as it is depraved through the corruption of sin, it begins to be good only when it has been renewed by God. Nor do we say that a man does anything good without willing it, but that it is only when his inclination is regulated by the Spirit of God. Hence, in so far as concerns this department, we see that the entire praise is ascribed to God, and that what sophists teach us is frivolous—that grace is offered to us, and placed, as it were, in the midst of us, that we may embrace it if we choose; for if God did not work in us efficaciously, he could not be said to produce in us a good inclination. As to the second department, we must entertain the same view. "God," says he, "is Ὁ ἐνεργῶν τὸ ἐνεργεῖν—*he that worketh in us to do.*" He brings, therefore, to perfection those pious dispositions which he has implanted in us, that they may not be unproductive, as he promises by Ezekiel,—"I will cause them to walk in my commandments." (Ezek. xi. 20.) From this we infer that perseverance, also, is his free gift.

According to his good pleasure. Some explain this to mean —the good intention of the mind.[2] I, on the other hand, take it rather as referring to God, and understand by it his benevolent disposition, which they commonly call *beneplacitum,* (*good pleasure.*) For the Greek word εὐδοκία is very frequently

---

[1] See *Institutes,* vol. i. pp. 350, 353.
[2] " Aucuns exposent le mot Grec, bon propos et bon cœur, le rapportans aux hommes;"—" Some explain the Greek word as meaning, a good purpose and a good heart, making it refer to men."

everything from us. Accordingly, not satisfied with having assigned to God the production both of *willing* and of *doing* aright, he ascribes both to his unmerited mercy. By this means he shuts out the contrivance of the sophists as to *subsequent grace*, which they imagine to be the reward of merit. Hence he teaches, that the whole course of our life, if we live aright, is regulated by God, and that, too, from his unmerited goodness.

With fear and trembling. From this Paul deduces an exhortation—that they must *with fear work out their own salvation.* He conjoins, as he is accustomed, *fear* and *trembling,* for the sake of greater intensity, to denote—serious and anxious fear. He, accordingly, represses drowsiness as well as confidence. By the term *work* he reproves our indolence, which is always ingenious in seeking advantages.[1] Now it seems as if it had in the grace of God a sweet occasion of repose; for if He *worketh in us,* why should we not indulge ourselves at our ease? The Holy Spirit, however, calls us to consider, that he wishes to work upon living organs, but he immediately represses arrogance by recommending *fear* and *trembling.*

The inference, also, is to be carefully observed: "You have," says he, "all things from God; therefore be solicitous and humble." For there is nothing that ought to train us more to modesty and fear, than our being taught, that it is by the grace of God alone that we stand, and will instantly fall down, if he even in the slightest degree withdraw his hand. Confidence in ourselves produces carelessness and arrogance. We know from experience, that all who confide in their own strength, grow insolent through presumption, and at the same time, devoid of care, resign themselves to sleep. The remedy for both evils is, when, distrusting ourselves, we depend entirely on God alone. And assuredly, that man has made decided progress in the knowledge, both of the grace of God, and of his own weakness,

[1] " Ingenieuse a cercher ses auantages, et quelques vaines excuses;"— " Ingenious in seeking its advantages, and some vain pretexts."

strength, must necessarily be at the same time in a state of intoxicated security. Hence it is a shameless calumny that Papists bring against us,—that in extolling the grace of God, and putting down free-will, we make men indolent, shake off the fear of God, and destroy all feeling of concern. It is obvious, however, to every reader, that Paul finds matter of exhortation here—not in the doctrine of Papists, but in what is held by us. " God," says he, "*works all things in us;* therefore submit to him with *fear.*" I do not, indeed, deny that there are many who, on being told that there is in us nothing that is good, indulge themselves the more freely in their vices; but I deny that this is the fault of the doctrine, which, on the contrary, when received as it ought to be, produces in our hearts a feeling of concern.

Papists, however, pervert this passage so as to shake the assurance of faith, for the man that trembles[2] is in uncertainty. They, accordingly, understand Paul's words as if they meant that we ought, during our whole life, to waver as to assurance of salvation. If, however, we would not have Paul contradict himself, he does not by any means exhort us to hesitation, inasmuch as he everywhere recommends confidence and (πληροφορίαν) *full assurance.* The solution, however, is easy, if any one is desirous of attaining the true meaning without any spirit of contention. There are two kinds of fear; the one produces anxiety along with humility; the other hesitation. The *former* is opposed to fleshly confidence and carelessness, equally as to arrogance; the latter, to assurance of faith. Farther, we must take notice, that, as believers repose with assurance upon the grace of God, so, when they direct their views to their own frailty, they do not by any means resign themselves carelessly to sleep, but are by *fear* of dangers stirred up to prayer. Yet, so far is this *fear* from disturbing tranquillity of conscience, and shaking confidence, that it rather confirms it. For distrust of ourselves leads us to lean more confidently upon the

[1] " Cerche songneusement et implore;"—" Diligently seeks and implores."
[2] " Car celuy qui tremble, disent-ils;"—" For he that trembles, say they."

submit themselves to God with true self-renunciation.

Work out your own salvation. As Pelagians of old, so Papists at this day make a proud boast of this passage, with the view of extolling man's excellence. Nay more, when the preceding statement is mentioned to them by way of objection, *It is God that worketh in us,* &c., they immediately by this shield ward it off (so to speak)— *Work out your own salvation.* Inasmuch, then, as the work is ascribed to God and man in common, they assign the half to each. In short, from the word *work* they derive free-will; from the term *salvation* they derive the merit of eternal life. I answer, that *salvation* is taken to mean the entire course of our calling, and that this term includes all things, by which God accomplishes that perfection, to which he has predestinated us by his gracious choice. This no one will deny, that is not obstinate and impudent. We are said to perfect it, when, under the regulation of the Spirit, we aspire after a life of blessedness. It is God that calls us, and offers to us salvation; it is our part to embrace by faith what he gives, and by obedience act suitably to his calling; but we have neither from ourselves. Hence we act only when he has prepared us for acting.

The word which he employs properly signifies—to continue until the end; but we must keep in mind what I have said, that Paul does not reason here as to how far our ability extends, but simply teaches that God acts in us in such a manner, that he, at the same time, does not allow us to be inactive,[1] but exercises us diligently, after having stirred us up by a secret influence.[2]

14. *Without murmurings.* These are fruits of that humility to which he had exhorted them. For every man that has learned carefully to submit himself to God, without claiming anything for himself, will also conduct himself agreeably among men. When every one makes it his care to please him-

---

[1] " Deuenir paresseux et oisifs ;"—" To become idle and indolent."

[2] " Mais apres nous auoir poussez et incitez par vne inspiration secrete et cachee, nous employe et exerce songneusement ;"—" But, after having stimulated and incited us by a secret and hidden inspiration, he diligently employs and exercises us."

the *first* place, accordingly, he forbids malignity and secret enmities; and then, *secondly*, open contentions. He adds, *thirdly*, that they give no occasion to others to complain of them—a thing which is wont to arise from excessive moroseness. It is true that hatred is not in all cases to be dreaded; but care must be taken, that we do not make ourselves odious through our own fault, so that the saying should be fulfilled in us, *They hated me without a cause.* (Psalm xxxv. 19.) If, however, any one wishes to extend it farther, I do not object to it. For murmurings and disputations spring up, whenever any one, aiming beyond measure at his own advantage,[1] gives to others occasion of complaint.[2] Nay, even this expression may be taken in an active sense, so as to mean—not troublesome or querulous. And this signification will not accord ill with the context, for a querulous temper ($\mu\epsilon\mu\psi\iota\mu o\iota\rho\iota\alpha$)[3] is the seed of almost all quarrels and slanderings. He adds *sincere,* because these pollutions will never come forth from minds that have been purified.

15. *The sons of God, unreprovable.* It ought to be rendered—*unreprovable,* BECAUSE *ye are the sons of God.* For God's adoption of us ought to be a motive to a blameless life, that we may in some degree resemble our Father. Now, although there never has been such perfection in the world as to have nothing worthy of reproof, those are, nevertheless, said to be *unreprovable* who aim at this with the whole bent of their mind, as has been observed elsewhere.[4]

In the midst of a wicked generation. Believers, it is true, live on earth, intermingled with the wicked;[5] they breathe the

---

[1] "Cerchant outre mesure son proufit et vtilite particuliere;"—"Seeking beyond measure his own particular profit and advantage."

[2] "Le vice qui est en plusieurs qu'ils sont pleins de complaints contre les autres;"—"The fault that is in very many—that they are full of complaints as to others."

[3] The term is used by Aristotle. See *Arist.* Virt. et Vit. 7. 6.—*Ed.*

[4] Our Author most probably refers to what he had stated when commenting on 1 *Cor.* i. 8. See CALVIN on the *Corinthians,* vol. i. pp. 58, 59.—*Ed.*

[5] "Mesles auec les infideles et meschans;"—"Mingled with the unbelieving and the wicked."

scarcely be found a single pious family that was not surrounded on all sides by unbelievers. So much the more does Paul stir up the Philippians to guard carefully against all corruptions. The meaning therefore is this: "You are, it is true, inclosed in the midst of the wicked; but, in the mean time, bear in mind that you are, by God's adoption, separated from them: let there be, therefore, in your manner of life, conspicuous marks by which you may be distinguished. Nay more, this consideration ought to stir you up the more to aim at a pious and holy life, that we may not also be a part of the *crooked generation*,[2] entangled by their vices and contagion."

As to his calling them a *wicked and crooked generation*, this corresponds with the connection of the passage. For he teaches us that we must so much the more carefully take heed on this account—that many occasions of offence are stirred up by unbelievers, which disturb their right course; and the whole life of unbelievers is, as it were, a labyrinth of various windings, that draw us off from the right way. They are, however, notwithstanding, epithets of perpetual application, that are descriptive of unbelievers of all nations and in all ages. For if the heart of man is wicked and unsearchable, (Jer. xvii. 9,) what will be the fruits springing from such a root? Hence we are taught in these words, that in the life of man there is nothing pure, nothing right, until he has been renewed by the Spirit of God.

Among whom shine ye. The termination of the Greek word is doubtful, for it might be taken as the *indicative—ye shine;* but the *imperative* suits better with the exhortation. He would have unbelievers be as lamps, which shine amidst the darkness of the world, as though he had said, "Unbelievers, it is true, are children of the night, and there is in the world nothing but darkness; but God has enlightened you for this end, that the purity of your life may shine forth

[1] "Et lors mesme que S. Paul escriuoit ceci;"—"And even at the time that St. Paul wrote this."
[2] "De la generation peruerse et maudite;"—"Of the perverse and accursed generation."

will arise upon thee, and his glory will be seen upon thee." (Isaiah lx. 2.) He adds immediately afterwards, "The Gentiles shall walk in thy light, and kings in the brightness of thy countenance." Though Isaiah speaks there rather of doctrine, while Paul speaks here of an exemplary life, yet, even in relation to doctrine, Christ in another passage specially designates the Apostles the *light of the world.* (Matt v. 14.)

16. *Holding forth the word of life.* The reason why they ought to be luminaries is, that they carry the *word of life,* by which they are enlightened, that they may give light also to others. Now he alludes to lamps, in which wicks are placed that they may burn, and he makes us resemble the lamps; while he compares the word of God to the wick, from which the light comes. If you prefer another figure—we are candlesticks: the doctrine of the gospel is the candle, which, being placed in us, diffuses light on all sides. Now he intimates, that we do injustice to the word of God, if it does not shine forth in us in respect of purity of life. This is the import of Christ's saying, "*No man lighteth a candle, and putteth it under a bushel,*" &c. (Matt. v. 15.) We are said, however, to *carry the word of life* in such a way as to be, in the mean time, carried by it,[1] inasmuch as we are founded upon it. The manner, however, of carrying it, of which Paul speaks, is, that God has intrusted his doctrine with us on condition, not that we should keep the light of it under restraint, as it were, and inactive, but that we should hold it forth to others. The sum is this: that all that are enlightened with heavenly doctrine carry about with them a light, which detects and discovers their crimes,[2] if they do not walk in holiness and chastity; but that this light has been kindled up, not merely that they may themselves be guided in the right way, but that they may also shew it to others.

That I may have glory. That he may encourage them the more, he declares that it will turn out to his glory, if he has not laboured among them in vain. Not as if those who

---

[1] "Soustenus ou portez d'elle;"—"Sustained or carried by it."
[2] "Leur turpitude et vilenie;"—"Their disgrace and villany."

ministry is a singular blessing from God, let us not feel surprised, if God, among his other gifts, makes this the crowning one. Hence, as Paul's Apostleship is now rendered illustrious by so many Churches, gained over to Christ through his instrumentality, so there can be no question that such trophies[1] will have a place in Christ's kingdom, as we will find him saying a little afterwards, *You are my crown.* (Phil. iv. 1.) Nor can it be doubted, that the greater the exploits, the triumph will be the more splendid.[2]

Should any one inquire how it is that Paul now glories in his labours, while he elsewhere forbids us to *glory* in any but *in the Lord,* (1 Cor. i. 31 ; 2 Cor. x. 17,) the answer is easy— that, when we have prostrated ourselves, and all that we have before God, and have placed in Christ all our ground of glorying, it is, at the same time, allowable for us to glory through Christ in God's benefits, as we have seen in the First Epistle to the Corinthians.[3] The expression, *at the day of the Lord,* is intended to stimulate the Philippians to perseverance, while the tribunal of Christ is set before their view, from which the reward of faith is to be expected.

17. Yea, and if I be offered upon the sacrifice and service of your faith, I joy, and rejoice with you all.
18. For the same cause also do ye joy, and rejoice with me.
19. But I trust in the Lord Jesus to send Timotheus shortly unto you, that I also may be of good comfort when I know your state.
20. For I have no man like-minded, who will naturally care for your state.
21. For all seek their own, not the things which are Jesus Christ's.

17. Quin etiam si immoler super hostia et sacrificio fidei vestrae, gaudeo et congaudeo vobis omnibus.
18. De hoc ipso gaudete, et congaudete mihi.
19. Spero autem in Domino, Timotheum brevi me ad vos missurum, ut ego tranquillo sim animo, postquam statum vestrum cognoverim.
20. Neminem enim habeo pari animo praeditum, qui germane res vestras curaturus sit.
21. Omnes enim quae sua sunt quaerunt: non quae sunt Christi Iesu.

[1] " Telles conquestes et marques de triomphe ;"—" Such conquests and tokens of triumph." The term *tropaea* made use of by our Author, (corresponding to the Greek term τρόπαια,) properly signifies, monuments of the enemy's *defeat,* (τροπή.)—*Ed.*

[2] " Tant plus qu'il y aura de faits cheualeureux, que le triomphe aussi n'en soit d'autant plus magnifique et honourable ;"—" The more there are of illustrious deeds, the triumph also will be so much the more magnificent and honourable."

[3] See CALVIN on the Corinthians, vol. i. pp. 94, 95.

23. Him therefore I hope to send presently, so soon as I shall see how it will go with me.	23. Hunc igitur spero me missurum, simulac mea negotia videro.
24. But I trust in the Lord that I also myself shall come shortly.	24. Confido autem in Domino quod ipse quoque brevi sim venturus.

17. *If I should be offered.*[1] The Greek word is σπένδομαι, and accordingly there appears to be an allusion to those animals, by the slaughter of which agreements and treaties were confirmed among the ancients. For the Greeks specially employ the term σπονδὰς to denote the victims by which treaties are confirmed. In this way, he calls his death the confirmation of their faith, which it certainly would be. That, however, the whole passage may be more clearly understood, he says that he offered sacrifice to God, when he consecrated them by the gospel. There is a similar expression in Romans xv. 16; for in that passage he represents himself as a priest, who *offers up* the Gentiles to God by the gospel. Now, as the gospel is a spiritual sword for slaying victims,[2] so faith is, as it were, the oblation; for there is no faith without mortification, by means of which we are consecrated to God.

He makes use of the terms, θυσίαν καὶ λειτουργίαν—*sacrifice and service,* the *former* of which refers to the Philippians, who had been offered up to God; and the *latter* to Paul, for it is the very act of sacrificing. The term, it is true, is equivalent to *administration,* and thus it includes functions and offices of every kind; but here it relates properly to the service of God—corresponding to the phrase made use of by the Latins—*operari sacris*—(to be *employed in sacred rites.*[3]) Now Paul says that he will rejoice, if he shall be offered up upon a sacrifice of this nature—that it

---

[1] Paul's statement here is interpreted by Dr. John Brown as equivalent to the following:—" If my life be poured out as a libation over your conversion to Christ, 'I joy and rejoice with you all.' It could not be better sacrificed than in the cause of his glory and your salvation."—Brown's Discourses and Sayings of our Lord illustrated, vol. iii. p. 379.—*Ed.*

[2] "Pour tuer les bestes qu'on doit sacrifier;"—"For killing the animals that ought to be sacrificed."

[3] See *Liv.* l. i. c. 31, *ad fin.*—*Ed.*

with our own blood what we teach.

From this, however, a useful lesson is to be gathered as to the nature of faith—that it is not a vain thing, but of such a nature as to consecrate man to God. The ministers of the gospel have, also, here a singular consolation in being called priests of God, to present victims to him;[1] for with what ardour ought that man to apply himself to the pursuit of preaching, who knows that this is an acceptable sacrifice to God! The wretched Papists, having no knowledge of this kind of sacrifice, contrive another, which is utter sacrilege.

I rejoice with you, says he—so that if it should happen that he died, they would know that this took place for their profit, and would receive advantage from his death.

18. *Rejoice ye.* By the alacrity which he thus discovers, he encourages the Philippians, and enkindles in them a desire to meet death with firmness,[2] inasmuch as believers suffer no harm from it. For he has formerly taught them that death would be *gain* to himself, (Phil. i. 21;) here, on the other hand, he is chiefly concerned that his death may not disconcert the Philippians.[3] He, accordingly, declares that it is no ground of sorrow; nay, that they have occasion of joy, inasmuch as they will find it to be productive of advantage. For, although it was in itself a serious loss to be deprived of such a teacher, it was no slight compensation that the gospel was confirmed by his blood. In the mean time, he lets them know that to himself personally death would be matter of joy. The rendering of Erasmus, taking it in the present tense, *Ye rejoice,* is altogether unsuitable.

19. *But I hope.* He promises them the coming of Timothy, that, from their expecting him, they may bear up more

[1] " Pour luy offrir en sacrifice les ames des fideles;"—" To offer to him in sacrifice the souls of the believers."

[2] " Les enflambe a mourir constamment, et receuoir la mort d'vn cœur magnanime;"—" Enkindles them to die with firmness, and meet death with magnanimity."

[3] " Que sa mort ne trouble et estonne les Philippians;"—" That his death may not distress and alarm the Philippians."

from giving way, so this consideration, too, was fitted to encourage greatly the Philippians: "There will one come very shortly, who will set himself in opposition to the contrivances of our enemies." But if the mere expectation of him had so much influence, his presence would exert a much more powerful effect. We must take notice of the condition[1] —in respect of which he submits himself to the providence of God, forming no purpose, but with *that* leading the way, as assuredly it is not allowable to determine anything as to the future, except, so to speak, under the Lord's hand. When he adds, *that I may be in tranquillity*, he declares his affection towards them, inasmuch as he was so much concerned as to their dangers, that he was not at ease until he received accounts of their prosperity.

20. *I have no man like-minded.* While some draw another meaning from the passage, I interpret it thus: "I have no one equally well-affected for attending to your interests." For Paul, in my opinion, compares Timothy with others, rather than with himself, and he pronounces this eulogium upon him, with the express design that he may be the more highly esteemed by them for his rare excellence.

21. *For all seek their own things.* He does not speak of those who had openly abandoned the pursuit of piety, but of those very persons whom he reckoned brethren, nay, even those whom he admitted to familiar intercourse with him. These persons, he nevertheless says, were so warm in the pursuit of their own interests, that they were unbecomingly cold in the work of the Lord. It may seem at first view as if it were no great fault to seek one's own profit; but how insufferable it is in the servants of Christ, appears from this, that it renders those that give way to it utterly useless. For it is impossible that the man who is devoted to self, should apply himself to the interests of the Church. Did then, you will say, Paul cultivate the society of men that were worthless and mere pretenders? I answer, that it is not to

---

[1] " En ces mots, *au Seigneur Jesus,* il faut noter la condition;"—" In these words, *in the Lord Jesus,* we must notice the condition."

the Church, but that, taken up with their own individual interests, they were to some extent negligent to the promotion of the public advantage of the Church. For it must necessarily be, that one or other of two dispositions prevails over us—either that, overlooking ourselves, we are devoted to Christ, and those things that are Christ's, or that, unduly intent on our own advantage, we serve Christ in a superficial manner.

From this it appears, how great a hinderance it is to Christ's ministers to seek their own interests. Nor is there any force in these excuses: "I do harm to no one"—"I must have a regard, also, to my own advantage"—"I am not so devoid of feeling as not to be prompted by a regard to my own advantage." For you must give up your own right if you would discharge your duty: a regard to your own interest must not be put in preference to Christ's glory, or even placed upon a level with it. Whithersoever Christ calls you, you must go promptly, leaving off all other things. Your calling ought to be regarded by you in such a way, that you shall turn away all your powers of perception from everything that would impede you. It might be in your power to live elsewhere in greater opulence, but God has bound you to the Church, which affords you but a very moderate sustenance: you might elsewhere have more honour, but God has assigned you a situation, in which you live in a humble style:[1] you might have elsewhere a more salubrious sky, or a more delightful region, but it is here that your station is appointed. You might wish to have to do with a more humane people: you feel offended with their ingratitude, or barbarity, or pride; in short, you have no sympathy with the disposition or the manners of the nation in which you are, but you must struggle with yourself, and do violence in a manner to opposing inclinations, that you may[2] keep

[1] "Sans estre en plus grande reputation;"—"Without being in very great reputation."
[2] "En sorte que tu te contentes du lieu qui t'est ordonné, et que t'employes a ta charge;"—"So as to content yourself with the place that is appointed for you, and employ yourself in your own department."

serve God.

If, however, Paul reproves so severely those who were influenced by a greater concern for themselves than for the Church, what judgment may be looked for by those who, while altogether devoted to their own affairs, make no account of the edification of the Church? However they may now flatter themselves, God will not spare them. An allowance must be given to the ministers of the Church to seek their own interests, so as not to be prevented from seeking the kingdom of Christ; but in that case they will not be represented as seeking their own interests, as a man's life is estimated according to its chief aim. When he says *all*, we are not to understand the term denoting universality, as though it implied that there was no exception, for there were others also, such as Epaphroditus,[2] but there were few of these, and he ascribes to all what was very generally prevalent.

When, however, we hear Paul complaining, that in that golden age, in which all excellences flourished, that there were so few that were rightly affected,[3] let us not be disheartened, if such is our condition in the present day: only let every one take heed to himself, that he be not justly reckoned to belong to that catalogue. I should wish, however, that Papists would answer me one question—where Peter was at that time, for he must have been at Rome, if what they say is true. O the sad and vile description that Paul gave of him! They utter, therefore, mere fables, when they pretend that he at that time presided over the Church of Rome. Observe, that the edification of the Church is termed the *things of Christ*, because we are truly engaged in his work, when we labour in the cultivation of his vineyard.

[1] See CALVIN on the Corinthians, vol. i. p. 249.

[2] " Car il y en auoit d'autres qui auoyent plus grand soin de l'Eglise de Dieu, que d'eux-mesmes, comme Epaphrodite ;"—" For there were others of them that had greater concern as to the Church of God, than as to themselves, such as Epaphroditus."

[3] " Qu'il y auoit si peu de gens sages et qui eussent vn cœur entier a nostre Seigneur ;"—" That there were so few persons that were wise, and had devotedness of heart to our Lord."

mood, *know ye;* (for there had scarcely been opportunity during that short time to make trial,) but this is not of great moment. What is chiefly to be noticed is, that he furnishes Timothy with an attestation of fidelity and modesty. In evidence of his fidelity, he declares, that he had *served with him in the gospel,* for such a connection was a token of true sincerity. In evidence of his modesty, he states, that he had *submitted to him as to a father.* It is not to be wondered, that this virtue is expressly commended by Paul, for it has in all ages been rare. At the present day, where will you find one among the young that will give way to his seniors, even in the smallest thing? to such an extent does impertinence triumph and prevail in the present age! In this passage, as in many others, we see how diligently Paul makes it his aim to put honour upon pious ministers, and that not so much for their own sakes, as on the ground of its being for the advantage of the whole Church, that such persons should be loved and honoured, and possess the highest authority.

24. *I trust that I myself.* He adds this, too, lest they should imagine that anything had happened to change his intention as to the journey of which he had previously made mention. At the same time, he always speaks conditionally —*If it shall please the Lord.* For although he expected deliverance from the Lord, yet there having been, as we have observed, no express promise, this expectation was by no means settled, but was, as it were, suspended upon the secret purpose of God.

25. Yet I supposed it necessary to send to you Epaphroditus, my brother, and companion in labour, and fellow-soldier, but your messenger, and he that ministered to my wants.

26. For he longed after you all, and was full of heaviness, because that ye had heard that he had been sick.

27. For indeed he was sick nigh unto death: but God had mercy on

25. Porro necessarium existimavi Epaphroditum, fratrem et cooperarium, et commilitonem meum, Apostolum autem vestrum, et ministrum necessitatis meæ mittere ad vos.

26. Quandoquidem desiderabat vos omnes, et erat anxius animi, propterea quod audieratis ipsum infirmatum fuisse.

27. Et certe infirmatus fuit, ut esset morti vicinus, sed Deus miser-

28. I sent him therefore the more carefully, that, when ye see him again, ye may rejoice, and that I may be the less sorrowful.

29. Receive him therefore in the Lord with all gladness; and hold such in reputation:

30. Because for the work of Christ he was nigh unto death, not regarding his life, to supply your lack of service toward me.

28. Studiosius itaque misi illum, ut eo viso rursus gaudeatis, et ego magis vacem dolore.

29. Excipite ergo illum in Domino cum omni gaudio: et qui tales sunt, in pretio habete:

30. Quia propter opus Christi usque ad mortem accessit, exponens periculo animam, ut sufficeret quod deerat vestro erga me ministerio, (*vel*, *officio*.)

25. *I thought it necessary to send to you Epaphroditus.* After having encouraged them by the promise of his own coming and that of Timothy, he fortifies them also for the present, by sending previously Epaphroditus, that in the mean time, while he waited the issue of his own affairs, (for this was the cause of his delay,) they might not be in want of a pastor who should take care that matters were properly managed. Now, he recommends Epaphroditus by many distinctions—that he is his *brother*, and helper in the affairs of the gospel—that he is his *fellow-soldier*, by which term he intimates what is the condition of the ministers of the gospel; that they are engaged in an incessant warfare, for Satan will not allow them to promote the gospel without maintaining a conflict. Let those, then, who prepare themselves for edifying the Church, know that war is denounced against them, and prepared. This, indeed, is common to all Christians—to be soldiers in the camp of Christ,[1] for Satan is the enemy of all. It is, however, more particularly applicable to the ministers of the word, who go before the army and bear the standard. Paul, however, more especially might boast of his military service,[2] inasmuch as he was exercised to a very miracle in every kind of contest. He accordingly

---

[1] " De batailler sous l'enseigne de Christ;"—" To fight under Christ's banner."

[2] " S. Paul pouuoit se vanter plus que pas on des autrés, que sa condition estoit semblable a celle d'vn gendarme;"—" St. Paul might boast more than any other that his condition resembled that of a soldier."

The term *Apostle* here, as in many other passages, is taken generally to mean any evangelist,[1] unless any one prefers to understand it as meaning an ambassador sent by the Philippians, so that it may be understood as conjoining these two things—an ambassador to afford service to Paul.[2] The former signification, however, is in my opinion more suitable. He mentions also, among other things, to his praise, that he had *ministered to him in prison*—a matter which will be treated of more fully ere long.

26. *He longed after you.* It is a sign of a true pastor, that while he was at a great distance, and was willingly detained by a pious engagement, he was nevertheless affected with concern for his flock, and a longing after them; and on learning that his sheep were distressed on his account,[3] he was concerned as to their grief. On the other hand, the anxiety of the Philippians for their pastor is here discovered.

27. *But God had mercy on him.* He had expressed the severity of the disease—that Epaphroditus had been sick, so that life was despaired of, in order that the goodness of God might shine forth more clearly in his restored health. It is, however, surprising that he should ascribe it to the mercy of God that Epaphroditus had had his period of life prolonged, while he had previously declared that he desired death in preference to life. (Phil. i. 23.) And what were better for us than that we should remove hence to the kingdom of God, delivered from the many miseries of this world, and more especially, rescued from that bondage of sin in which he elsewhere exclaims that he is *wretched,* (Rom. vii. 24,) to attain the full enjoyment of that liberty of the Spirit, by which we become connected with the Son of God?[4] It were tedious to enumerate all the things which tend to

[1] " Pour tous prescheurs de l'euangile ;"—" For all preachers of the gospel."

[2] " Ambassade pour administrer a Sainct Paul en sa necessite ;"—" An ambassador to minister to St. Paul in his necessity."

[3] " Pour l'amour de luy;"—" From love to him."

[4] " Par laquelle nous soyons parfaitement conioints auec le Fils de Dieu;"—" By which we are perfectly united with the Son of God."

God, when it does nothing but lengthen out our miseries? I answer, that all these things do not prevent this life from being, nevertheless, considered in itself, an excellent gift of God. More especially those who live to Christ are happily exercised here in hope of heavenly glory; and accordingly, as we have had occasion to see a little ago, life is gain to them.[1] Besides, there is another thing, too, that is to be considered—that it is no small honour that is conferred upon us, when God glorifies himself in us; for it becomes us to look not so much to life itself, as to the end for which we live.

But on me also, lest I should have sorrow. Paul acknowledges that the death of Epaphroditus would have been bitterly painful to him, and he recognises it as an instance of God's sparing mercy toward himself, that he had been restored to health. He does not, therefore, make it his boast that he has the *apathy* (*ἀπάθειαν*) of the Stoics, as if he were a man of iron, and exempt from human affections.[2] "What then!" some one will say, "where is that unconquerable magnanimity?—where is that indefatigable perseverance?" I answer, that Christian patience differs widely from philosophical obstinacy, and still more from the stubborn and fierce sternness of the Stoics. For what excellence were there in patiently enduring the cross, if there were in it no feeling of pain and bitterness? But when the consolation of God overcomes that feeling, so that we do not resist, but, on the contrary, give our back to the endurance of the rod, (Isaiah l. 5,) we in that case present to God a sacrifice of obedience that is acceptable to him. Thus Paul acknowledges that he felt some uneasiness and pain from his bonds, but that he nevertheless cheerfully endured these same bonds for the sake of Christ.[3] He acknowledges that he would have felt the death of Epaphroditus an event hard to

[1] CALVIN seems to refer here to what he had said when commenting on Phil. i. 21.—*Ed.*

[2] CALVIN, in the French version, makes reference to what he has said on this subject in the *Institutes*. See *Institutes*, vol. ii. p. 281.—*Ed.*

[3] " Pour l'amour de Christ;"—" From love to Christ."

reluctance was not yet fully removed; for we give proof of our obedience, only when we bridle our depraved affections, and do not give way to the infirmity of the flesh.¹

Two things, therefore, are to be observed: in the *first* place, that the dispositions which God originally implanted in our nature are not evil in themselves, because they do not arise from the fault of corrupt nature, but come forth from God as their Author; of this nature is the grief that is felt on occasion of the death of friends: in the *second* place, that Paul had many other reasons for regret in connection with the death of Epaphroditus, and that these were not merely excusable, but altogether necessary. This, in the first place, is invariable in the case of all believers, that, on occasion of the death of any one, they are reminded of the anger of God against sin; but Paul was the more affected with the loss sustained by the Church, which he saw would be deprived of a singularly good pastor at a time when the good were so few in number. Those who would have dispositions of this kind altogether subdued and eradicated, do not picture to themselves merely men of flint, but men that are fierce and savage. In the depravity of our nature, however, everything in us is so perverted, that in whatever direction our minds are bent, they always go beyond bounds. Hence it is that there is nothing that is so pure or right in itself, as not to bring with it some contagion. Nay more, Paul, as being a man, would, I do not deny, have experienced in his grief something of human error,² for he was subject to infirmity, and required to be tried with temptations, in order that he might have occasion of victory by striving and resisting.

28. *I have sent him the more carefully.* The presence of Epaphroditus was no small consolation to him; yet to such

¹ " Ne nous laissons point vaincre par l'infirmite de nostre chair;"— " Do not allow ourselves to be overcome by the infirmity of our flesh."

² " Mesme ie ne nie pas que sainct Paul (comme il estoit homme) ne se trouué surprins de quelque exces vicieux en sa douleur;"—" Nay more, I do not deny that St. Paul (inasmuch as he was a man) might find himself overtaken with some faulty excess in his grief."

his departure, because it grieved him that, on his account, he was taken away from the flock that was intrusted to him, and was reluctant to avail himself of his services, though otherwise agreeable to him, when it was at the expense of loss to them. Hence he says, that he will feel more happiness in the joy of the Philippians.

29. *Receive him with all joy.* He employs the word *all* to mean sincere and abundant. He also recommends him again to the Philippians; so intent is he upon this, that all that approve themselves as good and faithful pastors may be held in the highest estimation: for he does not speak merely of one, but exhorts that all such should be held in estimation; for they are precious pearls from God's treasuries, and the rarer they are, they are so much the more worthy of esteem. Nor can it be doubted that God often punishes our ingratitude and proud disdain, by depriving us of good pastors, when he sees that the most eminent that are given by him are ordinarily despised. Let every one, then, who is desirous that the Church should be fortified against the stratagems and assaults of wolves, make it his care, after the example of Paul, that the authority of good pastors be established;[1] as, on the other hand, there is nothing upon which the instruments of the devil are more intent, than on undermining it by every means in their power.

30. *Because for the work of Christ.* I consider this as referring to that infirmity, which he had drawn down upon himself by incessant assiduity. Hence he reckons the distemper of Epaphroditus among his excellences, as it certainly was a signal token of his ardent zeal. Sickness, indeed, is not an excellence, but it is an excellence not to spare yourself that you may serve Christ. Epaphroditus felt that his health would be in danger if he applied himself beyond measure; yet he would rather be negligent as to health than be deficient in duty; and that he may commend this conduct the more to the Philippians, he says that it was

[1] " Soit establie et demeure entiere;"—" Be established, and remain entire."

Epaphroditus, having been sent for this purpose, acted in their stead.[2] He speaks of the services rendered to him as the *work of the Lord,* as assuredly there is nothing in which we can better serve God, than when we help his servants who labour for the truth of the gospel.

CHAPTER III.

1. Finally, my brethren, rejoice in the Lord. To write the same things to you, to me indeed *is* not grievous, but for you *it is* safe.
2. Beware of dogs, beware of evil workers, beware of the concision.
3. For we are the circumcision, which worship God in the spirit, and rejoice in Christ Jesus, and have no confidence in the flesh.
4. Though I might also have confidence in the flesh. If any other man thinketh that he hath whereof he might trust in the flesh, I more:
5. Circumcised the eighth day, of the stock of Israel, *of* the tribe of Benjamin, an Hebrew of the Hebrews; as touching the law, a Pharisee;
6. Concerning zeal, persecuting the Church; touching the righteousness which is in the law, blameless.

1. Quod reliquum est, fratres mei, gaudete in Domino; eadem scribere vobis, me quidem haud piget, vobis autem tutum est.
2. Videte canes, videte malos operarios, videte concisionem.
3 Nos enim sumus circumcisio, qui spiritu Deum colimus, et gloriamur in Christo Iesu, non autem in carne confidimus.
4. Tametsi ego etiam in carne fiduciam habeo. Si quis alius videtur confidere in carne, ego magis:
5. Circumcisus die octavo, ex genere Israel, tribu Beniamin, Hebraeus ex Hebraeis, secundum legem Pharisaeus:
6. Secundum zelum persequens Ecclesiam, secundum iustitiam, quae est in lege, irreprehensibilis.

1. *Rejoice in the Lord.* This is a conclusion from what goes before, for as Satan never ceased to distress them with daily rumours, he bids them divest themselves of anxiety and be of good courage. In this way he exhorts them to constancy, that they may not fall back from the doctrine which they have once received. The phrase *henceforward* denotes a continued course, that, in the midst of many hinderances, they may not cease to exercise holy joy. It is a

[1] " Vn accomplissement, ou moyen de suppleer ce qui defailloit de leur seruice;"—" A filling up, or a means of supplying what was defective in their service."
[2] " Faisoit en cest endroit ce qu'ils deuoyent faire;"—" Did in this matter what they ought to have done."

name unpleasant,[2] we take such satisfaction in the simple tasting of God's grace, that all annoyances, sorrows, anxieties, and griefs are sweetened.

To write the same things to you. Here he begins to speak of the false Apostles, with whom, however, he does not fight hand to hand, as in the Epistle to the Galatians, but in a few words severely[3] exposes them, as far as was sufficient. For as they had simply made an attempt upon the Philippians, and had not made an inroad upon them,[4] it was not so necessary to enter into any regular disputation with the view of refuting errors, to which they had never lent an ear. Hence he simply admonishes them to be diligent and attentive in detecting impostors and guarding against them.

In the *first* place, however, he calls them *dogs;* the metaphor being grounded upon this—that, for the sake of filling their belly, they assailed true doctrine with their impure barking. Accordingly, it is as though he had said,—impure or profane persons; for I do not agree with those who think that they are so called on the ground of envying others, or biting them.[5]

In the *second* place, he calls them *evil workers,* meaning, that, under the pretext of building up the Church, they did nothing but ruin and destroy everything; for many are busily occupied[6] who would do better to remain idle. As the public crier[7] on being asked by Gracchus in mockery,

[1] " De nous troubler et effaroucher;"—" To trouble and frighten us."
[2] " Fascheux et ennuyeux;"—" Disagreeable and irksome."
[3] " Il les rembarre rudement et auec authorite;"—" He baffles them sternly and with authority."
[4] " Pource qu'ils auoyent seulement fait leurs efforts, et essayé de diuertir les Philippiens, et ne les auoyent gaignez et abbatus;"—" As they had merely employed their efforts, and had attempted to turn aside the Philippians, and had not prevailed over them and subdued them."
[5] " Pour autant qu'ils portoyent enuie auec autres, ou les mordoyent et detractoyent d'eux;"—" On the ground of their bearing envy to others, and biting and calumniating them."
[6] " Car il y en a plusieurs qui se tourmentent tant et plus, et se meslent de beaucoup de choses;"—" For there are many that torture themselves on this occasion and on that, and intermeddle with many things."
[7] " Comme anciennement a Rome ce crier public;"—" As anciently at Rome that public crier."

was the ringleader of a ruinous sedition. Hence Paul would have a distinction made among *workers*, that believers may be on their guard against those that are *evil*.

In the *third* term employed, there is an elegant (προσωνομασία) *play upon words*. They boasted that they were the *circumcision:* he turns aside this boasting by calling them the *concision*,[1] inasmuch as they tore asunder the unity of the Church. In this we have an instance tending to shew that the Holy Spirit in his organs[2] has not in every case avoided wit and humour, yet so as at the same time to keep at a distance from such pleasantry as were unworthy of his majesty. There are innumerable examples in the Prophets, and especially in Isaiah, so that there is no profane author that abounds more in agreeable plays upon words, and figurative forms of expression. We ought, however, more carefully still to observe the vehemence with which Paul inveighs against the false Apostles, which will assuredly break forth wherever there is the ardour of pious zeal. But in the mean time we must be on our guard lest any undue warmth or excessive bitterness should creep in under a pretext of zeal.

When he says, that to *write the same things is not grievous to him*, he seems to intimate that he had already written on some other occasion to the Philippians. There would, however, be no inconsistency in understanding him as meaning, that he now by his writings reminds them of the same things as they had frequently heard him say, when he was with them. For there can be no doubt that he had often intimated to them in words, when he was with them, how much they ought to be on their guard against such pests: yet he does not grudge to repeat these things, because the

---

[1] "*The Concision*—that is, those who rend and divide the Church. Compare Rom. xvi. 17, 18. They gloried in being the περιτομὴ, (*the circumcision*,) which name and character St. Paul will not here allow them, but claims it for Christians in the next words, and calls them the κατατομὴ, or *concision*, expressing his contempt of their pretences, and censure of their practices."—*Pierce.—Ed.*

[2] "En ses organes et instrumens c'est a dire ses seruiteurs par lesquels il a parle ;"—"In his organs and instruments, that is to say, his servants, by whom he has spoken."

not merely to supply the flock with pasture, and to rule the sheep by his guidance, but to drive away the wolves when threatening to make an attack upon the fold, and that not merely on one occasion, but so as to be constantly on the watch, and to be indefatigable. For as *thieves and robbers* (John x. 8) are constantly on the watch for the destruction of the Church, what excuse will the pastor have if, after courageously repelling them in several instances, he gives way on occasion of the ninth or tenth attack?

He says also, that a repetition of this nature is profitable to the Philippians, lest they should be—as is wont to happen occasionally—of an exceedingly fastidious humour, and despise it as a thing that was superfluous. For many are so difficult to please, that they cannot bear that the same thing should be said to them a second time, and, in the mean time, they do not consider that what is inculcated upon them daily is with difficulty retained in their memory ten years afterwards. But if it was profitable to the Philippians to listen to this exhortation of Paul—to be on their guard against wolves, what do Papists mean who will not allow that any judgment should be formed as to their doctrine? For to whom, I pray you, did Paul address himself when he said, *Beware?* Was it not to those whom they do not allow to possess any right to judge? And of the same persons Christ says, in like manner, *My sheep hear my voice, and they follow me; they flee from a stranger, and they hear not his voice.* (John x. 5, 27.)

3. *For we are the circumcision*—that is, we are the true seed of Abraham, and heirs of the testament which was confirmed by the sign of circumcision. For the true circumcision is *of the spirit* and *not of the letter*, inward, and situated in the heart, not visible according to the flesh. (Rom. ii. 29.)

By *spiritual worship* he means that which is recommended to us in the gospel, and consists of confidence in God, and invocation of him, self-renunciation, and a pure conscience. We must supply an antithesis, for he censures, on the other hand, legal worship, which was exclusively pressed upon

they observe the ceremonies of the law, they boast on false grounds that they are the people of God; but we are the truly circumcised, who worship God in spirit and in truth." (John iv. 23.)

But here some one will ask, whether *truth* excludes the sacraments, for the same thing might be said as to Baptism and the Lord's Supper. I answer, that this principle must always be kept in view, that figures were abolished by the advent of Christ, and that circumcision gave way to baptism. It follows, also, from this principle, that the pure and genuine worship of God is free from the legal ceremonies, and that believers have the true circumcision without any figure.

And we glory in Christ. We must always keep in view the antithesis. "We have to do with the reality, while they rest in the symbols: we have to do with the substance, while they look to the shadows." And this suits sufficiently well with the corresponding clause, which he adds by way of contrast—*We have no confidence in the flesh.* For under the term *flesh* he includes everything of an external kind in which an individual is prepared to glory, as will appear from the context, or, to express it in fewer words, he gives the name of *flesh* to everything that is apart from Christ. He thus reproves, and in no slight manner, the perverse zealots of the law, because, not satisfied with Christ, they have recourse to grounds of glorying apart from him. He has employed the terms *glorying*, and *having confidence*, to denote the same thing. For confidence lifts up a man, so that he ventures even to glory, and thus the two things are connected.

4. *Though I might also.* He does not speak of the disposition exercised by him, but he intimates, that he has also ground of glorying, if he were inclined to imitate their folly. The meaning therefore is, "My glorying, indeed, is placed in Christ, but, were it warrantable to glory in the flesh, I have also no want of materials." And from this we learn in what manner to reprove the arrogance of those who glory in something apart from Christ. If we are ourselves

boasting, without retorting upon them also our grounds of glorying, that they may understand that it is not through envy that we reckon of no value, nay, even voluntarily renounce those things on which they set the highest value. Let, however, the conclusion be always of this nature—that all confidence in the flesh is vain and preposterous.

If any one has confidence in the flesh, I more. Not satisfied with putting himself on a level with any one of them, he even gives himself the preference to them. Hence he cannot on this account be suspected, as though he were envious of their excellence, and extolled Christ with the view of making his own deficiencies appear the less inconsiderable. He says, therefore, that, if it were coming to be matter of dispute, he would be superior to others. For they had nothing (as we shall see erelong) that he had not on his part equally with them, while in some things he greatly excelled them. He says, not using the term in its strict sense, that he has *confidence in the flesh*, on the ground that, while not placing confidence in them, he was furnished with those grounds of fleshly glorying, on account of which they were puffed up.

5. *Circumcised on the eighth day.* It is literally—" The *circumcision of the eighth day.*" There is no difference, however, in the sense, for the meaning is, that he was circumcised in the proper manner, and according to the appointment of the law.[1] Now this customary circumcision was reckoned of superior value; and, besides, it was a token of the race to which he belonged; on which he touches immediately afterwards. For the case was not the same as to foreigners, for after they had become proselytes they were circumcised in youth, or when grown up to manhood, and sometimes even in old age. He says, accordingly, that he is of the *race of Israel.* He names the tribe,[2]—not, in my

[1] " Circoncis deuëment et selon l'ordonnance et les obseruations de la loy;"—" Circumcised duly and according to the appointment and the observances of the law."

[2] " Il note la tribu et le chef de la lignee de laquelle il estoit descendu;"— " He names the tribe and the head of the line from which he was descended."

more fully that he belonged to the race of Israel, as it was the custom that every one was numbered according to his particular tribe. With the same view he adds still farther, that he is an *Hebrew of the Hebrews.* For this name was the most ancient, as being that by which Abraham himself is designated by Moses. (Gen. xiv. 13.)[1] The sum, therefore, is this —that Paul was descended from the seed of Jacob from the most ancient date, so that he could reckon up grandfathers and great-grandfathers, and could even go still farther back.

According to the law, a Pharisee. Having spoken of the nobility of his descent, he now proceeds to speak of special endowments of persons, as they are called. It is very generally known, that the sect of the Pharisees was celebrated above the others for the renown in which it was held for sanctity and for doctrine. He states, that he belonged to that sect. The common opinion is, that the Pharisees were so called from a term signifying *separation ;*[2] but I approve rather of what I learned at one time from Capito, a man of sacred memory,[3] that it was because they boasted that they were endowed with the gift of *interpreting* Scripture, for פרש, (*parash,*) among the Hebrews, conveys the idea of *interpretation.*[4] While others declared themselves to be *literals,*[5] they preferred to be regarded as *Pharisees,*[6] as being in possession of the interpretations of the ancients. And assuredly it is manifest that, under the pretext of antiquity, they corrupted the whole of Scripture by their inventions; but as they, at the same time, retained some sound interpretations, handed down by the ancients, they were held in the highest esteem.

[1] See CALVIN *on the Corinthians,* vol. ii. pp. 357, 358.
[2] " Que les Pharisiens ont este ainsi nommez, pource qu'ils estoyent separez d'auec les autres, comme estans saincts;"—" That the Pharisees were so called, because they were separated from others, as being holy."
[3] See CALVIN *on the Corinthians,* vol. ii. p. 82.
[4] The reader will find the etymology of the term *Pharisees,* discussed at considerable length in the *Harmony,* vol. i. p. 281, *n.* 4.—*Ed.*
[5] The meaning is, that in interpreting Scripture, they did not go beyond the bare letter.—*Ed.*
[6] See *Harmony,* vol. i. pp. 281, 282, and vol. iii. p. 74.

God than sects, for in it is communicated the truth of God, which is the bond of unity. Besides this, Josephus tells us in the 13th book of his Antiquities, that all the sects took their rise during the high priesthood of Jonathan. Paul employs the term *law*, not in its strict sense, to denote the doctrine of religion, however much corrupted it was at that time, as Christianity is at this day in the Papacy. As, however, there were many that were in the rank of teachers, who were less skilful, and exercised,[1] he makes mention also of his *zeal*. It was, indeed, a very heinous sin on the part of Paul to *persecute the Church*, but as he had to dispute with unprincipled persons, who, by mixing up Christ with Moses, pretended zeal for the law, he mentions, on the other hand, that he was so keen a zealot of the law, that on that ground he *persecuted the Church*.

6. *As to the righteousness which is in the law.* There can be no doubt he means by this the entire righteousness of the law, for it were too meagre a sense to understand it exclusively of the ceremonies. The meaning, therefore, is more general—that he cultivated an integrity of life, such as might be required on the part of a man that was devoted to the law. To this, again, it is objected, that the *righteousness of the law* is perfect in the sight of God. For the sum of it is —that men be fully devoted to God, and what beyond this can be desired for the attainment of perfection? I answer, that Paul speaks here of that *righteousness* which would satisfy the common opinion of mankind. For he separates the law from Christ. Now, what is the law without Christ but a dead letter? To make the matter plainer, I observe, that there are two righteousnesses of the law. The one is *spiritual*—perfect love to God, and our neighbours: it is contained in doctrine, and had never an existence in the life of any man. The other is *literal*—such as appears in the view of men, while, in the mean time, hypocrisy reigns in the heart, and there is in the sight of God nothing but iniquity. Thus, the law has two aspects; the one has an eye to God,

[1] " Exercez en l'Ecriture;"—" Exercised in Scripture."

tainly, and almost unrivalled; yet let us observe in what esteem he held it.

7. But what things were gain to me, those I counted loss for Christ.	7. Verum quae mihi lucra erant, ea existimavi propter Christum iacturam.
8. Yea doubtless, and I count all things *but* loss for the excellency of the knowledge of Christ Jesus my Lord: for whom I have suffered the loss of all things, and do count them *but* dung, that I may win Christ.	8. Quin etiam omnia existimo iacturam esse, propter eminentiam cognitionis Christi Iesu Domini mei: propter quem omnium iacturam feci et existimo reiectamenta esse, ut Christum lucrifaciam.
9. And be found in him, not having mine own righteousness, which is of the law, but that which is through the faith of Christ, the righteousness which is of God by faith:	9. Et inveniam[1] in ipso, non habens meam iustitiam quae ex Lege est, sed quae est per fidem Christi: quae, inquam, ex Deo est iustitia in fide.
10. That I may know him, and the power of his resurrection, and the fellowship of his sufferings, being made conformable unto his death;	10. Ut cognoscam ipsum, et potentiam resurrectionis eius, et communicationem passionum eius, dum configuror morti eius,
11. If by any means I might attain unto the resurrection of the dead.	11. Si quo modo perveniam ad resurrectionem mortuorum.

7. *What things were gain to me.* He says, that those things were *gain* to him, for ignorance of Christ is the sole reason why we are puffed up with a vain confidence. Hence, where we see a false estimate of one's own excellence, where we see arrogance, where we see pride, *there* let us be assured that Christ is not known. On the other hand, so soon as Christ shines forth, all those things that formerly dazzled our eyes with a false splendour instantly vanish, or at least are disesteemed. Those things, accordingly, which had been *gain* to Paul when he was as yet blind, or rather had imposed upon him under an appearance of *gain*, he acknowledges to have been *loss* to him, when he has been enlightened. Why *loss?* Because they were hinderances in the way of his coming to Christ. What is more hurtful than anything that keeps us back from drawing near to Christ? Now he speaks chiefly of his own *righteousness*, for we are not received by Christ, except as naked and emptied of our own righteousness. Paul, accordingly, acknowledges that nothing

[1] " Et que ie les retrouue en iceluy, *ou*, soye trouué en iceluy;"—" And that I may find them in him, *or*, be found in him."

8. *Nay more, I reckon.* He means, that he continues to be of the same mind, because it often happens, that, transported with delight in new things, we forget everything else, and afterwards we regret it. Hence Paul, having said that he renounced all hinderances, that he might gain Christ, now adds, that he continues to be of this mind.

For the sake of the excellency of the knowledge. He extols the gospel in opposition to all such notions as tend to beguile us. For there are many things that have an appearance of excellence, but the knowledge of Christ surpasses to such a degree everything else by its sublimity,[1] that, as compared with it, there is nothing that is not contemptible. Let us, therefore, learn from this, what value we ought to set upon the knowledge of Christ alone. As to his calling him *his Lord*, he does this to express the intensity of his feeling.

For whom I have suffered the loss of all things. He expresses more than he had done previously; at least he expresses himself with greater distinctness. It is a similitude taken from seamen, who, when urged on by danger of shipwreck, throw everything overboard, that, the ship being lightened, they may reach the harbour in safety. Paul, then, was prepared to lose everything that he had, rather than be deprived of Christ.

But it is asked, whether it is necessary for us to renounce riches, and honours, and nobility of descent, and even external righteousness, that we may become *partakers of Christ,* (Heb. iii. 14,) for all these things are gifts of God, which, in themselves, are not to be despised? I answer, that the Apostle does not speak here so much of the things themselves, as of the quality of them. It is, indeed, true, that the kingdom of heaven is like a *precious pearl,* for the purchase of which no one should hesitate to sell everything that he has. (Matt. xiii. 46.) There is, however, a difference between the substance of things and the quality. Paul did not reckon it necessary to disown connection with his own tribe and with the race of Abraham, and make himself an alien, that he

---

[1] " Par son excellence et hautesse ;"— " By its excellence and loftiness."

should become unchaste; that from being sober, he should become intemperate; and that from being respectable and honourable, he should become dissolute; but that he should divest himself of a false estimate of his own righteousness, and treat it with contempt. We, too, when treating of the righteousness of faith, do not contend against the substance of works, but against that quality with which the sophists invest them, inasmuch as they contend that men are justified by them. Paul, therefore, divested himself—not of works, but of that mistaken confidence in works, with which he had been puffed up.

As to riches and honours, when we have divested ourselves of attachment to them, we will be prepared, also, to renounce the things themselves, whenever the Lord will require this from us, and so it ought to be. It is not expressly necessary that you be a poor man, in order that you may be a Christian; but if it please the Lord that it should be so, you ought to be prepared to endure poverty. In fine, it is not lawful for Christians to have anything apart from Christ. I consider as *apart from Christ* everything that is a hinderance in the way of Christ alone being our ground of glorying, and having an entire sway over us.

And I count them but refuse. Here he not merely by words, but also by realities, amplifies greatly what he had before stated. For those who cast their merchandise and other things into the sea, that they may escape in safety, do not, therefore, despise riches, but act as persons prepared rather to live in misery and want,[1] than to be drowned along with their riches. They part with them, indeed, but it is with regret and with a sigh; and when they have escaped, they

---

[1] *Pierce* adduces the two following instances of the same form of expression as made use of among the Romans—*Plautus* says, (*Trucul.* Act ii. sc vii. ver. 5,) when speaking of one that was chargeable with prodigality—" Qui bona sua pro *stercore* habet, foras jubet ferri," (" who counts his goods but *dung*, and orders them to be carried out of the house.") Thus, also, *Apuleius*, (*Florid*, c. 14,) speaks of *Crates*, when he turned Cynic: " Rem familiarem abjicit velut onus *stercoris*, magis labori quam usui:"—(" He casts away his goods as a heap of *dung*, that was more troublesome than useful.")—*Ed.*

that he formerly reckoned precious, but that they were like *dung*, offensive to him, or were disesteemed like things that are thrown away in contempt. Chrysostom renders the word—*straws*. Grammarians, however, are of opinion, that σκύβαλον is employed as though it were κυσίβαλον—*what is thrown to dogs*.[1] And certainly there is good reason why everything that is opposed to Christ should be offensive to us, inasmuch as it is an *abomination in the sight of God*. (Luke xvi. 15.) There is good reason why it should be offensive to us also, on the ground of its being an unfounded imagination.

That I may gain Christ. By this expression he intimates that we cannot *gain Christ* otherwise than by losing everything that we have. For he would have us rich by his grace alone: he would have him alone be our entire blessedness. Now, in what way we must suffer the loss of all things, has been already stated—in such a manner that nothing will turn us aside from confidence in Christ alone. But if Paul, with such innocence and integrity of life, did not hesitate to reckon his own righteousness to be *loss* and *dung*, what mean those Pharisees of the present day, who, while covered over with every kind of wickedness, do nevertheless feel no shame in extolling their own merits in opposition to Christ?

9. *And may find them in him.* The verb is in the passive voice, and hence all others have rendered it, *I may be found.* They pass over the context, however, in a very indifferent manner, as though it had no peculiar force. If you read it in the passive voice, an *antithesis* must be understood—that Paul was lost before he was found in Christ, as a rich merchant is like one *lost*, so long as he has his vessel laden with riches; but when they have been thrown overboard, he is *found*.[2] For here that saying[3] is admirably in point—" I

[1] Such is the etymology given by *Suidas*, " τὸ τοῖς κυσὶ βαλλόμενον;"— " what is *thrown to dogs.*"—*Ed.*

[2] " Mais apres que les richesses sont iettees en la mer, il est trouué, pource qu'il commence a avoir esperance d'eschapper, d'autant que le vaisseau est allegé;"—" But after his riches have been thrown into the sea, he is found, inasmuch as he begins to have hope of escaping, because the vessel has been lightened."

[3] " Le prouerbe ancien;"—" The ancient proverb."

signification, and means—to recover what you have voluntarily given up, (as Budaeus shews by various examples,) I have not hesitated to differ from the opinion of others. For, in this way, the meaning will be more complete, and the doctrine the more ample—that Paul renounced everything that he had, that he might recover them in Christ; and this corresponds better with the word *gain*, for it means that it was no trivial or ordinary *gain*, inasmuch as Christ contains everything in himself. And, unquestionably, we lose nothing when we come to Christ naked and stript of everything, for those things which we previously imagined, on false grounds, that we possessed, we then begin really to acquire. He, accordingly, shews more fully, how great the riches of Christ, because we obtain and *find* all things in him.

Not having mine own righteousness. Here we have a remarkable passage, if any one is desirous to have a particular description of the *righteousness of faith*, and to understand its true nature. For Paul here makes a comparison between two kinds of *righteousness*. The *one* he speaks of as belonging to the man, while he calls it at the same time the *righteousness of the law;* the *other*, he tells us, is from God, is obtained through faith, and rests upon faith in Christ. These he represents as so directly opposed to each other, that they cannot stand together. Hence there are two things that are to be observed here. In the *first* place, that the *righteousness of the law* must be given up and renounced, that you may be righteous through faith; and *secondly*, that the *righteousness of faith* comes forth from God, and does not belong to the individual. As to both of these we have in the present day a great controversy with Papists; for on the one hand, they do not allow that the *righteousness of faith* is altogether from God, but ascribe it partly to man; and, on the other hand, they mix them together, as if the one did not destroy the other. Hence we must carefully examine the several words made use of by Paul, for there is not one of them that is not very emphatic.

He says, that believers have no righteousness of their

be ours. Hence he leaves no room whatever for the righteousness of works. Why he calls it the righteousness of the law, he shews in Romans x. 5; because this is the sentence of the law, *He that doeth these things shall live in them.* The law, therefore, pronounces the man to be righteous through works. Nor is there any ground for the cavil of Papists, that all this must be restricted to ceremonies. For in the *first* place, it is a contemptible frivolity to affirm that Paul was righteous only through ceremonies; and *secondly,* he in this way draws a contrast between those two kinds of righteousness—the one being of man, the other, from God. He intimates, accordingly, that the one is the reward of works, while the other is a free gift from God. He thus, in a general way, places man's merit in opposition to Christ's grace; for while the law brings works, faith presents man before God as naked, that he may be clothed with the righteousness of Christ. When, therefore, he declares that the righteousness of faith is from God, it is not simply because faith is the gift of God, but because God justifies us by his goodness, or because we receive by faith the righteousness which he has conferred upon us.

10. *That I may know him.* He points out the efficacy and nature of faith—that it is the knowledge of Christ, and that, too, not bare or indistinct, but in such a manner that the power of his resurrection is felt. *Resurrection* he employs as meaning, the completion of redemption, so that it comprehends in it at the same time the idea of death. But as it is not enough to know Christ as crucified and raised up from the dead, unless you experience, also, the fruit of this, he speaks expressly of efficacy.[1] Christ therefore is rightly known, when we feel how powerful his death and resurrection are, and how efficacious they are in us. Now all things are there furnished to us—expiation and destruction of sin, freedom from condemnation, satisfaction, victory over death, the attainment of righteousness, and the hope of a blessed immortality.

[1] " De l'efficace ou puissance;"—" Of the efficacy or power."

us through the resurrection of Christ, and is obtained by us through faith, he proceeds to treat of the exercises of the pious, and that in order that it might not seem as though he introduced an inactive faith, which produces no effects in the life. He also intimates, indirectly, that these are the exercises in which the Lord would have his people employ themselves; while the false Apostles pressed forward upon them the useless elements of ceremonies. Let every one, therefore, who has become through faith a partaker of all Christ's benefits, acknowledge that a condition is presented to him—that his whole life be conformed to his death.

There is, however, a twofold participation and fellowship in the death of Christ. The *one* is inward—what the Scripture is wont to term the *mortification of the flesh*, or the *crucifixion of the old man*, of which Paul treats in the sixth chapter of the Romans; the *other* is outward—what is termed the *mortification of the outward man*. It is the endurance of the Cross, of which he treats in the eighth chapter of the same Epistle, and here also, if I do not mistake. For after introducing along with this the *power of his resurrection*, Christ crucified is set before us, that we may follow him through tribulations and distresses; and hence the resurrection of the dead is expressly made mention of, that we may know that we must die before we live. This is a continued subject of meditation to believers so long as they sojourn in this world.

This, however, is a choice consolation, that in all our miseries we are partakers of Christ's Cross, if we are his members; so that through afflictions the way is opened up for us to everlasting blessedness, as we read elsewhere, (2 Tim. ii. 11,) *If we die with him, we shall also live with him; if we suffer with him, we shall also reign with him.* We must all therefore be prepared for this—that our whole life shall represent nothing else than the image of death, until it produce death itself, as the life of Christ is nothing else than a prelude of death. We enjoy, however, in the

resurrection. Hence Paul says, that he is conformed to his death, that he may attain the glory of the resurrection. The phrase, *if by any means,* does not indicate doubt, but expresses difficulty, with a view to stimulate our earnest endeavour;[1] for it is no light contest, inasmuch as we must struggle against so many and so serious hinderances.

12. Not as though I had already attained, either were already perfect; but I follow after, if that I may apprehend that for which also I am apprehended of Christ Jesus.
13. Brethren, I count not myself to have apprehended: but *this* one thing *I do,* forgetting those things which are behind, and reaching forth unto those things which are before,
14. I press toward the mark, for the prize of the high calling of God in Christ Jesus.
15. Let us therefore, as many as be perfect, be thus minded: and if in any thing ye be otherwise minded, God shall reveal even this unto you.
16. Nevertheless, whereto we have already attained, let us walk by the same rule, let us mind the same thing.
17. Brethren, be followers together of me, and mark them which walk so, as ye have us for an ensample.

12. Non quod iam apprehenderim, aut iam perfectus sim: sequor autem, si ego quoque apprehendam, quemadmodum[2] et apprehensus sum a Christo Iesu.
13. Fratres, ego me ipsum nondum arbitror apprehendisse, unum autem, ea quae retro sunt oblitus, ad ea quae ante sunt me extendens,
14. Secundum scopum sequor ad palmam supernae vocationis Dei in Christo Iesu.
15. Quicunque perfecti sumus, hoc sentiamus: et si quod aliter sentitis, etiam hoc vobis Deus revelabit.
16. Caeterum quo perveniamus, ut idem sentiamus, eadem procedamus regula.
17. Simul imitatores mei estote, fratres, et considerate eos qui sic ambulant: quemadmodum nos habetis pro exemplari.

12. *Not as though I had already apprehended.* Paul insists upon this, that he may convince the Philippians that he thinks of nothing but Christ—knows nothing else—desires nothing else—is occupied with no other subject of meditation. In connection with this, there is much weight in what he now adds—that he himself, while he had given up all hinderances, had nevertheless not attained that object

---

[1] " Afin de nous resueiller et aiguiser a nous y addonner de tant plus grande affection ;"—" That it may arouse and stimulate us to devote ourselves to it with so much the greater zeal."

[2] " *Comme,* ou, *pour laquelle cause* ;"—" *As,* or, *for which cause.*"

was this incumbent on the Philippians, who were still far behind him?

It is asked, however, what it is that Paul says he has not yet attained? For unquestionably, so soon as we are by faith ingrafted into the body of Christ, we have already entered the kingdom of God, and, as it is stated in Ephesians ii. 6, we already, in hope, *sit in heavenly places.* I answer, that our salvation, in the mean time, is in hope, so that the inheritance indeed is secure; but we nevertheless have it not as yet in possession. At the same time, Paul here looks at something else—the advancement of faith, and of that mortification of which he had made mention. He had said that he aimed and eagerly aspired at the resurrection of the dead through fellowship in the Cross of Christ. He adds, that he has not as yet arrived at this. At what? At the attainment of having entire fellowship in Christ's sufferings, having a full taste of the power of his resurrection, and knowing him perfectly. He teaches, therefore, by his own example, that we ought to make progress, and that the knowledge of Christ is an attainment of such difficulty, that even those who apply themselves exclusively to it, do nevertheless not attain perfection in it so long as they live. This, however, does not detract in any degree from the authority of Paul's doctrine, inasmuch as he had acquired as much as was sufficient for discharging the office committed to him. In the mean time, it was necessary for him to make progress, that this divinely-furnished instructor of all might be trained to humility.

As also I have been apprehended. This clause he has inserted by way of correction, that he might ascribe all his endeavours to the grace of God. It is not of much importance whether you read *as,* or *in so far as;* for the meaning in either case remains the same—that Paul was apprehended by Christ, that he might apprehend Christ; that is, that he did nothing except under Christ's influence and guidance. I have chosen, however, the more distinct rendering, as it seemed to be optional.

as though he were still in suspense, but repeats what he had said before—that he still aimed at making farther progress, because he had not yet attained the end of his calling. He shews this immediately after, by saying that he was intent on this one thing, leaving off everything else. Now, he compares our life to a race-course, the limits of which God has marked out to us for running in. For as it would profit the runner nothing to have left the starting-point, unless he went forward to the goal, so we must also pursue the course of our calling until death, and must not cease until we have obtained what we seek. Farther, as the way is marked out to the runner, that he may not fatigue himself to no purpose by wandering in this direction or in that, so there is also a goal set before us, towards which we ought to direct our course undeviatingly; and God does not permit us to wander about heedlessly. Thirdly, as the runner requires to be free from entanglement, and not stop his course on account of any impediment, but must continue his course, surmounting every obstacle, so we must take heed that we do not apply our mind or heart to anything that may divert the attention, but must, on the contrary, make it our endeavour, that, free from every distraction, we may apply the whole bent of our mind exclusively to God's calling. These three things Paul comprehends in one similitude. When he says that he *does this one thing*, and forgets all things that are behind, he intimates his assiduity, and excludes everything fitted to distract. When he says that he *presses toward the mark*, he intimates that he is not wandering from the way.

Forgetting those things that are behind. He alludes to runners, who do not turn their eyes aside in any direction, lest they should slacken the speed of their course, and, more especially, do not look behind to see how much ground they have gone over, but hasten forward unremittingly towards the goal. Thus Paul teaches us, that he does not think of what he has been, or of what he has done, but simply presses forward towards the appointed goal, and that, too, with such ardour, that he runs forward to it, as it were, with

Should any one remark, by way of objection, that the remembrance of our past life is of use for stirring us up, both because the favours that have been already conferred upon us give us encouragement to entertain hope, and because we are admonished by our sins to amend our course of life, I answer, that thoughts of this nature do not turn away our view from what is before us to what is behind, but rather help our vision, so that we discern more distinctly the goal. Paul, however, condemns here such looking back, as either destroys or impairs alacrity. Thus, for example, should any one persuade himself that he has made sufficiently great progress, reckoning that he has done enough, he will become indolent, and feel inclined to *deliver up the lamp*² to others; or, if any one looks back with a feeling of regret for the situation that he has abandoned, he cannot apply the whole bent of his mind to what he is engaged in. Such was the nature of the thoughts from which Paul's mind required to be turned away, if he would in good earnest follow out Christ's calling. As, however, there has been mention made here of endeavour, aim, course, perseverance, lest any one should imagine that salvation consists in these things, or should even ascribe to human industry what comes from another quarter, with the view of pointing out the cause of all these things, he adds—*in Christ Jesus.*

15. *As many as are perfect.* Lest any one should understand this as spoken of the generality of mankind, as though he were explaining the simple elements to those that are mere children in Christ, he declares that it is a rule which all that are perfect ought to follow. Now, the rule is this— that we must renounce confidence in all things, that we may

---

¹ The participle referred to is ἐπικτεινόμενος, which, as is remarked by Dr. Bloomfield, "is highly appropriate to the *racer,* whether on foot, or on horseback, or in the chariot; since the racer *stretches his head and hands forward* in anxiety to reach the goal."—*Ed.*

² A proverbial expression, founded on the circumstance that in certain games at Athens the runners had to carry a lamp, or burning torch, in such a way that it should not go out, and, on any one of the competitors giving up the contest, he *delivered up the lamp,* or torch, to his successor. See Auct. ad Herenn. l. 4, c. 46; Lucret. l. 2, v. 77.—*Ed.*

which may be the means of conducting us to a blessed resurrection. Where now will be that state of perfection which monks dream of—where the confused medley of such contrivances—where, in short, the whole system of Popery, which is nothing else than an imaginary perfection, that has nothing in common with this rule of Paul? Undoubtedly, whoever will understand this single term, will clearly perceive that everything that is taught in the Papacy, as to the attainment of righteousness and salvation, is nauseous dung.

If in anything otherwise. By the same means he both humbles them, and inspires them with good hope, for he admonishes them not to be elated in their ignorance, and at the same time he bids them be of good courage, when he says that we must wait for the revelation of God. For we know how great an obstacle to truth obstinacy is. This, therefore, is the best preparation for docility—when we do not take pleasure in error. Paul, accordingly, teaches indirectly, that we must make way for the revelation of God, if we have not yet attained what we seek. Farther, when he teaches that we must advance by degrees, he encourages them not to draw back in the middle of the course. At the same time, he maintains beyond all controversy what he has previously taught, when he teaches that others who differ from him will have a revelation given to them of what they do not as yet know. For it is as though he had said,— "The Lord will one day shew you that the very thing which I have stated is a perfect rule of true knowledge and of right living." No one could speak in this manner, if he were not fully assured of the reasonableness and accuracy of his doctrine. Let us in the mean time learn also from this passage, that we must bear for a time with ignorance in our weak brethren, and forgive them, if it is not given them immediately to be altogether of one mind with us. Paul felt assured as to his doctrine, and yet he allows those who could not as yet receive it time to make progress, and he does not cease on that account to regard them as brethren, only he cautions them against flattering themselves in their igno-

as unsuitable and inappropriate.

16. *Nevertheless, so far as we have attained.* Even the Greek manuscripts themselves differ as to the dividing of the clauses, for in some of them there are two complete sentences. If any one, however, prefer to divide the verse, the meaning will be as Erasmus has rendered it.[2] For my part, I rather prefer a different reading, implying that Paul exhorts the Philippians to imitate him, that they may at last reach the same goal, so as to *think the same thing,* and *walk by the same rule.* For where sincere affection exists, such as reigned in Paul, the way is easy to a holy and pious concord. As, therefore, they had not yet learned what true perfection was, in order that they might attain it he wishes them to be imitators of him; that is, to seek God with a *pure conscience,* (2 Tim. i. 3,) to arrogate nothing to themselves, and calmly to subject their understandings to Christ. For in the imitating of Paul all these excellences are included—pure zeal, fear of the Lord, modesty, self-renunciation, docility, love, and desire of concord. He bids them, however, be at one and the same time imitators of him; that is, all with one consent, and with one mind.

Observe, that the goal of perfection to which he invites the Philippians, by his example, is, that they *think the same thing,* and *walk by the same rule.* He has, however, assigned the first place to the doctrine in which they ought to harmonize, and the rule to which they should conform themselves.

17. *Mark them.* By this expression he means, that it is all one to him what persons they single out for themselves for imitation, provided they conform themselves to that purity of which he was a pattern. By this means all sus-

[1] The rendering of the Vulgate (*revelavit*) is followed in the Rheims version—(1582)—*hath reuealed.—Ed.*

[2] The rendering of Erasmus is as follows:—" Eadem incedamus regulâ, ut simus concordes;"—" Let us walk by the same rule, *that we may be of the same mind.*" The words inserted in the common text κανόνι τὸ αὐτὸ φρονεῖν (*rule—mind the same thing,*) are omitted, as is noticed by Granville Penn, in the *Vat.* and *Alex.* MSS., the *Copt.* and *Ethiop.* versions, and by Hilary and Augustine.—*Ed.*

time he warns them that all are not to be imitated indiscriminately, as he afterwards explains more fully.

18. (For many walk, of whom I have told you often, and now tell you even weeping, *that they are* the enemies of the cross of Christ:	18. Multi enim ambulant (quos saepe dicebam vobis, ac nunc etiam flens dico, inimicos esse crucis Christi:
19. Whose end *is* destruction, whose god *is their* belly, and *whose* glory *is* in their shame, who mind earthly things.)	19. Quorum finis perditio, quorum deus venter est, et gloria in confusione ipsorum terrena cogitantes.)
20. For our conversation is in heaven; from whence also we look for the Saviour, the Lord Jesus Christ:	20. Nostra autem conversatio in coelis est, e quibus etiam salvatorem respectamus, Dominum Iesum Christum.
21. Who shall change our vile body, that it may be fashioned like unto his glorious body, according to the working whereby he is able even to subdue all things unto himself.	21. Qui transformabit corpus nostrum humile, ut sit conforme corpori suo glorioso, secundum efficaciam, qua potest etiam sibi subiicere omnia.

18. *For many walk.* The simple statement, in my opinion, is this: *Many walk who mind earthly things*, meaning by this, that there are many who creep upon the ground,[1] not feeling the power of God's kingdom. He mentions, however, in connection with this, the marks by which such persons may be distinguished. These we will examine, each in its order. By *earthly things* some understand ceremonies, and the outward elements of the world, which cause true piety to be forgotten. I prefer, however, to view the term as referring to carnal affection, as meaning that those who are not regenerated by the Spirit of God think of nothing but the world. This will appear more distinctly from what follows; for he holds them up to odium on this ground—that, being desirous exclusively of their own honour, ease, and gain, they had no regard to the edification of the Church.

Of whom I have told you often. He shews that it is not without good reason that he has often warned the Philippians, inasmuch as he now endeavours to remind them by letter of the same things as he had formerly spoken of to them when present with them. His tears, also, are an evi-

[1] " Qui ont leurs affections enracines en la terre;"—" Who have their affections rooted in the earth."

but by pious zeal, inasmuch as he sees that the Church is miserably destroyed[1] by such pests. It becomes us, assuredly, to be affected in such a manner, that on seeing that the place of pastors is occupied by wicked and worthless persons, we shall sigh, and give evidence, at least by our tears, that we feel deeply grieved for the calamity of the Church.

It is of importance, also, to take notice of whom Paul speaks—not of open enemies, who were avowedly desirous that doctrine might be undermined—but of impostors and profligates, who trampled under foot the power of the gospel, for the sake of ambition or of their own belly. And unquestionably persons of this sort, who weaken the influence of the ministry by seeking their own interests,[2] sometimes do more injury than if they openly opposed Christ. We must, therefore, by no means spare them, but must point them out with the finger, as often as there is occasion. Let them complain afterwards, as much as they choose, of our severity, provided they do not allege anything against us that it is not in our power to justify from Paul's example.

That they are the enemies of the cross of Christ. Some explain *cross* to mean the whole mystery of redemption, and they explain that this is said of them, because, by preaching the law, they made void the benefit of Christ's death. Others, however, understand it as meaning, that they shunned the cross, and were not prepared to expose themselves to dangers for the sake of Christ. I understand it, however, in a more general way, as meaning that, while they pretended to be friends, they were, nevertheless, the worst enemies of the gospel. For it is no unusual thing for Paul to employ the term *cross* to mean the entire preaching of the gospel. For as he says elsewhere, *If any man is in Christ, let him be a new creature.* (2 Cor. v. 17.)[3]

[1] " Perdue et ruinee;"—" Destroyed and ruined."
[2] " Ne regardans qu'a eux-mesmes et a leur proufit, font perdre toute la faueur et la force du ministere;"—" Looking merely to themselves and their own advantage, undermine all the influence and power of the ministry."
[3] Such is CALVIN's rendering of the passage referred to. See CALVIN on the Corinthians, vol. ii. pp. 229, 233.—*Ed.*

the more carefully on their guard, that they may not involve themselves in the ruin of those persons. As, however, profligates of this description, by means of show and various artifices, frequently dazzle the eyes of the simple for a time, in such a manner that they are preferred even to the most eminent servants of Christ, the Apostle declares, with great confidence,[1] that the glory with which they are now puffed up will be exchanged for ignominy.

Whose god is the belly. As they pressed the observance of circumcision and other ceremonies, he says that they did not do so from zeal for the law, but with a view to the favour of men, and that they might live peacefully and free from annoyance. For they saw that the Jews burned with a fierce rage against Paul, and those like him, and that Christ could not be proclaimed by them in purity with any other result, than that of arousing against themselves the same rage. Accordingly, consulting their own ease and advantage, they mixed up these corruptions with the view of mitigating the flames of others.[2]

20. *But our conversation is in heaven.* This statement overturns all empty shows, in which pretended ministers of the gospel are accustomed to glory, and he indirectly holds up to odium all their objects of aim,[3] because, by flying about above the earth, they do not aspire towards heaven. For he teaches that nothing is to be reckoned of any value except God's spiritual kingdom, because believers ought to lead a heavenly life in this world. "They *mind earthly things:* it is therefore befitting that we, whose *conversation is in heaven,* should be separated from them."[4] We are, it is true,

---

[1] " Hardiment et d'vne grande asseurance;"—" Boldly, and with great confidence."

[2] " Pour esteindre et appaiser le feu des autres;"—" For the sake of mitigating and allaying the fire of others." CALVIN's meaning appears to be, that they made it their endeavour to screen themselves as far as possible from the *fiery rage* of those around them.—*Ed.*

[3] " Toutes leurs inuentions et façons de faire;"—" All their contrivances and modes of acting."

[4] " Que nous soyons diuisez et separez d'auec eux;"—" That we be divided and separated from them."

Lord than wheat. Farther, we are exposed to the common inconveniences of this earthly life; we require, also, meat and drink, and other necessaries, but we must, nevertheless, be conversant with heaven in mind and affection. For, on the one hand, we must pass quietly through this life, and, on the other hand, we must be dead to the world that Christ may live in us, and that we, in our turn, may live to him. This passage is a most abundant source of many exhortations, which it were easy for any one to elicit from it.

Whence also. From the connection that we have with Christ, he proves that our citizenship[1] is a heaven, for it is not seemly that the members should be separated from their Head. Accordingly, as Christ is in heaven, in order that we may be conjoined with him, it is necessary that we should in spirit dwell apart from this world. Besides, *where our treasure is, there is our heart also.* (Matt. vi. 21.) Christ, who is our blessedness and glory, is in heaven: let our souls, therefore, dwell with him on high. On this account he expressly calls him *Saviour.* Whence does salvation come to us? Christ will come to us from heaven as a *Saviour.* Hence it were unbefitting that we should be taken up with this earth.[2] This epithet, *Saviour,* is suited to the connection of the passage; for we are said to be in heaven in respect of our minds on this account, that it is from that source alone that the hope of salvation beams forth upon us. As the coming of Christ will be terrible to the wicked, so it rather turns away their minds from heaven than draws them thither: for they know that he will come to them as a Judge, and they shun him so far as is in their power. From these words of Paul pious minds derive the sweetest consolation, as instructing them that the coming of Christ is to be desired by them, inasmuch as it will bring salvation to them. On the other hand, it is a sure token of incredulity, when persons tremble on any mention being made of it. See the *eighth*

[1] *Politiam*—a term corresponding to that employed in the original, πολίτευμα.—*Ed.*
[2] "Que nous soyons occupez et enueloppez en terre;"—"That we should be occupied and entangled with the earth."

tented with Christ alone.

Farther, we learn from this passage that nothing mean or earthly is to be conceived of as to Christ, inasmuch as Paul bids us look upward to heaven, that we may seek him. Now, those that reason with subtlety that Christ is not shut up or hid in some corner of heaven, with the view of proving that his body is everywhere, and fills heaven and earth, say indeed something that is true, but not the whole: for as it were rash and foolish to mount up beyond the heavens, and assign to Christ a station, or seat, or place of walking, in this or that region, so it is a foolish and destructive madness to draw him down from heaven by any carnal consideration, so as to seek him upon earth. Up, then, with our hearts,[1] that they may be with the Lord.

21. *Who will change.* By this argument he stirs up the Philippians still farther to lift up their minds to heaven, and be wholly attached to Christ—because this body which we carry about with us is not an everlasting abode, but a frail tabernacle, which will in a short time be reduced to nothing. Besides, it is liable to so many miseries, and so many dishonourable infirmities, that it may justly be spoken of as *vile* and full of ignominy. Whence, then, is its restoration to be hoped for? From heaven, at Christ's coming. Hence there is no part of us that ought not to aspire after heaven with undivided affection. We see, on the one hand, in life, but chiefly in death, the present meanness of our bodies; the glory which they will have, conformably to Christ's body, is incomprehensible by us: for if the disciples could not endure the slight taste which he afforded[2] in his transfiguration, (Matt. xvii. 6,) which of us could attain its fulness? Let us for the present be contented with the evidence of our adoption, being destined to know the riches of our inheritance when we shall come to the enjoyment of them.

[1] *Sursum corda.* Our Author most probably alludes to the circumstance, that this expression was wont to be made use of among Christians in ancient times, when the ordinance of the supper was about to be administered. See CALVIN's *Institutes*, vol. iii. p. 440.—*Ed.*

[2] " De sa gloire;"—" Of his glory."

the resurrection, Paul on this account places before our eyes the boundless power of God, that it may entirely remove all doubt; for distrust arises from this—that we measure the thing itself by the narrowness of our own understanding. Nor does he simply make mention of *power*, but also of *efficacy*, which is the effect, or power shewing itself in action, so to speak. Now, when we bear in mind that God, who created all things out of nothing, can command the earth, and the sea, and the other elements, to render back what has been committed to them,[1] our minds are immediately roused up to a firm hope—nay, even to a spiritual contemplation of the resurrection.

But it is of importance to take notice, also, that the right and power of raising the dead, nay more, of doing everything according to his own pleasure, is assigned to the person of Christ—an encomium by which his Divine majesty is illustriously set forth. Nay, farther, we gather from this, that the world was created by him, for to *subject all things to himself* belongs to the Creator alone.

CHAPTER IV.

1. Therefore, my brethren, dearly beloved and longed for, my joy and crown, so stand fast in the Lord, *my* dearly beloved.
2. I beseech Euodias, and beseech Syntyche, that they be of the same mind in the Lord.
3. And I entreat thee also, true yoke-fellow, help those women which laboured with me in the gospel, with Clement also, and *with* other my fellow-labourers, whose names *are* in the book of life.

1. Itaque, fratres mei dilecti et desiderati, gaudium et corona mea, sic state in Domino, dilecti.
2. Evodian hortor, et Syntychen hortor, ut unum sentiant in Domino.
3. Sane rogo etiam te, germane compar, adiuva eas, quae in evangelio idem mecum certamen sustinuerunt, cum Clemente etiam, et reliquis adiutoribus meis, quorum nomina sunt in libro vitae.

1. *Therefore, my brethren.* He concludes his doctrine, as he is wont, with most urgent exhortations, that he may fix

---

[1] " Qu'il leur auoit donné en garde;"—" What he had given to them to keep."

tions,¹ which at the same time are not dictated by flattery, but by sincere affection. He calls them his *joy* and *crown;* because, delighted to see those who had been gained over through his instrumentality persevering in the faith,² he hoped to attain that triumph, of which we have spoken,³ when the Lord will reward with a *crown* those things which have been accomplished under his guidance.

When he bids them *so stand fast in the Lord,* he means that their condition is approved of by him. At the same time, the particle *so* might be taken as referring to the doctrine going before; but the former view is more suitable, so that, by praising their present condition, he exhorts them to perseverance. They had already, it is true, given some evidence of their constancy. Paul, however, well knowing human weakness, reckons that they have need of confirmation for the future.

2. *I exhort Euodias and Syntyche.* It is an almost universally received opinion that Paul was desirous to settle a quarrel, I know not of what sort, between those two women. While I am not inclined to contend as to this, the words of Paul do not afford ground enough for such a conjecture to satisfy us that it really was so. It appears, from the testimony which he gives in their favour, that they were very excellent women; for he assigns to them so much honour as to call them fellow-soldiers in the gospel.⁴ Hence, as their agreement was a matter of great moment,⁵ and, on

---

¹ "Et les appelant par noms amiables et gracieux, il tasche de gaigner leurs cœurs;"—"And calling them by lovely and kind names, he endeavours to gain their hearts."

² "Estant ioyeux de les veoir perseuerer en la foy, a laquelle ils auoyent este amenez par son moyen;"—"Being delighted to see them persevere in the faith, to which they had been brought through his instrumentality."

³ CALVIN seems to refer here to what he had said when commenting on Phil. ii. 16. See p. 72.—*Ed.*

⁴ "Il les appelle ses compagnes de guerre, d'autant qu'elles ont bataillé auec luy en l'euangile;"—"He calls them his companions in war, inasmuch as they had struggled hard with him in the gospel."

⁵ "C'estoit vne chose grandement requise et necessaire qu'elles fussent d'vn consentement;"—"It was a thing greatly requisite and necessary that they should be in a state of agreement."

We must take notice, however, that, whenever he speaks of agreement, he adds also the bond of it—*in the Lord.* For every combination will inevitably be accursed, if apart from the Lord, and, on the other hand, nothing is so disjoined, but that it ought to be reunited in Christ.

3. *I entreat thee, also, true yoke-fellow.* I am not inclined to dispute as to the gender of the noun, and shall, accordingly, leave it undetermined,[1] whether he addresses here a man or a woman. At the same time there is excessive weakness in the argument of Erasmus, who infers that it is a woman from the circumstance, that mention is made here of other women—as though he did not immediately subjoin the name of Clement in the same connection. I refrain, however, from that dispute: only I maintain that it is not Paul's wife that is designated by this appellation. Those who maintain this, quote Clement and Ignatius as their authorities. If they quoted correctly, I would not certainly despise men of such eminence. But as writings are brought forward from Eusebius[2] which are spurious, and were contrived by ignorant monks,[3] they are not deserving of much credit among readers of sound judgment.[4]

Let us, therefore, inquire as to the thing itself, without taking any false impression from the opinions of men. When Paul wrote the First Epistle to the Corinthians, he was, as he mentions, at that time unmarried. (1 Cor. vii. 8.) *To the unmarried,* says he, *and widows, I say: it is good that they should continue even as I am.* He wrote that Epistle at Ephesus,[5] when he was prepared to leave it. Not long after, he proceeded to Jerusalem, where he was put in prison, and

---

[1] " Je le laisse a disputer aux autres;"—" I leave it to others to dispute as to this."

[2] " Comme ainsi soit qu'on mette en auant ie ne scay quels faux escrits sous le nom d'Eusebe;"—" As they set forth I know not what spurious writings under the name of Eusebius."

[3] " Et adioustez a son histoire;"—" And added to his history."

[4] " Ils ne meritent point enuers les lecteurs de bon iugement, qu'on y adiouste grande foy;"—" They do not deserve, as to readers of good judgment, that much credit should be attached to them."

[5] See CALVIN on the Corinthians, vol. ii. pp. 70, 72, 78.

spent by him partly in journeying, and partly in prison. In addition to this, he was even at that time prepared to endure imprisonment and persecutions, as he himself testifies, according to Luke. (Acts xxi. 13.) I am, at the same time, well aware what objection is usually brought forward in opposition to this—that Paul, though married, refrained from conjugal intercourse. The words, however, convey another meaning, for he is desirous that unmarried persons may have it in their power to remain in the same condition with himself. Now, what is that condition but celibacy? As to their bringing forward that passage—*Is it not lawful for me to lead about a wife?* (1 Cor. ix. 5,) for the purpose of proving he had a wife, it is too silly to require any refutation.[1] But granting that Paul was married, how came his wife to be at Philippi—a city which we do not read of his entering on more than two occasions, and in which it is probable he never remained so much as two whole months? In fine, nothing is more unlikely than that he speaks here of his wife; and to me it does not seem probable that he speaks of any female. I leave it, however, to the judgment of my readers. The word which Paul makes use of here (συλλάμ-βανεσθαι) means, to take hold of a thing and embrace it along with another person, with the view of giving help.[2]

Whose names are in the book of life. The *book of life* is the roll of the righteous, who are predestinated to life, as in the writings of Moses. (Exod. xxxii. 32.) God has this roll beside himself in safe keeping. Hence the book is nothing else than His eternal counsel, fixed in His own breast. In place of this term, Ezekiel employs this expression—*the writing of the house of Israel.* With the same view it is said in Psalm lxix. 29, *Let them be blotted out of the book of the living, and let them not be written among the righteous;* that is, let them not be numbered among the elect of

---

[1] See CALVIN on the Corinthians, vol. i. pp. 234, 235, 292.
[2] It is defined by Wahl, in his *Clavis N. T. Philologica*, as follows: *Una manum admoveo*, i.e., *opitulor, opem fero, iuvo;* (*I lend a helping-hand;* that is, *I assist, I bring assistance, I aid*.)—*Ed.*

Should any one allege, that Paul therefore acts rashly in usurping to himself the right of pronouncing as to the secrets of God, I answer, that we may in some measure form a judgment from the token by which God manifests his election, but only in so far as our capacity admits. In all those, therefore, in whom we see the marks of adoption shine forth, let us in the mean time reckon those to be the sons of God until the *books are opened*, (Rev. xx. 12,) which will thoroughly bring all things to view. It belongs, it is true, to God alone now to *know them that are his*, (2 Tim. ii. 19,)[1] and to separate at least the lambs from the kids ;[2] but it is our part to reckon in charity all to be lambs who, in a spirit of obedience, submit themselves to Christ as their Shepherd,[3] who betake themselves to his fold, and remain there constantly. It is our part to set so high a value upon the gifts of the Holy Spirit, which he confers peculiarly on his elect, that they shall be to us the seals, as it were, of an election which is hid from us.

4. Rejoice in the Lord alway: *and* again I say, Rejoice.	4. Gaudete in Domino semper, iterum dico, gaudete.
5. Let your moderation be known unto all men. The Lord *is* at hand.	5. Moderatio vestra nota sit omnibus hominibus. Dominus prope est.
6. Be careful for nothing : but in every thing by prayer and supplication, with thanksgiving, let your requests be made known unto God.	6. De nulla re sitis solliciti: sed in omnibus, oratione et precatione, cum gratiarum actione, petitiones vestrae innotescant apud Deum.
7. And the peace of God, which passeth all understanding, shall keep your hearts and minds through Christ Jesus.	7. Et pax Dei, quae exsuperat omnem intelligentiam, custodiet corda vestra et cogitationes vestras in Christo Iesu.
8. Finally, brethren, whatsoever things are true, whatsoever things *are* honest, whatsoever things *are* just, whatsoever things *are* pure, whatsoever things *are* lovely, whatsoever things *are* of good report ; if *there be* any virtue, and if *there be* any praise, think on these things.	8. Quod reliquum est, fratres, quaecunque sunt vera, quaecunque gravia, quaecunque iusta, quaecunque pura, quaecunque amabilia, quaecunque honesta: si qua virtus, et qua laus, haec cogitate.
9. Those things, which ye have both learned, and received, and	9. Quae et didicistis, et suscepistis, et audistis, et vidistis in me :

[1] See CALVIN on the Psalms, vol. iii. pp. 73, 74.
[2] " Les agneux des boucs ;"—" The lambs from the goats."
[3] " Christ vray Pasteur ;"—" Christ the true Shepherd."

4. *Rejoice in the Lord.* It is an exhortation suited to the times; for, as the condition of the pious was exceedingly troublous, and dangers threatened them on every side, it was possible that they might give way, overcome by grief or impatience.[1] Hence he enjoins it upon them, that, amidst circumstances of hostility and disturbance, they should nevertheless *rejoice in the Lord*,[2] as assuredly these spiritual consolations, by means of which the Lord refreshes and gladdens us, ought *then* most of all to show their efficacy when the whole world tempts us to despair. Let us, however, in connection with the circumstances of the times, consider what efficacy there must have been in this word uttered by the mouth of Paul, who might have had special occasion of sorrow.[3] For if they are appalled by persecutions, or imprisonments, or exile, or death, here is the Apostle setting himself forward, who, amidst imprisonments, in the very heat of persecution, and in fine, amidst apprehensions of death, is not merely himself joyful, but even stirs up others to joy. The sum, then, is this—that come what may, believers, having the Lord standing on their side,[4] have amply sufficient ground of joy.

The repetition of the exhortation serves to give greater force to it: Let this be your strength and stability, to *rejoice in the Lord*, and that, too, not for a moment merely, but so that your joy in him may be perpetuated.[5] For unquestionably it differs from the joy of the world in this respect—that we know from experience that the joy of the world is deceptive, frail, and fading, and Christ even pro-

---

[1] " Il se pouuoit faire que les Philippiens, estans vaincus de tristesse ou impatience, venissent a perdre courage;"—" It might be, that the Philippians, being overcome by grief or impatience, might come to lose heart."

[2] " Non obstant les troubles et les fascheries qu'ils voyoyent deuant leurs yeux;"—" Notwithstanding the troubles and annoyances that they saw before their eyes."

[3] " Qui plus que tous les autres pouuoit auoir matiere de se contrister;"—" Who might more than all others have had occasion to indulge sorrow."

[4] " Ont le Seigneur pour eux;"—" Have the Lord for them."

[5] " Que vostre ioye se continue en iceluy iusques a la fin;"—" That your joy may maintain itself in him until the end."

from us.

5. *Your moderation.* This may be explained in two ways. We may understand him as bidding them rather give up their right, than that any one should have occasion to complain of their sharpness or severity. " Let all that have to deal with you have experience of your equity and humanity." In this way to *know,* will mean to *experience.* Or we may understand him as exhorting them to endure all things with equanimity.¹ This latter meaning I rather prefer; for τὸ ἐπιεικές is a term that is made use of by the Greeks themselves to denote moderation of spirit—when we are not easily moved by injuries, when we are not easily annoyed by adversity, but retain equanimity of temper. In accordance with this, Cicero makes use of the following expression,—" My mind is tranquil, which takes everything in good part."² Such equanimity—which is as it were the mother of patience —he requires here on the part of the Philippians, and, indeed, such as will manifest itself to all, according as occasion will require, by producing its proper effects. The term *modesty* does not seem appropriate here, because Paul is not in this passage cautioning them against haughty insolence, but directs them to conduct themselves peaceably in everything, and exercise control over themselves, even in the endurance of injuries or inconveniences.

The Lord is at hand. Here we have an *anticipation,* by which he obviates an objection that might be brought forward. For carnal sense rises in opposition to the foregoing statement. For as the rage of the wicked is the more inflamed in proportion to our mildness,³ and the more they see us prepared for enduring, are the more emboldened to inflict injuries, we are with difficulty induced to *possess our*

¹ " En douceur et patience;"—" With sweetness and patience."
² " Tranquillus animus meus, qui aequi boni facit omnia." CALVIN here gives the sense, but not the precise words, of Cicero, which are as follows: " Tranquillissimus autem animus meus, qui totum istuc aequi boni facit;" —" My mind, however, is most tranquil, which takes all that in good part." See Cic. Att. 7, 7.—*Ed.*
³ " D'autant'plus que nous-nous monstrons gracieux et debonnaires;" —" The more that we show ourselves agreeable and gentle."

sheep will quickly be devoured by wolves." Hence we conclude, that the ferocity of the wicked must be repressed by corresponding violence, that they may not insult us with impunity.[1] To such considerations Paul here opposes confidence in Divine providence. He replies, I say, that *the Lord is at hand*, whose power can overcome their audacity, and whose goodness can conquer their malice. He promises that he will aid us, provided we obey his commandment. Now, who would not rather be protected by the hand of God alone, than have all the resources of the world at his command?

Here we have a most beautiful sentiment, from which we learn, in the *first* place, that ignorance of the providence of God is the cause of all impatience, and that this is the reason why we are so quickly, and on trivial accounts, thrown into confusion,[2] and often, too, become disheartened because we do not recognise the fact that the Lord cares for us. On the other hand, we learn that this is the only remedy for tranquillizing our minds—when we repose unreservedly in his providential care, as knowing that we are not exposed either to the rashness of fortune, or to the caprice of the wicked,[3] but are under the regulation of God's fatherly care. In fine, the man that is in possession of this truth, that God is present with him, has what he may rest upon with security.

There are, however, two ways in which *the Lord* is said to be *at hand*—either because his judgment is at hand, or because he is prepared to give help to his own people, in which sense it is made use of here; and also in Psalm cxlv. 18, *The Lord is near to all that call upon him.* The meaning therefore is,—" Miserable were the condition of the pious, if the Lord were at a distance from them." But as he has received them under his protection and guardianship, and

---

[1] " Afin qu'ils ne s'esleuent point a l'encontre de nous a leur plaisir et sans resistance;"—" That they may not rise up against us at their pleasure, and without resistance."

[2] " Que nous sommes tout incontinent et pour vn rien troublez et esmeus;"—" That we are all at once and for nothing troubled and moved."

[3] " Ni au plaisir desbordé des meschans;"—" Nor to the unbridled inclination of the wicked."

intimidated by the rage of the wicked. It is well known, and matter of common occurrence, that the term *solicitudo* (*carefulness*) is employed to denote that *anxiety* which proceeds from distrust of Divine power or help.

6. *But in all things.* It is the singular number that is made use of by Paul, but is the neuter gender; the expression, therefore, ἐν παντὶ, is equivalent to *in omni negotio*, (*in every matter*,) for προσευχὴ (*prayer*) and δέησις (*supplication*) are feminine nouns. In these words he exhorts the Philippians, as David does all the pious in Psalm lv. 23, and Peter also in 1 Peter v. 7, to *cast all their care upon the Lord.* For we are not made of iron,[1] so as not to be shaken by temptations. But this is our consolation, this our solace —to deposit, or (to speak with greater propriety) to disburden in the bosom of God everything that harasses us. Confidence, it is true, brings tranquillity to our minds, but it is only in the event of our exercising ourselves in prayers. Whenever, therefore, we are assailed by any temptation, let us betake ourselves forthwith to prayer, as to a sacred asylum.[2]

The term *requests* he employs here to denote desires or wishes. He would have us make these known to God by prayer and supplication, as though believers poured forth their hearts before God, when they commit themselves, and all that they have, to Him. Those, indeed, who look hither and thither to the vain comforts of the world, may appear to be in some degree relieved; but there is one sure refuge—leaning upon the Lord.

With thanksgiving. As many often pray to God amiss,[3] full of complaints or of murmurings, as though they had just ground for accusing him, while others cannot brook delay, if he does not immediately gratify their desires, Paul on this account conjoins thanksgiving with prayers. It is as

---

[1] " Car nous ne sommes de fer ni d'acier (comme on dit) ne si insensibles;"—" For we are not of iron nor steel, as they say, nor so insensible."
[2] " Comme a vne franchise;"—" As to a privilege."
[3] " Autrement qu'ils ne doyuent;"—" Otherwise than they ought."

way, that we, nevertheless, subject our affections to his good pleasure, and give thanks while presenting petitions. And, unquestionably, gratitude[1] will have this effect upon us—that the will of God will be the grand sum of our desires.

7. *And the peace of God.* Some, by turning the future tense into the optative mood, convert this statement into a prayer, but it is without proper foundation. For it is a promise in which he points out the advantage of a firm confidence in God, and invocation of him. "If you do that," says he, "*the peace of God will keep your minds and hearts.*" Scripture is accustomed to divide the soul of man, as to its frailties, into two parts—the *mind* and the *heart*. The *mind* means the *understanding*, while the *heart* denotes all the *dispositions* or *inclinations*. These two terms, therefore, include the entire soul, in this sense,—" The peace of God will guard you, so as to prevent you from turning back from God in wicked thoughts or desires."

It is on good ground that he calls it the *peace of God*, inasmuch as it does not depend on the present aspect of things,[2] and does not bend itself to the various shiftings of the world,[3] but is founded on the firm and immutable word of God. It is on good grounds, also, that he speaks of it as *surpassing all understanding or perception*, for nothing is more foreign to the human mind, than in the depth of despair to exercise, nevertheless, a feeling of hope, in the depth of poverty to see opulence, and in the depth of weakness to keep from giving way, and, in fine, to promise ourselves that nothing will be wanting to us when we are left destitute of all things; and all this in the grace of God alone, which is not itself known otherwise than through the word, and the inward earnest of the Spirit.

[1] " La recognoissance des benefices de Dieu;"—" Gratitude for God's benefits."

[2] " De ces choses basses;"—" Of these low things."

[3] " N'est point en branle pour chanceler selon les changemens diuers du monde;"—" Is not in suspense so as to turn about according to the various shiftings of the world."

mends *truth*, which is nothing else than the integrity of a good conscience, with the fruits of it : *secondly, gravity,* or *sanctity,* for τὸ σεμνόν[1] denotes both—an excellence which consists in this, that we walk in a manner *worthy of our vocation,* (Eph. iv. 1,) keeping at a distance from all profane filthiness : *thirdly, justice,* which has to do with the mutual intercourse of mankind—that we do not injure any one, that we do not defraud any one : and, *fourthly, purity,* which denotes chastity in every department of life. Paul, however, does not reckon all these things to be sufficient, if we do not at the same time endeavour to make ourselves agreeable to all, in so far as we may lawfully do so in the Lord, and have regard also to our good name. For it is in this way that I understand the words προσφιλῆ καὶ εὔφημα.

If any praise,[2] that is, *anything praiseworthy,* for amidst such a corruption of manners there is so great a perversity in men's judgments that praise is often bestowed[3] upon what is blameworthy, and it is not allowable for Christians to be desirous even of true praise among men, inasmuch as they are elsewhere forbidden to *glory, except in God alone.* (1 Cor. i. 31.) Paul, therefore, does not bid them try to gain applause or commendation by virtuous actions, nor even to regulate their life according to the judgments of the people, but simply means, that they should devote themselves to the performance of good works, which merit commendation, that the wicked, and those who are enemies of the gospel, while they deride Christians and cast reproach upon them, may, nevertheless, be constrained to commend their deportment.

[1] " The word σεμνὸν means that which has *dignity* connected with it. Hence σεμνός and μεγαλοπρεπής are joined together by *Aristotle,* as quoted by *Wetstein,* and in 2 Macc. viii. 15."—*Storr.* See *Biblical Cabinet,* vol. xl. p. 178, *note.*—*Ed.*

[2] " The *Clermont* copy reads here, εἴ τις ἔπαινος ἐπιστήμης, *If there be any praise of knowledge.* Instead of ἐπιστήμης, the Valesian readings have παιδείας, with which the *Vulg. Latin* agrees, reading, *If there be any praise of discipline,* (*disciplinae,*) as does also the *Ethiopic,* and two ancient Commentators mentioned by Dr. Mills."—*Pierce.*—*Ed.*

[3] " Bien souuent on louë ;"—" Very frequently they praise."

Now *meditation* comes first, afterwards follows *action*.

9. *What things ye have learned, and received, and heard.* By this accumulation of terms he intimates, that he was assiduous in inculcating these things. " This was my doctrine—my instruction—my discourse among you." Hypocrites, on the other hand, insisted upon nothing but ceremonies. Now, it was a dishonourable thing to abandon the holy instruction,[2] which they had wholly imbibed, and with which they had been thoroughly imbued.

You have seen in me. Now, the main thing in a public speaker[3] should be, that he may speak, not with his mouth merely, but by his life, and procure authority for his doctrine by rectitude of life. Paul, accordingly, procures authority for his exhortation on this ground, that he had, by his life no less than by his mouth, been a leader and master of virtues.

And the God of peace. He had spoken of the *peace of God;* he now more particularly confirms what he had said, by promising that God himself, the Author of peace, will be with them. For the presence of God brings us every kind of blessing: as though he had said, that they would feel that God was present with them to make all things turn out well and prosperously, provided they apply themselves to pious and holy actions.

10. But I rejoiced in the Lord greatly, that now at the last your care of me hath flourished again;	10. Gavisus sum autem in Domino valde, quod aliquando reviguistis in studio mei, de quo etiam

---

[1] " Like the Latin terms *cogitare, meditari,* the Greek μιλιτᾷν signifies to *contemplate* a thing, with the view of *finding means for effecting it.* . . . According to this view, ταῦτα λογίζισθι, in the passage before us, will be equivalent to ταῦτα ποιιῖν λογίζισθι, ' think to do these things,'—' give diligence to do them.' "—*Storr.* See *Biblical Cabinet,* vol. xl. p. 180, note.—*Ed.*

[2] " C'eust este vne chose dishonneste aux Philippiens de delaisser la sainte doctrine et instruction ;"—" It would have been a dishonourable thing for the Philippians to abandon the holy doctrine and instruction."

[3] " En vn prescheur ;"—" In a preacher."

want: for I have learned, in whatsoever state I am, *therewith* to be content.	riam loquar; ego enim didici, in quibus sum, iis contentus esse.
12. I know both how to be abased, and I know how to abound: every where, and in all things, I am instructed both to be full and be hungry, both to abound and to suffer need.	12. Novi et humilis esse, novi et excellere: ubique et in omnibus institutus sum, et saturari, et esurire, et abundare, et penuriam pati.
13. I can do all things through Christ which strengtheneth me.	13. Omnia possum in Christo, qui me corroborat.
14. Notwithstanding ye have well done that ye did communicate with my affliction.	14. Caeterum benefecistis simul communicando afflictioni meae.

10. *But I rejoiced.* He now declares the gratitude of his mind towards the Philippians, that they may not regret their beneficence,[1] as is usually the case when we think that our services are despised, or are reckoned of no account. They had sent him by Epaphroditus supplies for the relief of his necessity; he declares that their present had been acceptable to him, and he says, that he rejoiced that they had plucked up new vigour so as to exercise care respecting him. The metaphor is borrowed from trees, the strength of which is drawn inward, and lies concealed during winter, and begins to flourish[2] in spring. But immediately afterwards subjoining a correction, he qualifies what he had said, that he may not seem to reprove their negligence in the past. He says, therefore, that they had formerly, too, been concerned respecting him, but that the circumstances of the times had not admitted of his being sooner relieved by their benignity. Thus he throws the blame upon the want of opportunity. I take the phrase ἐφ' ᾧ as referring to the person of Paul, and that is its proper signification, as well as more in accordance with the connection of Paul's words.

11. *Not that I speak with respect to want.* Here we have a *second* correction, by which he guards against its being suspected that his spirit was pusillanimous and broken down

[1] " Afin qu'ils ne se repentent point de luy auoir assisté;"—" That they may not regret their having assisted him."

[2] " A reprendre vigueur et fleurir;"—" To recover strength and flourish."

whom he was a pattern of life. Accordingly he declares, that he had been gratified by their liberality in such a way that he could at the same time endure want with patience. *Want* refers here to disposition, for that man can never be poor in mind, who is satisfied with the lot which has been assigned to him by God.

In what state I am, says he, that is, " Whatever my condition may be, I am satisfied with it." Why? because saints know that they thus please God. Hence they do not measure sufficiency by abundance, but by the will of God, which they judge of by what takes place, for they are persuaded that their affairs are regulated by his providence and good pleasure.

12. *I know both how to be abased.* There follows here a distinction, with the view of intimating that he has a mind adapted to bear any kind of condition.[1] Prosperity is wont to puff up the mind beyond measure, and adversity, on the other hand, to depress. From both faults he declares himself to be free. *I know,* says he, *to be abased*—that is, to endure abasement with patience. Περισσεύειν is made use of twice, but in the former instance it is employed as meaning, to *excel;* in the *second* instance, as meaning, to *abound,* so as to correspond with the things to which they are exposed. If a man knows to make use of present abundance in a sober and temperate manner, with thanksgiving, prepared to part with everything whenever it may be the good pleasure of the Lord, giving also a share to his brother, according to the measure of his ability, and is also not puffed up, that man has learned to *excel,* and to *abound.* This is a peculiarly excellent and rare virtue, and much superior to the endurance of poverty. Let all who wish to be Christ's disciples exercise themselves in acquiring this knowledge which was possessed by Paul, but in the mean time let them

[1] " Il fait yci vne diuision, disant qu'il est tellement disposé en son cœur qu'il scait se comporter et en prosperite et en adversite ;"—" He makes a distinction here, saying that he is prepared in his mind in such a manner, that he knows how to conduct himself both in prosperity and in adversity."

when they come to be deprived of their riches.

13. *I can do all things through Christ.* As he had boasted of things that were very great,[1] in order that this might not be attributed to pride or furnish others with occasion of foolish boasting, he adds, that it is by Christ that he is endowed with this fortitude. "*I can do all things,*" says he, "but it is in Christ, not by my own power, for it is Christ that supplies me with strength." Hence we infer, that Christ will not be less strong and invincible in us also, if, conscious of our own weakness, we place reliance upon his power alone. When he says *all things,* he means merely those things which belong to his calling.

14. *Nevertheless ye did well.* How prudently and cautiously he acts, looking round carefully in both directions, that he may not lean too much to the one side or to the other. By proclaiming in magnificent terms his steadfastness, he meant to provide against the Philippians supposing that he had given way under the pressure of want.[2] He now takes care that it may not, from his speaking in high terms, appear as though he despised their kindness—a thing that would not merely shew cruelty and obstinacy, but also haughtiness. He at the same time provides for this, that if any other of the servants of Christ should stand in need of their assistance they may not be slow to give him help.

15. Now, ye Philippians, know also, that in the beginning of the gospel, when I departed from Macedonia, no church communicated with me, as concerning giving and receiving, but ye only.	15. Nostis autem et vos Philippenses, quod initio Evangelii, quando exivi ex Macedonia, nulla mecum Ecclesia in ratione dati et accepti, nisi vos soli.
16. For even in Thessalonica ye sent once and again unto my necessity.	16. Nam et Thessalonicam semel atque iterum mihi, quod opus erat, misistis:
17. Not because I desire a gift; but I desire fruit that may abound to your account.	17. Non quia requiram donum, sed requiro fructum, qui exsuperet in rationem vestram.

[1] "De choses grandes et excellentes;"—"Of things great and excellent."
[2] "Qu'il fust abbattu, et eust perdu courage estant en indigence;"—"That he had been overcome, and had lost heart, being in poverty."

from you, an odour of a sweet smell, a sacrifice acceptable, well-pleasing to God.	sunt a vobis in odorem bonae fragrantiae, sacrificium acceptum gratum Deo.
19. But my God shall supply all your need according to his riches in glory by Christ Jesus.	19. Deus autem meus implebit, quicquid vobis opus est, secundum divitias suas in gloria per Christum Iesum.
20. Now unto God and our Father *be* glory for ever and ever. Amen.	20. Porro Deo et Patri nostro gloria in secula seculorum. Amen.
21. Salute every saint in Christ Jesus. The brethren which are with me greet you.	21. Salutate omnes sanctos in Christo Iesu. Salutant vos qui mecum sunt fratres.
22. All the saints salute you, chiefly they that are of Cesar's household.	22. Salutant vos omnes sancti: maxime qui sunt ex domo Cæsaris.
23. The grace of our Lord Jesus Christ *be* with with you all. Amen.	23. Gratia Domini nostri Iesu Christi cum omnibus vobis. Amen.
It was written to the Philippians from Rome by Epaphroditus.	Scripta est a Roma per Epaphroditum.

15. *And ye know.* I understand this to have been added by way of excuse, inasmuch as he often received something from them, for if the other Churches had discharged their duty, it might have seemed as though he were too eager to receive. Hence in clearing himself he praises them, and in praising them he modestly excuses others. We must also, after Paul's example, take heed lest the pious, on seeing us too much inclined to receive from others, should on good grounds reckon us to be insatiable. *You also know,* says he. "I do not require to call in other witnesses, for ye yourselves also know." For it frequently happens, that when one thinks that others are deficient in duty, he is the more liberal in giving assistance. Thus the liberality of some escapes the notice of others.

In the matter of giving and receiving. He alludes to pecuniary matters, in which there are two parts, the one *receiving,* the other *expending.* It is necessary that these should be brought to an equality by mutual compensation. There was an account of this nature carried on between Paul and the Churches.[1] While Paul administered the

---

[1] "Il y auoit quelque telle condition et conuenance entre Sainct Paul et les Eglises;"—"There was some such condition and correspondence between St. Paul and the Churches."

support of his life, as he says elsewhere, *If we dispense to you spiritual things, is it a great matter if you give in return carnal things?* (1 Cor. ix. 11.) Hence, if the other churches had relieved Paul's necessities, they would have been giving nothing gratuitously, but would have been simply paying their debt, for they ought to have acknowledged themselves indebted to him for the gospel. This, however, he acknowledges, had not been the case, inasmuch as they had not laid out anything on his account. What base ingratitude, and how very unseemly, to treat such an Apostle with neglect, to whom they knew themselves to be under obligation beyond their power to discharge! On the other hand, how great the forbearance of this holy man, to bear with their inhumanity with so much gentleness and indulgence, as not to make use of one sharp word by way of accusing them!

17. *Not that I demand a gift.* Again he repels an unfavourable opinion that might be formed of immoderate cupidity, that they might not suppose that it was an indirect hint,[1] as if they ought singly to stand in the room of all,[2] and as if he abused their kindness. He accordingly declares, that he consulted not so much his own advantage as theirs. "While I receive from you," says he, "there is proportionably much advantage that redounds to yourselves; for there are just so many articles that you may reckon to have been transferred to the table of accounts." The meaning of this word[3] is connected with the similitude formerly employed of exchange or compensation in pecuniary matters.

18. *I have received all things, and abound.* He declares

---

[1] "Pour les induire a continuer;"—"To induce them to hold on."

[2] "Comme si eux deussent tenir la place de tous, et faire pour les autres;"—"As if they ought to hold the place of all, and to act in the room of others."

[3] CALVIN evidently refers to the word λόγον, (*account,*) which the Apostle had made use of in the fifteenth verse, in the phrase εἰς λόγον δόσεως καὶ λήψεως, (*in the matter of giving and receiving.*) It is noticed by *Beza*, that the Rabbins make use of a corresponding phrase מתן ומשא (*mattan umassa*)—*giving and taking.*—*Ed.*

saying, that he *has been filled.* It was undoubtedly a moderate sum that they had sent, but he says, that by means of that moderate sum he is filled to satiety. It is, however, a more distinguished commendation that he bestows upon the gift in what follows, when he calls it a *sacrifice acceptable, and presented as the odour of a good fragrance.* For what better thing can be desired than that our acts of kindness should be sacred offerings, which God receives from our hands, and takes pleasure in their sweet odour? For the same reason Christ says, *Whatsoever ye shall have done unto one of the least of these, ye have done it unto me.*

The similitude of *sacrifices,* however, adds much emphasis, by which we are taught, that the exercise of love which God enjoins upon us, is not merely a benefit conferred upon man, but is also a spiritual and sacred service which is performed to God, as we read in the Epistle to the Hebrews, that he is *well pleased with such sacrifices.* (Heb. xiii. 16.) Alas for our indolence![1]—which appears in this, that while God invites us with so much kindness to the honour of priesthood, and even puts sacrifices in our hands, we nevertheless do not sacrifice to him, and those things which were set apart for sacred oblations we not only lay out for profane uses, but squander them wickedly upon the most polluted contaminations.[2] For the altars, on which sacrifices from our resources ought to be presented, are the poor, and the servants of Christ. To the neglect of these some squander their resources on every kind of luxury, others upon the palate, others upon immodest attire, others upon magnificent dwellings.[3]

[1] " Or maudite soit nostre paresse ;"—" But accursed be our indolence."
[2] " Les consumons prodigalement et meschamment en choses infames et abominables ;"—" We lay them out lavishly and wickedly on things infamous and abominable."
[3] " Les vns dependent tout leur bien en toutes de dissolutions, les autres en gouermandise et yurognerie, les autres en brauetes excessiues, les autres a bastir des palais somptueux ;"—" Some lay out all their wealth on all kinds of luxuries, others on eating and drinking, others superfluous elegance of dress, others in building sumptuous palaces."

ing, I approve more of the other. He expressly makes mention of God as *his*, because he owns and acknowledges as done to himself whatever kindness is shewn to his servants. They had therefore been truly sowing in the Lord's field, from which a sure and abundant harvest might be expected. Nor does he promise them merely a reward in the future life, but even in respect of the necessities of the present life: "Do not think that you have impoverished yourselves; God, whom I serve, will abundantly furnish you with everything necessary for you." The phrase, *in glory*, ought to be taken in place of the adverb *gloriously*, as meaning *magnificently*, or *splendidly*. He adds, however, *by Christ*, in whose name everything that we do is acceptable to God.

20. *Now to our God and Father.* This may be taken as a general thanksgiving, by which he closes the epistle; or it may be viewed as bearing more particularly upon the last clause in reference to the liberality shewn to Paul.[2] For in respect of the assistance which the Philippians had afforded him, it became him to reckon himself indebted to them for it in such a manner as to acknowledge, that this aid had been afforded to them by the mercy of God.

22. *The brethren that are with me salute you.* In these salutations he names first of all his intimate associates,[3] afterwards all the saints in general, that is, the whole Church at Rome, but chiefly those of the household of Nero—a thing well deserving to be noticed; for it is no common evidence of divine mercy, that the gospel had made its way into that sink of all crimes and iniquities. It is also the more to be admired, in proportion as it is a rare thing for holiness to reign in the courts of sovereigns. The conjecture formed by some, that Seneca is here referred to among others, has no

---

[1] " Comme si c'estoit vn souhait que sainct Paul feist;"—" As if it were a wish that St. Paul expressed."

[2] " La liberalite de laquelle les Philippiens auoyent vsé enuers sainct Paul;"—" The liberality which the Philippians had exercised towards St. Paul."

[3] " Les compagnons, qui demeuroyent auec luy;"—" His associates who lived with him."

long to the *household of Cesar*, but was a senator, and had at one time held the office of praetor.[1]

[1] " Some imagine," says Dr. A. Clarke, " that *Seneca*, the preceptor of Nero, and the poet *Lucan*, were converted by St. Paul; and there are still extant, and in a MS. now before me, letters which profess to have passed between Paul and *Seneca;* but they are worthy of neither. They have been printed in some editions of *Seneca's* works."—*Ed.*

END OF THE COMMENTARY ON THE EPISTLE TO
THE PHILIPPIANS.

COMMENTARY

ON

THE EPISTLE TO THE COLOSSIANS.

THE ARGUMENT

ON

THE EPISTLE OF PAUL TO THE COLOSSIANS.

THERE were three neighbouring cities in Phrygia, as made mention of by PAUL in this Epistle—LAODICEA, HIERAPOLIS, and COLOSSE—which, as *Orosius*[1] informs us, were overthrown[2] by an earthquake in the times of the emperor *Nero*. Accordingly, not long after this Epistle was written, three Churches of great renown perished by a mournful as well as horrible occurrence—a bright mirror truly of divine judgment, if we had but eyes to see it. The COLOSSIANS had been, not indeed by PAUL, but with fidelity and purity by EPAPHRAS and other ministers, instructed in the gospel; but immediately afterwards, Satan had, with his *tares*, crept in, (Matt. xiii. 25,)[3] according to his usual and invariable manner, that he might there pervert the right faith.[4]

Some are of opinion that there were two classes of men that endeavoured to draw aside the COLOSSIANS from the purity of the gospel;—that, on the one hand, the philosophers, by disputing in reference to stars, fate, and trifles of a like nature, and that the Jews, on the other hand, by urging the observance of their ceremonies, had raised up many mists with the view of throwing Christ into the shade.[5] Those, however, who are of this opinion are in-

[1] Orosius, (Paulus,) a "Spanish presbyter, a native of Tarragona, flourished under Arcadius and Honorius."—*Smith's* Dictionary of Greek Biography and Mythology.—*Ed.*

[2] "Toutes trois furent destructes et renversees;"—"They were, all the three, destroyed and overthrown."

[3] "Satan y estoit entré cauteleusement auec son yuroye;"—"Satan had entered in there craftily with his tares."

[4] "Pour y corrompre et peruertir la vraye foy;"—"That he might there corrupt and pervert the true faith."

[5] "Auoyent comme fait leuer beaucoup de brouillars pour offusquer la clarte de Christ, voire pour la suffoquer;"—"Had, as it were, raised up many mists with the view of darkening Christ's brightness; nay, more, with the view of choking it."

heavenly creatures. For as to their adding also the term *elements*,[1] it is worse than ridiculous. As, however, it is not my intention to refute the opinions of others, I shall simply state what appears to me to be the truth, and what may be inferred by sound reasoning.

In the first place, it is abundantly evident, from PAUL's words, that those profligates were intent upon this—that they might mix up Christ with Moses, and might retain the shadows of the law along with the gospel. Hence it is probable that they were Jews. As, however, they coloured over their fallacies with specious disguises,[2] PAUL, on this account, calls it a *vain philosophy.* (Col. ii. 8.) At the same time, in employing that term, he had in his eye, in my opinion, the speculations with which they amused themselves, which were subtle, it is true, but at the same time useless and profane : for they contrived a way of access to God through means of angels, and put forth many speculations of that nature, such as are contained in the books of Dionysius on the Celestial Hierarchy,[3] drawn from the school of the Platonists. This, therefore, is the principal object at which he aims—to teach that all things are in Christ, and that he alone ought to be reckoned amply sufficient by the Colossians.

The order, however, which he follows is this :—After the inscription usually employed by him, he commends them, with the view of leading them to listen to him more attentively. He then, with the view of shutting up the way against all new and strange contrivances, bears testimony to the doctrine which they had previously received from EPAPHRAS. Afterwards, in entreating that the Lord would increase their faith, he intimates that something is still wanting to them, that he may pave the way for imparting to them more solid instruction. On the other hand, he extols with suitable commendations the grace of God towards them, that they may not lightly esteem it. Then follows the instruction, in which he teaches that all parts of our salvation are to be found in Christ

---

[1] " Car quant au mot d'elemens, sur lequel aussi ils fondent leur opinion ;"—" For as to the word elements, on which also they found their opinion."

[2] " Pource qu'ils couuroyent de belles couleurs leurs fallaces et tromperies, et fardoyent leur doctrine ;"—" As they covered over their fallacies and deceptions with beautiful colours, and painted their doctrine."

[3] See CALVIN on the Corinthians, vol. ii. p. 370, *n.* 3.

blessing that they possessed, in order that they might the more carefully make it their aim to retain him to the end.¹ And, truly, even this one article were of itself perfectly sufficient to lead us to reckon this Epistle, short as it is, to be an inestimable treasure; for what is of greater importance in the whole system of heavenly doctrine than to have Christ drawn to the life, that we may distinctly behold² his excellence, his office, and all the fruits that arise to us from it?

For in this respect especially we differ from Papists, that while we are both of us called Christians, and profess to believe in Christ, they picture to themselves one that is torn, disfigured, divested of his excellence, denuded of his office, in fine, such as to be a spectre³ rather than Christ himself: we, on the other hand, embrace him such as he is here described by PAUL—loving and efficacious. This Epistle, therefore, to express it in one word, distinguishes the true Christ from a fictitious one⁴—than which nothing better or more excellent can be desired. Towards the end of the *First Chapter* he again endeavours to secure authority for himself from the station assigned him,⁵ and in magnificent terms extols the dignity of the gospel.

In the *Second Chapter* he opens up more distinctly than he had done the reason which had induced him to write—that he might provide against the danger which he saw to be impending over them, while he touches, in passing, on the affection which he cherishes towards them, that they may know that their welfare is the object of his concern. From this he proceeds to exhortation, by which he applies the foregoing doctrine, as it were, to present

---

¹ " Et pour les faire plus songneux de la retenir iusqu'a la fin, et s'arrester tousiours en luy, il recite que par Christ ils sont entrez en participation de tout bien et benediction;"—" And with the view of making them more careful to retain him unto the end, and remain always in him, he reminds them that it is through Christ that they have begun to participate of every benefit and blessing."

² " Afin que nous puissions aiseement veoir et contempler;"—" That we may be able easily to perceive and contemplate."

³ " Tel, que c'est plustost vn phantasme qu' vn vray Christ;"—" Such, that it is rather a phantasm than a true Christ."

⁴ " Imaginatif, ou faict a plaiser;"—" Imaginary, or fictitious."

⁵ " Pour estre plus authorizé entr' eux, il fait derechef mention de la charge qu'il auoit receuë de Dieu;"—" That he may have more authority among them, he again makes mention of the charge which he had received from God."

cumcision, abstinence from food, and of other outward exercises—in which they mistakingly made the service of God to consist; and also of the absurd worship of angels, whom they put in Christ's room. Having made mention of circumcision, he takes occasion to notice also, in passing, what is the office, and what is the nature of ceremonies—from which he lays it down as a settled point that they have been abrogated by Christ. These things are treated of till the end of the *Second Chapter.*

In the *Third Chapter,* in opposition to those vain prescriptions, to the observance of which the false apostles were desirous to bind believers, he makes mention of those true offices of piety in which the Lord would have us employ ourselves; and he begins with the very *spring-head*—that is, mortification of the flesh and newness of life. From this he derives the *streams*—that is, particular exhortations, some of which apply to all Christians alike, while others relate more especially to particular individuals, according to the nature of their calling.

In the beginning of the *Fourth Chapter* he follows out the same subject: afterwards, having commended himself to their prayers, he shews by many tokens[3] how much he loves them, and is desirous to promote their welfare.

---

[1] " A son propos, et a ce dont ils auoyent affaire ;"—" To his subject, and to what they had to do with."

[2] " Monstrant, que tout ce qui hors Christ, n'est que vanite ;"—" Shewing that everything that is apart from Christ is mere vanity."

[3] " Par plusieurs signes et tesmoignages ;"—" By many signs and evidences."

COMMENTARY

ON

THE EPISTLE OF PAUL TO THE COLOSSIANS.

CHAPTER I.

1. Paul, an apostle of Jesus Christ by the will of God, and Timotheus *our* brother,
2. To the saints and faithful brethren in Christ which are at Colosse: Grace *be* unto you, and peace, from God our Father, and the Lord Jesus Christ.
3. We give thanks to God and the Father of our Lord Jesus Christ, praying always for you,
4. Since we heard of your faith in Christ Jesus, and of the love *which ye have* to all the saints;
5. For the hope which is laid up for you in heaven, whereof ye heard before in the word of the truth of the gospel;
6. Which is come unto you, as *it is* in all the world; and bringeth forth fruit, as *it doth* also in you, since the day ye heard *of it,* and knew the grace of God in truth:
7. As ye also learned of Epaphras our dear fellow-servant, who is for you a faithful minister of Christ;
8. Who also declared unto us your love in the Spirit.

1. Paulus apostolus Iesu Christi, per voluntatem Dei, et Timotheus frater,
2. Sanctis qui sunt Colossis, et fidelibus fratribus in Christo; gratia vobis et pax a Deo et Patre nostro, et Domino Iesu Christo.
3. Gratias agimus Deo. et Patri Domini nostri Iesu Christi, semper pro vobis orantes,
4. Audita fide vestra, quae est in Christo Iesu, et caritate erga omnes sanctos,
5. Propter spem repositam vobis in coelis, de qua prius audistis, per sermonem veritatis, nempe Evangelii,
6. Quod ad vos pervenit: quemadmodum et in universo mundo fructificat et propagatur, sicut etiam in vobis, ex quo die audistis, et cognovistis gratiam Dei in veritate.
7. Quemadmodum et didicistis ab Epaphra, dilecto converso nostro, qui est fidelis erga vos minister Christi:
8. Qui etiam nobis manifestavit caritatem vestram in Spiritu.

1. *Paul an Apostle.* I have already, in repeated instances, explained the design of such inscriptions. As, however, the COLOSSIANS had never seen him, and on that account his authority was not as yet so firmly established

will of God. From this it followed, that he did not act rashly in writing to persons that were not known by him, inasmuch as he was discharging an embassy with which God had intrusted him. For he was not bound to one Church merely, but his Apostleship extended to all. The term *saints* which he applies to them is more honourable, but in calling them *faithful brethren,* he allures them more winningly to listen to him. As for other things, they may be found explained in the foregoing Epistles.

3. *We give thanks to God.* He praises the faith and love of the Colossians, that he may encourage them the more to alacrity and constancy of perseverance. Farther, by shewing that he has a persuasion of this kind respecting them, he procures their friendly regards, that they may be the more favourably inclined and teachable for receiving his doctrine. We must always take notice that he makes use of thanksgiving in place of congratulation, by which he teaches us, that in all our joys we must readily call to remembrance the goodness of God, inasmuch as everything that is pleasant and agreeable to us is a kindness conferred by him. Besides, he admonishes us, by his example, to acknowledge with gratitude not merely those things which the Lord confers upon us, but also those things which he confers upon others.

But for what things does he give thanks to the Lord? For the *faith* and *love* of the Colossians. He acknowledges, therefore, that both are conferred by God: otherwise the gratitude were pretended. And what have we otherwise than through his liberality? If, however, even the smallest favours come to us from that source, how much more ought this same acknowledgment to be made in reference to those two gifts, in which the entire sum of our excellence consists?

To the God and Father.[2] Understand the expression thus —*To God who is the Father of Christ.* For it is not lawful for

---

[1] " Son simple et priué nom ;"—" His simple and private name."
[2] " *A Dieu qui est le Pere.* Il y auroit mot a mot, A Dieu et Pere ;"— " *To God who is the Father.* It were literally, To God and Father."

ing the door to us, if we are desirous to have access to the true God. For on this account, also, is he a Father to us, because he has embraced us in his only begotten Son, and in him also sets forth his paternal favour for our contemplation.

Always for us. Some explain it thus—*We give thanks to God always for you,* that is, *continually.* Others explain it to mean—*Praying always for you.* It may also be interpreted in this way, "Whenever we pray for you, we at the same time give thanks to God;" and this is the simple meaning, "We give thanks to God, and we at the same time pray." By this he intimates, that the condition of believers is never in this world perfect, so as not to have, invariably, something wanting. For even the man who has begun admirably well, may fall short in a hundred instances every day; and we must ever be making progress while we are as yet on the way. Let us therefore bear in mind that we must rejoice in the favours that we have already received, and give thanks to God for them in such a manner, as to seek at the same time from him perseverance and advancement.

4. *Having heard of your faith.* This was a means of stirring up his love towards them, and his concern for their welfare, when he heard that they were distinguished by *faith* and *love.* And, unquestionably, gifts of God that are so excellent ought to have such an effect upon us as to stir us up to love them wherever they appear. He uses the expression, faith *in Christ,* that we may always bear in mind that Christ is the proper object of faith.

He employs the expression, *love towards the saints,* not with the view of excluding others, but because, in proportion as any one is joined to us in God, we ought to embrace him the more closely with a special affection. True love, therefore, will extend to mankind universally, because they all are our flesh, and *created in the image of God,* (Gen. ix. 6;) but in respect of degrees, it will begin with those who are of the *household of faith.* (Gal. vi. 10.)

5. *For the hope which is laid up for you in heaven.* For the *hope* of eternal life will never be inactive in us, so as

for him in heaven will aspire thither, looking down upon this world. Meditation, however, upon the heavenly life stirs up our affections both to the worship of God, and to exercises of love. The Sophists pervert this passage for the purpose of extolling the merits of works, as if the hope of salvation depended on works. The reasoning, however, is futile. For it does not follow, that because hope stimulates us to aim at upright living, it is therefore founded upon works, inasmuch as nothing is more efficacious for this purpose than God's unmerited goodness, which utterly overthrows all confidence in works.

There is, however, an instance of *metonymy* in the use of the term *hope*, as it is taken for the thing hoped for. For the hope that is in our hearts is the glory which we hope for in heaven. At the same time, when he says, that there is a *hope* that is *laid up for us in heaven*, he means, that believers ought to feel assured as to the promise of eternal felicity, equally as though they had already a treasure laid up[1] in a particular place.

Of which ye heard before. As eternal salvation is a thing that surpasses the comprehension of our understanding, he therefore adds, that the assurance of it had been brought to the Colossians by means of the gospel; and at the same time he says in the outset,[2] that he is not to bring forward anything new, but that he has merely in view to confirm them in the doctrine which they had previously received. Erasmus has rendered it—*the true word of the gospel.* I am also well aware that, according to the Hebrew idiom, the genitive is often made use of by Paul in place of an epithet; but the words of Paul here are more emphatic.[3] For he calls the gospel, κατ' ἐξοχήν, (*by way of eminence,*) the *word of truth,* with the view of putting honour upon it, that they may more steadfastly and firmly adhere to the revelation

---

[1] " Vn tresor en seure garde;"—" A treasure in safe keeping."

[2] " Il dit auant que passer plus outre;"—" He says before proceeding farther."

[3] " Ont yci plus grande signifiance, et emportent plus;"—" Have here more significancy, and are more emphatic."

6. *As also in all the world it brings forth fruit.* This has a tendency both to confirm and to comfort the pious—to see the effect of the gospel far and wide in gathering many to Christ. The faith of it does not, it is true, depend on its success, as though *we* should believe it on the ground that *many* believe it. Though the whole world should fail, though heaven itself should fall, the conscience of a pious man must not waver, because God, on whom it is founded, does nevertheless remain true. This, however, does not hinder our faith from being confirmed, whenever it perceives God's excellence, which undoubtedly shews itself with more power in proportion to the number of persons that are gained over to Christ.

In addition to this, in the multitude of the believers at that time there was beheld an accomplishment of the many predictions which extend the reign of Christ from the East to the West. Is it a trivial or common aid to faith, to see accomplished before our eyes what the Prophets long since predicted as to the extending of the kingdom of Christ through all countries of the world? What I speak of, there is no believer that does not experience in himself. Paul accordingly had it in view to encourage the Colossians the more by this statement, that, by seeing in various places the fruit and progress of the gospel, they might embrace it with more eager zeal. $Aὐξανόμενον$, which I have rendered *propagatur*, (*is propagated*,) does not occur in some copies; but, from its suiting better with the context, I did not choose to omit it. It also appears from the commentaries of the ancients that this reading was always the more generally received.[2]

Since the day ye heard it, and knew the grace. Here he praises them on account of their docility, inasmuch as they immediately embraced sound doctrine; and he praises them on account of their constancy, inasmuch as they persevered

---

[1] The term *apposition*, in grammar, signifies the putting of two nouns in the same case.—*Ed.*

[2] "This" (καὶ αὐξανόμενον) "is the reading of the *Vatican* and all the *most* ancient authorities."—*Penn.—Ed.*

tasted of the gospel but the man that knew himself to be reconciled to God, and took hold of the salvation that is held forth in Christ.

In truth means *truly* and *without pretence ;* for as he had previously declared that the gospel is undoubted truth, so he now adds, that it had been purely administered by them, and that *by Epaphras.* For while all boast that they preach the gospel, and yet at the same time there are many *evil workers,* (Phil. iii. 2,) through whose ignorance, or ambition, or avarice, its purity is adulterated, it is of great importance that faithful ministers should be distinguished from the less upright. For it is not enough to hold the term gospel, unless we know that this is the true gospel—what was preached by Paul and Epaphras. Hence Paul confirms the doctrine of Epaphras by giving it his approbation, that he may induce the Colossians to adhere to it, and may, by the same means, call them back from those profligates who endeavoured to introduce strange doctrines. He at the same time dignifies Epaphras with a special distinction, that he may have more authority among them; and lastly, he presents him to the Colossians in an amiable aspect, by saying that he had borne testimony to him of their love. Paul everywhere makes it his particular aim, that he may, by his recommendation, render those who he knows serve Christ faithfully, very dear to the Churches; as, on the other hand, the ministers of Satan are wholly intent on alienating, by unfavourable representations,[1] the minds of the simple from faithful pastors.

Love in the Spirit I take to mean, *spiritual love,* according to the view of Chrysostom, with whom, however, I do not agree in the interpretation of the preceding words. Now, *spiritual love* is of such a nature as has no view to the world, but is consecrated to the service of piety,[2] and has, as it were, an internal root, while carnal friendships depend on external causes.

[1] " Par faux rapports et calomnies ;"—" By false reports and calumnies."
[2] " Mais est commencee et comme consacree a l'adueu de la piete et cognoissance de Dieu ;"—" But is commenced and, as it were, consecrated to the service of piety and the knowledge of God."

might be filled with the knowledge of his will in all wisdom and spiritual understanding;	cognitione voluntatis ipsius, in omni sapientia et prudentia¹ spirituali:
10. That ye might walk worthy of the Lord unto all pleasing, being fruitful in every good work, and increasing in the knowledge of God;	10. Ut ambuletis digne Deo, in omne obsequium, in omni bono opere fructificantes, et crescentes in cognitione Dei:
11. Strengthened with all might, according to his glorious power, unto all patience and long-suffering with joyfulness.	11. Omni robore roborati, secundum potentiam gloriae ipsius, in omnem tolerantiam et patientiam, cum gaudio.

9. *For this cause we also.* As he has previously shewn his affection for them in his thanksgivings, so he now shews it still farther in the earnestness of his prayers in their behalf.² And, assuredly, the more that the grace of God is conspicuous in any, we ought in that proportion specially to love and esteem them, and to be concerned as to their welfare. But what does he pray for in their behalf? That they may know God more fully; by which he indirectly intimates, that something is still wanting in them, that he may prepare the way for imparting instruction to them, and may secure their attention to a fuller statement of doctrine. For those who think that they have already attained everything that is worthy of being known, despise and disdain everything farther that is presented to them. Hence he removes from the Colossians an impression of this nature, lest it should be a hinderance in the way of their cheerfully making progress, and allowing what had been begun in them to receive an additional polish. But what knowledge does he desire in their behalf? The knowledge of *the divine will,* by which expression he sets aside all inventions of men, and all speculations that are at variance with the word of God. For his will is not to be sought anywhere else than in his word.

---

¹ " *Prudence,* ou *intelligence;*"—" *Prudence,* or *understanding.*"

² " Comme il a ci dessus demonstré l'amour qu'il auoit enuers eux, en protestant qu'il s'esiouit de leurs auancemens, et en rend graces a Dieu, aussi le fait-il maintenant en son affection vehemente, et continuation de prier;"—" As he has already shewn the love which he cherished towards them, by declaring that he rejoices in their proficiency, and gives thanks to God for it, so he does the same now by his intense eagerness and perseverance in prayer."

rule of right knowledge. For if any one is desirous simply to know those things which it has pleased God to reveal, that is the man who accurately knows what it is to be truly wise. If we desire anything beyond that, this will be nothing else than to be foolish, by not keeping within due bounds. By the word συνέσεως, which we render *prudentiam*, (prudence,) I understand—that discrimination which proceeds from intelligence. Both are called *spiritual* by Paul, because they are not attained in any other way than by the guidance of the Spirit. For the *animal man does not perceive the things that are of God.* (1 Cor. ii. 14.) So long as men are regulated by their own carnal perceptions, they have also their own wisdom, but it is of such a nature as is mere vanity, however much they may delight themselves in it. We see what sort of theology there is under the Papacy, what is contained in the books of philosophers, and what wisdom profane men hold in estimation. Let us, however, bear in mind, that the wisdom which is alone commended by Paul is comprehended in the *will of God.*

10. *That ye may walk worthy of God.* In the *first* place he teaches, what is the end of *spiritual understanding,* and for what purpose we ought to make proficiency in God's school—that we may *walk worthy of God,* that is, that it may be manifest in our life, that we have not in vain been taught by God. Whoever they may be that do not direct their endeavours towards this object, may possibly toil and labour much, but they do nothing better than wander about in endless windings, without making any progress.[1] Farther, he admonishes us, that if we would *walk worthy of God,* we must above all things take heed that we regulate our whole course of life according to the will of God, renouncing our own understanding, and bidding farewell to all the inclinations of our flesh.

This also he again confirms by saying—*unto all obedience,*

[1] " Mais ils ne feront que tracasser çà et là, et tourner a l'entour du pot (comme on dit) sans s'auancer;"—" But they will do nothing else than hurry hither and thither, and go about the bush (as they say) without making progress."

view this definition of Paul—that it is such a life as, leaving the opinions of men, and leaving, in short, all carnal inclination, is regulated so as to be in subjection to God alone. From this follow good works, which are the fruits that God requires from us.

Increasing in the knowledge of God. He again repeats, that they have not arrived at such perfection as not to stand in need of farther increase; by which admonition he prepares them, and as it were leads them by the hand, to an eagerness for proficiency, that they may shew themselves ready to listen, and teachable. What is here said to the Colossians, let all believers take as said to themselves, and draw from this a common exhortation—that we must always make progress in the doctrine of piety until death.

11. *Strengthened with all might.* As he has previously prayed that they might have both a sound understanding and the right use of it, so also now he prays that they may have courage and constancy. In this manner he puts them in mind of their own weakness, for he says, that they will not be strong otherwise than by the Lord's help; and not only so, but with the view of magnifying this exercise of grace the more, he adds, *according to his glorious power.* " So far from any one being able to stand, through dependence on his own strength, the power of God shews itself illustriously in helping our infirmity." Lastly, he shews in what it is that the strength of believers ought to display itself —*in all patience and long-suffering.* For they are constantly, while in this world, exercised with the cross, and a thousand temptations daily present themselves, so as to weigh them down, and they see nothing of what God has promised. They must, therefore, arm themselves with an admirable patience, that what Isaiah says may be accomplished, *In hope and in silence shall be your strength.*[1] (Isaiah xxx. 15.) It is preferable to connect with this sentence the clause, *with joy.* For although the other reading is more commonly to be met

[1] Lowth's rendering of the passage is similar: " In silence, and in pious confidence, shall be your strength."—*Ed.*

sustained otherwise than by alacrity of mind, and will never be maintained with fortitude by any one that is not satisfied with his condition.

12. Giving thanks unto the Father, which hath made us meet to be partakers of the inheritance of the saints in light:	12. Gratias agentes Deo et Patri,[1] qui nos fecit idoneos ad participationem hereditatis sanctorum in lumine.
13. Who hath delivered us from the power of darkness, and hath translated *us* into the kingdom of his dear Son;	13. Qui eripuit nos ex potestate tenebrarum, et transtulit in regnum Filii sui dilecti:
14. In whom we have redemption through his blood, *even* the forgiveness of sins:	14. In quo habemus redemptionem per sanguinem eius, remissionem peccatorum:
15. Who is the image of the invisible God, the first-born of every creature:	15. Qui est imago Dei invisibilis, primogenitus universae creaturae.
16. For by him were all things created that are in heaven, and that are in earth, visible and invisible, whether *they be* thrones, or dominions, or principalities, or powers; all things were created by him, and for him:	16. Quoniam in ipso creata sunt omnia, tum quae in coelis sunt, tum quae super terram; visibilia et invisibilia; sive throni, sive dominationes, sive principatus, sive potestates.
17. And he is before all things, and by him all things consist.	17. Omnia per ipsum, et in ipsum creata sunt: et ipse est ante omnia, et omnia in ipso constant.

12. *Giving thanks.* Again he returns to thanksgiving, that he may take this opportunity of enumerating the blessings which had been conferred upon them through Christ, and thus he enters upon a full delineation of Christ. For this was the only remedy for fortifying the Colossians against all the snares, by which the false Apostles endeavoured to entrap them—to understand accurately what Christ was. For how comes it that we are *carried about with so many strange doctrines,* (Heb. xiii. 9,) but because the excellence of Christ is not perceived by us? For Christ alone makes all other things suddenly vanish. Hence there is nothing that Satan so much endeavours to accomplish as to bring on mists with the view of obscuring Christ, because he knows,

---

[1] " *A Dieu et Pere, qui nous a faits,* ou, au Pere, qui nous a faits;"— " *To God and the Father, who hath made us,* or, to the Father, who hath made us."

as well as restoring pure doctrine—to place Christ before the view such as he is with all his blessings, that his excellence may be truly perceived.

The question here is not as to the name. Papists in common with us acknowledge one and the same Christ; yet in the mean time how great a difference there is between us and them, inasmuch as they, after confessing Christ to be the Son of God, transfer his excellence to others, and scatter it hither and thither, and thus leave him next to empty,[1] or at least rob him of a great part of his glory, so that he is called, it is true, by them the Son of God, but, nevertheless, he is not such as the Father designed he should be towards us. If, however, Papists would cordially embrace what is contained in this chapter, we would soon be perfectly agreed, but the whole of Popery would fall to the ground, for it cannot stand otherwise than through ignorance of Christ. This will undoubtedly be acknowledged by every one that will but consider the main article[2] of this first chapter; for his grand object here is that we may know that Christ is the beginning, middle, and end—that it is from him that all things must be sought—that nothing is, or can be found, apart from him. Now, therefore, let the readers carefully and attentively observe in what colours Paul depicts Christ to us.

Who hath made us meet. He is still speaking of the *Father*, because he is the beginning, and efficient cause (as they speak) of our salvation. As the term *God* is more distinctly expressive of majesty, so the term *Father* conveys the idea of clemency and benevolent disposition. It becomes us to contemplate both as existing in God, that his majesty may inspire us with fear and reverence, and that his fatherly love may secure our full confidence. Hence it is not without good reason that Paul has conjoined these two things,

[1] " Ils le laissent quasi vuide et inutile;"—" They leave him in a manner empty and useless."
[2] *Statum.* The term is commonly employed among the Latins like στάσις among the Greeks, to mean the *point at issue.* See *Cic. Top.* 25. —*Ed.*

ancient Greek manuscripts.¹ At the same time there will be no inconsistency in saying, that he contents himself with the single term, *Father*. Farther, as it is necessary that his incomparable grace should be expressed by the term *Father*, so it is also not less necessary that we should, by the term *God*, be roused up to admiration of so great goodness, that he, who is God, has condescended thus far.²

But for what kindness does he give thanks to God? For his having *made* him, and others, *meet to be partakers of the inheritance of the saints*. For we are born children of wrath, exiles from God's kingdom. It is God's adoption that alone *makes us meet*. Now, adoption depends on an unmerited election. The Spirit of regeneration is the seal of adoption. He adds, *in light*, that there might be a contrast—as opposed to the darkness of Satan's kingdom.³

13. *Who hath delivered us.* Mark, here is the beginning of our salvation—when God delivers us from the depth of ruin into which we were plunged. For wherever his grace is not, *there* is darkness,⁴ as it is said in *Isaiah*, (lx. 2,) *Behold darkness shall cover the earth, and thick darkness the nations; but the Lord shall arise upon thee, and his glory shall be seen upon thee.* In the first place, we ourselves are called darkness, and afterwards the whole world, and Satan, the Prince of darkness,⁵ under whose tyranny we are held captive, until we are set free by Christ's hand.⁶ From this you may gather that the whole world, with all its pretended

---

¹ It is stated by *Beza*, that some Greek manuscripts have τῷ Θεῷ καὶ Πατρὶ, (*to God and the Father,*) and that this is the reading in some copies of the Vulgate. *Wiclif* (1380) reads, "To God and to the Fadir." Rheims (1582) "To God and the Father."—*Ed.*

² "S'est abbaisé iusques là de vouloir estre nostre Pere;"—"Has abased himself so far as to be willing to be our Father."

³ "Afin qu'il y eust vne opposition entre les tenebres du royaume de Satan, et la lumiere du royaume de Dieu;"—"That there might be a contrast between the darkness of Satan's kingdom, and the light of God's kingdom."

⁴ "Là il n'y a que tenebres;"—"*-There* is nothing but darkness."

⁵ "One of the names which the Jews gave to Satan was חשׁך—*darkness.*"—*Illustrated Commentary.*—*Ed.*

⁶ "Iusqu'a ce que nous soyons deliurez et affranchis par la puissance de Christ;"—"Until we are delivered and set free by the power of Christ."

of Christ, there is no light.

Hath translated us into the kingdom. These form already the beginnings of our blessedness—when we are *translated into the kingdom* of Christ, because we *pass from death into life.* (1 John iii. 14.) This, also, Paul ascribes to the grace of God, that no one may imagine that he can attain so great a blessing by his own efforts. As, then, our deliverance from the slavery of sin and death is the work of God, so also our passing into the kingdom of Christ. He calls Christ the Son of his love, or the Son that is beloved by God the Father, because it is in him alone that his soul takes pleasure, as we read in Matt. xvii. 5, and in whom all others are beloved. For we must hold it as a settled point, that we are not acceptable to God otherwise than through Christ. Nor can it be doubted, that Paul had it in view to censure indirectly the mortal enmity that exists between men and God, until love shines forth in the Mediator.

14. *In whom we have redemption.* He now proceeds to set forth in order, that all parts of our salvation are contained in Christ, and that he alone ought to shine forth, and to be seen conspicuous above all creatures, inasmuch as he is the beginning and end of all things. In the *first* place, he says that we have *redemption*,[1] and immediately explains it as meaning the *remission of sins;* for these two things agree together by *apposition*.[2] For, unquestionably, when God remits our transgressions, he exempts us from condemnation to eternal death. This is our liberty, this our glorying in the face of death—that our sins are not imputed to us. He says that this redemption was procured through the *blood of Christ*, for by the sacrifice of his death all the sins of the world have been expiated. Let us, therefore, bear in mind,

---

[1] " Redemption et deliurance ;"—" Redemption and deliverance."
[2] The following explanation of the meaning of the term *apposition* is furnished in a marginal note in our author's French version : " C'est quand deux noms substantifs appartenans a vne mesme chose, sont mis ensemble sans conionction, comme par declaration l'vn et l'autre ;"—" This is when two substantive nouns, relating to the same thing, are placed together without being conjoined, as if by way of explanation, the one and the other."

15. *Who is the image of the invisible God.* He mounts up higher in discoursing as to the glory of Christ. He calls him the *image of the invisible God,* meaning by this, that it is in him alone that God, who is otherwise invisible, is manifested to us, in accordance with what is said in John i. 18, —*No man hath ever seen God: the only begotten Son, who is in the bosom of the Father, hath himself manifested him to us.* I am well aware in what manner the ancients were accustomed to explain this; for having a contest to maintain with Arians, they insist upon the equality of the Son with the Father, and his (ὁμοουσίαν) *identity of essence,*[2] while in the mean time they make no mention of what is the chief point —in what manner the Father makes himself known to us in Christ. As to Chrysostom's laying the whole stress of his defence on the term *image,* by contending that the creature cannot be said to be the *image* of the Creator, it is excessively weak; nay more, it is set aside by Paul in 1 Cor. xi. 7, whose words are—*The man is the* IMAGE *and glory of God.*

That, therefore, we may not receive anything but what is solid, let us take notice, that the term *image* is not made use of in reference to essence, but has a reference to us; for Christ is called the *image of God* on this ground—that he makes God in a manner visible to us. At the same time, we gather also from this his (ὁμοουσία) *identity of essence,* for Christ would not truly represent God, if he were not the essential Word of God, inasmuch as the question here is not as to those things which by communication are suitable also to creatures, but the question is as to the perfect wisdom, goodness, righteousness, and power of God, for the representing of which no creature were competent. We shall have, therefore, in this term, a powerful weapon in opposition to the Arians, but, notwithstanding, we must begin with that reference[3] that I have mentioned; we must not insist upon the essence alone. The sum is this—that God in himself,

---

[1] " Blasphemes execrables;"—" Execrable blasphemies."
[2] See CALVIN on the Corinthians, vol. ii. p. 196, *n.* 1.
[3] " Relation et correspondance;"—" Reference and correspondence."

of men, and that he is revealed to us in Christ alone, that we may behold him as in a mirror. For in Christ he shews us his righteousness, goodness, wisdom, power, in short, his entire self. We must, therefore, beware of seeking him elsewhere, for everything that would set itself off as a representation of God, apart from Christ, will be an idol.

The first-born of every creature. The reason of this appellation is immediately added—*For in him all things are created,* as he is, three verses afterwards, called the *first-begotten from the dead,* because by him we all rise again. Hence, he is not called the *first-born,* simply on the ground of his having preceded all creatures in point of time, but because he was begotten by the Father, that they might be created by him, and that he might be, as it were, the substance or foundation of all things. It was then a foolish part that the Arians acted, who argued from this that he was, consequently, a creature. For what is here treated of is, not what he is in himself, but what he accomplishes in others.

16. *Visible and invisible.* Both of these kinds were included in the foregoing distinction of *heavenly* and *earlhy* things; but as Paul meant chiefly to make that affirmation in reference to Angels, he now makes mention of things invisible. Not only, therefore, have those heavenly creatures which are visible to our eyes, but spiritual creatures also, been created by the Son of God. What immediately follows, *whether thrones,* &c., is as though he had said—"by whatever name they are called."

By *thrones* some understand *Angels.* I am rather, however, of opinion, that the heavenly palace of God's majesty is meant by the term, which we are not to imagine to be such as our mind can conceive of, but such as is suitable to God himself. We see the sun and moon, and the whole adorning of heaven, but the glory of God's kingdom is hid from our perception, because it is spiritual, and above the heavens. In fine, let us understand by the term *thrones* that seat of blessed immortality which is exempted from all change.

if they swayed any separate kingdom, or were endowed with peculiar power,[1] but because they are the ministers of Divine power and dominion.[2] It is customary, however, that, in so far as God manifests his power in creatures, his names are, in that proportion, transferred to them. Thus he is himself alone *Lord* and *Father*, but those are also called *lords* and *fathers* whom he dignifies with this honour. Hence it comes that angels, as well as judges, are called *gods*.[3] Hence, in this passage also, angels are signalized by magnificent titles, which intimate, not what they can do of themselves, or apart from God, but what God does by them, and what functions he has assigned to them. These things it becomes us to understand in such a manner as to detract nothing from the glory of God alone; for he does not communicate his power to angels as to lessen his own; he does not work by them in such a manner as to resign his power to them; he does not desire that his glory should shine forth in them, so as to be obscured in himself. Paul, however, designedly extols the dignity of angels in terms thus magnificent, that no one may think that it stands in the way of Christ alone having the pre-eminence over them. He makes use, therefore, of these terms, as it were by way of concession, as though he had said, that all their excellence detracts nothing from Christ,[4] however honourable the titles with which they are adorned. As for those who philosophize on these terms with excessive subtlety, that they may draw from them the different orders of angels, let them regale themselves with their dainties, but they are assuredly very remote from Paul's design.

17. *All things were created by him, and for him.* He places angels in subjection to Christ, that they may not

[1] " Ayent vertu ou puissance d'eux-mesmes;"—" Have power or authority of themselves."

[2] " Sont executeurs de la puissance Diuine, et ministres de sa domination;"—" Are the executors of God's power, and ministers of his dominion."

[3] See CALVIN on John, vol. i. p. 419.

[4] " N'oste rien a la gloire de Christ;"—" Takes nothing from the glory of Christ."

creation ought to be viewed as having a relation *to* him, as their legitimate end; *thirdly*, because he himself existed always, prior to their creation; *fourthly*, because he sustains them by his power, and upholds them in their condition. At the same time, he does not affirm this merely as to angels, but also as to the whole world. Thus he places the Son of God in the highest seat of honour, that he may have the *pre-eminence* over angels as well as men, and may bring under control all creatures in heaven and in earth.

18. And he is the head of the body, the church; who is the beginning, the first-born from the dead; that in all *things* he might have the pre-eminence:

19. For it pleased *the Father,* that in him should all fulness dwell:

20. And (having made peace through the blood of his cross) by him to reconcile all things unto himself; by him, *I say*, whether *they be* things in earth, or things in heaven.

18. Et ipse est caput corporis Ecclesiae, ipse principium, primogenitus mortuis, ut sit in omnibus ipse primas tenens:

19. Quoniam in ipso placuit omnem plenitudinem inhabitare.

20. Et per ipsum reconciliare omnia sibi, pacificando per sanguinem crucis eius, per ipsum, tam quae sunt super terram, quam quae sunt in coelis.

18. *The head of the body.* Having discoursed in a general way of Christ's excellence, and of his sovereign dominion over all creatures, he again returns to those things which relate peculiarly to the Church. Under the term *head* some consider many things to be included. And, unquestionably, he makes use afterwards, as we shall find, of the same metaphor in this sense—that as in the human body it serves as a root, from which vital energy is diffused through all the members, so the life of the Church flows out from Christ, &c. (Col. ii. 19.) Here, however, in my opinion, he speaks chiefly of government. He shews, therefore, that it is Christ that alone has authority to govern the Church, that it is he to whom alone believers ought to have an eye, and on whom alone the unity of the body depends.

Papists, with the view of supporting the tyranny of their idol, allege that the Church would be (ἀκέφαλον) *without a head,*[1] if the Pope did not, as a head, exercise rule in it.

---

[1] See *Institutes*, vol. ii. p. 11.

her head; for as Christ claims for himself this title, so he truly exercises the office. I am also well aware of the cavil by which they attempt to escape—that the Pope is a ministerial head. The name, however, of *head* is too august to be rightfully transferred to any mortal man,[1] under any pretext, especially without the command of Christ. Gregory shews greater modesty, who says (in his 92d Epistle, 4th Book) that Peter was indeed one of the chief members of the Church, but that he and the other Apostles were members under one head.

He is the beginning. As ἀρχὴ is sometimes made use of among the Greeks to denote the end, to which all things bear a relation, we might understand it as meaning, that Christ is in this sense (ἀρχὴ) *the end.* I prefer, however, to explain Paul's words thus—that he is the *beginning*, because he is the *first-born from the dead;* for in the resurrection there is a restoration of all things, and in this manner the commencement of the second and new creation, for the former had fallen to pieces in the ruin of the first man. As, then, Christ in rising again had made a commencement of the kingdom of God, he is on good grounds called the *beginning;* for *then* do we truly begin to have a being in the sight of God, when we are renewed, so as to be new creatures. He is called the *first-begotten from the dead,* not merely because he was the first that rose again, but because he has also restored life to others, as he is elsewhere called the *first-fruits of those that rise again.* (1 Cor. xv. 20.)

That he may in all things. From this he concludes, that supremacy belongs to him in all things. For if he is the Author and Restorer of all things, it is manifest that this honour is justly due to him. At the same time the phrase *in omnibus* (*in all things*) may be taken in two ways—either *over all creatures,* or, *in everything.* This, however, is of no

---

[1] " Est si honorable et magnifique qu'il ne peut estre transferé a homme mortel;"—" Is so honourable and magnificent, that it cannot be transferred to a mortal man."

19. *Because it hath pleased the Father that in him.* With the view of confirming what he has declared respecting Christ, he now adds, that it was so arranged in the providence of God. And, unquestionably, in order that we may with reverence adore this mystery, it is necessary that we should be led back to that fountain. "This," says he, "has been in accordance with the counsel of God, that *all fulness may dwell in him.*" Now, he means a fulness of righteousness, wisdom, power, and every blessing. For whatever God has he has conferred upon his Son, that he may be glorified in him, as is said in John v. 20. He shews us, however, at the same time, that we must draw from the fulness of Christ everything good that we desire for our salvation, because such is the determination of God—not to communicate himself, or his gifts to men, otherwise than by his Son. "Christ is all things to us: apart from him we have nothing." Hence it follows, that all that detract from Christ, or that impair his excellence, or rob him of his offices, or, in fine, take away a drop from his fulness, overturn, so far as is in their power, God's eternal counsel.

20. *And by him to reconcile all things to himself.* This, also, is a magnificent commendation of Christ, that we cannot be joined to God otherwise than through him. In the first place, let us consider that our happiness consists in our cleaving to God, and that, on the other hand, there is nothing more miserable than to be alienated from him. He declares, accordingly, that we are blessed through Christ alone, inasmuch as he is the bond of our connection with God, and, on the other hand, that, apart from him, we are most miserable, because we are shut out from God.[1] Let us, however, bear in mind, that what he ascribes to Christ belongs peculiarly to him, that no portion of this praise may be transferred to any other.[2] Hence we must consider the contrasts to these things to be understood—that if this is Christ's prero-

---

[1] "Bannis de la compagnie de Dieu;"—"Banished from the society of God."

[2] "Tant excellent soit-il;"—"However excellent he may be."

pacificators, through whom access to God might be opened up.

Making peace through the blood of his cross. He speaks of the Father,—that he has been made propitious to his creatures by the blood of Christ. Now he calls it the *blood of the cross,* inasmuch as it was the pledge and price of the making up of our peace with God, because it was poured out upon the cross. For it was necessary that the Son of God should be an expiatory victim, and endure the punishment of sin, that we might be *the righteousness of God in him.* (2 Cor. v. 21.) The *blood of the cross,* therefore, means the blood of the sacrifice which was offered upon the cross for appeasing the anger of God.

In adding *by him,* he did not mean to express anything new, but to express more distinctly what he had previously stated, and to impress it still more deeply on their minds—that Christ alone is the author of reconciliation, as to exclude all other means. For there is no other that has been crucified for us. Hence it is he alone, by whom and for whose sake we have God propitious to us.

Both upon earth and in heaven. If you are inclined to understand this as referring merely to rational creatures, it will mean, men and angels. There were, it is true, no absurdity in extending it to all without exception; but that I may not be under the necessity of philosophizing with too much subtlety, I prefer to understand it as referring to angels and men; and as to the latter, there is no difficulty as to their having need of a peace-maker in the sight of God. As to angels, however, there is a question not easy of solution. For what occasion is there for reconciliation, where there is no discord or hatred? Many, influenced by this consideration, have explained the passage before us in this manner—that angels have been brought into agreement with men, and that by this means heavenly creatures have been restored to favour with earthly creatures. Another meaning, however, is conveyed by Paul's words, *that God hath reconciled to himself.* That explanation, therefore, is forced.

cause they were previously alienated from him by sin, and because they would have had him as a Judge to their ruin,[1] had not the grace of the Mediator interposed for appeasing his anger. Hence the nature of the peace-making between God and men was this, that enmities have been abolished through Christ, and thus God becomes a Father instead of a Judge.

Between God and angels the state of matters is very different, for there was *there*[2] no revolt, no sin, and consequently no separation. It was, however, necessary that angels, also, should be made to be at peace with God, for, being creatures, they were not beyond the risk of falling, had they not been confirmed by the grace of Christ. This, however, is of no small importance for the perpetuity of peace with God, to have a fixed standing in righteousness, so as to have no longer any fear of fall or revolt. Farther, in that very obedience which they render to God, there is not such absolute perfection as to give satisfaction to God in every respect, and without the need of pardon. And this beyond all doubt is what is meant by that statement in Job iv. 18, *He will find iniquity in his angels.* For if it is explained as referring to the devil, what mighty thing were it? But the Spirit declares there, that the greatest purity is vile,[3] if it is brought into comparison with the righteousness of God. We must, therefore, conclude, that there is not on the part of angels so much of righteousness as would suffice for their being fully joined with God. They have, therefore, need of a peace-maker, through whose grace they may wholly cleave to God. Hence it is with propriety that Paul declares, that the grace of Christ does not reside among mankind alone, and on the other hand makes it common also to angels. Nor is there any injustice done to angels, in sending them to a Mediator, that they may, through his kindness, have a well-grounded peace with God.

[1] " A leur confusion et ruine ;"—" To their confusion and ruin."
[2] " En eux ;"—" Among them."
[3] " Que la plus grande purete qu'on pourroit trouuer, ne sera que vilenie et ordure ;"—" That the greatest purity that could be found will be nothing but filth and pollution."

Christ be their peace-maker also? I answer, No, not even of wicked men: though I confess that there is a difference, inasmuch as the benefit of redemption is offered to the latter, but not to the former.[2] This, however, has nothing to do with Paul's words, which include nothing else than this, that it is through Christ alone, that all creatures, who have any connection at all with God, cleave to him.

21. And you, that were sometime alienated, and enemies in *your* mind by wicked works, yet now hath he reconciled
22. In the body of his flesh through death, to present you holy, and unblameable, and unreproveable, in his sight;
23. If ye continue in the faith grounded and settled, and *be* not moved away from the hope of the gospel, which ye have heard, *and* which was preached to every creature which is under heaven; whereof I Paul am made a minister:

21. Et vos quum aliquando essetis alienati, et inimici cogitatione in operibus malis,
22. Nunc reconciliavit in corpore carnis suae per mortem; ut sisteret vos sanctos et irreprehensibiles in conspectu suo:
23. Si quidem permanetis fide fundati et firmi, et non dimoveamini a spe Evangelii quod audistis: quod praedicatum est apud universam creaturam, quae sub coelo est: cuius factus sum ego Paulus minister.

21. *And whereas ye were formerly.* The general doctrine which he had set forth he now applies particularly to them, that they may feel that they are guilty of very great ingratitude, if they allow themselves to be drawn away from Christ to new inventions. And this arrangement must be carefully observed, because the particular application of a doctrine, so to speak, affects the mind more powerfully. Farther, he leads their views to experience, that they may recognise in themselves the benefit of that redemption of which he had made mention. "You are yourselves a sample[3] of that grace which I declare to have been offered to mankind through Christ. For ye were *alienated,* that is, from God. Ye were *enemies;* now ye are received into favour: whence comes this? It is because God, being appeased by the death

---

[1] "Sous ombre de ce mot, *Toutes choses;*"—"Under the pretext of this word, *All things.*"
[2] "Est offert aux meschans et reprouuez, et non pas aux diables;"—"Is offered to the wicked and reprobate, but not to devils."
[3] "Vn miroir;"—"A mirror."

has previously declared as to the Father, he now affirms respecting Christ; for we must necessarily explain it thus, *in the body of* HIS *flesh.*

The term διανοίας (*thought*) I explain, as employed by way of amplification, as though he had said, that they were altogether, and in the whole of their mental system, *alienated from God,* that no one may imagine, after the manner of philosophers, that the alienation is merely in a particular part, as Popish theologians restrict it to the lower appetites. "Nay," says Paul, "what made you odious to God, had taken possession of your whole mind." In fine, he meant to intimate, that man, whatever he may be, is wholly at variance with God, and is an enemy to him. The old interpreter renders it (*sensum*) *sense.* Erasmus renders it *mentem,* (*mind.*) I have made use of the term *cogitationis,* to denote what the French call *intention.* For such is the force of the Greek word, and Paul's meaning requires that it should be rendered so.

Farther, while the term *enemies* has a passive as well as active signification, it is well suited to us in both respects, so long as we are apart from Christ. For we are born children of wrath, and every thought of the flesh is *enmity against God.* (Rom. viii. 7.)

In wicked works. He shews from its effects the inward hatred which lies hid in the heart. For as mankind endeavour to free themselves from all blame, until they have been openly convicted, God shews them their impiety by outward works, as is more amply treated of in Rom. i. 19. Farther, what is told us here as to the Colossians, is applicable to us also, for we differ nothing in respect of nature. There is only this difference, that some are called from their mother's womb, whose malice God anticipates, so as to prevent them from breaking forth into open fruits, while others, after having wandered during a great part of their life, are brought back to the fold. We all, however, stand in need of Christ as our peace-maker, because we are the slaves of sin, and where sin is, *there* is enmity between God and men.

which the Son of God had in common with us. He meant, therefore, to intimate, that the Son of God had put on the same nature with us, that he took upon him this vile earthly body, subject to many infirmities, that he might be our Mediator. When he adds, *by death,* he again calls us back to sacrifice. For it was necessary that the Son of God should become man, and be a partaker of our flesh, that he might be our brother: it was necessary that he should by dying become a sacrifice, that he might make his Father propitious to us.

That he might present us holy. Here we have the second and principal part of our salvation—newness of life. For the entire blessing of redemption consists mainly in these two things, remission of sins, and spiritual regeneration. (Jer. xxxi. 33.) What he has already spoken of was a great matter, that righteousness has been procured for us through the death of Christ, so that, our sins being remitted, we are acceptable to God. Now, however, he teaches us, that there is in addition to this another benefit equally distinguished— the gift of the Holy Spirit, by which we are renewed in the image of God. This, also, is a passage worthy of observation, as shewing that a gratuitous righteousness is not conferred upon us in Christ, without our being at the same time regenerated by the Spirit to the obedience of righteousness, as he teaches us elsewhere, that *Christ is made to us righteousness and sanctification.* (1 Cor. i. 30.) The *former* we obtain by a gratuitous acceptance;[1] and the *latter* by the gift of the Holy Spirit, when we are made new creatures. There is however an inseparable connection between these two blessings of grace.

Let us, however, take notice, that this holiness is nothing more than begun in us, and is indeed every day making progress, but will not be perfected until Christ shall appear for the restoration of all things. For the Cœlestinians[2] and

[1] " Par l'acceptation gratuite de Dieu, c'est a dire pource qu'il nous accepte et ha agreables;"—" By God's gratuitous acceptance, that is, because he accepts of us, and regards us with favour."

[2] The followers of Cœlestius, who, along with Pelagius, held views

sion of sins. For they conceived of a perfection in this world which could satisfy the judgment of God, so that mercy was not needed. Paul, however, does not by any means shew us here what is accomplished in this world, but what is the end of our calling, and what blessings are brought to us by Christ.

23. *If ye continue.* Here we have an exhortation to perseverance, by which he admonishes them that all the grace that had been conferred upon them hitherto would be vain, unless they persevered in the purity of the gospel. And thus he intimates, that they are still only making progress, and have not yet reached the goal. For the stability of their faith was at that time exposed to danger through the stratagems of the false apostles. Now he paints in lively colours assurance of faith when he bids the Colossians be *grounded and settled* in it. For faith is not like mere opinion, which is shaken by various movements, but has a firm steadfastness, which can withstand all the machinations of hell. Hence the whole system of Popish theology will never afford even the slightest taste of true faith, which holds it as a settled point, that we must always be in doubt respecting the present state of grace, as well as respecting final perseverance. He afterwards takes notice also of a relationship[1] which subsists between faith and the gospel, when he says that the Colossians will be *settled* in the faith, only in the event of their not falling back from the *hope of the gospel;* that is, the hope which shines forth upon us through means of the gospel, for where the gospel is, *there* is the hope of everlasting salvation. Let us, however, bear in mind, that the sum of all is contained in Christ. Hence he enjoins it upon them here to shun all doctrines which lead away from Christ, so that the minds of men are otherwise occupied.

Which ye have heard. As the false apostles themselves, who tear and rend Christ in pieces, are accustomed proudly
subversive of the doctrine of original sin, the necessity of divine grace, and other doctrines of a kindred character.—*Ed.*

[1] " Vne relation et correspondence mutuelle ;"—" A mutual relationship and correspondence."

of the gospel, that the truth of the gospel may be brought into confusion,¹ Paul, on this account, expressly declares, that *that* was the genuine,² *that* the undoubted gospel, which the Colossians had heard, namely, from Epaphras, that they might not lend an ear to doctrines at variance with it. He adds, besides, a confirmation of it, that it is the very same as was preached over the whole world. It is, I say, no ordinary confirmation when they hear that they have the whole Church agreeing with them, and that they follow no other doctrine than what the Apostles had alike taught and was everywhere received.

It is, however, a ridiculous boasting of Papists, in respect of their impugning our doctrine by this argument, that it is not preached everywhere with approbation and applause, inasmuch as we have few that assent to it. For though they should burst, they will never deprive us of this—that we at this day teach nothing but what was preached of old by Prophets and Apostles, and is obediently received by the whole band of saints. For Paul did not mean that the gospel should be approved of by the consent of all ages³ in such a way that, if it were rejected, its authority would be shaken. He had, on the contrary, an eye to that commandment of Christ, *Go, preach the gospel to every creature;* (Mark xvi. 15;) which commandment depends on so many predictions of the Prophets, foretelling that the kingdom of Christ would be spread over the whole world. What else then does Paul mean by these words than that the Colossians had also been watered by those *living streams,* which, *springing forth from Jerusalem,* were to flow out through the whole world? (Zech. xiv. 8.)

We also do not glory in vain, or without remarkable fruit

---

¹ " Demeure en confus, et qu'on ne scache que c'est ;"—" May remain in confusion, and it may not be known what it is."

² " Vray et naturel ;"—" True and genuine."

³ " Car Sainct Paul n' a pas voulu dire que l'approbation de l'Euangile dependist du consentement de tous siecles ;"—" For St. Paul did not mean to say, that the approbation of the Gospel depended on the consent of all ages."

Lord, which is received by all the Churches, and in the profession of which all pious persons have lived and died. It is also no common help for fortifying us against so many assaults, that we have the consent of the whole Church— such, I mean, as is worthy of so distinguished a title. We also cordially subscribe to the views of Augustine, who refutes the Donatists[2] by this argument particularly, that they bring forward a gospel that is in all the Churches unheard of and unknown. This truly is said on good grounds, for if it is a true gospel that is brought forward, while not ratified by any approbation on the part of the Church, it follows, that vain and false are the many promises in which it is predicted that the preaching of the gospel will be carried through the whole world, and which declare that the *sons of God shall be gathered* from all nations and countries, &c. (Hosea i. 10, 11.) But what do Papists do? Having bid farewell to Prophets and Apostles, and passing by the ancient Church, they would have their revolt from the gospel be looked upon as the consent of the universal Church. Where is the resemblance? Hence, when there is a dispute as to the consent of the Church, let us return to the Apostles and their preaching, as Paul does here. Farther, lest any one should explain too rigidly the term denoting universality,[3] Paul means simply, that it had been preached everywhere far and wide.

Of which I am made. He speaks also of himself personally, and this was very necessary, for we must always take care, that we do not rashly intrude ourselves into the office of teaching.[4] He accordingly declares, that this office was appointed him, that he may secure for himself right and authority. And, indeed, he so connects his apostleship with their faith, that they may not have it in their power to re-

[1] " Ne sans vn fruit singulier et consolation merueilleuse ;"—" Not without remarkable fruit, and wonderful consolation."
[2] The *Donatists* were a sect that sprung up in Africa during the fourth century, and were vigorously opposed by Augustine.—*Ed.*
[3] " Ce mot, *Toute* ;"—" This word, *All.*"
[4] " De prescher et enseigner ;"—" Of preaching and teaching."

24. Who now rejoice in my sufferings for you, and fill up that which is behind of the afflictions of Christ in my flesh for his body's sake, which is the church;	24. Nunc gaudeo in passionibus pro vobis, et adimpleo ea quae desunt afflictionibus Christi in carne mea, pro corpore eius, quod est Ecclesia :
25. Whereof I am made a minister, according to the dispensation of God which is given to me for you, to fulful the word of God;	25. Cuius factus sum minister, secundum dispensationem Dei, quae mihi data est erga vos, ad implendum sermonem Dei :
26. *Even* the mystery which hath been hid from ages and from generations, but now is made manifest to his saints :	26. Mysterium reconditum a saeculis et generationibus, quod nunc revelatum est sanctis eius.
27. To whom God would make known what *is* the riches of the glory of this mystery among the Gentiles; which is Christ in you, the hope of glory :	27. Quibus voluit Deus patefacere, quae sint divitiae gloriae mysterii huius in Gentibus, qui est Christus in vobis, spes gloriae :
28. Whom we preach, warning every man, and teaching every man in all wisdom; that we may present every man perfect in Christ Jesus :	28. Quem nos praedicamus, admonentes omnem hominem, et docentes omnem hominem in omni sapientia, ut sistamus omnem hominem perfectum in Christo Iesu.
29. Whereunto I also labour, striving according to his working, which worketh in me mightily.	29. In quam rem etiam laboro, decertans secundum potentiam eius, quae operatur in me potenter.

24. *I now rejoice.* He has previously claimed for himself authority on the ground of his calling. Now, however, he provides against the honour of his apostleship being detracted from by the bonds and persecutions, which he endured for the sake of the gospel. For Satan, also, perversely turns these things into occasions of rendering the servants of God the more contemptible. Farther, he encourages them by his example not to be intimidated by persecutions, and he sets forth to their view his zeal, that he may have greater weight.[1] Nay more, he gives proof of his affection towards them by no common pledge, when he declares that he willingly bears for their sake the afflictions which he endures. "But whence," some one will ask, "arises this *joy?*" From his seeing the fruit that springs from it. "The affliction that I endure on your account is

---

[1] " Et monstre le grand zele qu'il auoit, afin qu'il y ait plus de poids et authorite en ce qu'il dit ;"—" And shews the great zeal that he had, that there may be greater weight and authority in what he says."

says, that he *rejoiced in all necessities and afflictions,* on the ground of what he had heard as to their faith. (1 Thess. iii. 6, 7.)

And fill up what is wanting. The particle *and* I understand as meaning *for,* for he assigns a reason why he is joyful in his sufferings, because he is in this thing a partner with Christ, and nothing happier can be desired than this partnership.[2] He also brings forward a consolation common to all the pious, that in all tribulations, especially in so far as they suffer anything for the sake of the gospel, they are partakers of the cross of Christ, that they may enjoy fellowship with him in a blessed resurrection.

Nay more, he declares that there is thus *filled up what is wanting in the affliction of Christ.* For as he speaks in Rom. viii. 29, *Whom God elected, he also hath predestinated to be conformed to the image of Christ, that he may be the first-born among the brethren.* Farther, we know that there is so great a unity between Christ and his members, that the name of *Christ* sometimes includes the whole body, as in 1 Cor. xii. 12, for while discoursing there respecting the Church, he comes at length to the conclusion, that in Christ the same thing holds as in the human body. As, therefore, Christ has suffered *once* in his own person, so he suffers *daily* in his members, and in this way there are *filled up* those sufferings which the Father hath appointed for his body by his decree.[3] Here we have a *second* consideration, which ought to bear up our minds and comfort them in afflictions, that it is thus fixed and determined by the providence of God, that we must be conformed to Christ in the endurance of the cross, and that the fellowship that we have with him extends to this also.

[1] "M'est douce et gracieuse, pource qu'elle n'est point inutile ;"—" Is sweet and agreeable to me, because it is not unprofitable."

[2] " Ceste societe et conionction ;"—" This fellowship and connection."

[3] " It is worthy of remark, that the Apostle does not say παθηματα, the *passion* of Christ, but simply θλιψις, the *afflictions;* such as are common to all good men who bear a testimony against the ways and fashions of a wicked world. In these the Apostle had his share, in the *passion* of Christ he could have none."—*Dr. A. Clarke.—Ed.*

Church. He had previously stated that he suffered in behalf of the Colossians, and he now declares still farther, that the advantage extends to the whole Church. This advantage has been spoken of in Phil. i. 12. What could be clearer, less forced, or more simple, than this exposition, that Paul is joyful in persecution, because he considers, in accordance with what he writes elsewhere, that we must *carry about with us in our body the mortification of Christ, that his life may be manifested in us?* (2 Cor. iv. 10.) He says also in Timothy, *If* we suffer with him, we shall also reign with him: if we die with him, we shall also live with him, (2 Tim. ii. 11, 12,) and thus the issue will be blessed and glorious. *Farther*, he considers that we must not refuse the condition which God has appointed for his Church, that the members of Christ may have a suitable correspondence with the head; and, *thirdly*, that afflictions must be cheerfully endured, inasmuch as they are profitable to all the pious, and promote the welfare of the whole Church, by adorning the doctrine of the gospel.

Papists, however, disregarding and setting aside all these things,[1] have struck out a new contrivance in order that they may establish their system of indulgences. They give the name of *indulgences* to a remission of punishments, obtained by us through the merits of the martyrs. For, as they deny that there is a gratuitous remission of sins, and allege that they are redeemed by *satisfactory* deeds, when the *satisfactions* do not fill up the right measure, they call into their help the blood of the martyrs, that it may, along with the blood of Christ, serve as an expiation in the judgment of God. And this mixture they call the *treasure of the Church*,[2] the keys of which they afterwards intrust to whom they think fit. Nor are they ashamed to wrest this passage, with the view of supporting so execrable a blasphemy, as if

---

[1] "Mais quoy? Les Papistes laissans tout ceci;"—"But what? Papists leaving all this."

[2] See CALVIN'S *Institutes*, vol. ii. p. 237, and CALVIN on Corinthians, vol. i. p. 68.

They urge in their support the term ὑστερήματα, (*things wanting*,) as if Paul meant to say, that the sufferings which Christ has endured for the redemption of men were insufficient. There is no one, however, that does not see that Paul speaks in this manner, because it is necessary, that by the afflictions of the pious, the body of the Church should be brought to its perfection, inasmuch as the members are conformed to their head.[1] I should also be afraid of being suspected of calumny in repeating things so monstrous,[2] if their books did not bear witness that I impute nothing to them groundlessly.

They urge, also, what Paul says, that he suffers *for* the Church. It is surprising that this refined interpretation had not occurred to any of the ancients, for they all interpret it as we do, to mean, that the saints suffer *for* the Church, inasmuch as they confirm the faith of the Church. Papists, however, gather from this that the saints are redeemers, because they shed their blood for the expiation of sins. That my readers, however, may perceive more clearly their impudence, allow that the martyrs, as well as Christ, suffered *for* the Church, but in different ways, as I am inclined to express in Augustine's words rather than in my own. For he writes thus in his 84th treatise on John: "Though we brethren die for brethren, yet there is no blood of any martyr that is poured out for the remission of sins. This Christ did for us. Nor has he in this conferred upon us matter of imitation, but ground of thanksgiving." Also, in the fourth book to Bonifacius: "As the only Son of God be-

---

[1] " We are not to suppose that our Lord left any sufferings to be endured by Paul, or any one else, as the expiation of the sins or the ransom of the souls of his people. . . . The *filling up* spoken of by the Apostle is not the supplementing Christ's personal sufferings, but it is the completing that share allotted to himself as one of the members of Christ, as sufferings which, from the intimacy of union between the head and the members, may be called *his* sufferings. Christ lived in Paul, spoke in Paul, wrought in Paul, suffered in Paul; and in a similar sense, the sufferings of every Christian for Christ are the sufferings of Christ."—*Brown's* Expository Discourses on Peter, vol. iii. pp. 69, 70.—*Ed.*

[2] " Tels blasphemes horribles;"—" Such horrible blasphemies."

that we may through him, without merit, obtain undeserved favour." Similar to these is the statement of Leo Bishop of Rome; " The righteous *received* crowns, did not give them; and for the fortitude of believers there have come forth *examples of patience, not gifts of righteousness*. For their deaths were for themselves, and no one by his latter end paid the debt of another."[1]

Now, that this is the meaning of Paul's words is abundantly manifest from the context, for he adds, that he suffers *according to the dispensation that was given to him*. And we know that the ministry was committed to him, not of *redeeming* the Church, but of *edifying* it; and he himself immediately afterwards expressly acknowledges this. This is also what he writes to Timothy, *that he endures all things for the sake of the elect, that they may obtain the salvation which is in Christ Jesus*. (2 Tim. ii. 10.) Also, in 2 Cor. i. 4, that he willingly *endures all things for their consolation and salvation*. Let, therefore, pious readers learn to hate and detest those profane sophists, who thus deliberately corrupt and adulterate the Scriptures, in order that they may give some colour to their delusions.

25. *Of which I am made a minister.* Mark under what character he suffers for the Church—as being a *minister*, not to *give* the price of redemption, (as Augustine dexterously and piously expresses himself,) but to *proclaim* it. He calls himself, however, in this instance, a minister of the Church on a different ground from that on which he called himself elsewhere, (1 Cor. iv. 1,) a *minister of God*, and a little ago, (verse 23,) a *minister of the gospel*. For the Apostles serve God and Christ for the advancement of the glory of both: they serve the Church, and administer the gospel itself, with a view to promote salvation. There is, therefore, a different reason for the ministry in these expressions, but the one cannot subsist without the other. He says, how-

---

[1] The reader will find the same passage as above quoted by CALVIN in the *Institutes*, vol. ii. pp. 238, 239. See also CALVIN on the Corinthians, vol. i. p. 69, *n.* 1.—*Ed.*

To fulfil the word. He states the end of his ministry—that the word of God may be effectual, as it is, when it is obediently received. For this is the excellence of the gospel, that it is the *power of God unto salvation to every one that believeth.* (Rom. i. 16.) God, therefore, gives efficacy and influence to his word through means of the Apostles. For although preaching itself, whatever may be its issue, is the fulfilling of the word, yet it is the fruit that shews at length[1] that the seed has not been sown in vain.

26. *Hidden mystery.* Here we have a commendation of the gospel—that it is a wonderful secret of God. It is not without good reason that Paul so frequently extols the gospel by bestowing upon it the highest commendations in his power; for he saw that it was a *stumblingblock to the Jews, and foolishness to the Greeks.* (1 Cor. i. 23.) We see also at this day, in what hatred it is held by hypocrites, and how haughtily it is contemned by the world. Paul, accordingly, with the view of setting aside judgments so unfair and perverse, extols in magnificent terms the dignity of the gospel as often as an opportunity presents itself, and for that purpose he makes use of various arguments, according to the connection of the passage. Here he calls it a *sublime secret*, which was *hid from ages and generations,* that is, from the beginning of the world, through so many revolutions of ages.[2] Now, that it is of the gospel that he speaks, is evident from Rom. xvi. 25, Eph. iii. 9, and other similar passages.

The reason, however, why it is so called, is demanded. Some, in consequence of Paul's making express mention of the calling of the Gentiles, are of opinion, that the sole reason why it is so called is, that the Lord had, in a manner, contrary to all expectation, poured out his grace upon the Gentiles, whom he had appeared to have shut out for ever from participation in eternal life. Any one, however, that will examine the whole passage more narrowly, will perceive

---

[1] " Toutesfois c'est a proprement parler, le fruit qui monstre en fin ;"—" Yet it is, properly speaking, the fruit that shews at last."

[2] " D'annees et siecles ;"—" Of years and ages."

the Romans, to which I have referred. For the *first* is—that whereas God had, previously to the advent of Christ, governed his Church under dark coverings, both of words and of ceremonies, he has suddenly shone forth in full brightness by means of the doctrine of the gospel. The *second* is—that whereas nothing was previously seen but external figures, Christ has been exhibited, bringing with him the full truth, which had lain concealed. The *third* is, what I have mentioned—that the whole world, which had up to this time been estranged from God, is called to the hope of salvation, and the same inheritance of eternal life is offered to all. An attentive consideration of these things constrains us to reverence and adore this *mystery* which Paul proclaims, however it may be held in contempt by the world, or even in derision.

Which is now revealed. Lest any one should turn aside to another meaning the term *mystery*, as though he were speaking of a thing that was still secret and unknown, he adds, that it has now at length been published,[1] that it might be known by mankind. What, therefore, was in its own nature secret, has been made manifest by the will of God. Hence, there is no reason why its obscurity should alarm us, after the revelation that God has made of it. He adds, however, *to the saints*, for *God's arm* has not been *revealed* to all, (Isaiah liii. 1,) that they might understand his counsel.

27. *To whom God was pleased to make known.* Here he puts a bridle upon the presumption of men, that they may not allow themselves to be wise, or to inquire beyond what they ought, but may learn to rest satisfied with this one thing—that it has so pleased God. For the good pleasure of God ought to be perfectly sufficient for us as a reason. This, however, is said principally for the purpose of commending the grace of God; for Paul intimates, that mankind did by no means furnish occasion for God's making them participants of this secret, when he teaches that he

[1] "Publié et manifesté;"—"Published and manifested."

pleasure of God in opposition to all human merits and external causes.

What are the riches. We must always take notice, in what magnificent terms he speaks in extolling the dignity of the gospel. For he was well aware that the ingratitude of men is so great, that notwithstanding that this treasure is inestimable, and the grace of God in it is so distinguished, they, nevertheless, carelessly despise it, or at least think lightly of it. Hence, not resting satisfied with the term *mystery*, he adds *glory*, and that, too, not trivial or common. For *riches*, according to Paul, denote, as is well known, amplitude.[1] He states particularly, that those *riches* have been manifested among the Gentiles; for what is more wonderful than that the Gentiles, who had during so many ages been sunk in death, so as to appear to be utterly ruined, are all on a sudden reckoned among the sons of God, and receive the inheritance of salvation?

Which is Christ in you. What he had said as to the Gentiles generally he applies to the Colossians themselves, that they may more effectually recognise in themselves the grace of God, and may embrace it with greater reverence. He says, therefore, *which is Christ*, meaning by this, that all that secret is contained in Christ, and that all the riches of heavenly wisdom are obtained by them when they have Christ, as we shall find him stating more openly a little afterwards. He adds, *in you*, because they now possess Christ, from whom they were lately so much estranged, that nothing could exceed it. Lastly, he calls Christ the *hope of glory*, that they may know that nothing is wanting to them for complete blessedness when they have obtained Christ. This, however, is a wonderful work of God, that in *earthen* and frail *vessels* (2 Cor. iv. 7) the hope of heavenly glory resides.

28. *Whom we preach.* Here he applies to his own preaching everything that he has previously declared as to the wonderful and adorable secret of God; and thus he explains what he had already touched upon as to the *dispen-*

[1] "Signifient *magnificence*;"—"Denote *magnificence*."

his doctrine: for after having extolled the gospel in the highest terms, he now adds, that it is that divine secret which he preaches. It was not, however, without good reason that he had taken notice a little before, that Christ is the sum of that secret, that they might know that nothing can be taught that has more of perfection than Christ.

The expressions that follow have also great weight. He represents himself as the teacher of all men; meaning by this, that no one is so eminent in respect of wisdom as to be entitled to exempt himself from tuition. "God has placed me in a lofty position, as a public herald of his secret, that the whole world, without exception, may learn from me."

In all wisdom. This expression is equivalent to his affirming that his doctrine is such as to conduct a man to a wisdom that is perfect, and has nothing wanting; and this is what he immediately adds, that all that shew themselves to be true disciples will become *perfect.* See the second chapter of First Corinthians. (1 Cor. ii. 6.) Now, what better thing can be desired than what confers upon us the highest perfection? He again repeats, *in Christ,* that they may not desire to know anything but Christ alone. From this passage, also, we may gather a definition of true wisdom—that by which we are presented perfect in the sight of God, and that *in Christ,* and nowhere else.[1]

29. *For which thing.* He enhances, by two circumstances, the glory of his apostleship and of his doctrine. In the *first* place, he makes mention of his aim,[2] which is a token of the difficulty that he felt; for those things are for the most part the most excellent that are the most difficult. The *second* has more strength, inasmuch as he mentions that the power of God shines forth in his ministry. He does not speak, however, merely of the success of his preaching, (though in that too the blessing of God appears,) but also of the efficacy of the Spirit, in which God manifestly shewed himself; for on good grounds he ascribes his endeavours,

---

[1] " Et non en autre;"—" And not in another."
[2] " Son travaille et peine;"—" His labour and trouble."

CHAPTER II.

1. For I would that ye knew what great conflict I have for you, and *for* them at Laodicea, and *for* as many as have not seen my face in the flesh;
2. That their hearts might be comforted, being knit together in love, and unto all riches of the full assurance of understanding, to the acknowledgment of the mystery of God, and of the Father, and of Christ;
3. In whom are hid all the treasures of wisdom and knowledge.
4. And this I say, lest any man should beguile you with enticing words.
5. For though I be absent in the flesh, yet am I with you in the spirit, joying and beholding your order, and the stedfastness of your faith in Christ.

1. Volo autem vos scire, quantum certamen habeam pro vobis et iis qui sunt Laodiceae, et quicunque non viderunt faciem meam in carne;
2. Ut consolationem accipiant corda ipsorum, ubi compacti fuerint in caritate, et in omnes divitias certitudinis intelligentiae, in agnitionem mysterii Dei, et Patris, et Christi;
3. In quo sunt omnes thesauri sapientiae et intelligentiae absconditi.
4. Hoc autem dico, ne quis vos decipiat persuasorio sermone.
5. Nam etsi corpore sum absens, spiritu tamen sum vobiscum, gaudens et videns ordinem vestrum, et stabilitatem vestrae in Christum fidei.

1. *I would have you know.* He declares his affection towards them, that he may have more credit and authority; for we readily believe those whom we know to be desirous of our welfare. It is also an evidence of no ordinary affection, that he was concerned about them in the midst of death, that is, when he was in danger of his life; and that he may express the more emphatically the intensity of his affection and concern, he calls it a *conflict.* I do not find fault with the rendering of Erasmus—*anxiety;* but, at the same time, the force of the Greek word is to be noticed, for ἀγών is made use of to denote *contention.* By the same proof he confirms his statement, that his ministry is directed to them; for whence springs so anxious a concern as to their welfare, but from this, that the Apostle of the Gentiles was under obligation to embrace in his affection and concern even those who were unknown to him? As, however, there is commonly no love between those who are unknown to

seen my face in the flesh; for there is among the servants of God a sight different from that of the flesh, which excites love. As it is almost universally agreed that the First Epistle to Timothy was written from Laodicea, some, on this account, assign to Galatia that Laodicea of which Paul makes mention here, while the other was the metropolis of Phrygia Pacatiana.[1] It seems to me, however, to be more probable that that inscription is incorrect, as will be noticed in its proper place.

2. *That their hearts may receive consolation.* He now intimates what he desires for them, and shews that his affection is truly apostolic; for he declares that nothing else is desired by him than that they may be united together in faith and love. He shews, accordingly, that it was by no unreasonable affection (as happens in the case of some) that he had been led to take upon himself so great a concern for the Colossians and others, but because the duty of his office required it.

The term *consolation* is taken here to denote that true quietness in which they may repose. This he declares they will at length come to enjoy in the event of their being *united in love* and faith. From this it appears where the chief good is, and in what things it consists—when mutually agreed in one faith, we are also joined together in mutual love. This, I say, is the solid joy of a pious mind—this is the blessed life. As, however, love is here commended from its effect, because it fills the mind of the pious with true joy; so, on the other hand, the cause of it is pointed out by him, when he says, in *all fulness of understanding.*[2] The bond also of holy unity is the truth of God, when we embrace it with one consent; for peace and agreement with men flow forth from that fountain.

Riches of the assurance of understanding. As many, con-

[1] After the time of Constantine the Great, "Phrygia was divided into Phrygia Pacatiana and Phrygia Salutaris. . . . Colosse was the sixth city of the first division."—*Dr. A. Clarke.—Ed.*

[2] "*En toutes richesses de certitude d'intelligence;*"—"*In all riches of assurance of understanding.*"

pressly of the *riches of understanding*. By this phrase he means full and clear perception; and at the same time admonishes them, that according to the measure of understanding they must make progress also in love.

In the term *assurance*, he distinguishes between faith and mere opinion; for *that* man truly knows the Lord who does not vacillate or waver in doubt, but stands fast in a firm and constant persuasion. This constancy and stability Paul frequently calls (πληροφορίαν) *full assurance*, (which term he makes use of here also,) and always connects it with faith, as undoubtedly it can no more be separated from it than heat or light can be from the sun. The doctrine, therefore, of the schoolmen is devilish, inasmuch as it takes away assurance, and substitutes in its place *moral conjecture*,[1] as they term it.

Is an acknowledgment of the mystery. This clause must be read as added by way of *apposition,* for he explains what that knowledge is, of which he has made mention—that it is nothing else than the knowledge of the gospel. For the false apostles themselves endeavour to set off their impostures under the title of wisdom, but Paul retains the sons of God within the limits of the gospel exclusively, that they may desire to *know nothing else.* (1 Cor. ii. 2.) Why he uses the term *mystery* to denote the gospel, has been already explained. Let us, however, learn from this, that the gospel can be understood by faith alone—not by reason, nor by the perspicacity of the human understanding, because otherwise it is a thing that is hid from us.

The *mystery of God* I understand in a passive signification, as meaning—that in which God is revealed, for he immediately adds—*and of the Father, and of Christ*—by which expression he means that God cannot be known otherwise than *in Christ*, as, on the other hand, the Father must necessarily be known where Christ is known. For John affirms both: *He that hath the Son, hath the Father also : he that hath not the Son, hath also not the Father.* (1 John ii. 23.) Hence

[1] See CALVIN on the Corinthians, vol. i. p. 112, and vol. ii. p. 397.

as also, on the other hand, that man is ignorant of Christ, who is not led by him to the Father, and who does not in him embrace God wholly. In the mean time, it is a memorable passage for proving Christ's divinity, and the unity of his essence with the Father. For having spoken previously as to the knowledge of God, he immediately applies it to the Son, as well as to the Father, whence it follows, that the Son is God equally with the Father.

3. *In whom are all the treasures.* The expression *in quo* (*in whom*, or *in which*) may either have a reference collectively to everything he has said as to the *acknowledgment of the mystery,* or it may relate simply to what came immediately before, namely, *Christ.* While there is not much difference between the one or the other, I rather prefer the *latter* view, and it is the one that is more generally received. The meaning, therefore, is, that all the treasures of wisdom and knowledge are hid in Christ—by which he means, that we are perfect in wisdom if we truly know Christ, so that it is madness to wish to know anything besides Him. For since the Father has manifested himself wholly in Him, that man wishes to be wise apart from God, who is not contented with Christ alone. Should any one choose to interpret it as referring to the *mystery,* the meaning will be, that all the wisdom of the pious is included in the gospel, by means of which God is revealed to us in his Son.

He says, however, that the *treasures* are *hidden,* because they are not seen glittering with great splendour, but do rather, as it were, lie hid under the contemptible abasement and simplicity of the cross. For the *preaching of the cross* is always *foolishness to the world,* as we found stated in *Corinthians.* (1 Cor. i. 18.) I do not reckon that there is any great difference between *wisdom* and *understanding* in this passage, for the employment of two different terms serves only to give additional strength, as though he had said, that no knowledge, erudition, learning, wisdom, can be found elsewhere.

4. *This I say, that no man may deceive you.* As the con-

occupied with this persuasion—that the knowledge of Christ is of itself amply sufficient. And, unquestionably, this is the key that can close the door against all base errors.[1] For what is the reason why mankind have involved themselves in so many wicked opinions, in so many idolatries, in so many foolish speculations, but this—that, despising the simplicity of the gospel, they have ventured to aspire higher? All the errors, accordingly, that are in Popery, must be reckoned as proceeding from this ingratitude—that, not resting satisfied with Christ alone, they have given themselves up to strange doctrines.

With propriety, therefore, does the Apostle act in writing to the Hebrews, inasmuch as, when wishing to exhort believers not to allow themselves to be led astray[2] by strange or new doctrines, he first of all makes use of this foundation —*Christ yesterday, and to-day, and for ever.* (Heb. xiii. 8.) By this he means, that those are out of danger who remain in Christ, but that those who are not satisfied with Christ are exposed to all fallacies and deceptions. So Paul here would have every one, that would not be *deceived*, be fortified by means of this principle—that it is not lawful for a Christian man to know anything except Christ. Everything that will be brought forward after this, let it have ever so imposing an appearance, will, nevertheless, be of no value. In fine, there will be no *persuasiveness of speech*[3] that can turn aside so much as the breadth of a finger the minds of those that have devoted their understanding to Christ. It is a passage, certainly, that ought to be singularly esteemed. For as he who has taught men to know nothing except Christ, has provided against all wicked doctrines,[4] so there is the same reason why we should at this day destroy the

[1] " Tous erreurs et faussetez ;"—" All errors and impostures."

[2] " Qu'ils ne se laissent point distraire ça et la ;"—" That they do not allow themselves to be distracted hither and thither."

[3] *Pithanologia*—our author having here in view the Greek term made use of by Paul, πιθανολογία, (*persuasive speech.*) See CALVIN on 1 Corinthians, vol. i. p. 100; also *Plat. Theaet.* 163, A.—*Ed.*

[4] " Toutes fausses et meschantes doctrines ;"—" All false and wicked doctrines."

5. *For though I am absent in body.* Lest any one should object that the admonition was unseasonable, as coming from a place so remote, he says, that his affection towards them made him be *present with them in spirit,* and judge of what is expedient for them, as though he were present. By praising, also, their present condition, he admonishes them not to fall back from it, or turn aside.

Rejoicing, says he, AND *seeing,* that is—"BECAUSE *I see.*" For *and* means *for,* as is customary among the Latins and Greeks. "Go on as you have begun, for I know that hitherto you have pursued the right course, inasmuch as distance of place does not prevent me from beholding you with the eyes of the mind."

Order and steadfastness. He mentions two things, in which the perfection of the Church consists—*order* among themselves, and *faith* in Christ. By the term *order,* he means—agreement, no less than duly regulated morals, and entire discipline. He commends their *faith,* in respect of its constancy and steadfastness, meaning that it is an empty shadow of faith, when the mind wavers and vacillates between different opinions.[1]

6. As ye have therefore received Christ Jesus the Lord, *so* walk ye in him;
7. Rooted and built up in him, and stablished in the faith, as ye have been taught, abounding therein with thanksgiving.

6. Quemadmodum igitur suscepistis Christum Iesum Dominum, in ipso ambulate:
7. Radicati in ipso, et aedificati, et confirmati in fide, quemadmodum edocti estis, abundantes in ea cum gratiarum actione.

6. *As ye have received.* To commendation he adds exhortation, in which he teaches them that their having once received Christ will be of no advantage to them, unless they remain in him. Farther, as the false apostles held forth Christ's name with a view to deceive, he obviates this danger twice, by exhorting them to go on as they *had been taught,* and as they *had received Christ.* For in these words

---

[1] "Quand l'esprit est en branle, maintenant d'vne opinion, maintenant d'autre;"—"When the mind is in suspense, now of one opinion, then of another."

with so much constancy, as to be on their guard against every other doctrine and faith, in accordance with what Isaiah said, *This is the way, walk ye in it.* (Isaiah xxx. 21.) And, unquestionbly, we must act in such a manner, that the truth of the gospel, after it has been manifested to us, may be to us as a brazen wall[1] for keeping back all impostures.[2]

Now he intimates by *three* metaphors what steadfastness of faith he requires from them. The *first* is in the word *walk.* For he compares the pure doctrine of the gospel, as they had learned it, to a way that is sure, so that if any one will but keep it he will be beyond all danger of mistake. He exhorts them, accordingly, if they would not go astray, not to turn aside from the course on which they have entered.

The *second* is taken from trees. For as a tree that has struck its roots deep has a sufficiency of support for withstanding all the assaults of winds and storms, so, if any one is deeply and thoroughly fixed in Christ, as in a firm root, it will not be possible for him to be thrown down from his proper position by any machinations of Satan. On the other hand, if any one has not fixed his roots in Christ,[3] he will easily be *carried about with every wind of doctrine,* (Eph. iv. 14,) just as a tree that is not supported by any root.[4]

The *third* metaphor is that of a foundation, for a house that is not supported by a foundation quickly falls to ruins. The case is the same with those who lean on any other foundation than Christ, or at least are not securely founded on him, but have the building of their faith suspended, as it were, in the air, in consequence of their weakness and levity.

These two things are to be observed in the Apostle's words —that the stability of those who rely upon Christ is immovable, and their course is not at all wavering, or liable to

[1] *Murus aheneus.* Our author has probably in his eye the celebrated sentiment of Horace—" Hic *murus aheneus* esto—nil conscire sibi ;"— " Let this be the brazen wall—to be conscious to one's self of no crime." —(*Hor.* Ep. I. i. 60, 61.) See also *Hor.* Od. III. 3, 65.—*Ed.*

[2] " Toutes fallaces et astutes ;"—" All fallacies and wiles."

[3] " Si quelque vn n'ha la racine de son cœur plantee et fichee en Christ ;" —" If any one has not the root of his heart planted and fixed in Christ."

[4] " Que n'ha point les racines profondes ;"—" That has not deep roots."

Christ aye and until we have taken deep root in him. From this we may readily gather, that those who do not know Christ only wander into bypaths, and are tossed about in disquietude.

7. *And confirmed in the faith.* He now repeats without a figure the same thing that he had expressed by metaphors, —that the prosecution of the way, the support of the root, and of the foundation, is firmness and steadfastness of faith. And observe, that this argument is set before them in consequence of their having been well instructed, in order that they may safely and confidently secure their footing in the faith with which they had been made acquainted.

Abounding. He would not have them simply remain immovable, but would have them grow every day more and more. When he adds, *with thanksgiving*, he would have them always keep in mind from what source faith itself proceeds, that they may not be puffed up with presumption, but may rather with fear repose themselves in the gift of God. And, unquestionably, ingratitude is very frequently the reason why we are deprived of the light of the gospel, as well as of other divine favours.

8. Beware lest any man spoil you through philosophy and vain deceit, after the tradition of men, after the rudiments of the world, and not after Christ:

9. For in him dwelleth all the fulness of the Godhead bodily.

10. And ye are complete in him, which is the head of all principality and power:

11. In whom also ye are circumcised with the circumcision made without hands, in putting off the body of the sins of the flesh by the circumcision of Christ;

12. Buried with him in baptism, wherein also ye are risen with *him*

8. Videte ne quis vos praedetur per philosophiam et inanem deceptionem, secundum traditionem hominum secundum elementa mundi,[1] et non secundum Christum:

9. Quoniam in ipso habitat omnis plenitudo Deitatis corporaliter.[2]

10. Et estis in ipso completi, qui est caput omnis principatus et potestatis,

11. In quo etiam estis circumcisi circumcisione non manufacta, exuendo corpus peccatorum carnis, circumcisione, inquam, Christi.

12. Consepulti cum ipso per baptismum, in quo et consurrexistis

[1] " *Selon les rudimens du monde;*"—" *According to the rudiments of the world.*"

[2] " *Corporellement, ou, essenciellement;*"—" *Bodily, or, essentially.*"

8. *Beware lest any one plunder you.* He again instructs them as to the poison, which the antidote presented by him should be made use of to counteract. For although this, as we have stated, is a common remedy against all the impostures of the devil,[1] it had, nevertheless, at that time a peculiar advantage among the Colossians, to which it required to be applied. *Beware,* says he, *lest any one plunder you.* He makes use of a very appropriate term, for he alludes to *plunderers,* who, when they cannot carry off the flock by violence, drive away some of the cattle fraudulently. Thus he makes Christ's Church a sheep-fold, and the pure doctrine of the gospel the enclosures of the fold. He intimates, accordingly, that we who are the sheep of Christ repose in safety when we hold the unity of the faith, while, on the other hand, he likens the false apostles to *plunderers* that carry us away from the folds. Would you then be reckoned as belonging to Christ's flock? Would you remain in his folds? Do not deviate a nail's-breadth from purity of doctrine. For unquestionably Christ will act the part of the *good Shepherd* by protecting us if we but *hear his voice,* and *reject those of strangers.* In short, the *tenth* chapter of John is the exposition of the passage before us.

Through philosophy. As many have mistakingly imagined that *philosophy* is here condemned by Paul, we must point out what he means by this term. Now, in my opinion, he means everything that men contrive of themselves when wishing to be wise through means of their own understanding, and that not without a specious pretext of reason, so as to have a plausible appearance. For there is no difficulty in rejecting those contrivances of men which have nothing to set them off,[2] but in rejecting those that captivate men's minds by a false conceit of wisdom. Or should any one prefer to have it expressed in one word, *philosophy* is no-

---

[1] Our Author evidently refers to what he had said as to the advantage to be derived from *steadfastness in the faith.* See p. 178.—*Ed.*

[2] " Quand elles n'ont ni monstre ni couleur ;"—" When they have neither show nor appearance."

Of such a nature, I acknowledge, will all the subtleties of philosophers be, if they are inclined to add anything of their own to the pure word of God. Hence *philosophy* will be nothing else than a corruption of spiritual doctrine, if it is mixed up with Christ. Let us, however, bear in mind, that under the term *philosophy* Paul has merely condemned all spurious doctrines which come forth from man's head, whatever appearance of reason they may have. What immediately follows, as to *vain deceit*, I explain thus, " Beware of *philosophy,* which is nothing else than *vain deceit,*" so that this is added by way of *apposition.*[1]

According to the tradition of men. He points out more precisely what kind of *philosophy* he reproves, and at the same time convicts it of vanity on a twofold account—because it is *not according to Christ,* but according to the inclinations of men ;[2] and because it consists in the *elements of the world.* Observe, however, that he places Christ in opposition to the *elements of the world,* equally as to the *tradition of men,* by which he intimates, that whatever is hatched in man's brain is not in accordance with Christ, who has been appointed us by the Father as our sole Teacher, that he might retain us in the simplicity of his gospel. Now, that is corrupted by even a small portion of the leaven of *human traditions.* He intimates also, that all doctrines are foreign to Christ that make the worship of God, which we know to be spiritual, according to Christ's rule, to consist in the *elements of the world,*[3] and also such as fetter the minds of men by such trifles and frivolities, while Christ calls us directly to himself.

But what is meant by the phrase—*elements of the world ?*[4] There can be no doubt that it means ceremonies. For he

---

[1] See p. 148, *n.* 2.

[2] " Selon les ordonnances et plaisirs des hommes ;"—" According to the appointments and inclinations of men."

[3] " Es choses visibles de ce monde ;"—" In the visible things of this world."

[4] " *Rudimens,* ou *elemens du monde ;*"—" *Rudiments,* or *elements of the world.*"

a name is usually explained in two ways. Some think that it is a metaphor, so that the *elements* are the rudiments of children, which do not lead forward to mature doctrine. Others take it in its proper signification, as denoting things that are outward and are liable to corruption, which avail nothing for the kingdom of God. The former exposition I rather approve of, as also in Gal. iv. 3.

9. *For in him dwelleth.* Here we have the reason why those *elements of the world,* which are taught by men, do not accord with Christ—because they are additions for supplying a deficiency, as they speak. Now in Christ there is a perfection, to which nothing can be added. Hence everything that mankind of themselves mix up, is at variance with Christ's nature, because it charges him with imperfection. This argument of itself will suffice for setting aside all the contrivances of Papists. For to what purpose do they tend,[1] but to perfect what was commenced by Christ?[2] Now this outrage upon Christ[3] is not by any means to be endured. They allege, it is true, that they add nothing to Christ, inasmuch as the things that they have appended to the gospel are, as it were, a part of Christianity, but they do not effect an escape by a cavil of this kind. For Paul does not speak of an imaginary Christ, but of a Christ preached,[4] who has revealed himself by express doctrine.

Further, when he says that the *fulness of the Godhead* dwells in Christ, he means simply, that God is wholly found in him, so that he who is not contented with Christ alone, desires something better and more excellent than God. The sum is this, that God has manifested himself to us fully and perfectly in Christ.

Interpreters explain in different ways the adverb *bodily*. For my part, I have no doubt that it is employed—not in a

---

[1] " Toutes leurs inuentions ;"—" All their inventions."
[2] " Ce que Christ a commencé seulement ;"—" What Christ has only commenced."
[3] " Vn tel outrage fait au Fils de Dieu ;"—" Such an outrage committed upon the Son of God."
[4] " D'vn vray Christ ;"—" Of a true Christ."

that have ever been made. For God has often manifested himself to men, but it has been only in part. In Christ, on the other hand, he communicates himself to us wholly. He has also manifested himself to us otherwise, but it is in figures, or by power and grace. In Christ, on the other hand, he has appeared to us essentially. Thus the statement of John holds good: *He that hath the Son, hath the Father also.* (1 John ii. 23.) For those who possess Christ have God truly present, and enjoy Him wholly.

10. *And ye are complete in him.* He adds, that this perfect essence of Deity, which is in Christ, is profitable to us in this respect, that we are also perfect in him. "As to God's dwelling wholly in Christ, it is in order that we, having obtained him, may possess in him an entire perfection." Those, therefore, who do not rest satisfied with Christ alone, do injury to God in two ways, for besides detracting from the glory of God, by desiring something above his perfection, they are also ungrateful, inasmuch as they seek elsewhere what they already have in Christ. Paul, however, does not mean that the perfection of Christ is transfused into us, but that there are in him resources from which we may be filled, that nothing may be wanting to us.

Who is the head. He has introduced this clause again on account of the angels, meaning that the angels, also, will be ours, if we have Christ. But of this afterwards. In the mean time, we must observe this, that we are hemmed in, above and below, with railings,[2] that our faith may not deviate even to the slightest extent from Christ.

11. *In whom ye also are circumcised.* From this it appears, that he has a controversy with the false apostles, who mixed the law with the gospel, and by that means made Christ have, as it were, two faces. He specifies, however,

[1] "Σωματικῶς signifies *truly, really*, in opposition to *typically, figuratively*. There was a symbol of the Divine presence in the Hebrew *tabernacle*, and in the Jewish *temple;* but in the *body* of CHRIST the Deity, with all its plenitude of attributes, dwelt *really* and *substantially*, for so the word σωματικῶς means."—*Dr. A. Clarke.—Ed.*

[2] See CALVIN on the Corinthians, vol. i. p. 474, *n.* 2.

to Christ, because it destroys the spiritual *circumcision of Christ*. For circumcision was given to the Fathers that it might be the figure of a thing that was absent: those, therefore, who retain that figure after Christ's advent, deny the accomplishment of what it prefigures. Let us, therefore, bear in mind that outward *circumcision* is here compared with spiritual, just as a figure with the reality. The figure is of a thing that is absent: hence it puts away the presence of the reality. What Paul contends for is this—that, inasmuch as what was shadowed forth by a *circumcision made with hands*, has been completed in Christ, there is now no fruit or advantage from it.[1] Hence he says, that the circumcision which is made in the heart is the *circumcision of Christ*, and that, on this account, that which is outward is not now required, because, where the reality exists, that shadowy emblem vanishes,[2] inasmuch as it has no place except in the absence of the reality.

By the putting off of the body. He employs the term *body*, by an elegant metaphor, to denote a mass, made up of all vices. For as we are encompassed by our bodies, so we are surrounded on all sides by an accumulation of vices. And as the body is composed of various members, each of which has its own actings and offices, so from that accumulation of corruption all sins take their rise as members of the entire body. There is a similar manner of expression in Romans vi. 13.

He takes the term *flesh*, as he is wont, to denote corrupt nature. The *body of the sins of the flesh*, therefore, is the *old man with his deeds;* only, there is a difference in the manner of expression, for here he expresses more properly the mass of vices which proceed from corrupt nature. He says that we obtain this[3] through Christ, so that unquestionably an entire regeneration is his benefit. It is he that circumcises the foreskin of our heart, or, in other words,

---

[1] " Maintenant le fruit et l'vsage d'icelle est aneanti;"—" The fruit and advantage of it are now made void."

[2] " Le signe qui la figuroit s'esuanouit comme vn ombre;"—" The sign which prefigured it vanishes like a shadow."

[3] " Ce despouillement;"—" This divesture."

figure.

12. *Buried with him in baptism.* He explains still more clearly the manner of spiritual circumcision—because, being *buried with Christ,* we are partakers of his death. He expressly declares that we obtain this by means of baptism, that it may be the more clearly apparent that there is no advantage from circumcision under the reign of Christ. For some one might otherwise object : " Why do you abolish circumcision on this pretext—that its accomplishment is in Christ ? Was not Abraham, also, circumcised spiritually, and yet this did not hinder the adding of the sign to the reality ? *Outward* circumcision, therefore, is not superfluous, although that which is *inward* is conferred by Christ." Paul anticipates an objection of this kind, by making mention of baptism. Christ, says he, accomplishes in us spiritual circumcision, not through means of that ancient sign, which was in force under Moses, but by baptism. Baptism, therefore, is a sign of the thing that is presented to us, which while absent was prefigured by circumcision. The argument is taken from the economy[1] which God has appointed ; for those who retain circumcision contrive a mode of dispensation different from that which God has appointed.

When he says that we are *buried with Christ,* this means more than that we are *crucified* with him ; for burial expresses a continued process of mortification. When he says, that this is done through means of baptism, as he says also in Rom. vi. 4, he speaks in his usual manner, ascribing efficacy to the sacrament, that it may not fruitlessly signify what does not exist.[2] By baptism, therefore, we are *buried with Christ,* because Christ does at the same time accomplish efficaciously that mortification, which he there represents, that the reality may be conjoined with the sign.

[1] " Du gouuernement et dispensation que Dieu a ordonné en son Eglise ;" —" From the government and dispensation which God has appointed in his Church."

[2] " Afin que la signification ne soit vaine, comme d'vne chose qui n'est point ;"—" That the signification may not be vain, as of a thing that is not."

"We are not only," says he, "ingrafted into Christ's death, but we also rise to newness of life:" hence the more injury is done to Christ by those who endeavour to bring us back to circumcision. He adds, *by faith,* for unquestionably it is by it that we receive what is presented to us in baptism. But what *faith?* That of his *efficacy* or *operation,* by which he means, that faith is founded upon the power of God. As, however, faith does not wander in a confused and undefined contemplation, as they speak, of divine power, he intimates what *efficacy* it ought to have in view—that by which God *raised Christ from the dead.* He takes this, however, for granted, that, inasmuch as it is impossible that believers should be severed from their head, the same power of God, which shewed itself in Christ, is diffused among them all in common.

13. And you, being dead in your sins and the uncircumcision of your flesh, hath he quickened together with him, having forgiven you all trespasses;	13. Et vos, quum mortui essetis delictis et in praeputio carnis vestrae, simul vivificavit cum ipso, condonando vobis omnia peccata:
14. Blotting out the hand-writing of ordinances that was against us, which was contrary to us, and took it out of the way, nailing it to his cross;	14. Et deleto, quod contra nos erat, chirographo in decretis, quod erat nobis contrarium, et illud sustulit e medio affixum cruci,
15. *And,* having spoiled principalities and powers, he made a shew of them openly, triumphing over them in it.	15. Exspolians principatus et potestates, traduxit palam triumphans de his in illa, (*vel, in se ipso.*)

13. *And you, when ye were dead.* He admonishes the Colossians to recognise, what he had treated of in a general way, as applicable to themselves, which is by far the most effectual way of teaching. Farther, as they were Gentiles when they were converted to Christ, he takes occasion from this to shew them how absurd it is to pass over from Christ to the ceremonies of Moses. *Ye were,* says he, *dead in* UNCIRCUMCISION. This term, however, may be understood either in its proper signification, or figuratively. If you understand it in its proper sense, the meaning will be, "*Uncircumcision* is the badge of alienation from God; for

himself from *uncircumcision*, and, therefore, from death."[2] In this way he would not represent *uncircumcision* as the cause of death, but as a token that they were estranged from God. We know, however, that men cannot live otherwise than by cleaving to their God, who alone is their life. Hence it follows, that all wicked persons, however they may seem to themselves to be in the highest degree lively and flourishing, are, nevertheless, spiritually dead. In this manner this passage will correspond with Eph. ii. 11, where it is said, *Remember that, in time past, when ye were Gentiles, and called uncircumcision, by that circumcision which is made with hands in the flesh, ye were at that time without Christ, alienated from the commonwealth of Israel, and strangers to the promises.* Taking it metaphorically, there would, indeed, be an allusion to natural uncircumcision, but at the same time Paul would here be speaking of the obstinacy of the human heart, in opposition to God, and of a nature that is defiled by corrupt affections. I rather prefer the former exposition, because it corresponds better with the context; for Paul declares that uncircumcision was no hinderance in the way of their becoming partakers of Christ's life. Hence it follows, that circumcision derogated from the grace of God, which they had already obtained.

As to his ascribing death to uncircumcision, this is not as though it were the cause of it, but as being the badge of it, as also in that other passage in the Epistle to the Ephesians, which we have quoted. It is also customary in Scripture to denote deprivation of the reality by deprivation of the sign, as in Gen. iii. 22,—*Lest peradventure Adam eat of the fruit of life, and live.* For the tree did not confer life, but its being taken away was a sign of death.[3] Paul has in this place briefly expressed both. He says that these were *dead*

---

[1] " Là il n'y a que souillure et ordure;"—" *There*, there is nothing but filth and pollution."
[2] " Il vous a donc retirez de la mort;"—" He has, therefore, drawn you back from death."
[3] See CALVIN on Genesis, vol. i. p. 184.

ward pollution, an evidence of spiritual death.

By forgiving you. God does not quicken us by the mere remission of sins, but he makes mention here of this particularly, because that free reconciliation with God, which overthrows the righteousness of works, is especially connected with the point in hand, where he treats of abrogated ceremonies, as he discourses of more at large in the Epistle to the Galatians. For the false apostles, by establishing ceremonies, bound them with a halter, from which Christ has set them free.

14. *Having blotted out the hand-writing which was against us.* He now contends with the false apostles in close combat. For this was the main point in question,—whether the observance of ceremonies was necessary under the reign of Christ? Now Paul contends that ceremonies have been abolished, and to prove this he compares them to a *hand-writing,* by which God holds us as it were bound, that we may not be able to deny our guilt. He now says, that we have been freed from condemnation, in such a manner, that even the *hand-writing is blotted* out, that no remembrance of it might remain. For we know that as to debts the obligation is still in force, so long as the *hand-writing* remains; and that, on the other hand, by the erasing, or tearing of the hand-writing, the debtor is set free. Hence it follows, that all those who still urge the observance of ceremonies, detract from the grace of Christ, as though absolution were not procured for us through him; for they restore to the *hand-writing* its freshness, so as to hold us still under obligation.

This, therefore, is a truly theological reason for proving the abrogation of ceremonies, because, if Christ has fully redeemed us from condemnation, he must have also effaced the remembrance of the obligation, that consciences may be pacified and tranquil in the sight of God, for these two things are conjoined. While interpreters explain this passage in various ways, there is not one of them that satisfies me. Some think that Paul speaks simply of the moral law, but there is no ground for this. For Paul is accustomed to

(Eph. ii. 15,) and as we shall find he does shortly afterwards. More especially, the passage in Ephesians shews clearly, that Paul is here speaking of ceremonies.

Others, therefore, do better, in restricting it to ceremonies, but they, too, err in this respect, that they do not add the reason why it is called *hand-writing*, or rather they assign a reason different from the true one, and they do not in a proper manner apply this similitude to the context. Now, the reason is, that all the ceremonies of Moses had in them some acknowledgment of guilt, which bound those that observed them with a firmer tie, as it were, in the view of God's judgment. For example, what else were washings than an evidence of pollution? Whenever any victim was sacrificed, did not the people that stood by behold in it a representation of his death? For when persons substituted in their place an innocent animal, they confessed that they were themselves deserving of that death. In fine, in proportion as there were ceremonies belonging to it, just so many exhibitions were there of human guilt, and *hand-writings* of obligation.

Should any one object that they were sacraments of the grace of God, as Baptism and the Eucharist are to us at this day, the answer is easy. For there are two things to be considered in the ancient ceremonies—that they were suited to the time, and that they led men forward to the kingdom of Christ. Whatever was done at that time shewed in itself nothing but obligation. Grace was in a manner suspended until the advent of Christ—not that the Fathers were excluded from it, but they had not a present manifestation of it in their ceremonies. For they saw nothing in the sacrifices but the blood of beasts, and in their washings nothing but water. Hence, as to present view, condemnation remained; nay more, the ceremonies themselves sealed the condemnation. The Apostle speaks, also, in this manner in the whole of his Epistle to the Hebrews, because he places Christ in direct opposition to ceremonies. But how is it now? The Son of God has not only by his death de-

gated those ceremonies, that no remembrance of obligation might remain. This is full liberty—that Christ has by his blood not only blotted out our sins, but every *hand-writing* which might declare us to be exposed to the judgment of God. Erasmus in his version has involved in confusion the thread of Paul's discourse, by rendering it thus—" which was contrary to us by ordinances." Retain, therefore, the rendering which I have given, as being the true and genuine one.

Took it out of the way, fastening it to his cross. He shews the manner in which Christ has effaced the *hand-writing;* for as he fastened to the cross our curse, our sins, and also the punishment that was due to us, so he has also fastened to it that bondage of the law, and everything that tends to bind consciences. For, on his being fastened to the cross, he took all things to himself, and even bound them upon him, that they might have no more power over us.

15. *Spoiling principalities.* There is no doubt that he means devils, whom Scripture represents as acting the part of accusing us before God. Paul, however, says that they are disarmed, so that they cannot bring forward anything against us, the attestation of our guilt being itself destroyed. Now, he expressly adds this with the view of shewing, that the victory of Christ, which he has procured for himself and us over Satan, is disfigured by the false apostles, and that we are deprived of the fruit of it when they restore the ancient ceremonies. For if our liberty is the spoil which Christ has rescued from the devil, what do others, who would bring us back into bondage, but restore to Satan the spoils of which he had been stript bare?

Triumphing over them in it. The expression in the Greek allows, it is true, of our reading—*in himself;* nay more, the greater part of the manuscripts have ἐν αὐτῷ, with an aspirate. The connection of the passage, however, imperatively requires that we read it otherwise; for what would be meagre as applied to Christ, suits admirably as applied to the cross. For as he had previously compared the cross to

phal car, in which he shewed himself conspicuously to view.¹ For although in the cross there is nothing but curse, it was, nevertheless, swallowed up by the power of God in such a way, that it² has put on, as it were, a new nature. For there is no tribunal so magnificent, no throne so stately, no show of triumph so distinguished, no chariot so elevated,³ as is the gibbet on which Christ has subdued death and the devil, the prince of death; nay more, has utterly trodden them under his feet.

16. Let no man therefore judge you in meat, or in drink, or in respect of an holiday, or of the new-moon, or of the sabbath-*days;*

17. Which are a shadow of things to come; but the body *is* of Christ.

18. Let no man beguile you of your reward in a voluntary humility, and worshipping of angels, intruding into those things which he hath not seen, vainly puffed up by his fleshly mind;

19. And not holding the head, from which all the body by joints and bands having nourishment ministered, and knit together, increaseth with the increase of God.

16. Itaque ne quis vos iudicet⁴ vel in cibo, vel in potu, vel in parte⁵ diei festi, vel neomeniae, vel sabbatorum:

17. Quae sunt umbra futurorum, corpus autem Christi.

18. Ne quis palmam eripiat, volens in humilitate et cultu Angelorum, (id facere,) in ea quae non vidit se ingerens, frustra inflatus a mente carnis suae,

19. Et non tenens caput, ex quo totum corpus per iuncturas et connexiones subministratum et compactum crescit incremento Dei.

16. *Let no one therefore judge you.* What he had previously said of circumcision he now extends to the difference of meats and days. For circumcision was the first introduction to the observance of the law: other things⁶ followed afterwards. To *judge* means here, to hold one to be guilty of a crime, or to impose a scruple of conscience, so that we are no longer free. He says, therefore, that it is not in the power of men to make us subject to the observance of rites which Christ has by his death abolished, and exempts us

---

¹ " En grande magnificence ;"—" In great magnificence."
² " La croix ;"—" The cross."
³ " Tant eminent et honorable ;"—" So lofty and honourable."
⁴ " *Juge,* ou, *condamne ;*"—" *Judge,* or, *condemn.*"
⁵ " *En partie,* ou, *en distinction,* ou, *de la part,* ou, *au respect ;*"—" *In part,* or, *in distinguishing,* or, *of the part,* or, *in respect of.*"
⁶ " Les autres ceremonies ;"—" Other rites."

however, places Christ in contrast with all mankind, lest any one should extol himself so daringly as to attempt to take away what he has given him.

In respect of a festival-day. Some understand τὸ μέρος to mean *participation.* Chrysostom, accordingly, thinks that he used the term *part,* because they did not observe all festival-days, nor did they even keep holidays strictly, in accordance with the appointment of the law. This, however, is but a poor interpretation.[1] Consider whether it may not be taken to mean *separation,* for those that make a distinction of days, separate, as it were, one from another. Such a mode of partition was suitable for the Jews, that they might celebrate religiously[2] the days that were appointed, by separating them from others. Among Christians, however, such a division has ceased.

But some one will say, " We still keep up some observance of days." I answer, that we do not by any means observe days, as though there were any sacredness in holidays, or as though it were not lawful to labour upon them, but that respect is paid to government and order—not to days. And this is what he immediately adds.

17. *Which are a shadow of things to come.* The reason why he frees Christians from the observance of them is, that they were *shadows* at a time when Christ was still, in a manner, absent. For he contrasts shadows with revelation, and absence with manifestation. Those, therefore, who still adhere to those *shadows,* act like one who should judge of a man's appearance from his shadow, while in the mean time he had himself personally before his eyes. For Christ is now manifested to us, and hence we enjoy him as being present. *The body,* says he, *is of Christ,* that is, IN *Christ.* For the substance of those things which the ceremonies anciently prefigured is now presented before our eyes in Christ, inasmuch as he contains in himself everything that

---

[1] " Mais c'est vne coniecture bien maigre ;"—" But this is a very slender conjecture."
[2] " Estroittement ;"—" Strictly."

tion of Christ, or robs Christ of his excellence, and makes him in a manner void.¹ Accordingly, should any one of mortals assume to himself in this matter the office of judge, let us not submit to him, inasmuch as Christ, the only competent Judge, sets us free. For when he says, *Let no man judge you*, he does not address the false apostles, but prohibits the Colossians from yielding their neck to unreasonable requirements. To abstain, it is true, from swine's flesh, is in itself harmless, but the binding to do it is pernicious, because it makes void the grace of Christ.

Should any one ask, "What view, then, is to be taken of our sacraments? Do they not also represent Christ to us as absent?" I answer, that they differ widely from the ancient ceremonies. For as painters do not in the first draught bring out a likeness in vivid colours, and (εἰκονικῶς) *expressively*, but in the first instance draw rude and obscure lines with charcoal, so the representation of Christ under the law was unpolished, and was, as it were, a first sketch, but in our sacraments it is seen drawn out to the life. Paul, however, had something farther in view, for he contrasts the bare aspect of the *shadow* with the solidity of the *body*, and admonishes them, that it is the part of a madman to take hold of empty shadows, when it is in his power to handle the solid substance. Farther, while our sacraments represent Christ as absent as to view and distance of place, it is in such a manner as to testify that he has been once manifested, and they now also present him to us to be enjoyed. They are not, therefore, bare shadows, but on the contrary symbols² of Christ's presence, for they contain that *Yea and Amen* of all the *promises of God*, (2 Cor. i. 20,) which has been once manifested to us in Christ.

18. *Let no one take from you the palm.*³ He alludes to runners, or wrestlers, to whom the *palm* was assigned, on

¹ " Inutile et du tout vuide ;"—" Useless and altogether void."
² " Signes et tesmoignages ;"—" Signs and evidences."
³ " The Latin, ' *seducat*,' correctly gives the intention of καταβραβινίτω, which signifies, to cause a competitor to lose his prize, by *drawing him aside* from the goal, (*seorsim ducendo*, or *seducendo*.)"—*Penn.—Ed.*

them, therefore, that the false apostles aimed at nothing else than to snatch away from them the palm, inasmuch as they draw them aside from the rectitude of their course. Hence it follows that they must be shunned as the most injurious pests. The passage is also carefully to be marked as intimating, that all those who draw us aside from the simplicity of Christ cheat us out of the *prize of our high calling.* (Phil. iii. 14.)

Desirous in humility. Something must be understood; hence I have inserted in the text *id facere, (to do it.)* For he points out the kind of danger which they required to guard against. All are desirous to defraud you of the *palm,* who, under the pretext of humility, recommend to you the *worship of angels.* For their object is, that you may wander out of the way, leaving the one object of aim. I read *humility and worship of angels* conjointly, for the one follows the other, just as at this day the Papists make use of the same pretext when philosophizing as to the worship of saints. For they reason on the ground of man's abasement,[1] that we must, therefore, seek for mediators to help us. But for this very reason has Christ humbled himself—that we might directly betake ourselves to him, however miserable sinners we may be.

I am aware that the *worship of angels* is by many interpreted otherwise, as meaning such as has been delivered to men by angels; for the Devil has always endeavoured to set off his impostures under this title. The Pope at this day boasts, that all the trifles with which he has adulterated the pure worship of God are revelations. In like manner the Theurgians[2] of old alleged that all the superstitions that

---

[1] " Car ayans proposé l'indignite de l'homme, et presché d'humilite, de là ils concluent ;"—" For having set forth man's unworthiness, and having preached of humility, they conclude from this."

[2] The Theurgians were the followers of Ammonius Saccas, who prescribed an austere discipline with the view of " refining," as he pretended, " that faculty of the mind which receives the images of things, so as to render it capable of perceiving the demons, and of performing many marvellous things by their assistance." See *Mosheim's Ecclesiastical History,* vol. i. p. 174.—*Ed.*

here condemns all fanciful kinds of worship that are falsely set forth under the authority of angels.[2] But, in my opinion, he rather condemns the contrivance as to the worshipping of angels. It is on this account that he has so carefully applied himself to this in the very commencement of the Epistle, to bring angels under subjection, lest they should obscure the splendour of Christ.[3] In fine, as he had in the first chapter prepared the way for abolishing the ceremonies, so he had also for the removal of all other hinderances which draw us away from Christ alone.[4] In this class is the *worship of angels*.

Superstitious persons have from the beginning worshipped angels,[5] that through means of them there might be free access to God. The Platonists infected the Christian Church also with this error. For although Augustine sharply inveighs against them in his tenth book "On the City of God," and condemns at great length all their disputations as to the worship of angels, we see nevertheless what has happened. Should any one compare the writings of Plato with Popish theology, he will find that they have drawn wholly from Plato their prattling as to the *worship of angels*. The sum is this, that we must honour angels, whom Plato calls demons, χάριν τῆς εὐφήμου διαπορείας, (*for the sake of their auspicious intercession.*)[6] He brings forward this sentiment in Epinomis, and he confirms it in Cratylus,[7] and many other passages. In what respect do the Papists differ at all from this? "But," it will be said, "they do not deny that the Son of God is

[1] *Per manus,* (*from one hand to another.*) The reader will find the same proverbial expression made use of by CALVIN on the Corinthians, vol. i. pp. 150, 373, and vol. ii. p. 9.—*Ed.*

[2] "Lesquelles on fait receuoir au poure monde sous la fausse couuerture de l'authorite des anges;"—"Which they make the world receive under the false pretext of the authority of angels."

[3] "La splendeur de la maieste de Christ;"—"The splendour of Christ's majesty."

[4] "De seul vray but, qui est Christ;"—"From the only true aim, which is Christ."

[5] See CALVIN's *Institutes,* vol. i. p. 200.

[6] "A cause de l'heureuse intercession qu'ils font pour les hommes;"—"On account of the blessed intercession which they make for men."

[7] See CALVIN's *Institutes,* vol. i. p. 202.

assistance of the angels, and that, consequently, some worship must be rendered to them, so they placed angels in the seat of Christ, and honoured them with Christ's office. Let us know, then, that Paul here condemns all kinds of worship of human contrivance, which are rendered either to angels or to the dead, as though they were mediators, rendering assistance after Christ, or along with Christ.[1] For just so far do we recede from Christ, when we transfer the smallest part of what belongs to him to any others, whether they be angels or men.

Intruding into those things which he hath not seen. The verb ἐμβατεύειν, the participle of which Paul here makes use of, has various significations. The rendering which Erasmus, after Jerome, has given to it, *walking proudly*, would not suit ill, were there an example of such a signification in any author of sufficient note. For we see every day with how much confidence and pride rash persons pronounce an opinion as to things unknown. Nay, even in the very subject of which Paul treats, there is a remarkable illustration. For when the Sorbonnic divines put forth their trifles[2] respecting the intercession of saints or angels, they declare,[3] as though it were from an oracle,[4] that the dead[5] know and behold our necessities, inasmuch as they see all things in the reflex light of God.[6] And yet, what is less certain? Nay more, what is more obscure and doubtful? But such, truly, is their magisterial freedom, that they fearlessly and daringly assert what

---

[1] " Comme s'ils estoyent mediateurs ou auec Christ, ou en second lieu apres Christ, pour suppleer ce qui defaut de son costé;"—" As if they were mediators either with Christ, or in the second place after Christ, to supply what is wanting on his part."

[2] " Mettent en auant leurs mensonges;"—" Bring forward their falsehoods."

[3] " Ils prononcent et determinent comme par arrest;"—" They declare and determine as if by decree."

[4] " *Perinde atque ex tripode,*" (*just as though it were from the tripod.*) Our author manifestly alludes to the three-footed stool on which the Priestess of Apollo at Delphi sat, while giving forth oracular responses. —*Ed.*

[5] " Les saincts trespassez;"—" Departed saints."

[6] " En la reuerberation de la lumiere de Dieu;"—" In the reflection of the light of God."

This meaning, therefore, would be suitable, if that signification of the term were usual. It is, however, among the Greeks taken simply as meaning to *walk*. It also sometimes means to *inquire*. Should any one choose to understand it thus in this passage, Paul will, in that case, reprove a foolish curiosity in the investigation of things that are obscure, and such as are even hid from our view and transcend it.[1] It appears to me, however, that I have caught Paul's meaning, and have rendered it faithfully in this manner—*intruding into those things which he hath not seen.* For that is the common signification of the word ἐμβατεύειν—to enter upon an inheritance,[2] or to take possession, or to set foot anywhere. Accordingly, Budaeus renders this passage thus:—" Setting foot upon, or entering on the possession of those things which he has not seen." I have followed his authority, but have selected a more suitable term. For such persons in reality break through and intrude into secret things,[3] of which God would have no discovery as yet made to us. The passage ought to be carefully observed, for the purpose of reproving the rashness[4] of those who inquire farther than is allowable.

Puffed up in vain by a fleshly mind. He employs the expression *fleshly mind* to denote the perspicuity of the human intellect, however great it may be. For he places it in contrast with that spiritual wisdom which is revealed to us from heaven in accordance with that statement—*Flesh and blood hath not revealed it unto thee.* (Matt. xvi. 17.) Whoever, therefore, depends upon his own reason, inasmuch as the acuteness of the flesh is wholly at work in him,[5] Paul declares him to be *puffed up in vain.* And truly all the wisdom

---

[1] " Et surmontent toute nostre capacite;"—" And exceed all our capacity."

[2] Thus, ἐμβατεύειν εἰς τὴν οὐσίαν is made use of by Demosthenes, as meaning—" to *come in* to the property."—See *Dem.* 1086. 19.—*Ed.*

[3] " Es choses secretes et cachees;"—" Into things secret and hidden."

[4] " La fole outrecuidance;"—" The foolish presumption."

[5] " Pource qu'il n'est gouuerné que par la subtilite charnelle et naturelle;"—" Because he is regulated exclusively by carnal and natural acuteness."

nation of the Spirit. And observe, that those are said to be *puffed up* who insinuate themselves[1] under a show of humility. For it happens, as Augustine elegantly writes to Paulinus, by wonderful means, as to the soul of man, that it is more puffed up from a false humility than if it were openly proud.

19. *Not holding the head.* He condemns in the use of one word whatever does not bear a relation to Christ. He also confirms his statement on the ground that all things flow from him, and depend upon him. Hence, should any one call us anywhere else than to Christ, though in other respects he were big with heaven and earth, he is empty and full of wind: let us, therefore, without concern, bid him farewell. Observe, however, of whom he is speaking, namely, of those who did not openly reject or deny Christ, but, not accurately understanding his office and power, by seeking out other helps and means of salvation, (as they commonly speak,) were not firmly rooted in him.

From whom the whole body by joints. He simply means this, that the Church does not stand otherwise than in the event of all things being furnished to her by Christ, the *Head*, and, accordingly, that her entire safety[2] consists in him. The body, it is true, has its nerves, its *joints, and ligaments*, but all these things derive their vigour solely from the Head, so that the whole binding of them together is from that source. What, then, must be done? The constitution of the body will be in a right state, if simply the Head, which furnishes the several members with everything that they have, is allowed, without any hinderance, to have the pre-eminence. This Paul speaks of as the *increase of God*, by which he means that it is not every increase that is approved by God, but only that which has a relation to the Head. For we see that the kingdom of the Pope is not merely tall and large, but swells out into a monstrous size. As, how-

[1] " En la grace des hommes;"—" Into the favour of men."
[2] " Toute la perfection de son estre;"—" The entire perfection of her being."

body, and a confused mass that will fall to pieces of itself.

20. Wherefore, if ye be dead with Christ from the rudiments of the world, why, as though living in the world, are ye subject to ordinances,	20. Si igitur mortui estis cum Christo ab elementis huius mundi, quid tanquam viventibus in mundo decreta vobis perscribuntur?
21. (Touch not, taste not, handle not;	21. Ne esitaveris, ne gustaveris, ne attigeris:
22. Which all are to perish with the using,) after the commandments and doctrines of men?	22. Quae sunt omnia in corruptionem ipso abusu, secundum praecepta et doctrinas hominum,
23. Which things have indeed a shew of wisdom in will-worship, and humility, and neglecting of the body; not in any honour to the satisfying of the flesh.	23. Quae speciem[1] quidem habent sapientiae in superstitione,[2] et humilitate animi, et neglectu corporis:[3] non in honore aliquo ad expletionem carnis.[4]

20. *If ye are dead.* He had previously said, that the ordinances were fastened to the cross of Christ. (Ver. 14.) He now employs another figure of speech—that we are *dead* to them, as he teaches us elsewhere, that we are *dead to the law,* and the law, on the other hand, to us. (Gal. ii. 19.) The term death means abrogation,[5] but it is more expressive *and more emphatic,* (καὶ ἐμφατικώτερον.) He says, therefore, that the Colossians have nothing to do with ordinances. Why? Because they have died with Christ to ordinances; that is, after they died with Christ by regeneration, they were, through his kindness, set free from ordinances, that they may not belong to them any more. Hence he concludes that they are by no means bound by the ordinances, which the false apostles endeavoured to impose upon them.

21. *Eat not, taste not.* Hitherto this has been rendered—*Handle not,* but as another word immediately follows, which

---

[1] " *Espece,* ou, *forme ;*"—" *Appearance,* or, *form.*"

[2] " *Superstition,* ou, *deuotion volontaire ;*"—" *Superstition,* or, *will-worship.*"

[3] " *En mespris du corps,* ou, *en ce qu'elles n'espargnent le corps ;*"— " *In contempt of the body,* or, *inasmuch as they do not spare the body.*"

[4] " *Sans aucun honneur a rassasier la chair,* ou, *et ne ont aucun esgard au rassasiement d'iceluy :* ou, *mais ne font d'aucune estime, n'appartenans qu'a ce qui remplit le corps ;*"—" *Without any honour to the satisfying of the flesh,* or, *and they have no regard to the satisfying of it,* or, *but they hold it in no esteem, not caring as to what fills the body.*"

[5] " *Et abolissement ;*"—" *And abolishment.*"

ployed by the Greeks, among its other significations, in the sense of *eating*,[1] in accordance with the rendering that I have given. Plutarch makes use of it in the life of Cesar, when he relates that his soldiers, in destitution of all things, *ate* animals which they had not been accustomed previously to use as food.[2] And this arrangement is both in other respects natural and is also most in accordance with the connection of the passage; for Paul points out, (μιμητικῶς,) *by way of imitation*, to what length the waywardness of those who bind consciences by their laws is wont to proceed. From the very commencement they are unduly rigorous: hence he sets out with their prohibition—not simply against eating, but even against slightly partaking. After they have obtained what they wish they go beyond that command, so that they afterwards declare it to be unlawful to taste of what they do not wish should be eaten. At length they make it criminal even to *touch*. In short, when persons have once taken upon them to tyrannize over men's souls, there is no end of new laws being daily added to old ones, and new enactments starting up from time to time. How bright a mirror there is as to this in Popery! Hence Paul acts admirably well in admonishing us that human traditions are a labyrinth, in which consciences are more and more entangled; nay more, are snares, which from the beginning bind in such a way that in course of time they strangle in the end.

22. *All which things tend to corruption.* He sets aside, by a twofold argument, the enactments of which he has made mention—because they make religion consist in things outward and frail, which have no connection with the spiritual kingdom of God; and secondly, because they are from men, not from God. He combats the first argument, also, in Rom. xiv. 17, when he says, *The kingdom of God is not in*

[1] An example occurs in Homer's Odyssey, (iv. 60,) σίτου δ' ἅπτισθον καὶ χαίρετον.—" Take food and rejoice." See also *Xenoph. Mem.* 1. 3. 7.—*Ed.*

[2] The passage referred to is as follows:—" Ἐβρώθη δὲ καὶ φλοιός, ὡς λέγεται, καὶ ζώων ἀγεύστων πρότερον ἥψαντο."—" Even the bark of trees, it is said, was devoured, and they ate animals not previously tasted."—*Ed.*

himself says, *Whatever entereth into the mouth defileth not the man, because it goes down into the belly, and is cast forth.* (Matt. xv. 11.) The sum is this—that the worship of God, true piety, and the holiness of Christians, do not consist in drink, and food, and clothing, which are things that are transient and liable to corruption, and perish by abuse. For abuse is properly applicable to those things which are corrupted by the use of them. Hence enactments are of no value in reference to those things which tend to excite scruples of conscience. But in Popery you would scarcely find any other holiness, than what consists in little observances of corruptible things.

A *second* refutation is added[1]—that they originated with men, and have not God as their Author; and by this thunderbolt he prostrates and swallows up all traditions of men. For why? This is Paul's reasoning: "Those who bring consciences into bondage do injury to Christ, and make void his death. For whatever is of human invention does not bind conscience."

23. *Which have indeed a show.* Here we have the anticipation of an objection, in which, while he concedes to his adversaries what they allege, he at the same time reckons it wholly worthless. For it is as though he had said, that he does not regard their having a *show of wisdom.* But *show* is placed in contrast with *reality,* for it is an *appearance,* as they commonly speak, which deceives by resemblance.[2]

Observe, however, of what colours this *show* consists, according to Paul. He makes mention of three—self-invented worship,[3] humility, and neglect of the body. Superstition among the Greeks receives the name of ἐθελοϑρησκεία—the term which Paul here makes use of. He has, however, an eye to the etymology of the term, for ἐθελοϑρησκεία literally

---

[1] " Le second argument par lequel il refute telles ordonnances, est ;"— " The second argument by which he sets aside such enactments, is."

[2] " Par similitude qu'elle ha auec la verite ;"—" By the resemblance which it bears to the reality."

[3] " Le seruice forgé a plaisir, c'est a dire inuenté par les hommes ;"— " Worship contrived at pleasure, that is to say, invented by men."

Human traditions, therefore, are agreeable to us on this account, that they are in accordance with our understanding, for any one will find in his own brain the first outlines of them. This is the *first* pretext.

The *second* is humility, inasmuch as obedience both to God and men is pretended, so that men do not refuse even unreasonable burdens.[1] And for the most part traditions of this kind are of such a nature as to appear to be admirable exercises of humility.

They allure, also, by means of a *third* pretext, inasmuch as they seem to be of the greatest avail for the mortification of the flesh, while there is no sparing of the body. Paul, however, bids farewell to those disguises, for *what is in high esteem among men is often an abomination in the sight of God.* (Luke xvi. 15.) Farther, *that* is a treacherous obedience, and a perverse and sacrilegious humility, which transfers to men the authority of God; and *neglect of the body* is not of so great importance, as to be worthy to be set forth to admiration as the service of God.

Some one, however, will feel astonished, that Paul does not take more pains in pulling off those masks. I answer, that he on good grounds rests contented with the simple term *show*. For the principles which he had taken as opposed to this are incontrovertible—that the body is in Christ, and that, consequently, those do nothing but impose upon miserable men, who set before them shadows. *Secondly,* the spiritual kingdom of Christ is by no means taken up with frail and corruptible elements. *Thirdly,* by the death of Christ such observances were put an end to, that we might have no connection with them; and, *fourthly,* God is our only *Lawgiver.* (Isaiah xxxiii. 22.) Whatever may be brought forward on the other side, let it have ever so much splendour, is fleeting *show*.

Secondly, he reckoned it enough to admonish the Colossians, not to be deceived by the putting forth of empty things. There was no necessity for dwelling at greater

---

[1] "Iniques et dures a porter;"—"Unreasonable and hard to be borne."

be measured according to our views ; and that, consequently, any kind of service is not lawful, simply on the ground that it is agreeable to us. This, also, ought to be a commonly received point—that we owe to God such humility as to yield obedience simply to his commands, so as not to *lean to our own understanding,* &c., (Prov. iii. 5,)—and that the limit of humility towards men is this—that each one submit himself to others in love. Now, when they contend that the wantonness of the flesh is repressed by abstinence from meats, the answer is easy—that we must not therefore abstain from any particular food as being unclean, but must eat sparingly of what we do eat of, both in order that we may soberly and temperately make use of the gifts of God, and that we may not, impeded by too much food and drink, forget those things that are God's. Hence it was enough to say that these[1] were masks, that the Colossians, being warned, might be on their guard against false pretexts.

Thus, at the present day, Papists are not in want of specious pretexts, by which to set forth their own laws, however they may be—some of them impious and tyrannical, and others of them silly and trifling. When, however, we have granted them everything, there remains, nevertheless, this refutation by Paul, which is of itself more than sufficient for dispelling all their smoky vapours ;[2] not to say how far removed they[3] are from so honourable an appearance as that which Paul describes. The principal holiness of the Papacy,[4] at the present day, consists in monkhood, and of what nature that is, I am ashamed and grieved to make mention, lest I should stir up so abominable an odour. Farther, it is of importance to consider here, how prone, nay, how forward the mind of man is to artificial modes of worship.

[1] " Ces traditions ;"—" These traditions."
[2] " Tous les brouillars desquels ils taschent d'esblouir les yeux au poure monde ;"—" All the mists by which they endeavour to blind the eyes of the poor world."
[3] " Leurs traditions ;"—" Their traditions."
[4] " La premiere et la principale honnestete et sainctete de la Papaute ;" —" The first and principal decency and sanctity of the Papacy."

years after his death, as though he had never spoken a word. The zeal of men, therefore, for superstition is surpassingly mad, which could not be restrained by so plain a declaration of God from breaking forth, as historical records testify.

Not in any honour. Honour means *care,* according to the usage of the Hebrew tongue. *Honour widows,* (1 Tim. v. 3,) that is, take care of them. Now Paul finds fault with this, that they[2] teach to leave off care for the body. For as God forbids us to indulge the body unduly, so he commands that these be given it as much as is necessary for it. Hence Paul, in Rom. xiii. 14, does not expressly condemn care for the flesh, but such as indulges lusts. *Have no care,* says he, *for the flesh, to the gratifying of its lusts.* What, then, does Paul point out as faulty in those traditions of which he treats? It is that they gave no honour to the body for the *satisfying the flesh,* that is, according to the measure of necessity. For *satisfying* here means a mediocrity, which restricts itself to the simple use of nature, and thus stands in opposition to pleasure and all superfluous delicacies; for nature is content with little. Hence, to refuse what it requires for sustaining the necessity of life, is not less at variance with piety, than it is inhuman.

CHAPTER III.

1. If ye then be risen with Christ, seek those things which are above, where Christ sitteth on the right hand of God.

2. Set your affection on things above, not on things on the earth.

3. For ye are dead, and your life is hid with Christ in God.

4. When Christ, *who is* our life, shall appear, then shall ye also appear with him in glory.

1. Ergo si consurrexistis cum Christo, quae sursum sunt quaerite, ubi Christus est in dextera Dei sedens:

2. Quae sursum sunt cogitate, non quae super terram.

3. Mortui enim estis, et vita nostra abscondita est cum Christo in Deo.

4. Ubi autem Christus apparuerit, vita vestra, tunc etiam vos cum ipso apparebitis in gloria.

[1] " Peind yci au vif;"—" Paints here to the life."
[2] " Les traditions;"—" The traditions."

true exercises in which it becomes Christians to employ themselves; and this has no slight bearing upon the point in hand; for when we see what God would have us do, we afterwards easily despise the inventions of men. When we perceive, too, that what God recommends to us is much more lofty and excellent than what men inculcate, our alacrity of mind increases for following God, so as to disregard men. Paul here exhorts the Colossians to meditation upon the heavenly life. And what as to his opponents? They were desirous to retain their childish rudiments. This doctrine, therefore, makes the ceremonies be the more lightly esteemed. Hence it is manifest that Paul, in this passage, exhorts in such a manner as to confirm the foregoing doctrine; for, in describing solid piety and holiness of life, his aim is, that those vain *shows* of human traditions may vanish.[2] At the same time, he anticipates an objection with which the false apostles might assail him. What then? "Wouldst thou rather have men be idle than addict themselves to such exercises, of whatever sort they may be?" When, therefore, he bids Christians apply themselves to exercises of a greatly superior kind, he cuts off the handle for this calumny; nay more, he loads them with no small odium, on the ground that they impede the right course of the pious by worthless amusements.[3]

1. *If ye are risen with Christ.* Ascension follows resurrection: hence, if we are the members of Christ, we must ascend into heaven, because he, on being raised up from the dead, was *received up into heaven,* (Mark xvi. 19,) that he might draw us up with him. Now, we *seek those things which are above,* when in our minds[4] we are truly sojourners in this world, and are not bound to it. The word rendered *think upon* expresses rather assiduity and intensity of aim: "Let your whole meditation be as to this: to this apply

[1] " Recommandoyent estroittement;"—" Urgently recommended."
[2] " S'en aillent en fumee;"—" May vanish into smoke."
[3] " Par des amusemens plus que pueriles;"—" By worse than childish amusements."
[4] " De cœur et esprit;"—" In heart and spirit."

in heaven, how much less becoming were it to seek Christ upon the earth. Let us therefore bear in mind that *that* is a true and holy *thinking* as to Christ, which forthwith bears us up into heaven, that we may there adore him, and that our minds may dwell with him.

As to the *right hand of God*, it is not confined to heaven, but fills the whole world. Paul has made mention of it here to intimate that Christ encompasses us by his power, that we may not think that distance of place is a cause of separation between us and him, and that at the same time his majesty may excite us wholly to reverence him.

2. *Not the things that are on earth.* He does not mean, as he does a little afterwards, depraved appetites, which reign in earthly men, nor even riches, or fields, or houses, nor any other things of the present life, which we must *use, as though we did not use them,* (1 Cor. vii. 30, 31,)[1] but is still following out his discussion as to ceremonies, which he represents as resembling entanglements which constrain us to creep upon the ground. "Christ," says he, "calls us upwards to himself, while these draw us downwards." For this is the winding-up and exposition of what he had lately touched upon as to the abolition of ceremonies through the death of Christ. "The ceremonies are dead to you through the death of Christ, and you to them, in order that, being raised up to heaven with Christ, you may think only of those things that are above. Leave off therefore earthly things." I shall not contend against others who are of a different mind; but certainly the Apostle appears to me to go on step by step, so that, in the first instance, he places traditions as to trivial matters in contrast with meditation on the heavenly life, and afterwards, as we shall see, goes a step farther.

3. *For ye are dead.* No one can rise again with Christ, if he has not first died with him. Hence he draws an argument from *rising again* to *dying,* as from a consequent

[1] See CALVIN on the Corinthians, vol. i. p. 257.

we must *seek those things that are above?* It is because the life of the pious is *above.* Why does he now teach, that the things which are on earth are to be left off? Because they are dead to the world. "Death goes before that resurrection, of which I have spoken. Hence both of them must be seen in you."

It is worthy of observation, that our *life* is said to be *hid,* that we may not murmur or complain if our life, being buried under the ignominy of the cross, and under various distresses, differs nothing from death, but may patiently wait for the day of revelation. And in order that our waiting may not be painful, let us observe those expressions, *in God,* and *with Christ,* which intimate that our life is out of danger, although it does not appear. For, in the *first* place, God is faithful, and therefore will not deny what has been *committed* to him, (2 Tim. i. 12,) nor deceive in the guardianship which he has undertaken; and, *secondly,* the fellowship of Christ brings still greater security. For what is to be more desired by us than this—that our life remain with the very fountain of life? Hence there is no reason why we should be alarmed if, on looking around on every side, we nowhere see life. For we are *saved by hope. But those things which are already seen with our eyes are not hoped for.* (Rom. viii. 24.) Nor does he teach that our life is hid merely in the opinion of the world, but even as to our own view, because this is the true and necessary trial of our hope, that being encompassed, as it were, with death, we may seek life somewhere else than in the world.

4. *But when Christ, our life, shall appear.* Here we have a choice consolation—that the coming of Christ will be the manifestation of our life. And, at the same time, he admonishes us how unreasonable were the disposition of the man, who should refuse to bear up[2] until that day. For if our life is shut up in Christ, it must be *hid,* until he shall *appear.*

---

[1] " C'est a dire de ce qui suit a ce qui va deuant;"—" That is to say, from what follows to what comes before."

[2] " D'endurer et attendre;"—" To endure and wait."

tion, evil concupiscence, and covetousness, which is idolatry:	concupiscentiam malam, et avaritiam, quae est idololatria.
6. For which things' sake the wrath of God cometh on the children of disobedience.	6. Propter quae venit ira Dei in filios inobedientiae;
7. In the which ye also walked sometime, when ye lived in them.	7. In quibus vos quoque ambulabatis aliquando, quum viveretis in illis.
8. But now ye also put off all these; anger, wrath, malice, blasphemy, filthy communication out of your mouth.	8. Nunc autem deponite et vos omnia, iram, indignationem, malitiam, maledicentiam, turpiloquentiam ex ore vestro.

5. *Mortify therefore.* Hitherto he has been speaking of contempt of the world. He now proceeds further, and enters upon a higher philosophy, as to the *mortification of the flesh.* That this may be the better understood, let us take notice that there is a twofold *mortification.* The former relates to those things that are around us. Of this he has hitherto treated. The other is inward—that of the understanding and will, and of the whole of our corrupt nature. He makes mention of certain vices which he calls, not with strict accuracy, but at the same time elegantly, *members.* For he conceives of our nature as being, as it were, a mass made up of different vices. They are, therefore, our *members,* inasmuch as they in a manner stick close to us. He calls them also *earthly,* alluding to what he had said—*not the things that are on earth,* (ver. 2,) but in a different sense. " I have admonished you, that earthly things are to be disregarded: you must, however, make it your aim to mortify those vices which detain you on the earth." He intimates, however, that we are earthly, so long as the vices of our flesh are vigorous in us, and that we are made heavenly by the renewing of the Spirit.

After *fornication* he adds *uncleanness,* by which term he expresses all kinds of wantonness, by which lascivious persons pollute themselves. To these is added, πάθος, that is, *lust,* which includes all the allurements of unhallowed desire. This term, it is true, denotes mental perturbations of other kinds, and disorderly motions contrary to reason; but *lust* is not an unsuitable rendering of this passage. As to the rea-

say the same thing twice.

6. *On account of which things the wrath of God cometh.* I do not find fault with the rendering of Erasmus—*solet venire*—(*is wont to come,*) but as the present tense is often taken in Scripture instead of the future, according to the idiom of the Hebrew language, I have preferred to leave the rendering undecided, so that it might be accommodated to either meaning. He warns the Colossians, then, either of the ordinary judgments of God, which are seen daily, or of the vengeance which he has once denounced upon the wicked, and which impends over them, but will not be manifested until the last day. I willingly, however, admit the former meaning—that God, who is the perpetual Judge of the world, is accustomed to punish the crimes in question.

He says, however, expressly, that the wrath of God will come, or is wont to come, upon the unbelieving or disobedient, instead of threatening them with anything of this nature.[2] For God would rather that we should see his wrath upon the reprobate, than feel it in ourselves. It is true, that when the promises of grace are set before us, every one of the pious ought to embrace them equally as though they were designed for himself particularly; but, on the other hand, let us dread the threatenings of wrath and destruction in such a manner, that those things which are suitable for the reprobate, may serve as a lesson to us. God, it is true, is often said to be angry even with his children, and sometimes chastens their sins with severity. Paul speaks here, however, of eternal destruction, of which a mirror is to be seen only in the reprobate. In short, whenever God threatens, he shews, as it were, indirectly the punishment, that, beholding it in the reprobate, we may be deterred from sinning.

7. *In which ye walked.* Erasmus mistakingly refers this to men, rendering it, "*inter quos,*" ("among *whom,*") for there can be no doubt that Paul had in view the vices,

---

[1] " Est appelee *Idolatrie;*"—" Is called *Idolatry.*"
[2] " Plustot que de menacer les Colossiens de telles choses;'—" Instead of threatening the Colossians with such things."

differ from each other, as power does from action. *Living* holds the first place: *walking* comes afterwards, as in Gal. v. 25, *If ye live in the* SPIRIT, WALK *also in the Spirit.* By these words he intimates, that it were an unseemly thing that they should addict themselves any more to the vices, to which they had died through Christ. See the sixth chapter of the Epistle to the Romans. It is an argument from a withdrawment of the cause to a withdrawment of the effect.

8. *But now*—that is, after having ceased to *live in the flesh.* For the power and nature of *mortification* are such, that all corrupt affections are extinguished in us, lest sin should afterwards produce in us its wonted fruits. What I have rendered *indignationem,* (*indignation,*) is in the Greek θυμός—a term, which denotes a more impetuous passionateness than ὀργή, (*anger.*) Here, however, he enumerates, as may easily be perceived, forms of vice that were different from those previously mentioned.

9. Lie not one to another, seeing that ye have put off the old man with his deeds;	9. Ne mentiamini alii diversus alios, postquam exuistis veterem hominem cum actionibus suis:
10. And have put on the new *man,* which is renewed in knowledge after the image of him that created him:	10. Et induistis novum, qui renovatur in agnitionem, secundum imaginem eius, qui creavit eum:
11. Where there is neither Greek nor Jew, circumcision nor uncircumcision, Barbarian, Scythian, bond *nor* free: but Christ *is* all, and in all.	11. Ubi non est Graecus nec Judaeus, circumcisio nec praeputium, barbarus, Scytha, servus, liber: sed omnia et in omnibus Christus.
12. Put on therefore, as the elect of God, holy and beloved, bowels of mercies, kindness, humbleness of mind, meekness, long-suffering;	12. Induite igitur, tanquam electi Dei sancti et dilecti, viscera miserationum, comitatem, humilitatem, mansuetudinem, tolerantiam,
13. Forbearing one another, and forgiving one another, if any man have a quarrel against any: even as Christ forgave you, so also *do* ye.	13. Sufferentes vos mutuo, et condonantes si quis adversus alium litem habeat: quemadmodum Christus condonavit vobis, ita et vos.

9. *Lie not.* When he forbids *lying,* he condemns every sort of cunning, and all base artifices of deception. For I do not understand the term as referring merely to calumnies, but I view it as contrasted in a general way with sincerity. Hence it might be allowable to render it more briefly, and I

argument as to the fellowship, which believers have in the death and resurrection of Christ, but employs other forms of expression.

The *old man* denotes—whatever we bring from our mother's womb, and whatever we are by nature.[1] It is *put off* by all that are renewed by Christ. The *new man*, on the other hand, is that which is renewed by the Spirit of Christ to the obedience of righteousness, or it is nature restored to its true integrity by the same Spirit. The *old man*, however, comes first in order, because we are first-born from Adam, and afterwards are born again through Christ. And as what we have from Adam becomes old,[2] and tends towards ruin, so what we obtain through Christ remains for ever, and is not frail; but, on the contrary, tends towards immortality. This passage is worthy of notice, inasmuch as a definition of regeneration may be gathered from it. For it contains two parts—the *putting off* of the *old man*, and the *putting on* of the *new*, and of these Paul here makes mention. It is also to be noticed, that the *old man* is distinguished by his works, as a tree is by its fruits. Hence it follows, that the depravity that is innate in us is denoted by the term *old man*.

10. *Which is renewed in knowledge.* He shews in the *first* place, that newness of life consists in *knowledge*—not as though a simple and bare knowledge were sufficient, but he speaks of the illumination of the Holy Spirit, which is lively and effectual, so as not merely to enlighten the mind by kindling it up with the light of truth, but transforming the whole man. And this is what he immediately adds, that we are *renewed after the image of God.* Now, the *image of God* resides in the whole of the soul, inasmuch as it is not the reason merely that is rectified, but also the will. Hence, too, we learn, on the one hand, what is the end of our regeneration, that is, that we may be made like God, and that

---

[1] See CALVIN on the Romans, p. 224; also CALVIN on the Corinthians, vol. i. p. 188.
[2] " Deuient vieil et caduque ;"—" Becomes old and frail."

Moses in Gen. ix. 6,[1] the rectitude and integrity of the whole soul, so that man reflects, like a mirror, the wisdom, righteousness, and goodness of God. He speaks somewhat differently in the Epistle to the Ephesians, but the meaning is the same. See the passage—Eph. iv. 24. Paul, at the same time, teaches, that there is nothing more excellent at which the Colossians can aspire, inasmuch as this is our highest perfection and blessedness—to bear the image of God.

11. *Where there is neither Jew.* He has added this intentionally, that he may again draw away the Colossians from ceremonies. For the meaning of the statement is this, that Christian perfection does not stand in need of those outward observances, nay, that they are things that are altogether at variance with it. For under the distinction of *circumcision* and *uncircumcision*, of *Jew* and *Greek*, he includes, by *synecdoche*,[2] all outward things. The terms that follow, *barbarian, Scythian*,[3] *bond, free*, are added by way of amplification.

Christ is all, and in all, that is, Christ alone holds, as they say, the *prow* and the *stern*—the beginning and the end. Farther, by *Christ*, he means the spiritual righteousness of Christ, which puts an end to ceremonies, as we have formerly seen. They are, therefore, superfluous in a state of true perfection, nay more, they ought to have no place, inasmuch as injustice would otherwise be done to Christ, as though it were necessary to call in those helps for making up his deficiencies.

13. *Put on therefore.* As he has enumerated some parts of the *old man*, so he now also enumerates some parts of the

---

[1] " De laquelle Moyse fait mention au Gen. i. chap. c. 26, et ix. b. 6;"—" Of which Moses makes mention in Gen. i. 26, and ix. 6."

[2] *Synecdoche*, a figure of speech, by which a part is taken for the whole.—*Ed.*

[3] *Howe* supposes that Paul " may possibly refer here to a Scythian who, having an inclination to learning, betook himself to Athens, to study the principles of philosophy that were taught there. But meeting one day with a person that very insolently upbraided him on the account of his country, he gave him this smart repartee: ' True indeed it is, my country is a reproach to me; but you, for your part, are a reproach to your country.' "—*Howe's* Works, (Lond. 1822,) vol. v. p. 497.—*Ed.*

the effects and evidences of renovation." Hence the exhortation depends on the second clause, and, accordingly, he keeps up the metaphor in the word rendered *put on.*

He mentions, *first, bowels of mercy,* by which expression he means an earnest affection, with yearnings, as it were, of the *bowels: Secondly,* he makes mention of *kindness,* (for in this manner I have chosen to render χρηστότητα,) by which we make ourselves amiable. To this he adds *humility,* because no one will be kind and gentle but the man who, laying aside haughtiness, and high-mindedness, brings himself down to the exercise of modesty, claiming nothing for himself.

Gentleness—the term which follows—has a wider acceptation than *kindness,* for *that* is chiefly in look and speech, while *this* is also in inward disposition. As, however, it frequently happens, that we come in contact with wicked and ungrateful men, there is need of patience, that it may cherish mildness in us. He at length explains what he meant by *long-suffering*—that we embrace each other indulgently, and forgive also where any offence has been given. As, however, it is a thing that is hard and difficult, he confirms this doctrine by the example of Christ, and teaches, that the same thing is required from us, that as we, who have so frequently and so grievously offended, have nevertheless been received into favour, we should manifest the same kindness towards our neighbours, by forgiving whatever offences they have committed against us. Hence he says, *if any one have a quarrel against another.* By this he means, that even just occasions of *quarrel,* according to the views of men, ought not to be followed out.

As the chosen of God. Elect I take here to mean, set *apart.* " God has *chosen* you to himself, has sanctified you, and received you into his love on this condition, that ye be *merciful,* &c. To no purpose does the man that has not these excellences boast that he is *holy,* and *beloved* of God; to no purpose does he reckon himself among the number of believers."

15. And let the peace of God rule in your hearts, to the which also ye are called in one body; and be ye thankful.

16. Let the word of Christ dwell in you richly in all wisdom; teaching and admonishing one another in psalms, and hymns, and spiritual songs, singing with grace in your hearts to the Lord.

17. And whatsoever ye do in word or deed, *do* all in the name of the Lord Jesus, giving thanks to God and the Father by him.

15. Et pax Dei palmam obtineat[1] in cordibus vestris, ad quam etiam estis vocati in uno corpore, et grati sitis.

16. Sermo Christi inhabitet in vobis opulente in omni sapientia, docendo et commonefaciendo vos psalmis, hymnis, et canticis spiritualibus cum gratia, canentes in cordibus vestris Domino.

17. Et quiquid feceritis sermone vel opere, omnia in nomine Domini Iesu, gratiae agentes Deo et Patri, per ipsum.

14. *On account of all these things.* The rendering that has been given by others, "*super* omnia haec," (*above* all these things,) instead of *insuper*, (*over and above*,) is, in my opinion, meagre. It would be more suitable to render it, *Before* all these things. I have chosen, however, the more ordinary signification of the word ἐπί. For as all the things that he has hitherto enumerated flow from *love*, he now on good grounds exhorts the Colossians to cherish *love* among themselves, for the sake of these things—that they may be merciful, gentle, ready to forgive, as though he had said, that they would be such only in the event of their having *love*. For where *love* is wanting, all these things are sought for in vain. That he may commend it the more, he calls it the *bond of perfection*, meaning by this, that the troop of all the virtues[2] is comprehended under it. For this truly is the rule of our whole life, and of all our actions, so that everything that is not regulated according to it is faulty, whatever attractiveness it may otherwise possess. This is the reason why it is called here the *bond of perfection;* because there is nothing in our life that is well regulated if it be not directed towards it, but everything that we attempt is mere waste.

The Papists, however, act a ridiculous part in abusing this declaration, with the view of maintaining justification by

---

[1] "*Regne,* ou, *gouerne;*"—"*Reign,* or, *rule.*"

[2] *Virtutum omnium chorum.* See *Cic. l.* 3, Offic. *c. ult.—Ed.*

love." The answer is twofold ; for Paul here is not reasoning as to the manner in which men are made perfect in the sight of God, but as to the manner in which they may live perfectly among themselves. For the genuine exposition of the passage is this—that other things will be in a desirable state as to our life, if *love* be exercised among us. When, however, we grant that *love* is righteousness, they groundlessly and childishly take occasion from this to maintain, that we are justified by *love,* for where will perfect love be found ? We, however, do not say that men are justified by faith alone, on the ground that the observance of the law is not righteousness, but rather on this ground, that as we are all transgressors of the law, we are, in consequence of our being destitute of any righteousness of our own, constrained to borrow righteousness from Christ. There remains nothing, therefore, but the righteousness of faith, because perfect love is nowhere to be found.

15. *And the peace of God.* He gives the name of the *peace of God* to that which God has established among us, as will appear from what follows. He would have it *reign* in our hearts.[1] He employs, however, a very appropriate metaphor ; for as among wrestlers,[2] he who has vanquished all the others carries off the palm, so he would have the *peace of God* be superior to all carnal affections, which often hurry us on to contentions, disagreements, quarrels, secret grudges. He accordingly prohibits us from giving loose reins to corrupt affections of this kind. As, however, it is difficult to restrain them, he points out also the remedy, that the *peace of God* may carry the victory, because it must be a bridle, by which carnal affections may be restrained. Hence he says, *in our hearts;* because we constantly feel

[1] " *Rule in your hearts,* (βραβευέτω.) Let the peace of Christ *judge, decide,* and *govern* in your hearts, as the *brabeus,* or judge, does in the Olympic contests. . . . While peace rules, all is safe."—*Dr. A. Clarke.* —*Ed.*

[2] " Le mot Grec signifie aucunesfois, Enclins a rendre graces, et recognoistre les benefices que nous receuons ;"—" The Greek word means sometimes—having a disposition to give thanks, and to acknowledge the favours that we receive."

The clause, *to which ye are called*, intimates what manner of *peace* this is—that unity which Christ has consecrated among us under his own direction.[1] For God has *reconciled us to himself* in Christ, (2 Cor. v. 18,) with this view, that we may live in entire harmony among ourselves. He adds, *in one body*, meaning by this, that we cannot be in a state of agreement with God otherwise than by being united among ourselves as members of one body. When he bids us be *thankful*, I do not take this as referring so much to the remembrance of favours, as to sweetness of manners. Hence, with the view of removing ambiguity, I prefer to render it, "Be amiable." At the same time I acknowledge that, if gratitude takes possession of our minds,[2] we shall without fail be inclined to cherish mutual affection among ourselves.

16. *Let the word of Christ dwell.* He would have the doctrine of the gospel be familiarly known by them. Hence we may infer by what spirit those are actuated in the present day, who cruelly[3] interdict the Christian people from making use of it, and furiously vociferate, that no pestilence is more to be dreaded, than that the reading of the Scriptures should be thrown open to the common people. For, unquestionably, Paul here addresses men and women of all ranks; nor would he simply have them take a slight taste merely of the *word of Christ*, but exhorts that it should *dwell in them;* that is, that it should have a settled abode, and that *largely*, that they may make it their aim to advance and increase more and more every day. As, however, the desire of learning is extravagant on the part of many, while they pervert the word of the Lord for their own ambition, or for vain curiosity, or in some way corrupt it, he on this account adds, *in all wisdom*—that, being instructed by it, we may be wise as we ought to be.

[1] "En son nom et authorite;"—"In his own name and authority."

[2] "Si nous auons les cœurs et les sens abbreuuez de ceste affection de n'estre point ingrats;"—"If we have our hearts and minds thoroughly imbued with this disposition of being not unthankful."

[3] "Si estroitement et auec si grande cruaute;"—"So strictly and with such great cruelty."

mean profitable instruction, which tends to edification, as in Romans xii. 7—*He that teacheth, on teaching;* also in Timothy—" All Scripture is profitable for *teaching.*" (2 Tim. iii. 16.) This is the true use of Christ's word. As, however, doctrine is sometimes in itself cold, and, as one says,[1] when it is simply shewn what is right, virtue is praised[2] and left to starve,[3] he adds at the same time admonition, which is, as it were, a confirmation of doctrine and incitement to it. Nor does he mean that the *word of Christ* ought to be of benefit merely to individuals, that they may teach themselves, but he requires mutual teaching and admonition.

Psalms, hymns. He does not restrict the *word of Christ* to these particular departments, but rather intimates that all our communications should be adapted to edification, that even those which tend to hilarity may have no empty savour. " Leave to unbelievers that foolish delight which they take from ludicrous and frivolous jests and witticisms;[4] and let your communications, not merely those that are grave, but those also that are joyful and exhilarating, contain something profitable. In place of their obscene, or at least barely modest and decent songs, it becomes you to make use of hymns and songs that sound forth God's praise." Farther, under these three terms he includes all kinds of songs. They are commonly distinguished in this way—that a *psalm* is that, in the singing of which some musical instrument besides the tongue is made use of: a *hymn* is properly a song of praise, whether it be sung simply with the voice or otherwise; while an *ode* contains not merely praises, but exhortations and other matters. He would have the songs of

[1] " Comme a dit anciennement vn poëte Latin;"—" As a Latin poet has anciently said."

[2] " Probitas laudatur et alget;"—" Virtue is praised and starves,"— that is, is slighted. See Juv. i. 74.—*Ed.*

[3] " Il se trouue assez de gens qui louënt vertu, mais cependant elle se morfond: c'est a dire, il n'y en a gueres qui se mettent a l'ensuyure;"— ": There are persons enough who praise virtue, but in the mean time it starves; that is to say, there are scarcely any of them that set themselves to pursue it."

[4] " Plaisanteries pleines de vanite et niaiserie;"—" Pleasantries full of vanity and silliness."

his argument.

The clause, *in grace*, Chrysostom explains in different ways. I, however, take it simply, as also afterwards, in chapter iv. 6, where he says, " Let your speech be seasoned with salt, *in grace*," that is, by way of a dexterity that may be agreeable, and may please the hearers by its profitableness, so that it may be opposed to buffoonery and similar trifles.

Singing in your hearts. This relates to disposition; for as we ought to stir up others, so we ought also to sing from the heart, that there may not be merely an external sound with the mouth. At the same time, we must not understand it as though he would have every one sing inwardly to himself, but he would have both conjoined, provided the heart goes before the tongue.

17. *And whatsoever ye do.* We have already explained these things, and what goes before, in the Epistle to the Ephesians, where the same things are said almost word for word. As he had already begun to discourse in reference to different parts of the Christian life, and had simply touched upon a few precepts, it would have been too tedious a thing to follow out the rest one by one, he therefore concludes in a summary way, that life must be regulated in such a manner, that whatever we say or do may be wholly governed by the authority of Christ, and may have an eye to his glory as the mark.[1] For we shall fitly comprehend under this term the two following things—that all our aims[2] may set out with invocation of Christ, and may be subservient to his glory. From invocation follows the act of blessing God, which supplies us with matter of thanksgiving. It is also to be observed, that he teaches that we must give thanks to the Father *through Christ*, as we obtain through him every good thing that God confers upon us.

18. Wives, submit yourselves unto your own husbands, as it is fit in the Lord.	18. Mulieres, subditae estote proriis maritis, quemadmodum decet in Domino.

[1] " Comme a son but principal ;"—" As to its chief aim."
[2] " Toutes nos œuures et entreprinses ;"—" All our works and enterprises."

in all things: for this is well-pleasing unto the Lord.	tris per omnia: hoc enim placet Domino.
' 21. Fathers, provoke not your children *to anger*, lest they be discouraged.	21. Patres, ne provocetis liberos vestros, ne deiiciantur animis.
22. Servants, obey in all things *your* masters according to the flesh; not with eye-service, as men-pleasers; but in singleness of heart, fearing God:	22. Servi, obedite per omnia iis, qui secundum carnem sunt domini: non exhibitis ad oculum obsequiis, tanquam hominibus placere studentes, sed in simplicitate cordis, ut qui timeatis Deum.
23. And whatsoever ye do, do *it* heartily, as to the Lord, and not unto men;	23. Et quicquid feceritis, ex animo facite, tanquam Domino, et non hominibus:
24. Knowing that of the Lord ye shall receive the reward of the inheritance: for ye serve the Lord Christ.	24. Scientes quod a Domino recipietis mercedem hereditatis, nam Domino Christo servitis.
25. But he that doeth wrong shall receive for the wrong which he hath done: and there is no respect of persons.	25. Qui autem iniuste egerit, mercedem reportabit suae iniquitatis: et non est personarum acceptio. (*Deut.* x. 17.)

18. *Wives, be subject.* Now follow particular duties, as they are called,[1] which depend on the calling of individuals. In handling these it were superfluous to take up many words, inasmuch as I have already stated in the Epistle to the Ephesians almost everything that was necessary. Here I shall only add briefly such things as are more particularly suited to an exposition of the passage before us.

He commands *wives* to be *subject*. This is clear, but what follows is of doubtful signification—*as it is fit in the Lord.* For some connect it thus—" Be subject in the Lord, as it is fit." I, however, view it rather differently,—*As it is fit in the Lord*, that is, according to the appointment of the Lord, so that he confirms the subjection of wives by the authority of God. He requires *love* on the part of *husbands*, and *that they be not bitter*, because there is a danger lest they should abuse their authority in the way of tyranny.

20. *Children, obey your parents.* He enjoins it upon *children* to obey their parents,[2] without any exception. But

---

[1] " Les enseignemens concernans le deuoir particulier d'vn chacun ;"—" Instructions relating to the particular duty of each individual."
[2] " Leurs peres et meres ;"—" Their fathers and mothers."

without any reservation ? Now it were worse than unreasonable, that the authority of men should prevail at the expense of neglecting God. I answer, that here, too, we must understand as implied what he expresses elsewhere, (Eph. vi. 1) —*in the Lord.* But for what purpose does he employ a term of universality ? I answer again, that it is to shew, that obedience must be rendered not merely to just commands, but also to such as are unreasonable.[2] For many make themselves compliant with the wishes of their parents only where the command is not grievous or inconvenient. But, on the other hand, this one thing ought to be considered by children—that whoever may be their parents, they have been allotted to them by the providence of God, who by his appointment makes children subject to their parents.

In all things, therefore, that they may not refuse anything, however difficult or disagreeable—*in all things,* that in things indifferent they may give deference to the station which their parents occupy—*in all things,* that they may not put themselves on a footing of equality with their parents, in the way of questioning and debating, or disputing, it being always understood that conscience is not to be infringed upon.[3] He prohibits parents from exercising an immoderate harshness, lest their children should be so disheartened as to be incapable of receiving any honourable training ; for we see, from daily experience, the advantage of a liberal education.

22. *Servants, be obedient.* Anything that is stated here respecting *servants* requires no exposition, as it has been already expounded in commenting on Eph. vi. 1, with the exception of these two expressions,—*For we serve the Lord Christ ;* and, *He that will act unjustly will receive the reward of his iniquity.*

[1] " Les peres ou les meres ;"—" Fathers or mothers."

[2] " C'est a dire, fascheux et rigoureux ;"—" That is to say, grievous and rigorous."

[3] " Ou entrant en dispute auec eux, comme compagnon a compagnon, ainsi qu'on dit. Toutesfois, que ce soit tant que faire se pourra sans offenser Dieu ;"—" Or entering into dispute with them, as associate with associate, as they say. At the same time, let it be only in so far as it can be done without offending God."

supremacy of dominion, and is the supreme master. Here, truly, is choice consolation for all that are under subjection, inasmuch as they are informed that, while they willingly serve their masters, their services are acceptable to Christ, as though they had been rendered to him. From this, also, Paul gathers, that they will *receive* from him *a reward*, but it is the *reward of inheritance*, by which he means that the very thing that is bestowed in reward of works is freely given to us by God, for *inheritance* comes from adoption.

In the *second* clause he again comforts *servants*, by saying that, if they are oppressed by the unjust cruelty of their masters, God himself will take vengeance, and will not, on the ground that they are *servants*, overlook the injuries inflicted upon them, inasmuch as there is *no respect of persons with him*. For this consideration might diminish their courage, if they imagined that God had no regard for them, or no great regard, and that their miseries gave him no concern. Besides, it often happens that servants themselves endeavour to avenge injurious and cruel treatment. He obviates, accordingly, this evil, by admonishing them to wait patiently the judgment of God.

CHAPTER IV.

1. Masters, give unto *your* servants that which is just and equal; knowing that ye also have a Master in heaven.
2. Continue in prayer, and watch in the same with thanksgiving;
3. Withal praying also for us, that God would open unto us a door of utterance, to speak the mystery of Christ, for which I am also in bonds;
4. That I may make it manifest, as I ought to speak.

1. Domini, quod iustum est, servis exhibete, mutuamque aequabilitatem, scientes quod vos quoque Dominum habeatis in coelis.
2. Orationi instate, vigilantes in ea, cum gratiarum actione.
3. Orate simul et pro nobis, ut Deus aperiat nobis ianuam sermonis ad loquendum mysterium Christi, cuius etiam causa vinctus sum.
4. Ut manifestem illud, quemadmodum oportet me loqui.

1. *Masters, what is just.* He mentions first, *what is just*, by which term he expresses that kindness, as to which he

despise the condition of servants, so that they think that they are bound by no law, Paul brings them under control,[1] because both are equally under subjection to the authority of God. Hence that *equity* of which he makes mention.

And mutual equity. Some understand it otherwise, but I have no doubt that Paul here employed ἰσότητα to mean analogical[2] or distributive right,[3] as in *Ephesians*, τὰ αὐτὰ, (*the same things.*)[4] For masters have not their servants bound to them in such a manner as not to owe something to them in their turn, as analogical right to be in force among all ranks.[5]

2. *Continue in prayer.* He returns to general exhortations, in which we must not expect an exact order, for in that case he would have begun with prayer, but Paul had not an eye to that. Farther, as to prayer, he commends here two things; *first*, assiduity; *secondly*, alacrity, or earnest intentness. For, when he says, *continue*, he exhorts to perseverance, while he makes mention of *watching* in opposition to coldness, and listlessness.[6]

He adds, *thanksgiving*, because God must be solicited for present necessity in such a way that, in the mean time, we do not forget favours already received. Farther, we ought not to

---

[1] "Et rabbaisse leur presomption;"—"And beats down their presumption."

[2] Our author has here in view a definition of Aristotle, quoted by him when commenting on 2 Cor. viii. 13. See CALVIN on the Corinthians, vol. ii. p. 294.—*Ed.*

[3] "C'est a dire, qui est reglé et compassé selon la circonstance, qualité, ou vocation des personnes;"—"That is to say, which is regulated and proportioned according to the circumstances, station, or calling of individuals."

[4] "Comme aux Ephesiens il a vsé de ce mot, *Le mesme*, ou *Le semblable*, en ceste signification, comme il a este là touché;"—"As in the Ephesians he has made use of this word, *the same*, or *the like*, in this sense, as he has there noticed."

[5] "Comme il y a vn droict mutuel, reglé selon la consideration de l'office et vocation d'vn chacun, lequel droict doit auoir lieu entre tous estats;"— "As there is a mutual right, regulated according to a consideration of the office and calling of each individual, which right ought to have a place among all ranks."

[6] "Ou façon d'y proceder laschement, et comme par acquit;"—"Or a way of acting in it listlessly, and as a mere form."

contentedly whatever he gives. Thus a twofold *giving o thanks* is necessary. As to this point something has also been said in the Epistle to the Philippians. (Phil. iv. 6.)

3. *Pray also for us.* He does not say this by way of pretence, but because, being conscious to himself of his own necessity, he was earnestly desirous to be aided by their prayers, and was fully persuaded that they would be of advantage to them. Who then, in the present day, would dare to despise the intercessions of brethren, which Paul openly declares himself to stand in need of? And, unquestionably, it is not in vain that the Lord has appointed this exercise of love between us—that we pray for each other. Not only, therefore, ought each of us to pray for his brethren, but we ought also, on our part, diligently to seek help from the prayers of others, as often as occasion requires. It is, however, a childish[1] argument on the part of Papists, who infer from this, that the dead must be implored[2] to pray for us. For what is there here that bears any resemblance to this? Paul commends himself to the prayers of the brethren, with whom he knows that he has mutual fellowship according to the commandment of God: who will deny that this reason does not hold in the case of the dead? Leaving, therefore, such trifles, let us return to Paul.

As we have a signal example of modesty, in the circumstance that Paul calls others to his assistance, so we are also admonished, that it is a thing that is replete with the greatest difficulty, to persevere steadfastly in the defence of the gospel, and especially when danger presses. For it is not without cause that he desires that the Churches may assist him in this matter. Consider, too, at the same time, his amazing ardour of zeal. He is not solicitous as to his own safety;[3] he does not ask that prayers may be poured forth by the Churches on his behalf, that he may be delivered

[1] " Plus que puerile ;"—" Worse than childish."

[2] " Qu'il nous faut implorer l'aide des saincts trespassez ;"—" That we must implore the aid of departed saints."

[3] " Il ne se soucie point d'estre sauué des mains de ses ennemis ;"—" He does not feel anxiety to be saved from the hands of his enemies."

confession of the gospel; nay more, he fearlessly makes his own life a secondary matter, as compared with the glory of Christ and the spread of the gospel.

By a *door of utterance*, however, he simply means what, in Eph. vi. 19, he terms the *opening of the mouth*, and what Christ calls a *mouth and wisdom*. (Luke xxi. 15.) For the expression differs nothing from the other in meaning, but merely in form, for he here intimates, by an elegant metaphor, that it is in no degree easier for us to speak confidently respecting the gospel, than to break through a door that is barred and bolted. For this is truly a divine work, as Christ himself said, *It is not ye that speak, but the Spirit of your Father that speaketh in you.* (Matt. x. 20.) Having, therefore, set forward the difficulty, he stirs up the Colossians the more to prayer, by declaring that he cannot speak right, except in so far as his tongue is directed by the Lord. *Secondly*, he argues from the dignity[1] of the matter, when he calls the gospel the *mystery of Christ*. For we must labour in a more perfunctory manner in a matter of such importance. *Thirdly*, he makes mention also of his danger.

4. *As I ought.* This clause sets forth more strongly the difficulty, for he intimates that it is no ordinary matter. In the Epistle to the Ephesians, (Eph. vi. 20,) he adds, ἵνα παρρησιάσωμαι, (*that I may speak boldly,*) from which it appears that he desired for himself an undaunted confidence, such as befits the majesty of the gospel. Farther, as Paul here does nothing else than desire that grace may be given him for the discharge of his office, let us bear in mind that a rule is in like manner prescribed to us, not to give way to the fury of our adversaries, but to strive even to death in the publication of the gospel. As this, however, is beyond our power, it is necessary that we should *continue in prayer*, that the Lord may not leave us destitute of the spirit of confidence.

5. Walk in wisdom toward them that are without, redeeming the time.	5. Sapienter ambulate erga extraneos, tempus redimentes.
6. Let your speech *be* alway with grace, seasoned with salt, that ye	6. Sermo vester semper in gratia sit sale conditus: ut sciatis quomodo

[1] " La dignité et l'excellence;"—" The dignity and excellence.'

clare unto you, *who is* a beloved brother, and a faithful minister and fellow-servant in the Lord:	bis Tychicus dilectus frater et fidelis minister ac conservus in Domino.
8. Whom I have sent unto you for the same purpose, that he might know your estate, and comfort your hearts;	8. Quem misi ad vos hac de causa, ut sciretis statum meum, et consolaretur corda vestra:
9. With Onesimus, a faithful and beloved brother, who is *one* of you: they shall make known unto you all things which *are done* here.	9. Cum Onesimo fideli et dilecto fratre, qui est ex vobis. Omnia patefacient vobis quae hic sunt.

5. *Walk wisely.* He makes mention of *those that are without,* in contrast with those that are of the *household of faith.* (Gal. vi. 10.) For the Church is like a city of which all believers are the inhabitants, connected with each other by a mutual relationship, while unbelievers are strangers. But why would he have regard to be had to them, rather than to believers? There are three reasons: *first,* lest any *stumblingblock be put in the way of the blind,* (Lev. xix. 14,) for nothing is more ready to occur, than that unbelievers are driven from bad to worse through our imprudence, and their minds are wounded, so that they hold religion more and more in abhorrence. *Secondly,* it is lest any occasion may be given for detracting from the honour of the gospel, and thus the name of Christ be exposed to derision, persons be rendered more hostile, and disturbances and persecutions be stirred up. *Lastly,* it is lest, while we are mingled together, in partaking of food, and on other occasions, we be defiled by their pollutions, and by little and little become profane.

To the same effect, also, is what follows, *redeeming the time,* that is, because intercourse with them is dangerous. For in Eph. v. 16, he assigns the reason, *because the days are evil.* " Amidst so great a corruption as prevails in the world we must seize opportunities of doing good, and we must struggle against impediments." The more, therefore, that our path is blocked up with occasions of offence, so much the more carefully must we take heed lest our feet should stumble, or we should stop short through indolence.

6. *Your speech.* He requires suavity of speech, such as

impious, but also such as are worthless and idle. Hence he would have them *seasoned with salt.* Profane men have their seasonings of discourse,[1] but he does not speak of them; nay more, as witticisms are insinuating, and for the most part procure favour,[2] he indirectly prohibits believers from the practice and familiar use of them. For he reckons as tasteless everything that does not edify. The term *grace* is employed in the same sense, so as to be opposed to talkativeness, taunts, and all sorts of trifles which are either injurious or vain.[3]

That ye may know how. The man who has accustomed himself to caution in his communications will not fall into many absurdities, into which talkative and prating persons fall into from time to time, but, by constant practice, will acquire for himself expertness in making proper and suitable replies; as, on the other hand, it must necessarily happen, that silly talkers expose themselves to derision whenever they are interrogated as to anything; and in this they pay the just punishment of their silly talkativeness. Nor does he merely say *what,* but also *how,* and not to all indiscriminately, but to *every one.* For this is not the least important part of prudence—to have due regard to individuals.[4]

7. *My things.* That the Colossians may know what concern he has for them, he confirms them, by giving them, in a manner, a pledge. For although he was in prison, and was in danger of his life, making care for himself a secondary matter, he consults for their interests by sending Tychicus to them. In this the singular zeal, no less than

---

[1] *Sales.* The term is frequently employed by classical writers to denote *witticisms.* See *Cic.* Fam. ix. 15; *Juv.* ix. 11; *Hor.* Ep. ii. 2, 60.—*Ed.*

[2] "Et que par ce moyen il seroit a craindre que les fideles ne s'y addonnassent;"—"And as on this account it was to be feared that believers would addict themselves to this."

[3] "Ou s'en vont en fumee;"—"Or vanish into smoke."

[4] "Car c'est des principales parties de vraye prudence, de scauoir discerner les personnes pour parler aux vns et aux autres comme il est de besoin;"—"For it is one of the chief departments of true prudence, to know how to discriminate as to individuals, in speaking to one and to another, as there may be occasion."

imminent danger on account of the gospel, he, nevertheless, does not cease to employ himself in advancing the gospel, and takes care of all the Churches. Thus, the body, indeed, is under confinement, but the mind, anxious to employ itself in everything good, roams far and wide. His prudence shews itself in his sending a fit and prudent person to confirm them, as far as was necessary, and withstand the craftiness of the false apostles; and, farther, in his retaining Epaphras beside himself, until they should come to learn what and how great an agreement there was in doctrine among all true teachers, and might hear from Tychicus the same thing that they had previously learned from Epaphras. Let us carefully meditate on these examples, that they may stir us up to an imitation of the like pursuit.

He adds, *Onesimus*, that the embassy may have the more weight. It is, however, uncertain who this Onesimus was. For it can scarcely be believed that this is the slave of Philemon, inasmuch as the name of a thief and a fugitive would have been liable to reproach.[1] He distinguishes both of them by honourable titles, that they may do the more good, and especially Tychicus, who was to exercise the office of an instructor.

10. Aristarchus my fellow-prisoner saluteth you, and Marcus, sister's son to Barnabas; (touching whom ye received commandments: if he come unto you, receive him;)
11. And Jesus, which is called

10. Salutat vos Aristarchus, concaptivus meus, et Marcus, cognatus Barnabae, de quo accepistis mandata si venerit ad vos, ut suscipiatis ipsum.
11. Et Iesus qui dicitur Iustus,

---

[1] *Paley*, in his *Horae Paulinae*, finds the statement here made respecting Onesimus, "*who is one of you*," one of the many undesigned coincidences which he adduces in that admirable treatise, in evidence of the credibility of the New Testament. The train of his reasoning in this instance may be briefly stated thus—that while it appears from the Epistle to Philemon, that Onesimus was the servant or slave of Philemon, it is not stated in that Epistle to what city Philemon belonged; but that it appears from the Epistle, (Philem. 1, 2,) that he was of the same place, whatever that place was, with an eminent Christian, named Archippus, whom we find saluted by name amongst the Colossian Christians; while the expression made use of by Paul here respecting Onesimus, "*who is one of you*," clearly marks him out as being of the same city, viz., Colosse.—*Ed*.

12. Epaphras, who is *one* of you, a servant of Christ, saluteth you, always labouring fervently for you in prayers, that ye may stand perfect and complete in all the will of God.

13. For I bear him record, that he hath a great zeal for you, and them *that are* in Laodicea, and them in Hierapolis.

12. Salutat vos Epaphras, qui est ex vobis servus Christi, semper decertans pro vobis in precationibus, ut stetis perfecti et completi in omni voluntate Dei.

13. Testimonium enim illi reddo, quod multum studium vestri habeat, et eorum qui sunt Laodiceae et Hierapoli.

10. *Fellow-prisoner.* From this it appears that there were others that were associated with Paul,[1] after he was brought to Rome. It is also probable that his enemies exerted themselves, in the outset, to deter all pious persons from giving him help, by threatening them with the like danger, and that this for a time had the desired effect; but that afterwards some, gathering up courage, despised everything that was held out to them in the way of terror.

That ye receive him. Some manuscripts have *receive* in the imperative mood; but it is a mistake, for he expresses the nature of the *charge* which the Colossians had received—that it was a commendation of either Barnabas, or of Marcus. The latter is the more probable. In the Greek it is the infinitive mood,[2] but it may be rendered in the way I have done. Let us, however, observe, that they were careful in furnishing attestations, that they might distinguish good men from false brethren—from pretenders, from impostors, and multitudes of vagrants. The same care is more than simply necessary at the present day, both because good teachers are coldly received, and because credulous and foolish men lay themselves too open to be deceived by impostors.

11. *These only are fellow-workers,*—that is, of the circum-

---

[1] " D'autres furent mis prisonniers auec sainct Paul;"—" Some others were made prisoners along with St. Paul."

[2] " *Excipite* δἔξασθε, vel δἔξασθαι, *ut excipiatis,* si conjungas cum ἰλάβιτε, ut habet Syrus interpres, ut exprimatur quod fuerit illud mandatum;"—" *Receive ye,* δἔξασθε, or δἔξασθαι, *that ye may receive,* if you connect it with ἰλάβιτε, *(ye received,)* as the Syrian interpreter has it, so as to express what the charge was."—*Beza.—Ed.*

Jews at Rome who shewed themselves to be helpers to the gospel, nay more, that the whole nation was opposed to Christ. At the same time, by *workers* he means those only who were endowed with gifts that were necessary for promoting the gospel. But where was Peter at that time? Unquestionably, he has either been shamefully passed over here, and not without injustice, or else those speak falsely who maintain that he was then at Rome. Farther, he calls the gospel the *kingdom of God,* for it is the sceptre by which God reigns over us, and by means of it we are singled out to life eternal.[1] But of this form of expression we shall treat more fully elsewhere.

12. *Always striving.* Here we have an example of a good pastor, whom distance of place cannot induce to forget the Church, so as to prevent him from taking the care of it with him beyond the sea. We must notice, also, the strength of entreaty that is expressed in the word *striving.* For although the Apostle had it in view here to express intensity of affection, he at the same time admonishes the Colossians not to look upon the prayers of their pastor as useless, but, on the contrary, to reckon that they would afford them no small assistance. Lastly, let us infer from Paul's words, that the *perfection* of Christians is, when they *stand complete in the will of God,* that they may not suspend their scheme of life upon anything else.

14. Luke, the beloved physician, and Demas, greet you.	14. Salutat vos Lucas medicus dilectus, et Demas.
15. Salute the brethren which are in Laodicea, and Nymphas, and the church which is in his house.	15. Salutate fratres qui sunt Laodiceae, et Nympham, et Ecclesiam quae est domi ipsius;
16. And when this epistle is read among you, cause that it be read also in the church of the Laodiceans; and that ye likewise read the *epistle* from Laodicea.	16. Et quum lecta fuerit apud vos epistola, facite ut etiam in Laodicensium Ecclesia legatur: et eam quae ex Laodicea est ut vos legatis.
17. And say to Archippus, Take	17. Et dicite Archippo: Vide

---

[1] " Nous sommes receus a la vie eternelle;"—" We are received to life eternal."

18. The salutation by the hand of me Paul. Remember my bonds. Grace *be* with you. Amen.

¶ Written from Rome to the Colossians by Tychicus and Onesimus.

18. Salutatio, mea manu Pauli. Memores estote vinculorum meorum. Gratia vobiscum. AMEN.

Missa e Roma per Tychicum et Onesimum.

14. *Luke saluteth you.* I do not agree with those who understand this to be Luke the Evangelist; for I am of opinion that he was too well known to stand in need of such a designation, and he would have been signalized by a more magnificent eulogium. He would, undoubtedly, have called him his fellow-helper, or at least his companion and participant in his conflicts. I rather conjecture that he was absent at that time, and that it is another of the same name that is called a *physician,* to distinguish him from the other. *Demas,* of whom he makes mention, is undoubtedly the person of whom he complains—that he afterwards deserted him. (2 Tim. iv. 10.)

When he speaks of the Church which was in the house of Nymphas, let us bear in mind, that, in the instance of one household, a rule is laid down as to what it becomes all Christian households to be—that they be so many little Churches.[1] Let every one, therefore, know that this charge is laid upon him—that he is to train up his house in the fear of the Lord, to keep it under a holy discipline, and, in fine, to form in it the likeness of a Church.

16. *Let it be read in the Church of the Laodiceans.* Hence, though it was addressed to the Colossians, it was, nevertheless, necessary that it should be profitable to others. The same view must also be taken of all the Epistles. They were indeed, in the first instance, addressed to particular Churches, but, as they contain doctrine that is always in force, and is common to all ages, it is of no importance what title they bear, for the subject-matter belongs to us. It has been groundlessly supposed that the other Epistle of which he makes mention was written by Paul, and those labour under

[1] See CALVIN on the Corinthians, vol. ii. p. 78.

had been sent to Paul, the perusal of which might be profitable to the Colossians, as neighbouring towns have usually many things in common. There was, however, an exceedingly gross imposture in the circumstance that some worthless person, I know not who, had the audacity to forge, under this pretext, an Epistle that is so insipid,[1] that nothing can be conceived to be more foreign to Paul's spirit.

17. *Say to Archippus.* So far as I can conjecture, this Archippus was, in the mean time, discharging the office of pastor, during the absence of Epaphras ; but perhaps he was not of such a disposition as to be sufficiently diligent of himself without being stirred up. Paul, accordingly, would have him be more fully encouraged by the exhortation of the whole Church. He might have admonished him in his own name individually ; but he gives this charge to the Colossians that they may know that they must themselves employ incitements,[2] if they see their pastor cold, and the pastor himself does not refuse to be admonished by the Church. For the ministers of the word are endowed with signal authority, but such at the same time as is not exempt from laws. Hence, it is necessary that they should shew themselves teachable if they would duly teach others. As to Paul's calling attention again[3] to his *bonds,* he intimates by this that he was in no slight degree afflicted. For he was mindful of human infirmity, and without doubt he felt some twinges of it in himself, inasmuch as he was so very urgent that all pious persons should be mindful of his distresses. It is, however, no evidence of distrust, that he calls in from all quarters the helps that were appointed him by the Lord.

[1] " Contrefaire et mettre en auant vne lettre comme escrite par sainct Paul aux Laodiciens, voire si sotte et badine ;"—" To forge and put forward a letter as if written by St. Paul to the Laodiceans, and that too so foolish and silly."

[2] " Qu'eux-mesmes aussi doyuent faire des remonstrances et inciter leur pasteur ;"—" That they must themselves employ remonstrances and stir up their pastor."

[3] Paul had previously made mention of his *bonds,* in the 3d verse of the chapter.— *Ed.*

circulation, so that it was necessary to provide against imposition.[1]

[1] "Que des lors on faisoit courir des epistres a faux titre, et sous le nom des seruiteurs de Dieu : a laquelle meschancete il leur estoit force de remedier par quelque moyen;"—"That even then they put into circulation epistles under a false title, and in the name of the servants of God: to which wickedness he was under the necessity of employing a remedy by some means."

END OF THE COMMENTARY ON THE EPISTLE TO THE COLOSSIANS.

COMMENTARY

ON

THE FIRST EPISTLE TO THE THESSALONIANS.

THE AUTHOR'S DEDICATORY EPISTLE.

TO

MATURINUS CORDERIUS,

A MAN OF EMINENT PIETY AND LEARNING, PRINCIPAL OF THE COLLEGE OF LAUSANNE.

It is befitting that you should come in for a share in my labours, inasmuch as, under your auspices, having entered on a course of study, I made proficiency at least so far as to be prepared to profit in some degree the Church of God. When my father sent me, while yet a boy, to Paris, after I had simply tasted the first elements of the Latin tongue, Providence so ordered it that I had, for a short time, the privilege of having you as my instructor,[1] that I might be taught by you the true method of learning, in such a way that I might be prepared afterwards to make somewhat better proficiency. For, after presiding over the first class with the highest renown, on observing that pupils who had been ambitiously trained up by the other masters, produced nothing but mere show, nothing of solidity, so that they required to be formed by you anew, tired of this annoyance, you that year descended to the fourth class. This, indeed, was what you had in view, but to me it was a singular kindness on the part of God that I happened to have an auspicious commencement of such a course of training. And although I was permitted to have the use of it only for a short time, from the circumstance that we were soon afterwards advanced higher by an injudicious man, who regulated our studies according to his own pleasure, or rather his caprice, yet I derived so much assistance afterwards from your training, that it is with good reason that I acknowledge myself indebted to you for such progress as has since been made. And this I was desirous to testify to posterity, that, if any advantage shall accrue to them from my writings, they shall know that it has in some degree originated with you.

Geneva, 17th *February* 1550.

[1] See p. xvi.

ARGUMENT

ON

THE FIRST EPISTLE TO THE THESSALONIANS.

The greater part of this Epistle consists of exhortations. PAUL had instructed the THESSALONIANS in the right faith. On hearing, however, that persecutions were raging there,[1] he had sent Timothy with the view of animating them for the conflict, that they might not give way through fear, as human infirmity is apt to do. Having been afterwards informed by TIMOTHY respecting their entire condition, he employs various arguments to confirm them in steadfastness of faith, as well as in patience, should they be called to endure anything for the testimony of the gospel. These things he treats of in the *first three* Chapters.

In the beginning of the *Fourth* Chapter, he exhorts them, in general terms, to holiness of life, afterwards he recommends mutual benevolence, and all offices that flow from it. Towards the end, however, he touches upon the question of the resurrection, and explains in what way we shall all be raised up from death. From this it is manifest, that there were some wicked or light-minded persons, who endeavoured to unsettle their faith by unseasonably bringing forward many frivolous things.[2] Hence with the view of cutting off all pretext for foolish and needless disputations, he instructs them in few words as to the views which they should entertain.

In the *Fifth* Chapter he prohibits them, even more strictly, from inquiring as to *times;* but admonishes them to be ever on the watch, lest they should be taken unawares by Christ's sudden and unexpected approach. From this he proceeds to employ various exhortations, and then concludes the Epistle.

---

[1] " Ayant ouy qu'il y estoit suruenu des persecutions, et qu'elles continuoyent ;"—" Having heard that there were some persecutions that had broken out there, and that they were still continuing."

[2] " En mettant en auant sur ce propos beaucoup de choses frivoles et curieuses ;"—" By bringing forward upon this subject many frivolous and curious things."

COMMENTARY

ON

THE FIRST EPISTLE OF PAUL TO THE THESSALONIANS.

CHAPTER I.

1. Paul, and Silvanus, and Timotheus, unto the Church of the Thessalonians *which is* in God the Father, and *in* the Lord Jesus Christ: Grace *be* unto you, and peace, from God our Father, and the Lord Jesus Christ.

1. Paulus et Silvanus et Timotheus Ecclesiae Thessalonicensium, in Deo Patre, et Domino Iesu Christo, gratia vobis et pax a Deo Patre nostro, et Domino Iesu Christo.

THE brevity of the inscription clearly shews that PAUL'S doctrine had been received with reverence among the THESSALONIANS, and that without controversy they all rendered to him the honour that he deserved. For when in other Epistles he designates himself an Apostle, he does this for the purpose of claiming for himself authority. Hence the circumstance, that he simply makes use of his own name without any title of honour, is an evidence that those to whom he writes voluntarily acknowledged him to be such as he was. The ministers of Satan, it is true, had endeavoured to trouble this Church also, but it is evident that their machinations were fruitless. He associates, however, two others along with himself, as being, in common with himself, the authors of the Epistle. Nothing farther is stated here that has not been explained elsewhere, excepting that he says, " the Church *in God the Father, and in Christ ;*" by which terms (if I mistake not) he intimates, that there is truly among the Thessalonians a Church of God. This mark, therefore, is as it were an approval of a true and lawful Church. We may, however, at the same

short, there is no Church but what is founded upon God, is gathered under the auspices of Christ, and is united in his name.

2. We give thanks to God always for you all, making mention of you in our prayers;	2. Gratias agimus Deo semper de omnibus vobis, memoriam vestri facientes in precibus nostris,
3. Remembering without ceasing your work of faith, and labour of love, and patience of hope in our Lord Jesus Christ, in the sight of God and our Father;	3. Indesinenter[1] memores vestri, propter opus fidei, et laborem caritatis,[2] et patientiam spei Domini nostri Iesu Christi coram Deo et Patre nostro,
4. Knowing, brethren beloved, your election of God.	4. Scientes, fratres dilecti,[3] a Deo esse electionem vestram.
5. For our gospel came not unto you in word only, but also in power, and in the Holy Ghost, and in much assurance; as ye know what manner of men we were among you for your sake.	5. Quia Evangelium nostrum non fuit erga vos in sermone solum, sed in potentia, et in Spiritu sancto, et in certitudine multa: quemadmodum nostis quales fuerimus in vobis propter vos.

2. *We give thanks to God.* He praises, as he is wont, their faith and other virtues, not so much, however, for the purpose of praising them, as to exhort them to perseverance. For it is no small excitement to eagerness of pursuit, when we reflect that God has adorned us with signal endowments, that he may finish what he has begun, and that we have, under his guidance and direction, advanced in the right course, in order that we may reach the goal. For as a vain confidence in those virtues, which mankind foolishly arrogate to themselves, puffs them up with pride, and makes them careless and indolent for the time to come, so a recognition of the gifts of God humbles pious minds, and stirs them up to anxious concern. Hence, instead of congratula-

[1] " En nos prieres, sans cesse ayans souuenance; *ou*, En nos prieres sans cesse, Ayans souuenance;"—" In our prayers, without ceasing having remembrance; *or*, In our prayers without ceasing, Having remembrance."

[2] " De vous pour l'œuure de la foy, et pour le trauail de vostre charite; *ou*, de l'effect de vostre foy, et du trauail de vostre charite;"—" Of you for the work of faith, or for the labour of your love; *or*, of the effect of your faith, or of the labour of your love."

[3] " Freres bien-aimez, vostre election estre de Dieu; *ou*, freres bien-aimez de Dieu, vostre election; *ou*, vostre election, qui est de Dieu;"—" Brethren beloved, your election to be of God; *or*, brethren beloved of God, your election; *or*, your election, which is of God."

worthy of praise, is a kindness from God.[1] He also turns immediately to the future, in making mention of his *prayers.* We thus see for what purpose he commends their previous life.

3. *Unceasingly remembering you.* While the adverb *unceasingly* might be taken in connection with what goes before, it suits better to connect it in this manner. What follows might also be rendered in this way: *Remembering your work of faith and labour of love,* &c. Nor is it any objection to this that there is an article interposed between the pronoun ὑμῶν and the noun ἔργου,[2] for this manner of expression is frequently made use of by Paul. I state this, lest any one should charge the old translator with ignorance, from his rendering it in this manner.[3] As, however, it matters little as to the main point[4] which you may choose, I have retained the rendering of Erasmus.[5]

He assigns a reason, however, why he cherishes so strong an affection towards them, and prays diligently in their behalf—because he perceived in them those gifts of God which should stir him up to cherish towards them love and respect. And, unquestionably, the more that any one excels in piety and other excellences, so much the more ought we to hold him in regard and esteem. For what is more worthy of love than God? Hence there is nothing that should tend more to excite our love to individuals, than when the Lord manifests himself in them by the gifts of his Spirit. This is the highest commendation of all among the pious—this the most sacred bond of connection, by which they are more especially bound to each other. I have said, accordingly, that it

---

[1] "Est vn benefice procedant de la liberalite de Dieu;"—"Is a kindness proceeding from God's liberality."

[2] The words are ὑμῶν τοῦ ἔργου.—*Ed.*

[3] The rendering of the Vulgate is as follows: "*Sine intermissione memores operis fidei vestrae.*" Wiclif (1380) renders as follows: "With outen ceeysynge hauynge mynde of the werk of youre feithe." Cranmer, (1539,) on the other hand, renders thus: "And call you to remembraunce because of the worke of your fayth."—*Ed.*

[4] "Quant a la substance du propos;"—"As to the substance of the matter."

[5] The rendering of Erasmus is as follows: "Memores vestri propter opus fidei;"—"Mindful of you on account of your work of faith."

Work of faith I understand as meaning the *effect* of it. This *effect*, however, may be explained in two ways—*passively* or *actively*, either as meaning that faith was in itself a signal token of the power and efficacy of the Holy Spirit, inasmuch as he has wrought powerfully in the exciting of it, or as meaning that it afterwards produced outwardly its fruits. I reckon the effect to be in the root of faith rather than in its fruits.—" A rare energy of faith has shewn itself powerfully in you."

He adds *labour of love*, by which he means that in the cultivation of love they had grudged no trouble or labour. And, assuredly, it is known by experience, how laborious love is. That age, however, more especially afforded to believers a manifold sphere of labour, if they were desirous to discharge the offices of love. The Church was marvellously pressed down by a great multitude of afflictions :[1] many were stript of their wealth, many were fugitives from their country, many were thrown destitute of counsel, many were tender and weak.[2] The condition of almost all was involved. So many cases of distress did not allow *love* to be inactive.

To *hope* he assigns *patience*, as it is always conjoined with it, for *what we hope for, we in patience wait for*, (Rom. viii. 24,) and the statement should be explained to mean, that Paul remembers their patience in hoping for the coming of Christ. From this we may gather a brief definition of true Christianity—that it is a faith that is lively and full of vigour, so that it spares no labour, when assistance is to be given to one's neighbours, but, on the contrary, all the pious employ themselves diligently in offices of love, and lay out their efforts in them, so that, intent upon the hope of the manifestation of Christ, they despise everything else, and, armed with patience, they rise superior to the wearisomeness of length of time, as well as to all the temptations of the world.

[1] " D'afflictions quasi sans nombre ;"—" By afflictions, as it were, without number."
[2] " Foibles et debiles en la foy ;"—" Weak and feeble in faith."

immediately before. I explain it in this way. As he had spoken of his *prayers*, he declares that as often as he raises his thoughts to the kingdom of God, he, at the same time, recalls to his remembrance the *faith, hope,* and *patience,* of the Thessalonians, but as all mere pretence must vanish when persons come into the presence of God, this is added,[1] in order that the affirmation may have more weight. Farther, by this declaration of his good-will towards them he designed to make them more teachable and prepared to listen.[2]

4. *Knowing, brethren beloved.* The participle *knowing* may apply to Paul as well as to the Thessalonians. Erasmus refers it to the Thessalonians. I prefer to follow Chrysostom, who understands it of Paul and his colleagues, for it is (as it appears to me) a more ample confirmation of the foregoing statement. For it tended in no small degree to recommend them—that God himself had testified by many tokens, that they were acceptable and dear to him.

Election of God. I am not altogether dissatisfied with the interpretation given by Chrysostom—that God had made the Thessalonians illustrious, and had established their excellence. Paul, however, had it in view to express something farther; for he touches upon their calling, and as there had appeared in it no common marks of God's power, he infers from this that they had been specially called with evidences of a sure *election.* For the reason is immediately added —that it was not a bare preaching that had been brought to them, but such as was conjoined with the efficacy of the Holy Spirit, that it might obtain entire credit among them.

When he says, *in power, and in the Holy Spirit*, it is, in my opinion, as if he had said—in the power *of* the Holy Spirit, so that the latter term is added as explanatory of the former. *Assurance,* to which he assigned the third place, was

---

[1] " Ce poinct a nommeement este adiouste par Sainct Paul;"—" This point has been expressly added by St. Paul."

[2] " Car ce n'estoit vne petite consideration pour inciter St. Paul et les autres, a auoir les Thessaloniciens pour recommandez, et en faire esteme;"—" For it was no slight motive to induce St. Paul and others to hold the Thessalonians in estimation, and to regard them with esteem."

is, that Paul's gospel had been confirmed by solid proofs,[1] as though God had shewn from heaven that he had ratified their calling.[2] When, however, Paul brings forward the proofs by which he had felt assured that the calling of the Thessalonians was altogether from God, he takes occasion at the same time to recommend his ministry, that they may themselves, also, recognise him and his colleagues as having been raised up by God.

By the term *power* some understand miracles. I extend it farther, as referring to spiritual energy of doctrine. For, as we had occasion to see in the First Epistle to the Corinthians, Paul places it in contrast with *speech*[3]—the voice of God, as it were, living and conjoined with effect, as opposed to an empty and dead eloquence of men. It is to be observed, however, that the election of God, which is in itself hid, is manifested by its marks—when he gathers to himself the lost sheep and joins them to his flock, and holds out his hand to those that were wandering and estranged from him. Hence a knowledge of our election must be sought from this source. As, however, the secret counsel of God is a labyrinth to those who disregard his calling, so those act perversely who, under pretext of *faith* and *calling*, darken this first grace, from which faith itself flows. "By faith," say they, "we obtain salvation: there is, therefore, no eternal predestination of God that distinguishes between us and reprobates." It is as though they said— " Salvation is of faith: there is, therefore, no grace of God that illuminates us in faith." Nay rather, as gratuitous election must be conjoined with calling, as with its effect, so it must necessarily, in the mean time, hold the first place. It matters little as to the sense, whether you connect ὑπὸ with the participle *beloved* or with the term *election*.[4]

[1] " A là este comme seellé et ratifié par bons tesmoignages et approbations suffisantes;"—" Had been there, as it were, sealed and ratified by good testimonies and sufficient attestations."
[2] " Et en estoit l'autheur;"—" And was the author of it."
[3] See CALVIN on the Corinthians, vol. i. pp. 100, 101.
[4] " Au reste, les mots de ceste sentence sont ainsi couchez au texte

siderations, may entertain no doubt that they were elected by God. For it had been the design of God, in honouring Paul's ministry, that he might manifest to them their adoption. Accordingly, having said that they *know what manner of persons they had been*,[1] he immediately adds that he was such *for their sake*, by which he means that all this had been given them, in order that they might be fully persuaded that they were loved by God, and that their election was beyond all controversy.

6. And ye became followers of us, and of the Lord, having received the word in much affliction, with joy of the Holy Ghost:	6. Et vos imitatores nostri facti estis et Domini, dum sermonem amplexi estis in tribulatione multa, cum gaudio Spiritus sancti :
7. So that ye were ensamples to all that believe in Macedonia and Achaia.	7. Ita ut fueritis exemplaria omnibus credentibus in Macedonia et in Achaia.
8. For from you sounded out the word of the Lord not only in Macedonia and Achaia, but also in every place your faith to God-ward is spread abroad ; so that we need not to speak any thing.	8. A vobis enim personuit sermo Domini : nec in Macedonia tantum et in Achaia, sed etiam in omni loco, fides vestra quae in Deum est manavit : ita ut non opus habeamus quicquam loqui.

6. *And ye became imitators.* With the view of increasing their alacrity, he declares that there is a mutual agreement, and harmony, as it were, between his preaching and their faith. For unless men, on their part, answer to God, no proficiency will follow from the grace that is offered to them—not as though they could do this of themselves, but inasmuch as God, as he begins our salvation by calling us, perfects it also by fashioning our hearts to obedience. The sum, therefore, is this—that an evidence of Divine election

Grec de Sainct Paul, Sçachans freres bien-aimez de Dieu, vostre election : tellement que ce mot *de Dieu*, peut estre rapporté a deux endroits, ascauoir Bien-aimez de Dieu, ou vostre election estre de Dieu : mais c'est tout vn comment on le prene quant au sens ;"—" Farther, the words of this sentence are thus placed in the Greek text of St. Paul; knowing, brethren beloved of God, your election : in such a way, that this phrase *of God* may be taken as referring to two things, as meaning beloved of God, or, your election to be of God; but it is all one as to the sense in what way you take it."

[1] " Quels auoyent este St. Paul et ses compagnons ;"—" What manner of persons St. Paul and his associates had been."

faith of the Thessalonians, so that this conformity is a powerful attestation of it. He says, however, "Ye were imitators *of God and of us,*" in the same sense in which it is said, that *the people believed God and his servant Moses,* (Exod. xiv. 13,) not as though Paul and Moses had anything different from God, but because he wrought powerfully by them, as his ministers and instruments.[1] *While ye embraced.* Their readiness in receiving the gospel is called an *imitation* of God, for this reason, that as God had presented himself to the Thessalonians in a liberal spirit, so they had, on their part, voluntarily come forward to meet him.

He says, *with the joy of the Holy Spirit,* that we may know that it is not by the instigation of the flesh, or by the promptings of their own nature, that men will be ready and eager to obey God, but that this is the work of God's Spirit. The circumstance, that *amidst much tribulation* they had embraced the gospel, serves by way of amplification. For we see very many, not otherwise disinclined to the gospel, who, nevertheless, avoid it, from being intimidated through fear of the cross. Those, accordingly, who do not hesitate with intrepidity to embrace along with the gospel the afflictions that threaten them, furnish in this an admirable example of magnanimity. And from this it is so much the more clearly apparent, how necessary it is that the Spirit should aid us in this. For the gospel cannot be properly, or sincerely received, unless it be with ·a joyful heart. Nothing, however, is more at variance with our natural disposition, than to rejoice in afflictions.

7. *So that ye were.* Here we have another amplification—that they had stirred up even believers by their example; for it is a great thing to get so decidedly the start of those who had entered upon the course before us, as to furnish assistance to them for prosecuting their course. *Typus* (the word made use of by Paul) is employed by the Greeks in the same sense as *Exemplar* is among the Latins, and *Patron* among the French. He says, then, that the courage of the

[1] See CALVIN on the Corinthians, vol. ii. p. 288.

however, to render it *patterns*, that I might not needlessly make any change upon the Greek phrase made use of by Paul; and farther, because the plural number expresses, in my opinion, something more than if he had said that that Church as a body had been set forward for imitation, for the meaning is, that there were as many *patterns* as there were individuals.

8. *For from you sounded forth.* Here we have an elegant metaphor, by which he intimates that their faith was so lively,[1] that it did, as it were, by its *sound*, arouse other nations. For he says that the word of God *sounded forth* from them, inasmuch as their faith was *sonorous*[2] for procuring credit for the gospel. He says that this had not only occurred in neighbouring places, but this *sound* had also extended far and wide, and had been distinctly heard, so that the matter did not require to be published by him.[3]

9. For they themselves shew of us what manner of entering in we had unto you, and how ye turned to God from idols, to serve the living and true God,	9. Ipsi enim de vobis annuntiant, qualem habuerimus ingressum ad vos: et quomodo conversi fueritis ad Deum ab idolis, ut serviretis Deo viventi et vero:
10. And to wait for his Son from heaven, whom he raised from the dead, *even* Jesus, which delivered us from the wrath to come.	10. Et exspectaretis e cœlis Filium eius, quem excitavit a mortuis, Iesum qui nos liberat ab ira ventura.

He says that the report of their conversion had obtained great renown everywhere. What he mentions as to his *entering in among them,* refers to that power of the Spirit, by which God had signalized his gospel.[4] He says, however, that both things are freely reported among other nations, as things worthy of being made mention of. In the detail which follows, he shews, first, what the condition of mankind is,

[1] "Si viue et vertueuse;"—"So lively and virtuous."
[2] "Auoit resonné haut et clair;"—"Had resounded loud and clear."
[3] "Tellement que la chose n'ha point besoin d'estre par luy diuulgee et magnifiee d'auantage;"—"So that the matter does not need to be farther published and extolled by him."
[4] "Par laquelle Dieu auoit orné et magnifiquement authorizé son Euangile;"—"By which God had adorned and magnificently attested his gospel."

what is the fruit of the gospel. For although all do not worship idols, all are nevertheless addicted to idolatry, and are immersed in blindness and madness. Hence, it is owing to the kindness of God, that we are exempted from the impostures of the devil, and every kind of superstition. Some, indeed, he converts earlier, others later, but as alienation is common to all, it is necessary that we be converted to God, before we can serve God. From this, also, we gather the essence and nature of true faith, inasmuch as no one gives due credit to God but the man, who renouncing the vanity of his own understanding, embraces and receives the pure worship of God.

9. *To the living God.* This is the end of genuine conversion. We see, indeed, that many leave off superstitions, who, nevertheless, after taking this step, are so far from making progress in piety, that they fall into what is worse. For having thrown off all regard to God, they give themselves up to a profane and brutal contempt.[1] Thus, in ancient times, the superstitions of the vulgar were derided by Epicurus, Diogenes the Cynic, and the like, but in such a way that they mixed up the worship of God so as to make no difference between it and absurd trifles. Hence we must take care, lest the pulling down of errors be followed by the overthrow of the building of faith. Farther, the Apostle, in ascribing to God the epithets *true* and *living*, indirectly censures idols as being dead and worthless inventions, and as being falsely called gods. He makes the end of conversion to be what I have noticed—that they might *serve God.* Hence the doctrine of the gospel tends to this, that it may induce us to serve and obey God. For so long as we are the *servants of sin*, we are *free from righteousness*, (Rom. vi. 20,) inasmuch as we sport ourselves, and wander up and down, exempt from any yoke. No one, therefore, is properly converted to God, but the man who has learned to place himself wholly under subjection to him.

As, however, it is a thing that is more than simply diffi-

[1] " De toute religion ;"—" Of all religion."

fear of God and obedience to him—*waiting for Christ.* For unless we are stirred up to the hope of eternal life, the world will quickly draw us to itself. For as it is only confidence in the Divine goodness that induces us to serve God, so it is only the expectation of final redemption that keeps us from giving way.[1] Let every one, therefore, that would persevere in a course of holy life, apply his whole mind to an expectation of Christ's coming. It is also worthy of notice, that he uses the expression *waiting for Christ,* instead of the hope of everlasting salvation. For, unquestionably, without Christ we are ruined and thrown into despair, but when Christ shews himself, life and prosperity do at the same time shine forth upon us.[2] Let us bear in mind, however, that this is said to believers exclusively, for as for the wicked, as he will come to be their Judge, so they can do nothing but tremble in looking for him.

This is what he afterwards subjoins—that Christ *delivereth us from the wrath to come.* For this is felt by none but those who, being reconciled to God by faith, have conscience already pacified; otherwise,[3] his name is dreadful. Christ, it is true, delivered us by his death from the anger of God, but the import of that deliverance will become apparent on the last day.[4] This statement, however, consists of two departments. The *first* is, that the wrath of God and everlasting destruction are impending over the human race, inasmuch as *all have sinned, and come short of the glory of God.* (Rom. iii. 23.) The *second* is, that there is no way of escape but through the grace of Christ; for it is not without good grounds that Paul assigns to him this office. It is, however, an inestimable gift, that the pious, whenever mention is made of judgment, know that Christ will come as a Redeemer to them.

[1] " Que ne nous lassions et perdions courage;"—" That we do not give way and lose heart."
[2] " Jettent sur nous leurs rayons;"—" Cast upon us their rays."
[3] " Aux autres;"—" To others."
[4] " Mais au dernier iour sera veu a l'œil le fruit de ceste deliurance, et de quelle importance elle est;"—" But on the last day will be visible to the eye the fruit of that deliverance, and of what importance it is."

fail from looking at the present life. For as faith is a *looking at things that do not appear,* (Heb. xi. 1,) nothing is less befitting than that we should estimate the wrath of God, according as any one is afflicted in the world; as nothing is more absurd than to take hold of the transient blessings which we enjoy, that we may from them form an estimate of God's favour. While, therefore, on the one hand, the wicked sport themselves at their ease, and we, on the other hand, languish in misery, let us learn to fear the vengeance of God, which is hid from the eyes of flesh, and take our satisfaction in the secret delights of the spiritual life.[1]

10. *Whom he raised up.* He makes mention here of Christ's resurrection, on which the hope of our resurrection is founded, for death everywhere besets us. Hence, unless we learn to look to Christ, our minds will give way at every turn. By the same consideration, he admonishes them that Christ is to be *waited for from heaven,* because we will find nothing in the world to bear us up,[2] while there are innumerable trials to overwhelm us. Another circumstance must be noticed;[3] for as Christ rose for this end—that he might make us all at length, as being his members, partakers of the same glory with himself, Paul intimates that his resurrection would be vain, unless he again appeared as their Redeemer, and extended to the whole body of the Church the fruit and effect of that power which he manifested in himself.[4]

CHAPTER II.

1. For yourselves, brethren, know our entrance in unto you, that it was not in vain:

1. Ipsi enim nostis, fratres, quod ingressus noster ad vos non inanis fuerit:

---

[1] " En delices et plaisirs de la vie spirituelle, lesquels nous ne voyons point;"—" In the delights and pleasures of the spiritual life, which we do not see."

[2] " Et faire demeurer fermes;"—" And make us remain firm."

[3] " A laquelle ceci se rapporte;"—" To what this refers."

[4] " Laquelle il a vne fois monstree en sa personne;"—" Which he once shewed in his own person."

we were bold in our God to speak unto you the gospel of God with much contention.	proferendi apud vos evangelium Dei, cum multo certamine.
3. For our exhortation *was* not of deceit, nor of uncleanness, nor in guile:	3. Nam exhortatio nostra, non ex impostura, neque ex immunditia, neque in dolo:
4. But as we were allowed of God to be put in trust with the gospel, even so we speak; not as pleasing men, but God, which trieth our hearts.	4. Sed quemadmodum probati fuimus a Deo, ut crederetur nobis evangelium, sic loquimur, non quasi hominibus placentes, sed Deo qui probat corda nostra.

He now, leaving out of view the testimony of other Churches, reminds the Thessalonians of what they had themselves experienced,[1] and explains at large in what way he, and in like manner the two others, his associates, had conducted themselves among them, inasmuch as this was of the greatest importance for confirming their faith. For it is with this view that he declares his integrity—that the Thessalonians may perceive that they had been called to the faith, not so much by a mortal man, as by God himself. He says, therefore, that his *entering in unto them had not been vain*, as ambitious persons manifest much show, while they have nothing of solidity; for he employs the word *vain* here as contrasted with *efficacious*.

He proves this by *two* arguments. The *first* is, that he had suffered persecution and ignominy at Philippi; the *second* is, that there was a great conflict prepared at Thessalonica. We know that the minds of men are weakened, nay, are altogether broken down by means of ignominy and persecutions. It was therefore an evidence of a Divine work that Paul, after having been subjected to evils of various kinds and to ignominy, did, as if in a perfectly sound state, shew no hesitation in making an attempt upon a large and opulent city, with the view of subjecting the inhabitants of it to Christ. In this *entering in*, nothing is seen that savours of vain ostentation. In the *second* department the same Divine power is beheld, for he does not discharge his duty with applause and favour, but required to maintain a keen conflict. In the

[1] " Veuës et esprouuez;"—" Seen and experienced."

what he means when he says that he was *emboldened*. And, unquestionably, if all these circumstances are carefully considered, it cannot be denied that God there magnificently displayed his power. As to the history, it is to be found in the sixteenth and seventeenth chapters of the Acts.

3. *For our exhortation.* He confirms, by another argument, the Thessalonians in the faith which they had embraced—inasmuch as they had been faithfully and purely instructed in the word of the Lord, for he maintains that his doctrine was free from all deception and uncleanness. And with the view of placing this matter beyond all doubt, he calls their conscience to witness. The three terms which he makes use of may, it would seem, be distinguished in this manner: *imposture* may refer to the substance of doctrine, *uncleanness* to the affections of the heart, *guile* to the manner of acting. In the *first* place, therefore, he says that they had not been deluded or imposed upon by fallacies, when they embraced the kind of doctrine that had been delivered to them by him. *Secondly*, he declares his integrity, inasmuch as he had not come to them under the influence of any impure desire, but actuated solely by upright disposition. *Thirdly*, he says that he had done nothing fraudulently or maliciously, but had, on the contrary, manifested a simplicity befitting a minister of Christ. As these things were well known to the Thessalonians, they had a sufficiently firm foundation for their faith.

4. *As we have been approved.* He goes even a step higher, for he appeals to God as the Author of his apostleship, and he reasons in this manner: "God, when he assigned me this office, bore witness to me as a faithful servant; there is no reason, therefore, why men should have doubts as to my fidelity, which they know to have been *approved of by God.* Paul, however, does not glory in having been *approved of,* as though he were such of himself; for he does not dispute here as to what he had by nature, nor does he place his own power in collision with the grace of God, but simply says

[1] " Soustenu et fortifié;"—" Sustained and strengthened."

he has formed for himself according to his own pleasure.

Not as pleasing men. What is meant by *pleasing men* has been explained in the Epistle to the Galatians, (Gal. i. 10,) and this passage, also, shews it admirably. For Paul contrasts *pleasing* MEN, and *pleasing* GOD, as things that are opposed to each other. Farther, when he says—*God, who trieth our hearts,* he intimates, that those who endeavour to obtain the favour of men, are not influenced by an upright conscience, and do nothing from the heart. Let us know, therefore, that true ministers of the gospel ought to make it their aim to devote to God their endeavours, and to do it from the heart, not from any outward regard to the world, but because conscience tells them that it is right and proper. Thus it will be secured that they will not make it their aim to *please men,* that is, that they will not act under the influence of ambition, with a view to the favour of men.

5. For neither at any time used we flattering words, as ye know, nor a cloak of covetousness; God *is* witness:

6. Nor of men sought we glory, neither of you, nor *yet* of others, when we might have been burdensome, as the apostles of Christ.

7. But we were gentle among you, even as a nurse cherisheth her children:

8. So, being affectionately desirous of you, we were willing to have imparted unto you, not the gospel of God only, but also our own souls, because ye were dear unto us.

5. Neque enim unquam in sermone adulationis fuimus, quemadmodum nostis, neque in occasione avaritiae: Deus testis.

6. Nec quaesivimus ab hominibus gloriam, neque a vobis, neque ab aliis.

7. Quum possemus in pondere esse tanquam Christi Apostoli, facti tamen sumus mites in medio vestri, perinde acsi nutrix aleret filios suos.

8. Ita erga vos affecti, libenter voluissemus distribuere vobis non solum Evangelium Dei, sed nostras ipsorum animas, propterea quod cari nobis facti estis.

5. *For neither have we ever.* It is not without good reason that he repeats it so frequently, that the Thessalonians knew that what he states is true. For there is not a surer attestation, than the experience of those with whom we speak. And this was of the greatest importance to them, because Paul relates with what integrity he had conducted himself, with no other intention, than that his doctrine may have

that is desirous to *please men,* must of necessity stoop shamefully to flattery, while he that is intent upon duty with an earnest and upright disposition, will keep at a distance from all appearance of flattery.

When he adds, *nor for an occasion of covetousness,* he means that he had not, in teaching among them, been in quest of anything in the way of personal gain. Πρόφασις is employed by the Greeks to mean both *occasion* and *pretext,* but the former signification suits better with the passage, so as to be, as it were, a trap.[1] "I have not abused the gospel so as to make it an occasion of catching at gain." As, however, the malice of men has so many winding retreats, that avarice and ambition frequently lie concealed, he on this account calls God to witness. Now, he makes mention here of two vices, from which he declares himself to be exempt, and, in doing so, teaches that the servants of Christ should stand aloof from them. Thus, if we would distinguish the genuine servants of Christ from those that are pretended and spurious, they must be tried according to this rule, and every one that would serve Christ aright must also conform his aims and his actions to the same rule. For where avarice and ambition reign, innumerable corruptions follow, and the whole man passes away into vanity, for these are the two sources from which the corruption of the whole ministry takes its rise.

7. *When we might have exercised authority.* Some interpret it—*when we might have been burdensome,* that is, might have loaded you with expense, but the connection requires that τὸ βαρὺ should be taken to mean *authority.* For Paul says that he was so far removed from vain pomp, from boasting, from arrogance, that he even waived his just claim, so far as the maintenance of authority was concerned. For inasmuch as he was an Apostle of Christ, he deserved to be received with a higher degree of respect, but he had refrained

[1] "Tellement que ce soit vne ruse ou finesse, semblable a celle de ceux qui tendent les filets pour prendre les oiseaux;"—"So that it is a trick or artifice, similar to that of those who set traps for catching birds."

removed he was from haughtiness.²

What we have rendered *mild,* the old translator renders *Fuimus parvuli, (we have been little,)*³ but the reading which I have followed is more generally received among the Greeks; but whichever you may take, there can be no doubt that he makes mention of his voluntary abasement.⁴

As if a nurse. In this comparison he takes in two points that he had touched upon—that he had sought neither glory nor gain among the Thessalonians. For a mother in nursing her infant shews nothing of power or dignity. Paul says that he was such, inasmuch as he voluntarily refrained from claiming the honour that was due to him, and with calmness and modesty stooped to every kind of office. *Secondly,* a mother in nursing her children manifests a certain rare and wonderful affection, inasmuch as she spares no labour and trouble, shuns no anxiety, is wearied out by no assiduity, and even with cheerfulness of spirit gives her own blood to be sucked. In the same way, Paul declares that he was so disposed towards the Thessalonians, that he was prepared to lay out his life for their benefit. This, assuredly, was not the conduct of a man that was sordid or avaricious, but of one that exercised a disinterested affection, and he expresses this in the close—*because ye were dear unto us.* In the mean time, we must bear in mind, that all that would be ranked among true pastors must exercise this disposition of Paul—to have more regard to the welfare of the Church than to their own life, and not be impelled to duty by a regard to their own advantage, but by a sincere love to those to whom they know that they are conjoined, and laid under obligation.⁵

¹ " De toute apparence de preeminence et maieste ;"—" From all appearance of preeminence and majesty."
² " De toute hautesse et presomption ;"—" From all haughtiness and presumption."
³ The rendering of Wicliff (1380) is, as usual, in accordance with the Vulgate—" we weren made litil."—*Ed.*
⁴ " Abaissement et humilite ;"—" Abasement and humility."
⁵ " Pour vne vraye amour et non feinte qu'ils portent a ceux, ausquels ils scauent que Dieu les a conionts et liez ou obligez ;"—" From a true

not be chargeable unto any of you, we preached unto you the gospel of God.

10. Ye *are* witnesses, and God *also*, how holily, and justly, and unblameably, we behaved ourselves among you that believe:

11. As ye know how we exhorted and comforted, and charged every one of you, (as a father *doth* his children,)

12. That ye would walk worthy of God, who hath called you unto his kingdom and glory.

10. Vos testes estis et Deus, ut sancte, et iuste, et sine querela vobis, qui creditis, fuerimus.

11. Quemadmodum nostis, ut unumquemque vestrum, quasi pater suos liberos,

12. Exhortati simus, et monuerimus et obtestati simus, ut ambularetis digne Deo, qui vocavit vos in suum regnum et gloriam.

varemus quenquam vestrum, praedicavimus apud vos Evangelium Dei.

9. *For ye remember.* These things tend to confirm what he had stated previously—that to spare them he did not spare himself. He must assuredly have burned with a wonderful and more than human zeal, inasmuch as, along with the labour of teaching, he labours with his hand as an operative, with the view of earning a livelihood, and in this respect, also, refrained from exercising his right. For it is the law of Christ, as he also teaches elsewhere, (1 Cor. ix. 14,) that every church furnish its ministers with food and other necessaries. Paul, therefore, in laying no burden upon the Thessalonians, does something more than could, from the requirements of his office, have been required from him. In addition to this, he does not merely refrain from incurring public expense, but avoids burdening any one individually. Farther, there can be no doubt, that he was influenced by some good and special consideration in thus refraining from exercising his right,[1] for in other churches he exercised, equally with others, the liberty allowed him.[2] He received nothing from the Corinthians, lest he should give the false apostles a handle for glorying as to this matter. In the mean time, he did not hesitate to ask[3] from other churches, what was needed by him, for he writes that, while and unfeigned love which they bear to those, to whom they know that God has conjoined, and tied, or bound them."

[1] "Entre les Thessaloniciens;"—" Among the Thessalonians."

[2] "La liberte que Dieu donne;"—" The liberty that God gives."

[3] "Il n'a point fait de conscience de prendre lors des autres Eglises;"—" He made no scruple to take at that time from other Churches."

Hence, although the reason is not expressed here, we may, nevertheless, conjecture that the ground on which Paul was unwilling that his necessities should be ministered to, was—lest such a thing should put any hinderance in the way of the gospel. For this, also, ought to be matter of concern to good pastors—that they may not merely run with alacrity in their ministry, but may, so far as is in their power, remove all hinderances in the way of their course.

10. *Ye are witnesses.* He again calls God and them to witness, with the view of affirming his integrity, and cites, on the one hand, God as a witness of his conscience, and them,[2] on the other hand, as witnesses of what they had known by experience. *How holily,* says he, *and justly,* that is, with how sincere a fear of God, and with what fidelity and blamelessness towards men; and thirdly, *unreproachably,* by which he means that he had given no occasion of complaint or obloquy. For the servants of Christ cannot avoid calumnies, and unfavourable reports; for being hated by the world, they must of necessity be evil-spoken of among the wicked. Hence he restricts this to *believers,* who judge uprightly and sincerely, and do not revile malignantly and groundlessly.

11. *Every one as a father.* He insists more especially on those things which belong to his office. He has compared himself to a *nurse :* he now compares himself to a *father.* What he means is this—that he was concerned in regard to them, just as a *father* is wont to be as to his sons, and that he had exercised a truly paternal care in instructing and admonishing them. And, unquestionably, no one will ever be a good pastor, unless he shews himself to be a *father* to the Church that is committed to him. Nor does he merely declare himself to be such to the entire body,[3] but even to the individual members. For it is not enough that a pastor in the pulpit teach all in common, if he does not add also

[1] See CALVIN on the Corinthians, vol. ii. p. 347.
[2] " Les Thessaloniciens ;"—" The Thessalonians."
[3] " Tout le corps de ceste Eglise-la ;"—" The whole body of the Church there."

clares himself to be *free from the blood of all men,* because he did not cease to admonish all publicly, and also individually in private in their own houses. For instruction given in common is sometimes of little service, and some cannot be corrected or cured without particular medicine.

12. *Exhorted.* He shews with what earnestness he devoted himself to their welfare, for he relates that in preaching to them respecting piety towards God and the duties of the Christian life, it had not been merely in a perfunctory way,[1] but he says that he had made use of exhortations and *adjurations.* It is a lively preaching of the gospel, when persons are not merely told what is right, but are *pricked* (Acts ii. 37) by exhortations, and are called to the judgment-seat of God, that they may not fall asleep in their vices, for this is what is properly meant by *adjuring.* But if pious men, whose promptitude Paul so highly commends, stood in absolute need of being stimulated by stirring exhortations, nay, *adjurations,* what must be done with us, in whom sluggishness[2] of the flesh does more reign? In the mean time, as to the wicked, whose obstinacy is incurable, it is necessary to denounce upon them the horrible vengeance of God, not so much from hope of success, as in order that they may be rendered inexcusable.

Some render the participle παραμυθουμένοι, *comforted.* If we adopt this rendering, he means that he made use of consolations in dealing with the afflicted, who need to be sustained by the grace of God, and refreshed by tasting of heavenly blessings,[3] that they may not lose heart or become impatient. The other meaning, however, is more suitable to the context, that he *admonished;* for the three verbs, it is manifest, refer to the same thing.

[1] " Il n'y a point este par acquit, comme on dit ;"—" It had not been in the mere performance of a task, as they say."
[2] " La paresse et nonchalance de la chair ;"—" Indolence and negligence of the flesh."
[3] " Fortifiez ou soulagez en leur rafrechissant le goust des biens celestes ;" —" Strengthened or comforted in the way of refreshing their taste with heavenly blessings."

mercy of God, he admonished them not to fail as to their calling. His commendation of the grace of God is contained in the expression, *who hath called us into his kingdom.* For as our salvation is founded upon God's gracious adoption, every blessing that Christ has brought us is comprehended in this one term. It now remains that we answer God's call, that is, that we shew ourselves to be such children to him as he is a Father to us. For he who lives otherwise than as becomes a child of God, deserves to be cut off from God's household.

13. For this cause also thank we God without ceasing, because, when ye received the word of God which ye heard of us, ye received *it* not *as* the word of men, but (as it is in truth) the word of God, which effectually worketh also in you that believe.

14. For ye, brethren, became followers of the churches of God which in Judea are in Christ Jesus: for ye also have suffered like things of your own countrymen, even as they *have* of the Jews;

15. Who both killed the Lord Jesus and their own prophets, and have persecuted us; and they please not God, and are contrary to all men;

16. Forbidding us to speak to the Gentiles, that they might be saved, to fill up their sins alway: for the wrath is come upon them to the uttermost.

13. Quapropter nos quoque indesinenter gratias agimus Deo, quod, quum sermonem Dei praedicatum a nobis percepistis, amplexi estis, non ut sermonem hominum, sed quemadmodum revera est, sermonem Dei: qui etiam efficaciter agit in vobis credentibus.

14. Vos enim imitatores facti estis, fratres, Ecclesiarum Dei, quae sunt in Iudaea in Christo Iesu: quia eadem passi estis et vos a propriis tribulibus, quemadmodum et ipsi a Iudaeis,

15. Qui Dominum Iesum occiderunt, et proprios Prophetas, et nos persequuti sunt, et Deo non placent, et cunctis hominibus adversi sunt:

16. Qui obsistunt ne Gentibus loquamur, ut salvae fiant, ut compleantur eorum peccata semper: pervenit enim in eos ira usque in finem.

13. *Wherefore we give thanks.* Having spoken of his ministry, he returns again to address the Thessalonians, that he may always commend that mutual harmony of which he has previously made mention.[1] He says, therefore, that he gives thanks to God, because they had embraced *the word of God which they heard from his mouth, as the word of God, as it truly was.* Now, by these expressions he means, that it

[1] CALVIN refers here to the harmony which happily subsisted between the preaching of Paul and the faith of the Thessalonians. See p. 242.—*Ed.*

gained a footing, it is impossible but that a feeling of obligation to obey takes possession of our minds.[1] For who would not shudder at the thought of resisting God? who would not regard contempt of God with detestation? The circumstance, therefore, that the word of God is regarded by many with such contempt, that it is scarcely held in any estimation—that many are not at all actuated by fear, arises from this, that they do not consider that they have to do with God.

Hence we learn from this passage what credit ought to be given to the gospel—such as does not depend on the authority of men, but, resting on the sure and ascertained truth of God, raises itself above the world; and, in fine, is as far above mere opinion, as heaven is above earth:[2] and, *secondly*, such as produces of itself reverence, fear, and obedience, inasmuch as men, touched with a feeling of Divine majesty, will never allow themselves to sport with it. Teachers[3] are, in their turn, admonished to beware of bringing forward anything but the pure word of God, for if this was not allowable for Paul, it will not be so for any one in the present day. He proves, however, from the effect produced, that it was the word of God that he had delivered, inasmuch as it had produced that fruit of heavenly doctrine which the Prophets celebrate, (Isaiah lv. 11, 13; Jer. xxiii. 29,) in renewing their life,[4] for the doctrine of men could accomplish no such thing. The relative pronoun may be taken as referring either to *God* or to his *word*, but whichever way you choose, the meaning will come all to one, for as the Thessalonians felt in themselves a Divine energy, which proceeded from faith, they might rest assured that what they had heard was not a mere

---

[1] "Il ne se peut faire que nous ne venions quant et quant a auoir vne saincte affection d'obeir;"—"It cannot but be that we come at the same time to have a holy disposition to obey."

[2] "Aussi lois d'vne opinion, ou d'vn cuider;"—"As far above opinion, or imagination."

[3] "Les Docteurs, c'est a dire ceux qui ont la charge d'enseigner;"—"Teachers, that is to say, those that have the task of instructing."

[4] "En renouelant et reformant la vie des Thessaloniciens;"—"In renewing and reforming the life of the Thessalonians."

As to the expression, *the word of the preaching of God,* it means simply, as I have rendered it, *the word of God preached by man.* For Paul meant to state expressly that they had not looked upon the doctrine as contemptible, although it had proceeded from the mouth of a mortal man, inasmuch as they recognised God as the author of it. He accordingly praises the Thessalonians, because they did not rest in mere regard for the minister, but lifted up their eyes to God, that they might receive his word. Accordingly, I have not hesitated to insert the particle *ut,* (*that,*) which served to make the meaning more clear. There is a mistake on the part of Erasmus in rendering it, "the word of the hearing of God," as if Paul meant that God had been manifested. He afterwards changed it thus, "the word by which you learned God," for he did not advert to the Hebrew idiom.[1]

14. *For ye became imitators.* If you are inclined to restrict this to the clause in immediate connection with it, the meaning will be, that the power of God, or of his word, shews itself in their patient endurance, while they sustain persecutions with magnanimity and undaunted courage. I prefer, however, to view it as extending to the whole of the foregoing statement, for he confirms what he has stated, that the Thessalonians had in good earnest embraced the gospel, as being presented to them by God, inasmuch as they courageously endured the assaults which Satan made upon them, and did not refuse to suffer anything rather than leave off obedience to it. And, unquestionably, this is no slight test of faith when Satan, by all his machinations, has no success in moving us away from the fear of God.

In the mean time, he prudently provides against a dangerous temptation which might prostrate or harass them; for they endured grievous troubles from that nation which was the only one in the world that gloried in the name of God.

---

[1] " Car il n'a pas prins garde que c'estoit yci vne façon de parler prinse de la langue Hebraique;"—"For he did not take notice that it was a manner of expression taken from the Hebrew language."

oppose it with such inveterate hostility?" With the view of removing this occasion of offence,[1] he, in the *first* place, shews them that they have this in common with the first *Churches that were in Judea :* afterwards, he says that the Jews are determined enemies of God and of all sound doctrine. For although, when he says that they suffered from *their own countrymen,* this may be explained as referring to others rather than to the Jews, or at least ought not to be restricted to the Jews exclusively, yet as he insists farther in describing their obstinacy and impiety, it is manifest that these same persons are adverted to by him from the beginning. It is probable, that at Thessalonica some from that nation were converted to Christ. It appears, however, from the narrative furnished in the Acts, that *there,* no less than in Judea, the Jews were persecutors of the gospel. I accordingly take this as being said indiscriminately of Jews as well as of Gentiles, inasmuch as both endured great conflicts and fierce attacks from *their own countrymen.*

15. *Who killed the Lord Jesus.* As that people had been distinguished by so many benefits from God, in consequence of the glory of the ancient fathers, the very name[2] was of great authority among many. Lest this disguise should dazzle the eyes of any one, he strips the Jews of all honour, so as to leave them nothing but odium and the utmost infamy. "Behold," says he, "the virtues for which they deserve praise among the good and pious!—they killed their own prophets and at last the Son of God, they have persecuted me his servant, they wage war with God, they are detested by the whole world, they are hostile to the salvation of the Gentiles; in fine, they are destined to everlasting destruction." It is asked, why he says that Christ and the prophets were killed by the same persons? I answer, that this refers to the entire body,[3] for Paul means that there is nothing new or unusual in their resisting God, but that, on the contrary, they are,

---

[1] " Aux Thessaloniciens;"—" To the Thessalonians."
[2] " De Juif;"—" Of Jew."
[3] " A tout le corps du peuple;"—" To the whole body of the people."

16. *Who hinder us from speaking to the Gentiles.* It is not without good reason that, as has been observed,[1] he enters so much into detail in exposing the malice of the Jews.[2] For as they furiously opposed the Gospel everywhere, there arose from this a great stumblingblock, more especially as they exclaimed that the gospel was profaned by Paul, when he published it among the Gentiles. By this calumny they made divisions in the Churches, they took away from the Gentiles the hope of salvation, and they obstructed the progress of the gospel. Paul, accordingly, charges them with this crime—that they regard the salvation of the Gentiles with envy, but adds, that matters are so, in order that their *sins may be filled up,* that he may take away from them all reputation for piety; just as in saying previously, that they *pleased not God,* (verse 15,) he meant, that they were unworthy to be reckoned among the worshippers of God. The manner of expression, however, must be observed, implying that those who persevere in an evil course fill up by this means the measure of their judgment,[3] until they come to make it a heap. This is the reason why the punishment of the wicked is often delayed—because their impieties, so to speak, are not yet ripe. By this we are warned that we must carefully take heed lest, in the event of our adding from time to time[4] sin to sin, as is wont to happen generally, the heap at last reaches as high as heaven.

For wrath has come. He means that they are in an utterly hopeless state, inasmuch as they are vessels of the Lord's wrath. "The just vengeance of God presses upon them and pursues them, and will not leave them until they perish—as is the case with all the reprobate, who rush on headlong to death, to which they are destined." The Apostle, however, makes this declaration as to the entire body of the

---

[1] " See p. 259.
[2] " Il insiste si longuement a deschiffrer et toucher au vif la malice des Juifs;"—" He insists to so great a length in distinctly unfolding and touching to the quick the malice of the Jews."
[3] " Et condamnation;"—" And condemnation."
[4] " Chacun iour;"—" Every day."

true, of the whole nation generally, but we must keep in view the exception which he himself makes in Rom. xi. 5, —that the Lord will always have some seed remaining. We must always keep in view Paul's design—that believers must carefully avoid the society of those whom the just vengeance of God pursues, until they perish in their blind obstinacy. *Wrath*, without any additional term, means the judgment of God, as in Rom. iv. 15,—*the law worketh* WRATH ; also in Rom. xii. 19,—*neither give place unto* WRATH.

17. But we, brethren, being taken from you for a short time in presence, not in heart, endeavoured the more abundantly to see your face with great desire.	17. Nos vero, fratres, orbati vobis ad tempus horae[1] aspectu, non corde, abundantius studuimus faciem vestram videre in multo desiderio.
18. Wherefore we would have come unto you (even I Paul) once and again ; but Satan hindered us.	18. Itaque voluimus venire ad vos, ego quidem Paulus, et semel et bis, et obstitit nobis Satan.
19. For what *is* our hope, or joy, or crown of rejoicing ? *Are* not even ye in the presence of our Lord Jesus Christ at his coming ?	19. Quae enim nostra spes, vel gaudium, vel corona gloriationis ? annon etiam vos coram Domino nostro Iesu Christo in eius adventu ?
20. For ye are our glory and joy.	20. Vos enim estis gloria nostra et gaudium.

17. *But we, brethren, bereaved of you.* This excuse has been appropriately added, lest the Thessalonians should think that Paul had deserted them while so great an emergency demanded his presence. He has spoken of the persecutions which they endured from their own people: he, in the mean time, whose duty it was above all others to assist them, was absent. He has formerly called himself a *father ;* now, it is not the part of a *father* to desert his children in the midst of such distresses. He, accordingly, obviates all suspicion of contempt and negligence, by saying, that it was from no want of inclination, but because he had not opportunity. Nor does he say simply, "I was desirous to come to you, but my way was obstructed ;" but by the peculiar terms that he employs he expresses the intensity of his affection: "When," says he, "I was *bereaved* of you."[2] By the word

[1] " Pour vn moment du temps ;"—" For a moment of time."
[2] " The original word is here very emphatical. It is an allusion to that

expression of his feeling of desire—that it was with difficulty that he could endure their absence for a short time. It is not to be wondered, if length of time should occasion weariness or sadness; but we must have a strong feeling of attachment when we find it difficult to wait even a single hour. Now, by the *space of an hour*, he means—a small space of time.

This is followed by a correction—that he had been separated from them in *appearance, not in heart*, that they may know that distance of place does not by any means lessen his attachment. At the same time, this might not less appropriately be applied to the Thessalonians, as meaning that they, on their part, had felt united in *mind* while absent in *body;* for it was of no small importance for the point in hand that he should state how fully assured he was of their affection towards him in return. He shews, however, more fully his affection, when he says that he *endeavoured the more abundantly;* for he means that his affection was so far from being diminished by his leaving them, that it had been the more inflamed. When he says, *we would once and again*, he declares that it was not a sudden heat, that quickly cooled, (as we see sometimes happen,) but that he had been steadfast in this purpose,[2] inasmuch as he sought various opportunities.

18. *Satan hindered us.* Luke relates that Paul was in one instance hindered, (Acts xx. 3,) inasmuch as the Jews laid an ambush for him in the way. The same thing, or something similar, may have occurred frequently. It is not without good reason, however, that Paul ascribes the whole

grief, anxiety, and reluctance of heart, with which dying, affectionate parents take leave of their own children, when they are just going to leave them helpless orphans, exposed to the injuries of a merciless and wicked world, or that sorrow of heart with which poor destitute orphans close the eyes of their dying parents."—*Benson.—Ed.*

[1] " Le mot Grec signifie l'estat d'vn pere qui a perdu ses enfans, ou des enfans qui ont perdu leur pere ;"—" The Greek word denotes the condition of a father that has lost his children, or of children that have lost their father."

[2] *Hujus propositi tenacem.* See *Hor.* Od. 3, 3. 1.—*Ed.*

cipalities of the air, and spiritual wickednesses, &c. For, whenever the wicked molest us, they fight under Satan's banner, and are his instruments for harassing us. More especially, when our endeavours are directed to the work of the Lord, it is certain that everything that hinders proceeds from Satan; and would to God that this sentiment were deeply impressed upon the minds of all pious persons—that Satan is continually contriving, by every means, in what way he may hinder or obstruct the edification of the Church! We would assuredly be more careful to resist him; we would take more care to maintain sound doctrine, of which that enemy strives so keenly to deprive us. We would also, whenever the course of the gospel is retarded, know whence the hinderance proceeds. He says elsewhere, (Rom. i. 13,) that God had not permitted him, but both are true: for although Satan does his part, yet God retains supreme authority, so as to open up a way for us, as often as he sees good, against Satan's will, and in spite of his opposition. Paul accordingly says truly that God does not permit, although the hinderance comes from Satan.

19. *For what is our hope.* He confirms that ardour of desire, of which he had made mention, inasmuch as he has his happiness in a manner treasured up in them. "Unless I forget myself, I must necessarily desire your presence, for *ye are our glory and joy.*" Farther, when he calls them his *hope and the crown of his glory,* we must not understand this as meaning that he gloried in any one but God alone, but because we are allowed to glory in all God's favours, in their own place, in such a manner that he is always our object of aim, as I have explained more at large in the *first* Epistle to the Corinthians.[1] We must, however, infer from this, that Christ's ministers will, on the last day, according as they have individually promoted his kingdom, be partakers of glory and triumph. Let them therefore now learn to rejoice and glory in nothing but the prosperous issue of

[1] " Sur la premiere aux Corinth., chap. i. d. 31;"—" On 1 Corinthians i. 31."

that they will be actuated by that spirit of affection to the Church with which they ought. The particle *also* denotes that the Thessalonians were not the only persons in whom Paul triumphed, but that they held a place among many. The causal particle γάρ, (*for*,) which occurs almost immediately afterwards, is employed here not in its strict sense, by way of affirmation—" *assuredly* you are."

CHAPTER III.

1. Wherefore, when we could no longer forbear, we thought it good to be left at Athens alone,
2. And sent Timotheus, our brother, and minister of God, and our fellow-labourer in the gospel of Christ, to establish you, and to comfort you concerning your faith;
3. That no man should be moved by these afflictions: for yourselves know that we are appointed thereunto.
4. For verily, when we were with you, we told you before that we should suffer tribulation; even as it came to pass, and ye know.
5. For this cause, when I could no longer forbear, I sent to know your faith, lest by some means the tempter have tempted you, and our labour be in vain.

1. Quare non amplius sufferentes censuimus, ut Athenis relinqueremur soli:
2. Et misimus Timotheum fratrem nostrum, et ministrum Dei, et cooperarium nostrum in evangelio Christi, ut confirmaret vos, et vobis animum adderet ex fide nostra,
3. Ut nemo turbaretur in his afflictionibus: ipsi enim nostis quod in hoc sumus constituti.
4.. Etenim quum essemus apud vos, praediximus vobis quod essemus afflictiones passuri; quemadmodum etiam accidit, et nostis.
5. Quamobrem et ego non amplius sustinens, misi ut cognoscerem fidem vestram: ne forte tentasset vos, is qui tentat, et exinanitus esset labor noster.

1. *Wherefore, when we could no longer endure.* By the detail which follows, he assures them of the desire of which he had spoken. For if, on being detained elsewhere, he had sent no other to Thessalonica in his place, it might have seemed as though he were not so much concerned in regard to them; but when he substitutes Timothy in his place, he removes that suspicion, more especially when he prefers them before himself. Now that he esteemed them above himself, he shews from this, that he chose rather to be left alone than that they should be deserted: for these

that time no others with him; hence it was inconvenient and distressing for him to be without him. It is therefore a token of rare affection and anxious desire that he does not refuse to deprive himself of all comfort, with the view of relieving the Thessalonians. To the same effect is the word εὐδοκήσαμεν, which expresses a prompt inclination of the mind.[1]

2. *Our brother.* He assigns to him these marks of commendation, that he may shew the more clearly how much inclined he was to consult their welfare: for if he had sent them some common person, it could not have afforded them much assistance; and inasmuch as Paul would have done this without inconvenience to himself, he would have given no remarkable proof of his fatherly concern in regard to them. It is, on the other hand, a great thing that he deprives himself of a *brother* and *fellow-labourer,* and one to whom, as he declares in Phil. ii. 20, he found no equal, inasmuch as all aimed at the promotion of their own interests. In the mean time,[2] he procures authority for the doctrine which they had received from Timothy, that it may remain the more deeply impressed upon their memory.

It is, however, with good reason that he says that he had *sent Timothy* with this view—that they might receive a *confirmation of their faith* from his example. They might be intimidated by unpleasant reports as to persecutions; but Paul's undaunted constancy was fitted so much the more to animate them, so as to keep them from giving way. And, assuredly, the fellowship which ought to subsist between the saints and members of Christ extends even thus far— that the faith of one is the consolation of others. Thus, when the Thessalonians heard that Paul was going on with indefatigable zeal, and was by strength of faith surmounting all dangers and all difficulties, and that his faith continued everywhere victorious against Satan and the world, this brought them no small consolation. More especially we are,

---

[1] " Vne affection prompte et procedante d'vn franc cœur;"—" A prompt disposition, proceeding from a ready mind."
[2] " En parlant ainsi;"—" By speaking thus."

end of the Epistle to the Hebrews. (Heb. xiii. 7.) Paul, accordingly, means that they ought to be fortified by his example, so as not to give way under their afflictions. As, however, they might have been offended if Paul had entertained a fear lest they should all give way under persecutions, (inasmuch as this would have been an evidence of excessive distrust,) he mitigates this harshness by saying—*lest any one*, or, *that no one*. There was, however, good reason to fear this, as there are always some weak persons in every society.

3. *For ye yourselves know.* As all would gladly exempt themselves from the necessity of bearing the cross, Paul teaches that there is no reason why believers should feel dismayed on occasion of persecutions, as though it were a thing that was new and unusual, inasmuch as this is our condition, which the Lord has assigned to us. For this manner of expression—*we are appointed to it*—is as though he had said, that we are Christians on this condition. He says, however, that they *know* it, because it became them to fight the more bravely,[1] inasmuch as they had been forewarned in time. In addition to this, incessant afflictions made Paul contemptible among rude and ignorant persons. On this account he states that nothing had befallen him but what he had long before, in the manner of a prophet, foretold.

5. *Lest perhaps the tempter has tempted you.* By this term he teaches us that temptations are always to be dreaded, because it is the proper office of Satan to *tempt*. As, however, he never ceases to place ambushes for us on all sides, and to lay snares for us all around, so we must be on our watch, eagerly taking heed. And now he says openly what in the outset he had avoided saying, as being too harsh—that he had felt concerned lest his *labours* should be *vain*, if, peradventure, Satan should prevail. And this he does that they may be carefully upon their watch, and may stir themselves up the more vigorously to resistance.

---

[1] " Plus vaillamment et courageusement ;"—" More valiantly and courageously."

charity, and that ye have good remembrance of us always, desiring greatly to see us, as we also *to see* you;

7. Therefore, brethren, we were comforted over you in all our affliction and distress by your faith:

8. For now we live, if ye stand fast in the Lord.

9. For what thanks can we render to God again for you, for all the joy wherewith we joy for your sakes before our God;

10. Night and day praying exceedingly that we might see your face, and might perfect that which is lacking in your faith?

vestram, et quod bonam nostri memoriam habetis semper, desiderantes nos videre, quemadmodum et nos ipsi vos:

7. Inde consolationem percepimus fratres de vobis, in omni tribulatione et necessitate nostra per vestram fidem:

8. Quia nunc vivimus, si vos statis in Domino.

9. Quam enim gratiarum actionem possumus Deo reddere de vobis, in omni gaudio quod gaudemus propter vos coram Deo nostro;

10. Nocte ac die supra modum precantes, ut videamus faciem vestram, et suppleamus quae fidei vestrae desunt?

He shews here, by another argument, by what an extraordinary affection he was actuated towards them, inasmuch as he was transported almost out of his senses by the joyful intelligence of their being in a prosperous condition. For we must take notice of the circumstances which he relates. He was in *affliction* and *necessity*: there might have seemed, therefore, no room for cheerfulness. But when he hears what was much desired by him respecting the Thessalonians, as though all feeling of his distresses had been extinguished, he is carried forward to joy and congratulation. At the same time he proceeds, by degrees, in expressing the greatness of his joy, for he says, in the *first* place, we *received consolation*: afterwards he speaks of a joy that was plentifully poured forth.[1] This congratulation,[2] however, has the force of an exhortation; and Paul's intention was to stir up the Thessalonians to perseverance. And, assuredly, this must have been a most powerful excitement, when they learned that the holy Apostle felt so great consolation and joy from the advancement of their piety.

[1] " Ample et abondante;"—" Large and overflowing."
[2] " Ceste façon de tesmoigner la ioye qu'il sent de la fermete des Thessaloniciens;"—" This manner of testifying the joy which he feels in the steadfastness of the Thessalonians."

with which it is made use of by Paul, for in these two words he comprehends briefly the entire sum of true piety. Hence all that aim at this twofold mark during their whole life are beyond all risk of erring: all others, however much they may torture themselves, wander miserably. The third thing that he adds as to their *good remembrance* of him, refers to respect entertained for the Gospel. For it was on no other account that they held Paul in such affection and esteem.

8. *For now we live.* Here it appears still more clearly that Paul almost forgot himself for the sake of the Thessalonians, or, at least, making regard for himself a mere secondary consideration, devoted his first and chief thoughts to them. At the same time he did not do that so much from affection to men as from a desire for the Lord's glory. For zeal for God and Christ glowed in his holy breast to such a degree that it in a manner swallowed up all other anxieties. "*We live,*" says he, that is, "we are in good health, if you *persevere in the Lord.*" And under the adverb *now,* he repeats what he had formerly stated, that he had been greatly pressed down by *affliction* and *necessity;* yet he declares that whatever evil he endures in his own person does not hinder his joy. "Though in myself I am dead, yet in your welfare I *live.*" By this all pastors are admonished what sort of connection ought to subsist between them and the Church—that they reckon themselves happy when it goes well with the Church, although they should be in other respects encompassed with many miseries, and, on the other hand, that they pine away with grief and sorrow if they see the building which they have constructed in a state of decay, although matters otherwise should be joyful and prosperous.

9. *For what thanksgiving.* Not satisfied with a simple affirmation, he intimates how extraordinary is the greatness of his joy, by asking himself *what thanks he can render to God;* for by speaking thus he declares that he cannot find an expression of gratitude that can come up to the measure of his joy. He says that he rejoices *before God,* that is, truly and without any pretence.

men, while they live in this world, in such unqualified terms as not always to desire something better for them. For they are as yet in the way: they may fall back, or go astray, or even go back. Hence Paul is desirous to have opportunity given him of *supplying what is wanting in the faith* of the Thessalonians, or, which is the same thing, completing in all its parts their faith, which was as yet imperfect. Yet this is the faith which he had previously extolled marvellously. But from this we infer, that those who far surpass others are still far distant from the goal. Hence, whatever progress we may have made, let us always keep in view our *deficiencies*, (ὑστερήματα,)[2] that we may not be reluctant to aim at something farther.

From this also it appears how necessary it is for us to give careful attention to doctrine, for teachers[3] were not appointed merely with the view of leading men, in the course of a single day or month, to the faith of Christ, but for the purpose of perfecting the faith which has been begun. But as to Paul's claiming for himself what he elsewhere declares belongs peculiarly to the Holy Spirit, (1 Cor. xiv. 14,) this must be restricted to the ministry. Now, as the ministry of a man is inferior to the efficacy of the Spirit, and to use the common expression, is subordinate to it, nothing is detracted from it. When he says that he prayed *night and day beyond all ordinary measure*,[4] we may gather from these words how assiduous he was in praying to God, and with what ardour and earnestness he discharged that duty.

11. Now God himself and our Father, and our Lord Jesus Christ, direct our way unto you.

11. Ipse autem Deus et Pater noster, et Dominus noster Iesus Christus viam nostram ad vos dirigat.

[1] See p. 262.

[2] "Ὑστερήματα πίστεως.—*Afterings of faith,* as it may be significantly enough rendered, let but the novelty of the expression be pardoned."— *Howe's* Works, (London, 1822,) vol. iii. p. 70.—*Ed.*

[3] "Les Docteurs et ceux qui ont charge d'enseigner en l'Eglise;"— "Teachers and those that have the task of instructing in the Church."

[4] "*Night and day praying exceedingly*—Supplicating God at *all times;* mingling this with all my prayers; ὑπὲρ ἐκπερισσοῦ δεόμενοι, abounding and superabounding in my entreaties to God, to permit me to revisit you."— *Dr. A. Clarke.*—*Ed.*

even as we *do* toward you:

13. To the end he may stablish your hearts unblameable in holiness before God, even our Father, at the coming of our Lord Jesus Christ with all his saints.

et nos ipsi affecti sumus erga vos:

13. Ut confirmet corda vestra irreprehensibilia, in sanctitate coram Deo et Patre nostro, in adventu Domini nostri Iesu Christi, cum omnibus sanctis eius.

11. *Now God himself.* He now prays that the Lord, having removed Satan's obstructions, may open a door for himself, and be, as it were, the leader and director of his way to the Thessalonians. By this he intimates, that we cannot move a step with success,[1] otherwise than under God's guidance, but that when he holds out his hand, it is to no purpose that Satan employs every effort to change the direction of our course. We must take notice that he assigns the same office to God and to Christ, as, unquestionably, the Father confers no blessing upon us except through Christ's hand. When, however, he thus speaks of both in the same terms, he teaches that Christ has divinity and power in common with the Father.

12. *And the Lord fill you.* Here we have another prayer —that in the mean time, while his way is obstructed, the Lord, during his absence, may confirm the Thessalonians in holiness, and fill them with love. And from this again we learn in what the perfection of the Christian life consists— in love and pure holiness of heart, flowing from faith. He recommends love mutually cherished *towards each other*, and afterwards *towards all*, for as it is befitting that a commencement should be made with those that are of the *household of faith*, (Gal. vi. 10,) so our love ought to go forth to the whole human race. Farther, as the nearer connection must be cherished,[2] so we must not overlook those who are farther removed from us, so as to prevent them from holding their proper place.

He would have the Thessalonians abound in love and

---

[1] "Nous ne pouuons d'vn costé ne d'autre faire vn pas qui proufite et viene a bien;"—"We cannot on one side or another take a step that may be profitable or prosperous."

[2] "Il faut recognoistre et entretenir;"—"We must recognise and maintain."

same time increase in us, until it take possession of our whole heart, the corrupt love of self being extirpated. He prays that the love of the Thessalonians may be perfected by God, intimating that its increase, no less than its commencement, was from God alone. Hence it is evident how preposterous a part those act who measure our strength by the precepts of the Divine law. *The end of the law is love,* says Paul, (1 Tim. i. 5 ;) yet he himself declares that it is a work of God. When, therefore, God marks out our life,[1] he does not look to what we can do, but requires from us what is above our strength, that we may learn to ask from him power to accomplish it. When he says—*as we also towards you,* he stimulates them by his own example.

13. *That he may confirm your hearts.* He employs the term *hearts* here to mean *conscience,* or the innermost part of the soul; for he means that a man is acceptable to God only when he brings holiness of heart; that is, not merely external, but also internal. But it is asked, whether by means of holiness we stand at God's judgment-seat, for if so, to what purpose is remission of sins? Yet Paul's words seem to imply this—that their consciences might be *irreproveable in holiness.* I answer, that Paul does not exclude remission of sins, through which it comes that our holiness, which is otherwise mixed up with many pollutions, bears God's eye, for faith, by which God is pacified towards us, so as to pardon our faults,[2] precedes everything else, as the foundation comes before the building. Paul, however, does not teach us what or how great the holiness of believers may be, but desires that it may be increased, until it attain its perfection. On this account he says—*at the coming of our Lord,* meaning that the completion of those things, which the Lord now begins in us, is delayed till that time.

With all his saints. This clause may be explained in two ways, either as meaning that the Thessalonians, *with all*

[1] " Nous prescrit en ses commandemens la regle de viure;"—" Prescribes to us in his commandments the rule of life."
[2] " Nous fautes et infirmitez vicieuses;"—" Our faults and culpable infirmities."

second meaning, in so far as concerns the construction of the words, I have at the same time no doubt that Paul employed the term *saints* for the purpose of admonishing us that we are called by Christ for this end—that we may be gathered *with all his saints.* For this consideration ought to whet our desire for holiness.

CHAPTER IV.

1. Furthermore then, we beseech you, brethren, and exhort *you* by the Lord Jesus, that as ye have received of us how ye ought to walk and to please God, *so* ye would abound more and more.
2. For ye know what commandments we gave you by the Lord Jesus.
3. For this is the will of God, *even* your sanctification, that ye should abstain from fornication:
4. That every one of you should know how to possess his vessel in sanctification and honour;
5. Not in the lust of concupiscence, even as the Gentiles which know not God.

1. Ergo quod reliquum est, fratres, rogamus vos et obsecramus in Domino Iesu, quemadmodum accepistis a nobis, quomodo oporteat vos ambulare et placere Deo, ut abundetis magis:
2. Nostis enim quae praecepta dederimus vobis per Dominum Iesum.
3. Haec enim est voluntas Dei, sanctificatio vestra: ut vos abstineatis ab omni scortatione.
4. Et sciat unusquisque vestrum suum vas possidere in sanctificatione et honore:
5. Non in affectu concupiscentiae, quemadmodum et Gentes, quae non noverunt Deum.

1. *Furthermore.* This chapter contains various injunctions, by which he trains up the Thessalonians to a holy life, or confirms them in the exercise of it. They had previously learned what was the rule and method of a pious life: he calls this to their remembrance. *As*, says he, *ye have been taught.* Lest, however, he should seem to take away from them what he had previously assigned them, he does not simply exhort them to *walk* in such a manner, but to *abound more and more.* When, therefore, he urges them to make progress, he intimates that they are already in the way. The sum is this, that they should be more especially careful to make progress in the doctrine which they had received, and this Paul places in contrast with frivolous and vain pursuits, in which

due regulation of life scarcely obtains a place, even the most inferior. Paul, accordingly, reminds them in what manner they had been instructed, and bids them aim at this with their whole might. Now, there is a law that is here enjoined upon us—that, *forgetting the things that are behind,* we always aim at farther progress, (Phil. iii. 13,) and pastors ought also to make this their endeavour. Now, as to his *beseeching,* when he might rightfully enjoin—it is a token of humanity and modesty which pastors ought to imitate, that they may, if possible, allure people to kindness, rather than violently compel them.[1]

3. *For this is the will of God.* This is doctrine of a general nature, from which, as from a fountain, he immediately deduces special admonitions. When he says that *this is the will of God,* he means that we have been called by God with this design. "For this end ye are Christians—this the gospel aims at—that ye may *sanctify* yourselves *to God."* The meaning of the term *sanctification* we have already explained elsewhere in repeated instances—that renouncing the world, and clearing ourselves from the pollutions of the flesh, we offer ourselves to God as if in sacrifice, for nothing can with propriety be offered to Him, but what is pure and holy.

That ye abstain. This is one injunction, which he derives from the fountain of which he had immediately before made mention; for nothing is more opposed to holiness than the defilement of *fornication,* which pollutes the whole man. On this account he assigns the *lust of concupiscence* to the *Gentiles, who know not God.* "Where the knowledge of God reigns, lusts must be subdued."

By the *lust of concupiscence,* he means all base lusts of the flesh, but, at the same time, by this manner of expression, he brands with dishonour all desires that allure us to pleasure and carnal delights, as in Rom. xiii. 14, he bids us *have no care for the flesh in respect of the lust thereof.* For when men give indulgence to their appetites, there are no

[1] "Que de les contraindre rudement et d'vne façon violente ;"—"Rather than constrain them rudely and in a violent manner."

As for the expression, *that every one of you may know to possess his vessel*, some explain it as referring to a *wife*,[2] as though it had been said, "Let husbands dwell with their wives in all chastity." As, however, he addresses husbands and wives indiscriminately, there can be no doubt that he employs the term *vessel* to mean *body*. For every one has his body as a house, as it were, in which he dwells. He would, therefore, have us keep our body pure from all uncleanness.

And honour, that is, honourably, for the man that prostitutes his body to fornication, covers it with infamy and disgrace.

6. That no *man* go beyond and defraud his brother in *any* matter: because that the Lord *is* the avenger of all such, as we also have forewarned you, and testified.	6. Ne quis opprimat vel circumveniat in negotio fratrem suum: quia vindex erit Dominus omnium istorum, quemadmodum et praediximus vobis, et obtestati sumus.
7. For God hath not called us unto uncleanness, but unto holiness.	7. Non enim vocavit vos Deus ad immunditiam, sed ad sanctificationem.
8. He therefore that despiseth, despiseth not man, but God, who hath also given unto us his Holy Spirit.	8. Itaque qui hoc repudiat, non hominem repudiat, sed Deum, qui etiam dedit Spiritum suum sanctum in nos.

6. *Let no man oppress.* Here we have another exhortation, which flows, like a stream, from the doctrine of sanctification. "God," says he, "has it in view to sanctify us, *that no man may do injury to his brother.*" For as to Chrysostom's connecting this statement with the preceding one, and explaining ὑπερβαίνειν καὶ πλεονεκτεῖν to mean—neighing after the wives of others, (Jer. v. 8,) and eagerly desiring them, is too forced an exposition. Paul, accordingly, having adduced one instance of unchastity in respect of lasciviousness and lust, teaches that this also is a department of holiness—that we conduct ourselves righteously and harmlessly towards our neighbours. The *former* verb refers to violent oppressions—where the man that has more power emboldens

---

[1] "Il n'y a mesure ne fin de desbauchement et dissolution;"—"There is no measure or end of debauchery and wantonness."

[2] "Au regard du mari;"—"In relation to her husband."

for the most part, indulge themselves in lust and avarice, he reminds them of what he had formerly taught—that *God would be the avenger of all such things.* We must observe, however, what he says—we have *solemnly testified ;*[1] for such is the sluggishness of mankind, that, unless they are wounded to the quick, they are touched with no apprehension of God's judgment.

7. *For God hath not called us.* This appears to be the same sentiment with the preceding one—that *the will of God is our sanctification.* There is, however, a little difference between them. For after having discoursed as to the correcting of the vices of the flesh, he proves, from the end of our calling, that God desires this. For he sets us apart to himself as his peculiar possession.[2] Again, that God calls us to holiness, he proves by contraries, because he rescues us, and calls us back, from unchastity. From this he concludes, that all that reject this doctrine *reject not men, but God,* the Author of this calling, which altogether falls to the ground so soon as this principle as to newness of life is overthrown. Now, the reason why he rouses himself so vehemently is, because there are always wanton persons who, while they fearlessly despise God, treat with ridicule all threatenings of his judgment, and at the same time hold in derision all injunctions as to a holy and pious life. Such persons must not be taught, but must be beaten with severe reproofs as with the stroke of a hammer.

8.. *Who hath also given.* That he may the more effectually turn away the Thessalonians from such contempt and obstinacy, he reminds them that they had been endowed with the Spirit of God, *first,* in order that they may distinguish what proceeds from God ; *secondly,* that they make such a difference as is befitting between holiness and impurity ; and *thirdly,* that, with heavenly authority, they may pronounce judgment against all manner of unchastity—such

[1] " Nous vous auons testifié et comme adiuré ;"—" We have testified to you, and, as it were, adjured."

[2] " Comme pour son propre heritage et particulier ;"—" As for his peculiar and special inheritance."

cule all instructions that are given as to a holy life and the fear of God, those that are endowed with the Spirit of God have a very different testimony sealed upon their hearts. We must therefore take heed, lest we should extinguish or obliterate it. At the same time, this may refer to Paul and the other teachers, as though he had said, that it is not from human perception that they condemn unchastity, but they pronounce from the authority of God what has been suggested to them by his Spirit. I am inclined, however, to include both. Some manuscripts have the second person—*you,* which restricts the gift of the Spirit to the Thessalonians.

9. But as touching brotherly love, ye need not that I write unto you; for ye yourselves are taught of God to love one another.

10. And indeed ye do it toward all the brethren which are in all Macedonia: but we beseech you, brethren, that ye increase more and more;

11. And that ye study to be quiet, and to do your own business, and to work with your own hands, as we commanded you;

12. That ye may walk honestly toward them that are without, and *that* ye may have lack of nothing.

9. De fraterno autem amore non opus habetis, ut scribam vobis: ipsi enim vos a Deo estis edocti, ut diligatis invicem.

10. Etenim hoc facitis erga omnes fratres, qui sunt in tota Macedonia. Hortamur autem vos, fratres, ut abundetis magis,

11. Et altius contendatis, ut colatis quietem, et agatis res vestras, et laboretis manibus vestris, quemadmodum vobis denuntiavimus,

12. Ut ambuletis decenter erga extraneos, et nulla re opus habeatis.

9. *As to brotherly love.* Having previously, in lofty terms, commended their love, he now speaks by way of *anticipation,* saying, *ye need not that I write to you.* He assigns a reason—*because they had been divinely taught*—by which he means that love was engraven upon their hearts, so that there was no need of letters written on paper. For he does not mean simply what John says in his first Canonical[1]

[1] The Epistles of John, along with those of James, Peter, and Jude, "were termed *Canonical* by Cassiodorus in the middle of the sixth century, and by the writer of the prologue to these Epistles, which is erroneously ascribed to Jerome. . . . Du Pin says that some Latin writers have called these Epistles *Canonical,* either confounding the name with Catholic, or to denote that they are a part of the *Canon* of the books of the New Testament."—*Horne's* Introduction, vol. iv. p. 409. On the origin and import of the epithet *General,* or *Catholic,* usually applied to these

the Holy Spirit inwardly dictates efficaciously what is to be done, so that there is no need to give injunctions in writing. He subjoins an argument from the greater to the less; for as their love diffuses itself through the whole of Macedonia, he infers that it is not to be doubted that they *love one another.* Hence the particle *for* means *likewise,* or *nay more,* for, as I have already stated, he adds it for the sake of greater intensity.

10. *And we exhort you.* Though he declares that they were sufficiently prepared of themselves for all offices of love, he nevertheless does not cease to exhort them to make progress, there being no perfection in men. And, unquestionably, whatever appears in us in a high state of excellence, we must still desire that it may become better. Some connect the verb φιλοτιμεῖσθαι with what follows, as if he exhorted them to strive at the maintaining of peace; but it corresponds better with the expression that goes before. For after having admonished them to increase in love, he recommends to them a sacred emulation, that they may strive among themselves in mutual affection, or at least he enjoins that each one strive to conquer himself;[1] and I rather adopt this latter interpretation. That, therefore, their love may be perfect, he requires that there be a striving among them, such as is wont to be on the part of those who eagerly[2] aspire at victory. This is the best emulation, when each one strives to overcome himself in doing good. As to my not subscribing to the opinion of those who render the words, *strive to maintain peace,* this single reason appears to me to be sufficiently valid—that Paul would not in a thing of less difficulty have enjoined so arduous a conflict—which suits admirably well with advancement in love, where so many hinderances present themselves. Nor would I have any ob-

---

Epistles, the reader will find some valuable observations in *Brown's* Expository Discourses on Peter, vol. i. pp. 4, 5.—*Ed.*

[1] " En cest endroit;"—" In this matter."

[2] " Courageusement et d'vn grand desir;"—" Courageously and wait a great desire."

11. *Colatis quietem.* I have already stated that this clause must be separated from what goes before, for this is a new sentence. Now, to *be at peace,* means in this passage—to act peacefully and without disturbance, as we also say in French—*sans bruit, (without noise.)* In short, he exhorts them to be peaceable and tranquil. This is the purport of what he adds immediately afterwards—to *do your own business :* for we commonly see, that those who intrude themselves with forwardness into the affairs of others, make great disturbance, and give trouble to themselves and others. This, therefore, is the best means of a tranquil life, when every one, intent upon the duties of his own calling, discharges those duties which are enjoined upon him by the Lord, and devotes himself to these things : while the husbandman employs himself in rural labours, the workman carries on his occupation, and in this way every one keeps within his own limits. So soon as men turn aside from this, everything is thrown into confusion and disorder. He does not mean, however, that every one shall *mind his own business* in such a way as that each one should live apart, having no care for others, but has merely in view to correct an idle levity, which makes men noisy bustlers in public, who ought to lead a quiet life in their own houses.

Labour with your hands. He recommends manual labour on two accounts—that they may have a sufficiency for maintaining life, and that they may conduct themselves honourably even before unbelievers. For nothing is more unseemly than a man that is idle and good for nothing, who profits neither himself nor others, and seems born only to eat and drink. Farther, this labour or system of working extends far, for what he says as to *hands* is by way of *synecdoche ;* but there can be no doubt that he includes every useful employment of human life.

13. But I would not have you to be ignorant, brethren, concerning them which are asleep, that ye sorrow not, even as others which have no hope.

13. Nolo autem vos ignorare, fratres, de iis qui obdormierunt, ut ne contristemini, sicut et caeteri qui spem non habent.

bring with him. tum, adducet cum eo.

13. *But I would not have you ignorant.* It is not likely that the hope of a resurrection had been torn up among the Thessalonians by profane men, as had taken place at Corinth. For we see how he chastises the Corinthians with severity, but here he speaks of it as a thing that was not doubtful. It is possible, however, that this persuasion was not sufficiently fixed in their minds, and that they accordingly, in bewailing the dead, retained something of the old superstition. For the sum of the whole is this—that we must not bewail the dead beyond due bounds, inasmuch as we are all to be raised up again. For whence comes it, that the mourning of unbelievers has no end or measure, but because they have no hope of a resurrection? It becomes not us, therefore, who have been instructed as to a resurrection, to mourn otherwise than in moderation. He is to discourse afterwards as to the manner of the resurrection; and he is also on this account to say something as to *times;* but in this passage he meant simply to restrain excessive grief, which would never have had such an influence among them, if they had seriously considered the resurrection, and kept it in remembrance.

He does not, however, forbid us altogether to mourn, but requires moderation in our mourning, for he says, *that ye may not sorrow, as others who have no hope.* He forbids them to grieve in the manner of unbelievers, who give loose reins to their grief, because they look upon death as final destruction, and imagine that everything that is taken out of the world perishes. As, on the other hand, believers know that they quit the world, that they may be at last gathered into the kingdom of God, they have not the like occasion of grief. Hence the knowledge of a resurrection is the means of moderating grief. He speaks of the dead as *asleep,* agreeably to the common practice of Scripture—a term by which the bitterness of death is mitigated, for there is a great difference between *sleep* and *destruction.*[1] It

[1] " Entre dormir, et estre du tout reduit a neant ;"—" Between sleeping, and being altogether reduced to nothing."

up the man. Those, therefore, act a foolish part, who infer from this that souls sleep.¹

We are now in possession of Paul's meaning—that he lifts up the minds of believers to a consideration of the resurrection, lest they should indulge excessive grief on occasion of the death of their relatives, for it were unseemly that there should be no difference between them and unbelievers, who put no end or measure to their grief for this reason, that in death they recognise nothing but destruction.² Those that abuse this testimony, so as to establish among Christians Stoical indifference, that is, an iron hardness,³ will find nothing of this nature in Paul's words. As to their objecting that we must not indulge grief on occasion of the death of our relatives, lest we should resist God, this would apply in all adversities; but it is one thing to bridle our grief, that it may be made subject to God, and quite another thing to harden one's self so as to be like stones, by casting away human feelings. Let, therefore, the grief of the pious be mixed with consolation, which may train them to patience. The hope of a blessed resurrection, which is the mother of patience, will effect this.

14. *For if we believe.* He assumes this axiom of our faith, that Christ was raised up from the dead, that we might be partakers of the same resurrection: from this he infers, that we shall live with him eternally. This doctrine, however, as has been stated in 1 Cor. xv. 13, depends on another principle—that it was not for himself, but for us that Christ died and rose again. Hence those who have doubts as to the resurrection, do great injury to Christ: nay more, they do in a manner draw him down from heaven, as is said in Rom. x. 6.

---

¹ See CALVIN on the Corinthians, vol. ii. pp. 20, 21.

² "Ruine et destruction;"—" Ruin and destruction."

³ "Pour introduire et establir entre les Chrestiens ceste façon tant estrange, que les Stoiciens requeroyent en l'homme, ascauoir qu'il ne fust esmeu de douleur quelconque, mais qu'il fust comme de fer et stupide sans rien sentir;"—"For introducing and establishing among Christians that strange manner of acting, which the Stoics required on the part of an individual—that he should not be moved by any grief, but should be as it were of iron, and stupid, so as to be devoid of feeling."

into Christ, have death in common with him, that they may be partakers with him of life. It is asked, however, whether unbelievers will not also rise again, for Paul does not affirm that there will be a resurrection, except in the case of Christ's members. I answer, that Paul does not here touch upon anything but what suited his present design. For he did not design to terrify the wicked, but to correct[1] the immoderate grief of the pious, and to cure it, as he does, by the medicine of consolation.

15. For this we say unto you by the word of the Lord, that we which are alive *and* remain unto the coming of the Lord, shall not prevent them which are asleep.	15. Hoc enim vobis dicimus in sermone Domini, quod nos, qui vivemus et superstites erimus in adventum Domini, non praeveniemus eos, qui dormierunt.
16. For the Lord himself shall descend from heaven with a shout, with the voice of the archangel, and with the trump of God: and the dead in Christ shall rise first:	16. Quoniam ipse Dominus cum clamore, cum voce Archangeli et tuba Dei descendet e cœlo : ac mortui, qui in Christo sunt, resurgent primum.
17. Then we which are alive *and* remain shall be caught up together with them in the clouds, to meet the Lord in the air : and so shall we ever be with the Lord.	17. Deinde nos qui vivemus, ac residui erimus, simul cum ipsis rapiemur in nubibus, in occursum Domini in aera : et sic semper cum Domino erimus.
18. Wherefore comfort one another with these words.	18. Itaque consolamini vos mutuo in sermonibus istis.

15. *For this we say unto you.* He now briefly explains the manner in which believers will be raised up from death. Now, as he speaks of a thing that is very great, and is incredible to the human mind, and also promises what is above the power and choice of men, he premises that he does not bring forward anything that is his own, or that proceeds from men, but that the Lord is the Author of it. It is probable, however, that the *word of the Lord* means what was taken from his discourses.[2] For though Paul had learned by revelation all the secrets of the heavenly kingdom, it was, nevertheless, more fitted to establish in the minds of believers the belief of a resurrection, when he related those things that had

---

[1] " Mais seulement de corriger ou reprimer ;"—" But merely to correct or repress."

[2] " Prins des sermons de Christ ;"—" Taken from the sermons of Christ."

himself declared it."[1]

We who live. This has been said by him with this view—that they might not think that those only would be partakers of the resurrection who would be alive at the time of Christ's coming, and that those would have no part in it who had been previously taken away by death. "The order of the resurrection," says he, "will begin with them:[2] we shall accordingly not rise without them." From this it appears that the belief of a final resurrection had been, in the minds of some, slight and obscure, and involved in various errors, inasmuch as they imagined that the dead would be deprived of it; for they imagined that eternal life belonged to those alone whom Christ, at his last coming, would find still alive upon the earth. Paul, with the view of remedying these errors, assigns the first place to the dead, and afterwards teaches that those will follow who will be at that time remaining in this life.

As to the circumstance, however, that by speaking in the first person he makes himself, as it were, one of the number of those who will live until the last day, he means by this to arouse the Thessalonians to wait for it, nay more, to hold all believers in suspense, that they may not promise themselves some particular time: for, granting that it was by a special revelation that he knew that Christ would come at a somewhat later time,[3] it was nevertheless necessary that this doctrine should be delivered to the Church in common, that believers might be prepared at all times. In the mean time, it was necessary thus to cut off all pretext for the curiosity of many—as we shall find him doing afterwards at greater length. When, however, he says, *we that are alive,* he makes use of the present tense instead of the future, in accordance with the Hebrew idiom.

16. *For the Lord himself.* He employs the term κελεύσ-

[1] " L'a affermee et testifiee assureement par ses propos;"—" Has affirmed and testified it with certainty in his discourses."
[2] " Commencera par ceux qui seront decedez auparauant;"—" Will commence with those who shall have previously departed."
[3] " Ne viendroit si tost;"—" Would not come so soon."

nature of that arousing shout—that the archangel will discharge the office of a herald to summon the living and the dead to the tribunal of Christ. For though this will be common to all the angels, yet, as is customary among different ranks, he appoints one in the foremost place to take the lead of the others. As to the *trumpet*, however, I leave to others to dispute with greater subtlety, for I have nothing to say in addition to what I briefly noticed in the First Epistle to the Corinthians.[1] The Apostle unquestionably had nothing farther in view here than to give some taste of the magnificence and venerable appearance of the Judge, until we shall behold it fully. With this taste it becomes us in the mean time to rest satisfied.

The dead who are in Christ. He again says that the *dead who are in Christ*, that is, who are included in Christ's body, will *rise first*, that we may know that the hope of life is laid up in heaven for them no less than for the living. He says nothing as to the reprobate, because this did not tend to the consolation of the pious, of which he is now treating.

He says that those that survive will be *carried up together with them.* As to these, he makes no mention of death: hence it appears as if he meant to say that they would be exempted from death. Here Augustine gives himself much distress, both in the twentieth book on the City of God and in his Answer to Dulcitius, because Paul seems to contradict himself, inasmuch as he says elsewhere, that *seed cannot spring up again unless it die.* (1 Cor. xv. 36.) The solution, however, is easy, inasmuch as a sudden change will be like death. Ordinary death, it is true, is the separation of the soul from the body; but this does not hinder that the Lord may in a moment destroy this corruptible nature, so as to create it anew by his power, for thus is accomplished what Paul himself teaches must take place—that *mortality shall be swallowed up of life.* (2 Cor. v. 4.) What is stated in our Confession,[2] that "Christ will be the Judge of the

---

[1] See CALVIN on the Corinthians, vol. ii. pp. 59, 60.
[2] "En la confession de nostre foy;"—"In the confession of our faith."

that have not died will rise again. But, as I have said, that is a kind of death, when this flesh is reduced to nothing, as it is now liable to corruption. The only difference is this—that those who *sleep*[3] put off the *substance* of the body for some space of time, but those that will be suddenly changed will put off nothing but the *quality.*

17. *And so we shall be ever.* To those who have been once gathered to Christ he promises eternal life with him, by which statements the reveries of Origen and of the Chiliasts[4] are abundantly refuted. For the life of believers, when they have once been gathered into one kingdom, will have no end any more than Christ's. Now, to assign to Christ a thousand years, so that he would afterwards cease to reign, were too horrible to be made mention of. Those, however, fall into this absurdity who limit the life of believers to a thousand years, for they must live with Christ as long as Christ himself will exist. We must observe also what he says—*we shall be,* for he means that we profitably entertain a hope of eternal life, only when we hope that it has been expressly appointed for us.

18. *Comfort.* He now shews more openly what I have previously stated—that in the faith of the resurrection we have good ground of consolation, provided we are members of Christ, and are truly united to him as our Head. At the same time, the Apostle would not have each one to seek for himself assuagement of grief, but also to administer it to others.

[1] Our author manifestly refers here to the Formula of Confession, commonly called the "Apostles' Creed," which the reader will find explained at considerable length by CALVIN in the "Catechism of the Church of Geneva." See CALVIN's *Tracts,* vol. ii. pp. 39, 49.—*Ed.*

[2] "Sans aucune figure;"—"Without any figure." Our author, in his French translation, appends the following marginal note:—"C'est a dire sans le prendre comme ceux qui entendent par ces mots les bons et les mauuais;"—"That is to say, without taking it as those do, who understand by the words the good and the bad."

[3] "Ceux qui dorment, c'est a dire qui seront morts auant le dernier iour;"—"Those who sleep, that is to say, who will have died before the last day."

[4] See CALVIN's *Institutes,* vol. ii. pp. 615, 616.

1. But of the times and the seasons, brethren, ye have no need that I write unto you.	1. Porro de temporibus et articulis temporum non opus habetis, ut vobis scribatur.
2. For yourselves know perfectly, that the day of the Lord so cometh as a thief in the night.	2. Ipsi enim optime scitis, quod dies Domini tanquam fur in nocte sic veniet.
3. For when they shall say, Peace and safety, then sudden destruction cometh upon them, as travail upon a woman with child; and they shall not escape.	3. Quando enim dixerint, Pax et securitas, tunc repentinus ipsis superveniet interitus, quasi dolor partus mulieri praegnanti, nec effugient.
4. But ye, brethren, are not in darkness, that that day should overtake you as a thief.	4. Vos autem, fratres, non estis in tenebris, ut dies ille vos quasi fur opprimat.
5. Ye are all the children of light, and the children of the day: we are not of the night, nor of darkness.	5. Omnes vos filii lucis estis, et filii diei: non sumus noctis, neque tenebrarum.

1. *But as to times.* He now, in the third place, calls them back from a curious and unprofitable inquiry as to *times,* but in the mean time admonishes them to be constantly in a state of preparation for receiving Christ.[1] He speaks, however, by way of *anticipation,* saying, that they have no need that he should write as to those things which the curious desire to know. For it is an evidence of excessive incredulity not to believe what the Lord foretells, unless he marks out the day by certain circumstances, and as it were points it out with the finger. As, therefore, those waver between doubtful opinions who require that moments of time should be marked out for them, as if they would draw a conjecture[2] from some plausible demonstration, he accordingly says that discussions of this nature are not necessary for the pious. There is also another reason—that believers do not desire to know more than they are permitted to learn in God's school. Now Christ designed that the day of his coming should be hid from us, that, being in suspense, we might be as it were upon watch.

2. *Ye know perfectly.* He places exact knowledge in contrast with an anxious desire of investigation. But what is

---

[1] " Quand il viendra en iugement ;"—" When he will come to judgment."
[2] " De ce qu'ils en doyuent croire ;"—" Of what they must believe."

so as to take unbelievers by surprise, as a thief does those that are asleep. This, however, is opposed to evident tokens, which might portend afar off his coming to the world. Hence it were foolish to wish to determine the time precisely from presages or prodigies.

3. *For when they shall say.* Here we have an explanation of the similitude, *the day of the Lord will be like a thief in the night.* Why so? because it will come suddenly to unbelievers, when not looked for, so that it will take them by surprise, as though they were asleep. But whence comes that sleep? Assuredly from deep contempt of God. The prophets frequently reprove the wicked on account of this supine negligence, and assuredly they await in a spirit of carelessness not merely that last judgment, but also such as are of daily occurrence. Though the Lord threatens destruction,[2] they do not hesitate to promise themselves peace and every kind of prosperity. And the reason why they fall into this destructive indolence[3] is, because they do not see those things immediately accomplished, which the Lord declares will take place, for they reckon that to be fabulous that does not immediately present itself before their eyes. For this reason the Lord, in order that he may avenge this carelessness, which is full of obstinacy, comes all on a sudden, and contrary to the expectation of all, precipitates the wicked from the summit of felicity. He sometimes furnishes tokens of this nature of a sudden advent, but that will be the principal one, when Christ will come down to judge the world, as he himself testifies, (Matt. xxiv. 37,) comparing that time to the age of Noe, inasmuch as all will give way to excess, as if in the profoundest repose.

As the pains of child-bearing. Here we have a most apt similitude, inasmuch as there is no evil that seizes more suddenly, and that presses more keenly and more violently

---

[1] " Plenement et certainement;"—" Fully and certainly."

[2] " Leur denonce ruine et confusion;"—" Threatens them with ruin and confusion."

[3] " Ceste paresse tant dangereuse et mortelle;"—" This indolence so dangerous and deadly."

it, until she is seized amidst feasting and laughter, or in the midst of sleep.

4. *But ye, brethren.* He now admonishes them as to what is the duty of believers, that they look forward in hope to that day, though it be remote. And this is what is intended in the metaphor of *day* and *light.* The coming of Christ will take by surprise those that are carelessly giving way to indulgence, because, being enveloped in darkness, they see nothing, for no darkness is more dense than ignorance of God. We, on the other hand, on whom Christ has shone by the faith of his gospel, differ much from them, for that saying of Isaiah is truly accomplished in us, that *while darkness covers the earth, the Lord arises upon us, and his glory is seen in us.* (Isaiah lx. 2.) He admonishes us, therefore, that it were an unseemly thing that we should be caught by Christ asleep, as it were, or seeing nothing, while the full blaze of light is shining forth upon us. He calls them *children of light,* in accordance with the Hebrew idiom, as meaning—furnished with light; as also *children of the day,* meaning—those who enjoy the light of day.[1] And this he again confirms, when he says that we are *not of the night nor of darkness,* because the Lord has rescued us from it. For it is as though he had said, that we have not been enlightened by the Lord with a view to our walking in darkness.

6. Therefore let us not sleep, as *do* others; but let us watch and be sober.	6. Ergo ne dormiamus ut reliqui, sed vigilemus, et sobrii simus.
7. For they that sleep, sleep in the night; and they that be drunken, are drunken in the night.	7. Qui enim dormiunt, nocte dormiunt: et qui ebrii sunt, nocte ebrii sunt.
8. But let us, who are of the day, be sober, putting on the breastplate of faith and love; and for an helmet the hope of salvation.	8. Nos autem qui sumus diei, sobrii simus, induti thorace fidei et caritatis, et galea, spe salutis:
9. For God hath not appointed us to wrath, but to obtain salvation by our Lord Jesus Christ.	9. Quia non constituit nos Deus in iram, sed in acquisitionem salutis, per Dominum nostrum Iesum Christum:

[1] "It is 'day' with them. It is not only 'day' *round about* them, (so it is wherever the gospel is afforded to men,) but God hath made it 'day' *within.*"—*Howe's Works,* (Lond. 1822,) vol. vi. p. 294.—*Ed.*

6. *Therefore let us not sleep.* He adds other metaphors closely allied to the preceding one. For as he lately shewed that it were by no means seemly that they should be blind in the midst of light, so he now admonishes that it were dishonourable and disgraceful to sleep or be drunk in the middle of the day. Now, as he gives the name of *day* to the doctrine of the gospel, by which the Christ, the *Sun of righteousness* (Mal. iv. 2) is manifested to us, so when he speaks of sleep and drunkenness, he does not mean natural sleep, or drunkenness from wine, but stupor of mind, when, forgetting God and ourselves, we regardlessly indulge our vices. *Let us not sleep,* says he; that is, let us not, sunk in indolence, become senseless in the world. *As others,* that is, unbelievers,[1] from whom ignorance of God, like a dark night, takes away understanding and reason. *But let us watch,* that is, let us look to the Lord with an attentive mind. *And be sober,* that is, casting away the cares of the world, which weigh us down by their pressure, and throwing off base lusts, mount to heaven with freedom and alacrity. For this is spiritual sobriety, when we use this world so sparingly and temperately that we are not entangled with its allurements.

8. *Having put on the breastplate.* He adds this, that he may the more effectually shake us out of our stupidity, for he calls us as it were to arms, that he may shew that it is not a time to sleep. It is true that he does not make use of the term *war;* but when he arms us with a *breastplate* and a *helmet,* he admonishes us that we must maintain a warfare. Whoever, therefore, is afraid of being surprised by the enemy, must keep awake, that he may be constantly on watch. As, therefore, he has exhorted to vigilance, on the ground that the doctrine of the gospel is like the light of day, so he now

---

[1] "The *refuse,* as the word λοιποὶ emphatically signifies, or the reprobate and worst of men. . . . The word καθεύδωμεν, signifies a deeper or a more intense sleep. It is the word that is used in the Septuagint to signify the sleep of death." (Dan. xii. 2.)—*Howe's Works,* (Lond. 1822,) vol. vi. p. 290.—*Ed.*

hazardous a thing. For we see that soldiers, though in other situations they may be intemperate, do nevertheless, when the enemy is near, from fear of destruction, refrain from gluttony[1] and all bodily delights, and are diligently on watch so as to be upon their guard. As, therefore, Satan is on the alert against us, and tries a thousand schemes, we ought at least to be not less diligent and watchful.[2]

It is, however, in vain, that some seek a more refined exposition of the names of the kinds of armour, for Paul speaks here in a different way from what he does in Eph. vi. 14, for there he makes *righteousness* the *breastplate*. This, therefore, will suffice for understanding his meaning, that he designs to teach, that the life of Christians is like a perpetual warfare, inasmuch as Satan does not cease to trouble and molest them. He would have us, therefore, be diligently prepared and on the alert for resistance: farther, he admonishes us that we have need of arms, because unless we be well armed we cannot withstand so powerful[3] an enemy. He does not, however, enumerate *all the parts of armour*, (πανοπλίαν,) but simply makes mention of two, the *breastplate* and the *helmet*. In the mean time, he omits nothing of what belongs to spiritual armour, for the man that is provided with *faith*, *love*, and *hope*, will be found in no department unarmed.

9. *For God hath not appointed us.* As he has spoken of the *hope of salvation*, he follows out that department, and says that God has appointed us to this—that we *may obtain salvation through Christ*. The passage, however, might be explained in a simple way in this manner—that we must *put on the helmet of salvation*, because God wills not that we should perish, but rather that we should be saved. And this, indeed, Paul means, but, in my opinion, he has in view something farther. For as the day of Christ is for the

---

[1] " Et yurognerie ;"—" And drunkenness."
[2] " Pour le moins ne deuons-nous pas estre aussi vigilans que les gendarmes ?"—" Should we not at least be as vigilant as soldiers are ?"
[3] " Si puissant et si fort;"—" So powerful and so strong."

The Greek term περιποίησις means *enjoyment,* (as they speak,) as well as *acquisition.* Paul, undoubtedly, does not mean that God has called us, that we may procure salvation for ourselves, but that we may obtain it, as it has been acquired for us by Christ. Paul, however, encourages believers to fight strenuously, setting before them the certainty of victory; for the man who fights timidly and hesitatingly is half-conquered. In these words, therefore, he had it in view to take away the dread which arises from distrust. There cannot, however, be a better assurance of salvation gathered, than from the decree[2] of God. The term *wrath,* in this passage, as in other instances, is taken to mean the judgment or vengeance of God against the reprobate.

10. *Who died.* From the design of Christ's death he confirms what he has said, for if he died with this view—that he might make us partakers of his life, there is no reason why we should be in doubt as to our salvation. It is doubtful, however, what he means now by *sleeping* and *waking,* for it might seem as if he meant *life* and *death,* and this meaning would be more complete. At the same time, we might not unsuitably interpret it as meaning ordinary sleep. The sum is this—that Christ died with this view, that he might bestow upon us his life, which is perpetual and has no end. It is not to be wondered, however, that he affirms that we now *live with Christ,* inasmuch as we have, by entering through faith into the kingdom of Christ, *passed from death into life.* (John v. 24.) Christ himself, into whose body we are ingrafted, quickens us by his power, and the Spirit that dwelleth in us is *life, because of justification.*[3]

11. Wherefore comfort yourselves together, and edify one another, even as also ye do.	11. Quare exhortamini (*vel, consolamini*) vos invicem, et aedificate singuli singulos, sicut et facitis.

[1] "D'autant que volontiers nous auons en horreur et craignons le iour du Seigneur;"—"Inasmuch as we naturally regard with horror, and view with dread the day of the Lord."

[2] "Du decret et ordonnance de Dieu;"—"From the decree and appointment of God."

[3] "Comme il est dit en l'Epistre aux Rom. viii. b. 10;"—"As is stated in the Epistle to the Romans viii. 10."

and admonish you;	et admonent vos:
13. And to esteem them very highly in love for their works' sake. *And* be at peace among yourselves.	13. Ut eos habeatis in summo pretio cum caritate propter opus ipsorum: pacem habete cum ipsis, (*vel, inter vos.*)
14. Now we exhort you, brethren, warn them that are unruly, comfort the feeble-minded, support the weak, be patient toward all *men*.	14. Hortamur autem vos, fratres, monete inordinatos, consolamini pusillanimos, suscipite infirmos, patientes estote erga omnes.

11. *Exhort.* It is the same word that we had in the close of the preceding chapter, and which we rendered *comfort*, because the context required it, and the same would not suit ill with this passage also. For what he has treated of previously furnishes matter of both—of *consolation* as well as of *exhortation.* He bids them, therefore, communicate to one another what has been given them by the Lord. He adds, that they may *edify one another*—that is, may confirm each other in that doctrine. Lest, however, it might seem as if he reproved them for carelessness, he says at the same time that they of their own accord did what he enjoins. But, as we are slow to what is good, those that are the most favourably inclined of all, have always, nevertheless, need to be stimulated.

12. *And we beseech you.* Here we have an admonition that is very necessary. For as the kingdom of God is lightly esteemed, or at least is not esteemed suitably to its dignity, there follows also from this, contempt of pious teachers. Now, the most of them, offended with this ingratitude, not so much because they see themselves despised, as because they infer from this, that honour is not rendered to their Lord, are rendered thereby more indifferent, and God also, on just grounds, inflicts vengeance upon the world, inasmuch as he deprives it of good ministers,[1] to whom it is ungrateful. Hence, it is not so much for the advantage of ministers as of the whole Church, that those who faithfully preside over it should be held in esteem. And it is for this reason that Paul is so careful to recommend them. To *acknowledge* means here to *have regard* or respect; but Paul

[1] " Fideles ministres de la parolle;"—" Faithful ministers of the word."

ordinarily taken into consideration.

We must observe, however, with what titles of distinction he honours pastors. In the *first* place, he says that they *labour.* From this it follows, that all idle bellies are excluded from the number of pastors. Farther, he expresses the kind of labour when he adds, *those that admonish,* or instruct, *you.* It is to no purpose, therefore, that any, that do not discharge the office of an instructor, glory in the name of pastors. The Pope, it is true, readily admits such persons into his catalogue, but the Spirit of God expunges them from *his.* As, however, they are held in contempt in the world, as has been said, he honours them, at the same time, with the distinction of presidency.

Paul would have such as devote themselves to teaching, and preside with no other end in view than that of serving the Church, be held in no ordinary esteem. For he says literally—*let them be more than abundantly honoured,* and not without good ground, for we must observe the reason that he adds immediately afterwards—*on account of their work.* Now, this *work* is the edification of the Church, the everlasting salvation of souls, the restoration of the world, and, in fine, the kingdom of God and Christ. The excellence and dignity of this work are inestimable: hence those whom God makes ministers in connection with so great a matter, ought to be held by us in great esteem. We may, however, infer from Paul's words, that judgment is committed to the Church, that it may distinguish true pastors.[1] For to no purpose were these marks pointed out, if he did not mean that they should be taken notice of by believers. And while he commands that honour be given to those that *labour,* and to those that by teaching[2] govern properly and faithfully, he assuredly does not bestow any honour upon those that are idle and wicked, nor does he mark them out as deserving of it.

Preside in the Lord. This seems to be added to denote

---

[1] " Et les ministres fideles ;"—" And faithful ministers."
[2] " Et admonestant ;"—" And admonishing."

would have the government of the Church to be specially recognised as *his*, those that govern the Church in the name and by the commandment of Christ, are for this reason spoken of particularly as *presiding in the Lord*. We may, however, infer from this, how very remote those are from the rank of pastors and prelates who exercise a tyranny altogether opposed to Christ. Unquestionably, in order that any one may be ranked among lawful pastors, it is necessary that he should shew that he *presides* IN THE LORD, and has nothing apart from him. And what else is this, but that by pure doctrine he puts Christ in his own seat, that he may be the only Lord and Master?

13. *With love.* Others render it BY *love;* for Paul says IN *love,* which, according to the Hebrew idiom, is equivalent to *by* or *with.* I prefer, however, to explain it thus—as meaning that he exhorts them not merely to respect them,[1] but also love them. For as the doctrine of the gospel is lovely, so it is befitting that the ministers of it should be loved. It were, however, rather stiff to speak of *having in esteem* BY *love,* while the connecting together of love with honour suits well.

Be at peace. While this passage has various readings, even among the Greeks, I approve rather of the rendering which has been given by the old translator, and is followed by Erasmus—*Pacem habete cum eis, vel colite*—(*Have or cultivate peace with them.*)[2] For Paul, in my opinion, had in view to oppose the artifices of Satan, who ceases not to use every endeavour to stir up either quarrels, or disagreements, or enmities, between people and pastor. Hence we see daily how pastors are hated by their Churches for some trivial reason, or for no reason whatever, because this desire for the cultivation of peace, which Paul recommends so strongly, is not exercised as it ought.

14. *Admonish the unruly.* It is a common doctrine—that

---

[1] " De porter honneur aux fideles ministres;"—" To do honour to faithful ministers."

[2] Wiclif (1380) renders as follows: " Haue ye pees with hem."

arousing; but, as the dispositions of men are various, it is not without good reason that the Apostle commands that believers accommodate themselves to this variety. He commands, therefore, that the *unruly*[1] be admonished, that is, those who *live dissolutely*. The term *admonition*, also, is employed to mean sharp reproof, such as may bring them back into the right way, for they are deserving of greater severity, and they cannot be brought to repentance by any other remedy.

Towards the *faint-hearted* another system of conduct must be pursued, for they have need of consolation. The *weak* must also be assisted. By *faint-hearted,* however, he means those that are of a broken and afflicted spirit. He accordingly favours them, and the *weak,* in such a way as to desire that the *unruly* should be restrained with some degree of sternness. On the other hand, he commands that the *unruly* should be admonished sharply, in order that the weak may be treated with kindness and humanity, and that the *faint-hearted* may receive consolation. It is therefore to no purpose that those that are obstinate and intractable, demand that they be soothingly caressed, inasmuch as remedies must be adapted to diseases.

He recommends, however, *patience towards all,* for severity must be tempered with some degree of lenity, even in dealing with the *unruly.* This *patience,* however, is, properly speaking, contrasted with a feeling of irksomeness,[2] for nothing are we more prone to than to feel wearied out when we set ourselves to cure the diseases of our brethren. The man who has once and again comforted a person who is *faint-hearted,* if he is called to do the same thing a third time, will feel I know not what vexation, nay, even indignation, that will not permit him to persevere in discharging

---

[1] " The whole phraseology of this verse is military . . . . 'Ατάκτους— those who are *out of their ranks,* and are neither in a *disposition* nor *situation* to perform the work and duty of a soldier: those who will not do the work prescribed, and who will meddle with what is not commanded."—*Dr. A. Clarke.*—*Ed.*

[2] " A l'ennuy qu'on conçoit aiseement en tels affaires;"—." To the irksomeness which one readily feels in such matters."

of future success. Paul had in view to bridle impatience of this nature, by recommending to us moderation towards all.

15. See that none render evil for evil unto any *man;* but ever follow that which is good, both among yourselves, and to all *men.*	15. Videte, ne quis malum pro malo cuiquam reddat: sed semper benignitatem sectamini, et mutuam inter vos, et in omnes.
16. Rejoice evermore.	16. Semper gaudete.
17. Pray without ceasing.	17. Indesinenter orate.
18. In everything give thanks: for this is the will of God in Christ Jesus concerning you.	18. In omnibus gratias agite: haec enim Dei voluntas in Christo Iesu erga vos.
19. Quench not the Spirit.	19. Spiritum ne extinguatis.
20. Despise not prophesyings.	20. Prophetias ne contemnatis.
21. Prove all things: hold fast that which is good.	21. Omnia probate, quod bonum est tenete.
22. Abstain from all appearance of evil.	22. Ab omni specie mala abstinete.

15. *See that no one render evil for evil.* As it is difficult to observe this precept, in consequence of the strong bent of our nature to revenge, he on this account bids us take care to be on our guard. For the word *see* denotes anxious care. Now, although he simply forbids us to strive with each other in the way of inflicting injuries, there can, nevertheless, be no doubt that he meant to condemn, at the same time, every disposition to do injury. For if it is unlawful to *render evil for evil,* every disposition to injure is culpable. This doctrine is peculiar to Christians—not to retaliate injuries, but to endure them patiently. And lest the Thessalonians should think that revenge was prohibited only towards their brethren, he expressly declares that they are to *do evil to no one.* For particular excuses are wont to be brought forward in some cases. "What! why should it be unlawful for me to avenge myself on one that is so worthless, so wicked, and so cruel?" But as vengeance is forbidden us in every case, without exception, however wicked the man that has injured us may be, we must refrain from inflicting injury.

But always follow benignity. By this last clause he teaches that we must not merely refrain from inflicting vengeance, when any one has injured us, but must cultivate beneficence towards all. For although he means that it should in the

we may make it our aim to *overcome evil with good,* as he himself teaches elsewhere. (Rom. xii. 21.) The first step, therefore, in the exercise of patience, is, not to revenge injuries; the second is, to bestow favours even upon enemies.

16. *Rejoice always.* I refer this to moderation of spirit, when the mind keeps itself in calmness under adversity, and does not give indulgence to grief. I accordingly connect together these three things—to *rejoice always,* to *pray without ceasing,* and to *give thanks to God in* all things. For when he recommends constant praying, he points out the way of rejoicing perpetually, for by this means we ask from God alleviation in connection with all our distresses. In like manner, in Phil. iv. 4, having said, *Rejoice in the Lord always; again I say, Rejoice. Let your moderation be known to all. Be not anxious as to anything. The Lord is at hand.* He afterwards points out the means of this—*but in every prayer let your requests be made known to God, with giving of thanks.* In that passage, as we see, he presents as a source of joy a calm and composed mind, that is not unduly disturbed by injuries or adversities. But lest we should be borne down by grief, sorrow, anxiety, and fear, he bids us repose in the providence of God. And as doubts frequently obtrude themselves as to whether God cares for us, he also prescribes the remedy—that by prayer we disburden our anxieties, as it were, into his bosom, as David commands us to do in **Psalm xxxvii.** 5, and lv. 22; and Peter also, after his example. (1 Peter v. 7.) As, however, we are unduly precipitate in our desires, he imposes a check upon them—that, while we desire what we are in need of, we at the same time do not cease to give thanks.

He observes, here, almost the same order, though in fewer words. For, in the first place, he would have us hold God's benefits in such esteem, that the recognition of them and meditation upon them shall overcome all sorrow. And, unquestionably, if we consider what Christ has conferred upon us, there will be no bitterness of grief so intense as may not be alleviated, and give way to spiritual joy. For if this joy

that man to God, who does not set so high a value on the righteousness of Christ and the hope of eternal life, as to rejoice in the midst of sorrow. As, however, our minds are easily dispirited, until they give way to impatience, we must observe the remedy that he subjoins immediately afterwards. For on being cast down and laid low we are raised up again by prayers, because we lay upon God what burdened us. As, however, there are every day, nay, every moment, many things that may disturb our peace, and mar our joy, he for this reason bids us *pray without ceasing.* Now, as to this constancy in prayer, we have spoken of elsewhere.[2] *Thanksgiving*, as I have said, is added as a limitation. For many pray in such a manner, as at the same time to murmur against God, and fret themselves if he does not immediately gratify their wishes. But, on the contrary, it is befitting that our desires should be restrained in such a manner that, contented with what is given us, we always mingle thanksgiving with our desires. We may lawfully, it is true, ask, nay, sigh and lament, but it must be in such a way that the will of God is more acceptable to us than our own.

18. *For this is the will of God*—that is, according to Chrysostom's opinion—that we *give thanks.* As for myself, I am of opinion that a more ample meaning is included under these terms—that God has such a disposition towards us in Christ, that even in our afflictions we have large occasion of thanksgiving. For what is fitter or more suitable for pacifying us, than when we learn that God embraces us in Christ so tenderly, that he turns to our advantage and welfare everything that befalls us? Let us, therefore, bear in mind, that this is a special remedy for correcting our impatience—to turn away our eyes from beholding present evils that torment us, and to direct our views to a consideration of a different nature—how God stands affected towards us in Christ.

[1] " N'est point en nous, ou pour mieux dire, nous en sommes hors;"—" Is not in us, or as we may rather say, we are away from it."

[2] Our author probably refers here to what he has said on this subject when commenting on Eph. vi. 18.—*Ed.*

office of the Spirit to illuminate the understandings of men, and as he is on this account called our light, it is with propriety that we are said to *quench* him, when we make void his grace. There are some that think that it is the same thing that is said in this clause and the succeeding one. Hence, according to them, to *quench the Spirit* is precisely the same as to *despise prophesyings.* As, however, the Spirit is *quenched* in various ways, I make a distinction between these two things—that of a *general* statement, and a *particular.* For although *contempt of prophesying* is a *quenching of the Spirit,* yet those also *quench the Spirit* who, instead of stirring up, as they ought, more and more, by daily progress, the sparks that God has kindled in them, do, by their negligence, make void the gifts of God. This admonition, therefore, as to not *quenching the Spirit,* has a wider extent of meaning than the one that follows as to not *despising prophesyings.* The meaning of the *former* is: "Be enlightened by the Spirit of God. See that you do not lose that light through your ingratitude." This is an exceedingly useful admonition, for we see that those who have been *once enlightened,* (Heb. vi. 4,) when they reject so precious a gift of God, or, shutting their eyes, allow themselves to be hurried away after the vanity of the world, are struck with a dreadful blindness, so as to be an example to others. We must, therefore, be on our guard against indolence, by which the light of God is choked in us.

Those, however, who infer from this that it is in man's option either to *quench* or to *cherish* the light that is presented to him, so that they detract from the efficacy of grace, and extol the powers of free will, reason on false grounds. For although God works efficaciously in his elect, and does not merely present the light to them, but causes them to see, opens the eyes of their heart, and keeps them open, yet as the flesh is always inclined to indolence, it has need of being stirred up by exhortations. But what God commands by Paul's mouth, He himself accomplishes inwardly. In the mean time, it is our part to ask from the Lord, that he would

20. *Despise not prophesyings.* This sentence is appropriately added to the preceding one, for as the Spirit of God illuminates us chiefly by doctrine, those who give not teaching its proper place, do, so far as in them lies, *quench the Spirit,* for we must always consider in what manner or by what means God designs to communicate himself to us. Let every one, therefore, who is desirous to make progress under the direction of the Holy Spirit, allow himself to be taught by the ministry of prophets.

By the term *prophecy,* however, I do not understand the gift of foretelling the future, but as in 1 Cor. xiv. 3, the science of interpreting Scripture,[1] so that a *prophet* is an interpreter of the will of God. For Paul, in the passage which I have quoted, assigns to *prophets teaching for edification, exhortation,* and *consolation,* and enumerates, as it were, these departments. Let, therefore, prophecy in this passage be understood as meaning—interpretation made suitable to present use.[2] Paul prohibits us from *despising* it, if we would not choose of our own accord to wander in darkness.

The statement, however, is a remarkable one, for the commendation of external preaching. It is the dream of fanatics, that those are children who continue to employ themselves in the reading of the Scripture, or the hearing of the word, as if no one were spiritual, unless he is a despiser of doctrine. They proudly, therefore, despise the ministry of man, nay, even Scripture itself, that they may attain the Spirit. Farther, whatever delusions Satan suggests to them,[3] they presumptuously set forth as secret revelations of the Spirit. Such are the Libertines,[4] and other furies of that stamp. And the more ignorant that any one is, he is puffed up and swollen out with so much the greater arrogance. Let us, how-

---

[1] See CALVIN on the Corinthians, vol. i. pp. 415, 436.

[2] "Interpretation de l'Escriture applicquee proprement selon le temps, les personnes, et les choses presentes;"—"Interpretation of Scripture properly applied, according to time, persons, and things present."

[3] "Leur souffle aux aureilles;"—"Breathes into their ears."

[4] See CALVIN on the Corinthians, vol. ii. p. 7, *n.* 3.

21. *Prove all things.* As rash men and deceiving spirits frequently pass off their trifles under the name of *prophecy*, *prophecy* might by this means be rendered suspicious or even odious, just as many in the present day feel almost disgusted with the very name of *preaching*, as there are so many foolish and ignorant persons that from the pulpit blab out their worthless contrivances,[2] while there are others, also, that are wicked and sacrilegious persons, who babble forth execrable blasphemies.[3] As, therefore, through the fault of such persons it might be, that *prophecy* was regarded with disdain, nay more, was scarcely allowed to hold a place, Paul exhorts the Thessalonians to *prove all things*, meaning, that although all do not speak precisely according to set rule, we must, nevertheless, form a judgment, before any doctrine is condemned or rejected.

As to this, there is a twofold error that is wont to be fallen into, for there are some who, from having either been deceived by a false pretext of the name of God, or from their knowing that many are commonly deceived in this way, reject every kind of doctrine indiscriminately, while there are others that by a foolish credulity embrace, without distinction, everything that is presented to them in the name of God. Both of these ways are faulty, for the former class, saturated with a presumptuous prejudice of that nature, close up the way against their making progress, while the other class rashly expose themselves to all *winds* of errors. (Eph. iv. 14.) Paul admonishes the Thessalonians to keep the middle path between these two extremes, while he prohibits them from condemning anything without first examining it; and, on the other hand, he admonishes them to exercise judgment, before receiving, what may be brought forward, as undoubted truth. And unquestionably, this respect, at least, ought to be shewn to the name of God—that we do not *despise prophecy*, which is declared to have proceeded from him. As,

---

[1] "L'organe et instrument d'celuy;"—" His organ and instrument."
[2] "Leurs speculations ridicules;"—" Their ridiculous speculations."
[3] "Horribles et execrables;"—" Horrible and execrable."

sound doctrine. For it does not become the pious to shew such lightness, as indiscriminately to lay hold of what is false equally with what is true. From this we infer, that they have the spirit of judgment conferred upon them by God, that they may discriminate, so as not to be imposed upon by the impostures of men. For if they were not endowed with discrimination, it were in vain that Paul said—*Prove: hold fast that which is good.* If, however, we feel that we are left destitute of the power of *proving* aright; it must be sought by us from the same Spirit, who speaks by his prophets. But the Lord declares in this place by the mouth of Paul, that the course of doctrine ought not, by any faults of mankind, or by any rashness, or ignorance, or, in fine, by any abuse, to be hindered from being always in a vigorous state in the Church. For as the abolition of prophecy is the ruin of the Church, let us allow heaven and earth to be commingled, rather than that prophecy should cease.

Paul, however, may seem here to give too great liberty in teaching, when he would have *all things proved;* for things must be heard by us, that they may be *proved,* and by this means a door would be opened to impostors for disseminating their falsehoods. I answer, that in this instance he does not by any means require that an audience should be given to false teachers, whose *mouth* he elsewhere teaches (Tit. i. 11) *must be stopped,* and whom he so rigidly shuts out, and does not by any means set aside the arrangement, which he elsewhere recommends so highly (1 Tim. iii. 2) in the election of teachers. As, however, so great diligence can never be exercised as that there should not sometimes be persons prophesying, who are not so well instructed as they ought to be, and that sometimes good and pious teachers fail to hit the mark, he requires such moderation on the part of believers, as, nevertheless, not to refuse to hear. For nothing is more dangerous, than that moroseness, by which every kind of doctrine is rendered disgusting to us, while we do not allow ourselves to *prove* what is right.[1]

[1] " Tellement que nostre impatience ou chagrin nous empesche d'es-

from all things that bear upon their front an *appearance of evil.* In that case the meaning would be, that it is not enough to have an internal testimony of conscience, unless regard be at the same time had to brethren, so as to provide against occasions of offence, by avoiding every thing that can have the appearance of evil.

Those who explain the word *speciem* after the manner of dialecticians as meaning the subdivision of a general term, fall into an exceedingly gross blunder. For he[1] has employed the term *speciem* as meaning what we commonly term *appearance.* It may also be rendered either—*evil appearance,* or *appearance of evil.* The meaning, however, is the same. I rather prefer Chrysostom and Ambrose, who connect this sentence with the foregoing one. At the same time, neither of them explains Paul's meaning, and perhaps have not altogether hit upon what he intends. I shall state briefly my view of it.

In the first place, the phrase *appearance of evil,* or *evil appearance,* I understand to mean—when falsity of doctrine has not yet been discovered in such a manner, that it can on good grounds be rejected; but at the same time an unhappy suspicion is left upon the mind, and fears are entertained, lest there should be some poison lurking. He, accordingly, commands us to abstain from that kind of doctrine, which has an appearance of being evil, though it is not really so— not that he allows that it should be altogether rejected, but inasmuch as it ought not to be received, or to obtain belief. For why has he previously commanded that *what is good* should be *held fast,* while he now desires that we should *abstain* not simply from evil, but from *all appearance of evil ?* It is for this reason, that, when truth has been brought to light by careful examination, it is assuredly becoming in that case to give credit to it. When, on the other hand, there is any fear of false doctrine, or when the mind is involved

prouuer qui est la vraye ou la fausse;"—" So that our impatience or chagrin keeps us from proving what is true or false."

[1] " S. Paul;"—" St. Paul."

a doubtful and perplexed conscience. In short, he shews us in what way *prophecy* will be useful to us without any danger—in the event of our being attentive in *proving all things*, and our being free from lightness and haste.

23. And the very God of peace sanctify you wholly: and *I pray* God your whole spirit, and soul, and body, be preserved blameless unto the coming of our Lord Jesus Christ.	23. Ipse autem Deus pacis sanctificet vos totos : et integer spiritus vester, et anima et corpus sine reprehensione in adventu Domini nostri Iesu Christi custodiatur:
24. Faithful *is* he that calleth you, who also will do *it*.	24. Fidelis qui vos vocavit, qui et faciet.
25. Brethren, pray for us.	25. Fratres, orate pro nobis.
26. Greet all the brethren with an holy kiss.	26. Salutate fratres omnes in osculo sancto.
27. I charge you by the Lord, that this epistle be read unto all the holy brethren.	27. Adiuro vos per Dominum, ut legatur epistola omnibus sanctis fratribus.
28. The grace of our Lord Jesus Christ *be* with you. Amen.	28. Gratia Domini nostri Iesu Christi vobiscum. Amen.
¶ The first *epistle* unto the Thessalonians was written from Athens.	Ad Thessalonicenses prima scripta fuit ex Athenis.

23. *Now the God of peace himself.* Having given various injunctions, he now proceeds to prayer. And unquestionably doctrine is disseminated in vain,[1] unless God implant it in our minds. From this we see how preposterously those act who measure the strength of men by the precepts of God. Paul, accordingly, knowing that all doctrine is useless until God engraves it, as it were, with his own finger upon our hearts, beseeches God that he would *sanctify* the Thessalonians. Why he calls him here the *God of peace*, I do not altogether apprehend, unless you choose to refer it to what goes before, where he makes mention of brotherly agreement, and patience, and equanimity.[2]

We know, however, that under the term *sanctification* is included the entire renovation of the man. The Thessalonians, it is true, had been in part renewed, but Paul desires that God would perfect what is remaining. From this we infer, that we must, during our whole life, make progress in

---

[1] " Que proufitera-on de prescher la doctrine ?"—" What profit will be derived from preaching doctrine ?"

[2] " Repos d'esprit ;"—" Repose of mind."

For if it had been our part to co-operate with God, Paul would have spoken thus—" May God aid or promote your sanctification." But when he says, *sanctify you wholly*, he makes him the sole Author of the entire work.

And your entire spirit. This is added by way of exposition, that we may know what the *sanctification of the whole man* is, when he is kept *entire*, or pure, and unpolluted, in spirit, soul, and body, until the day of Christ. As, however, so complete an entireness is never to be met with in this life, it is befitting that some progress be daily made in purity, and something be cleansed away from our pollutions, so long as we live in the world.

We must notice, however, this division of the constituent parts of a man; for in some instances a man is said to consist simply of *body* and *soul*, and in that case the term *soul* denotes the immortal spirit, which resides in the body as in a dwelling. As the *soul*, however, has two principal faculties —the understanding and the will—the Scripture is accustomed in some cases to mention these two things separately, when designing to express the power and nature of the *soul;* but in that case the term *soul* is employed to mean the seat of the affections, so that it is the part that is opposed to the *spirit.* Hence, when we find mention made here of the term *spirit*, let us understand it as denoting reason or intelligence, as on the other hand by the term soul, is meant the will and all the affections.

I am aware that many explain Paul's words otherwise, for they are of opinion that by the term *soul* is meant vital motion, and by the *spirit* is meant that part of man which has been renewed; but in that case Paul's prayer were absurd. Besides, it is in another way, as I have said, that the term is wont to be made use of in Scripture. When Isaiah says, " *My* SOUL *hath desired thee in the night, my* SPIRIT *hath thought of thee,*" (Isaiah xxvi. 9,) no one doubts that he speaks of his understanding and affection, and thus

---

[1] " En l'estude et exercice de sainctete ;"—" In the study and exercise of holiness."

corresponds better with Paul's statement. For how is the whole man *entire*, except when his thoughts are pure and holy, when all his affections are right and properly regulated, when, in fine, the body itself lays out its endeavours and services only in good works? For the faculty of understanding is held by philosophers to be, as it were, a mistress: the affections occupy a middle place for commanding; the body renders obedience. We see now how well everything corresponds. For then is the man pure and entire, when he thinks nothing in his mind, desires nothing in his heart, does nothing with his body, except what is approved by God. As, however, Paul in this manner commits to God the keeping of the whole man, and all its parts, we must infer from this that we are exposed to innumerable dangers, unless we are protected by his guardianship.

24. *Faithful is he that hath called you.* As he has shewn by his prayer what care he exercised as to the welfare of the Thessalonians, so he now confirms them in an assurance of Divine grace. Observe, however, by what argument he promises them the never-failing aid of God—because he has *called* them; by which words he means, that when the Lord has once adopted us as his sons, we may expect that his grace will continue to be exercised towards us. For he does not promise to be a Father to us merely for one day, but adopts us with this understanding, that he is to cherish us ever afterwards. Hence our *calling* ought to be held by us as an evidence of everlasting grace, for he *will not leave the work of his hands incomplete.* (Psalm cxxxviii. 8.) Paul, however, addresses believers, who had not been merely called by outward preaching, but had been effectually brought by Christ to the Father, that they might be of the number of his sons.

26. *Salute all the brethren with an holy kiss.* As to the *kiss*, it was a customary token of salutation, as has been stated elsewhere.[1] In these words, however, he declares his affection towards all the saints.

---

[1] See CALVIN on the Corinthians, vol. ii. p. 78.

sons would suppress the Epistle, or whether he wished to provide against another danger—lest by a mistaken prudence and caution on the part of some, it should be kept among a few.[1] For there will always be found some who say that it is of no advantage to publish generally things that otherwise they recognise as very excellent. At least, whatever artifice or pretext Satan may have at that time contrived, in order that the Epistle might not come to the knowledge of all, we may gather from Paul's words with what earnestness and keenness he sets himself in opposition to it. For it is no light or frivolous thing to *adjure by the name of God.* We find, therefore, that the Spirit of God would have those things which he had set forth in this Epistle, through the ministry of Paul, to be published throughout the whole Church. Hence it appears, that those are more refractory than even devils themselves, who in the present day prohibit the people of God from reading the writings of Paul, inasmuch as they are no way moved by so strict an adjuration.

[1] " Qu'aucuns par vne prudence indiscrete, la communicassent seulement a quelque petit nombre sans en faire les autres participans ;"— " That some by an ill-advised prudence, would communicate it only to some small number without making others participate in it."

END OF THE COMMENTARY ON THE FIRST EPISTLE TO THE THESSALONIANS.

COMMENTARY

ON

THE SECOND EPISTLE TO THE THESSALONIANS.

THE AUTHOR'S DEDICATORY EPISTLE.

TO THAT DISTINGUISHED MAN

BENEDICT TEXTOR, PHYSICIAN.

WHILE you are reckoned to excel in the knowledge of your profession by those who are competent judges in that matter, I, for my part, have always regarded as a very high excellence that strict fidelity and diligence which you are accustomed to exercise, both in attending upon the sick, and in giving advice. But more especially in either restoring or establishing my own health, I have observed you to be so carefully intent, that it was easy to perceive that you were influenced not so much by regard to a particular individual, as by anxiety and concern for the common welfare of the Church. Another, perhaps, might think, that the kindness was smaller from its not having been shewn simply to himself as an individual; but as for me, I think myself on the contrary to be under a double obligation to you, on the ground, that while you omitted nothing whatever in discharging the office of a friend, you were at the same time equally concerned as to my ministry, too, which ought to be dearer to me than my life. The remembrance, besides, of my departed wife reminds me daily how much I owe you, not only because she was frequently through your assistance raised up, and was in one instance restored from a serious and dangerous distemper, but that even in that last disease, which took her away from us, you left nothing undone in the way of industry, labour, and effort, with a view to her assistance. Farther, as you do not allow me to give you any other remuneration, I have thought of inscribing your name upon this Commentary, in order that there may be some token of my good wishes towards you in return.

GENEVA, 1st *July* 1550.

THE ARGUMENT

ON

THE SECOND EPISTLE TO THE THESSALONIANS.

IT does not appear to me probable that this Epistle was sent from ROME, as the Greek manuscripts commonly bear; for he would have made some mention of his bonds, as he is accustomed to do in other Epistles. Besides, about the end of the third Chapter, he intimates that he is in danger from unreasonable[1] men. From this it may be gathered, that when he was going to Jerusalem, he wrote this Epistle in the course of the journey. It was also from an ancient date a very generally received opinion among the Latins, that it was written at ATHENS. The occasion, however, of his writing was this—that the THESSALONIANS might not reckon themselves overlooked, because Paul had not visited them, when hastening to another quarter. In the *first Chapter*, he exhorts them to patience. In the *second*, a vain and groundless fancy, which had got into circulation as to the coming of Christ being at hand, is set aside by him by means of this argument—that there must previously to that be a revolt in the Church, and a great part of the world must treacherously draw back from God, nay more, that Antichrist must reign in the temple of God. In the *third Chapter*, after having commended himself to their prayers, and having in a few words encouraged them to perseverance, he commands that those be severely chastised who live in idleness at the expense of others. If they do not obey admonitions, he teaches that they should be excommunicated.

[1] "Importuns et malins;"—"Unreasonable and wicked."

COMMENTARY

ON THE

SECOND EPISTLE OF PAUL TO THE THESSALONIANS.

CHAPTER I.

1. Paul, and Silvanus, and Timotheus, unto the church of the Thessalonians in God our Father, and the Lord Jesus Christ:

2. Grace unto you, and peace, from God our Father, and the Lord Jesus Christ.

3. We are bound to thank God always for you, brethren, as it is meet, because that your faith groweth exceedingly, and the charity of every one of you all toward each other aboundeth;

4. So that we ourselves glory in you in the churches of God, for your patience and faith in all your persecutions and tribulations that ye endure;

5. *Which is* a manifest token of the righteous judgment of God, that ye may be counted worthy of the kingdom of God, for which ye also suffer:

6. Seeing *it is* a righteous thing with God to recompense tribulation to them that trouble you;

7. And to you who are troubled rest with us.

1. Paulus et Silvanus et Timotheus Ecclesiae Thessalonicensium in Deo Patre nostro et Domino Iesu Christo,

2. Gratia vobis et pax a Deo Patre nostro et Domino Iesu Christo.

3. Gratias agere debemus Deo semper de vobis, fratres, quemadmodum dignum est, quia vehementer augescit fides vestra, et exuberat caritas mutua uniuscuiusque omnium vestrum;

4. Ut nos ipsi de vobis gloriemur in Ecclesia Dei, de tolerantia vestra et fide in omnibus persequutionibus vestris et afflictionibus quas sustinetis,

5. Ostensionem iusti iudicii Dei: ut digni habeamini regno Dei, pro quo et patimini.

6. Siquidem iustum est apud Deum reddere iis, qui vos affligunt, afflictionem:

7. Et vobis, qui affligimini, relaxationem nobiscum.

1. *To the Church of the Thessalonians which is in God.* As to the form of salutation, it were superfluous to speak. This only it is necessary to notice—that by a *Church in God and Christ* is meant one that has not merely been gathered together under the banner of faith, for the purpose of wor-

because while God adopts us to himself, and regenerates us, we from him begin to be in Christ. (1 Cor. i. 30.)

3. *To give thanks.* He begins with commendation, that he may have occasion to pass on to exhortation, for in this way we have more success among those who have already entered upon the course, when without passing over in silence their former progress, we remind them how far distant they are as yet from the goal, and stir them up to make progress. As, however, he had in the former Epistle commended their faith and love, he now declares the increase of both. And, unquestionably, this course ought to be pursued by all the pious—to examine themselves daily, and see how far they have advanced. This, therefore, is the true commendation of believers—their *growing* daily in *faith* and *love*. When he says *always*, he means that he is constantly supplied with new occasion. He had previously given thanks to God on their account. He says that he has now occasion to do so again, on the ground of daily progress. When, however, he gives thanks to God on this account, he declares that the enlargements, no less than the beginnings, of faith and love are from him, for if they proceeded from the power of men, thanksgiving would be pretended, or at least worthless. Farther, he shews that their proficiency was not trivial, or even ordinary, but most abundant. So much the more disgraceful is our slowness, inasmuch as we scarcely advance one foot during a long space of time.

As is meet. In these words Paul shews that we are bound to give thanks to God, not only when he does us good, but also when we take into view the favours bestowed by him upon our brethren. For wherever the goodness of God shines forth, it becomes us to extol it. Farther, the welfare of our brethren ought to be so dear to us, that we ought to reckon among our own benefits everything that has been conferred upon them. Nay more, if we consider the nature and sacredness of the unity of Christ's body, such a mutual fellowship will have place among us, that we shall reckon the benefits conferred upon an individual member as

Church.

4. *So that we ourselves glory in you.* He could not have bestowed higher commendation upon them, than by saying that he sets them forward before other Churches as a pattern, for such is the meaning of those words:—*We glory in you in the presence of other Churches.* For Paul did not boast of the faith of the Thessalonians from a spirit of ambition, but inasmuch as his commendation of them might be an incitement to make it their endeavour to imitate them. He does not say, however, that he glories in their faith and love, but in their *patience* and *faith.* Hence it follows, that *patience* is the fruit and evidence of *faith.* These words ought, therefore, to be explained in this manner:—" We glory in the patience which springs from faith, and we bear witness that it eminently shines forth in you;" otherwise the context would not correspond. And, undoubtedly, there is nothing that sustains us in tribulations as faith does; which is sufficiently manifest from this, that we altogether sink down so soon as the promises of God leave us. Hence, the more proficiency any one makes in faith, he will be so much the more endued with patience for enduring all things with fortitude, as on the other hand, softness and impatience under adversity betoken unbelief on our part; but more especially when persecutions are to be endured for the gospel, the influence of faith in that case discovers itself.

5. *A demonstration of the righteous judgment of God.* Without mentioning the exposition given by others, I am of opinion that the true meaning is this—that the injuries and persecutions which innocent and pious persons endure from the wicked and abandoned, shew clearly, as in a mirror, that God will one day be the judge of the world. And this statement is quite at antipodes with that profane notion, which we are accustomed to entertain, whenever it goes well with the good and ill with the wicked. For we think that the world is under the regulation of mere chance, and we leave God no control. Hence it is that impiety and contempt take possession of men's hearts, as Solomon speaks, (Eccl.

cerns himself as to the affairs of men. We hear what Ovid says,—"I am tempted to think that there are no gods."[1] Nay more, David confesses (Psalm lxxiii. 1-12) that, because he saw things in so confused a state in the world, he had well-nigh lost his footing, as in a slippery place. On the other hand, the wicked become more insolent through occasion of prosperity, as if no punishment of their crimes awaited them; just as Dionysius, when making a prosperous voyage,[2] boasted that the gods favoured the sacrilegious.[3] In fine, when we see that the cruelty of the wicked against the innocent walks abroad with impunity, carnal sense concludes that there is no judgment of God, that there are no punishments of the wicked, that there is no reward of righteousness.

Paul, however, declares on the other hand, that as God thus spares the wicked for a time, and winks at the injuries inflicted upon his people, His judgment to come is shewn us as in a mirror. For he takes for granted that it cannot but be that God, inasmuch as he is a just Judge, will one day restore peace to the miserable, who are now unjustly harassed, and will pay to the oppressors of the pious the reward that they have merited. Hence, if we hold this principle of faith, that God is the just Judge of the world, and that it is his office to render to every one a recompense according to his works, this second principle will follow incontrovertibly—that the present *disorderly state of matters* ($\dot{a}\tau a\xi i a\nu$) is a *demonstration* of the judgment, which does not yet appear. For if God is the righteous Judge of the world, those things that are now confused must, of

[1] "Solicitor nullos esse putare deos."—*Ovid* iii. Am. ix. 36. In order to see the appropriateness of the quotation, it is necessary to notice the connection of the words "Cum rapiant mala fata bonos. . . . Solicitor," &c. ;—"When misfortunes overtake the good, I am tempted," &c.—*Ed.*

[2] "Comme Denys le tyran, apres auoir pillé vn temple, s'estant mis sur le mer, et voyant qu'il auoit bon vent;"—"As Dionysius the tyrant, after he had plundered a temple, having embarked upon the sea, and observing that he had a favourable wind."

[3] Our author alludes to a saying of Dionysius the younger, tyrant of Sicily, on occasion of his plundering the temple of Proserpine. See CALVIN on the Psalms, vol. i. p. 141, vol. iii. p. 126, vol. v. p. 114.—*Ed.*

tion to the good, and walk abroad with unbridled violence, while the good are cruelly harassed without any fault on their part. From this it may be readily inferred, that God will one day ascend the judgment-seat, that he may remedy the state of matters in the world, so as to bring them into a better condition.

Hence the statement which he subjoins—that it is *righteous with God to appoint affliction*, &c., is the groundwork of this doctrine—that God furnishes tokens of a judgment to come when he refrains, for the present, from exercising the office of judge. And unquestionably, if matters were now arranged in a tolerable way, so that the judgment of God might be recognised as having been fully exercised, an adjustment of this nature would detain us upon earth. Hence God, in order that he may stir us up to the hope of a judgment to come, does, for the present, only to some extent judge the world. He furnishes, it is true, many tokens of his judgment, but it is in such a manner as to constrain us to extend our hope farther. A remarkable passage truly, as teaching us in what manner our minds ought to be raised up above all the impediments of the world, whenever we suffer any adversity—that the righteous judgment of God may present itself to our mind, which will raise us above this world. Thus death will be an image of life.

May be accounted worthy. There are no persecutions that are to be reckoned of such value as to make us *worthy of the kingdom of God,* nor does Paul dispute here as to the ground of worthiness, but simply takes the common doctrine of Scripture—that God destroys in us those things that are of the world, that he may restore in us a better life; and farther, that by means of afflictions he shews us the value of eternal life. In short, he simply points out the manner in which believers are prepared and, as it were, polished under God's anvil, inasmuch as, by afflictions, they are taught to renounce the world and to aim at God's heavenly kingdom. Farther, they are confirmed in the hope of

Luke xiii. 24.)

6. *To appoint affliction.* We have already stated why it is that he makes mention of the vengeance of God against the wicked—that we may learn to rest in the expectation of a judgment to come, because God does not as yet avenge the wicked, while it is, nevertheless, necessary that they should suffer the punishment of their crimes. Believers, however, at the same time, understand by this that there is no reason why they should envy the momentary and evanescent felicity of the wicked, which will ere long be exchanged for a dreadful destruction. What he adds as to the *rest* of the pious, accords with the statement of Paul, (Acts iii. 20,) where he calls the day of the last judgment the *day of refreshing.*

In this declaration, however, as to the good and the bad, he designed to shew more clearly how unjust and confused the government of the world would be, if God did not defer punishments and rewards till another judgment, for in this way the name of God were a thing that was dead.[1] Hence he is deprived of his office and power by all that are not intent on that righteousness of which Paul speaks.

He adds *with us,* that he may gain credit to his doctrine from his experience of belief in his own mind; for he shews that he does not philosophize as to things unknown, by putting himself into the same condition, and into the same rank with them. We know, however, how much more authority is due to those who have, by long practice, been exercised in those things which they teach, and do not require from others anything but what they are themselves prepared to do. Paul, therefore, does not, while himself in the shade, give instructions to the Thessalonians as to how they should fight in the heat of the sun, but, fighting vigorously, exhorts them to the same warfare.[2]

[1] "Morte et sans vertu;"—"Dead and powerless."
[2] "S. Paul, donc, enseignant les Thessaloniciens comment ils doyuent combattre au milieu des afflictions, ne parle point comme vn gendarme qui estant en l'ombre et a son aise, accourageroit les autres a faire leur deuoir a la campagne au milieu de la poussiere et a la chaleur du soleil :

8. In flaming fire, taking vengeance on them that know not God, and that obey not the gospel of our Lord Jesus Christ:	8. In igne flammanti, qui ultionem infliget iis, qui non noverunt Deum, et non obediunt evangelio Domini nostri Iesu Christi:
9. Who shall be punished with everlasting destruction from the presence of the Lord, and from the glory of his power;	9. Qui pœnam dabunt interitum aeternum a facie Domini, et a gloria potentiae ipsius,
10. When he shall come to be glorified in his saints, and to be admired in all them that believe, (because our testimony among you was believed,) in that day.	10. Quum venerit ut sanctificetur in sanctis suis, et admirabilis reddatur in omnibus, qui credunt (quia fides habita sit testimonio nostro erga vos) in illa die.

7. *When the Lord shall be manifested.* Here we have a confirmation of the foregoing statement. For as it is one of the articles of our faith, that Christ will come from heaven, and will not come in vain, faith ought to seek the end of his coming. Now this is—that he may come as a Redeemer to his own people; nay more, that he may judge the whole world. The description which follows has a view to this— that the pious may understand that God is so much the more concerned as to their afflictions in proportion to the dreadfulness of the judgment that awaits his enemies. For the chief occasion of grief and distress is this—that we think that God is but lightly affected with our calamities. We see into what complaints David from time to time breaks forth, while he is consumed by the pride and insolence of his enemies. Hence he has brought forward all this for the consolation of believers, while he represents the tribunal of Christ as full of horror,[1] that they may not be disheartened by their present oppressed condition, while they see themselves proudly and disdainfully trampled upon by the wicked.

What is to be the nature of that *fire*, and of what mate-

mais combattant luy-mesme vaillamment, il les exhorte a combattre de mesme;"—" St Paul, therefore, instructing the Thessalonians how they ought to fight in the midst of afflictions, does not speak like a soldier who, while in the shade and at his ease, would encourage others to do their duty in the campaign in the midst of dust, and in the heat of the sun; but, while fighting himself valiantly, he exhorts them to contend in like manner."

[1] " Plein d'horreur et d'espouvantement ;"—" Full of horror and terror."

view to teach—that Christ will be a most strict avenger of the injuries which the wicked inflict upon us. The metaphor, however, of *flame* and *fire*, is abundantly common in Scripture, when the anger of God is treated of.

By the *angels of his power*, he means those in whom he will exercise his power; for he will bring the angels with him for the purpose of displaying the glory of his kingdom. Hence, too, they are elsewhere called the *angels of his majesty*.

8. *Who will inflict vengeance.* That he may the better persuade believers that the persecutions which they endure will not go unpunished, he teaches that this also involves the interests of God himself, inasmuch as the same persons that persecute the pious are guilty of rebellion against God. Hence it is necessary that God should inflict vengeance upon them not merely with a view to our salvation, but also for the sake of his own glory. Farther, this expression, *who will inflict vengeance*, relates to Christ, for Paul intimates that this office is assigned to him by God the Father. It may be asked, however, whether it is lawful for us to desire vengeance, for Paul promises it, as though it could be lawfully desired. I answer, that it is not lawful to desire vengeance upon any one, inasmuch as we are commanded to wish well to all. Besides, although we may in a general way desire vengeance upon the wicked, yet, as we do not as yet discriminate them, we ought to desire the welfare of all. In the mean time, the ruin of the wicked may be lawfully looked forward to with desire, provided there reigns in our hearts a pure and duly regulated zeal for God, and there is no feeling of inordinate desire.

Who know not. He distinguishes unbelievers by these two marks—that they *know not God*, and *obey not the gospel of Christ*. For if obedience is not rendered to the gospel through faith, as he teaches in the *first* and in the *last* chapters of the Epistle to the Romans, unbelief is the occasion of resistance to it. He charges them at the same time with ignorance of God, for a lively acquaintance with God

devoid of light and intelligence, but because they have the understanding darkened in such a manner, that *seeing they do not see.* (Matt. xiii. 13.) It is not without good grounds that Christ declares that *this is life eternal, to know the true God,* &c. (John xvii. 3.) Accordingly, from the want of this salutary knowledge, there follows contempt of God, and in fine, death. On this point I have treated more fully in commenting on the first chapter of First Corinthians.[1]

9. *Everlasting destruction from the face.* He shews, by apposition,[2] what is the nature of the punishment of which he had made mention—destruction without end, and an undying death. The perpetuity of the death is proved from the circumstance, that it has the glory of Christ as its opposite. Now, this is eternal, and has no end. Accordingly, the influence of that death will never cease. From this also the dreadful severity of the punishment may be inferred, inasmuch as it will be great in proportion to the glory and majesty of Christ.

10. *When he shall come to be sanctified.* As he has hitherto discoursed as to the punishment of the wicked, he now returns to the pious, and says that Christ will come, that he may be *glorified* in them; that is, that he may irradiate them with his glory, and that they may be partakers of it. " Christ will not have this glory for himself individually; but it will be common to all the saints." This is the crowning and choice consolation of the pious, that when the Son of God will be manifested in the glory of his kingdom, he will gather them into the same fellowship with himself.[3] There is, however, an implied contrast between the present condition in which believers labour and groan, and that final restoration. For they are *now* exposed to the reproaches of the world, and are looked upon as vile and worthless; but *then* they will be precious, and full of dignity, when Christ will pour forth his glory upon them. The end of this is,

[1] See CALVIN on the Corinthians, vol. i. pp. 84-86.
[2] See p.148, *n.* 2.
[3] " Il les recueillera en plene conionction, et les fera ses consors;"— " He will gather them in full union, and will make them his partners."

intent upon the future manifestation of Christ's kingdom. For to what purpose does he make mention of His coming in power, but in order that they may in hope leap forward to that blessed resurrection which is as yet hid?

It is also to be observed, that after having made use of the term *saints*, he adds, by way of explanation—*those that believe*, by which he intimates that there is no holiness in men without faith, but that all are profane. In the close he again repeats the terms—*in that day*, for that expression is connected with this sentence. Now, he repeats it with this view, that he may repress the desires of believers, lest they should hasten forward beyond due bounds.

Because credit was given. What he had said in a general way as to saints, he now applies to the Thessalonians, that they may not doubt that they are of that number. "Because," says he, "my preaching has obtained credit among you, Christ has already enrolled you in the number of his own people, whom he will make partakers of his glory." He calls his doctrine a *testimony*, because the Apostles are Christ's *witnesses*. (Acts i. 8.) Let us learn, therefore, that the promises of God are ratified in us, when they gain credit with us.

11. Wherefore also we pray always for you, that our God would count you worthy of *this* calling, and fulfil all the good pleasure of *his* goodness, and the work of faith with power;
12. That the name of our Lord Jesus Christ may be glorified in you, and ye in him, according to the grace of our God and the Lord Jesus Christ.

11. In quam rem etiam oramus semper pro vobis: ut vos habeat dignos vocatione Deus noster, et impleat omne beneplacitum bonitatis, et opus fidei cum potentia:[1]
12. Quo glorificetur nomen Domini nostri Iesu Christi in vobis, et vos in ipso, secundum gratiam Dei nostri, et Domini Iesu Christi.

11. *On which account we pray always.* That they may know that they need continual help from God, he declares that he prays in their behalf. When he says *on this account*, he means, in order that they may reach that final goal of their course, as appears from the succeeding context, *that he*

[1] " Auec puissance, ou puissamment;"—" With power, or powerfully."

already *accounted them worthy of his calling.* He speaks, however, as to the end or completion, which depends on perseverance. For as we are liable to give way, our *calling* would not fail, so far as we are concerned, to prove sooner or later vain, if God did not confirm it. Hence he is said to *account us worthy*, when he conducts us to the point at which we aimed.

And fulfil. Paul goes to an amazing height in extolling the grace of God, for not contenting himself with the term *good pleasure,* he says that it flows from his goodness, unless perhaps any one should prefer to consider the beneficence[1] as arising from this *good pleasure,* which amounts to the same thing. When, however, we are instructed that the *gracious purpose* of God is the cause of our salvation, and that *that* has its foundation in the *goodness* of the same God, are we not worse than mad, if we venture to ascribe anything, however small, to our own merits? For the words are in no small degree emphatic. He might have said in one word, *that your faith may be fulfilled,* but he terms it *good pleasure.* Farther, he expresses the idea still more distinctly by saying, that God was prompted by nothing else than his own goodness, for he finds nothing in us but misery.

Nor does Paul ascribe to the grace of God merely the beginning of our salvation, but all departments of it. Thus that contrivance of the Sophists is set aside, that we are, indeed, anticipated by the grace of God, but that it is helped by subsequent merits. Paul, on the other hand, recognises in the whole progress of our salvation nothing but the pure grace of God. As, however, the *good pleasure* of God has been already accomplished in him, referring in the term subsequently employed by him to the effect which appears in us, he explains his meaning when he says—*and work of faith.* And he calls it a *work*, with regard to God, who works or produces faith in us, as though he had said—" that he may complete the building of faith which he has begun."

It is, also, not without good reason, that he says *with*

[1] " Ceste *bonté* et beneficence ;"—" This *goodness* and beneficence."

also, we know but too well from experience; and the reason, too, is not far to seek, if we consider how great our weakness is, how various are the hinderances that obstruct us on every side, and how severe are the assaults of Satan. Hence, unless the power of God afford us help in no ordinary degree, faith will never rise to its full height. For it is no easier task to bring faith to perfection in an individual, than to rear upon water a tower that may by its firmness withstand all storms and fury of tempests, and may surmount the clouds in height, for we are not less fluid than water, and it is necessary that the height of faith reach as high as heaven.

12. *That the name of our Lord Jesus Christ may be glorified.* He calls us back to the chief end of our whole life—that we may promote the Lord's glory. What he adds, however, is more especially worthy of notice, that those who have advanced the glory of Christ will also in their turn be glorified in him. For in this, first of all, the wonderful goodness of God shines forth—that he will have his glory be conspicuous in us who are covered over with ignominy. This, however, is a twofold miracle, that he afterwards irradiates us with his glory, as though he would do the same to us in return. On this account he adds, *according to the grace of God and Christ.* For there is nothing here that is ours either in the action itself, or in the effect or fruit, for it is solely by the guidance of the Holy Spirit that our life is made to contribute to the glory of God. And the circumstance that so much fruit arises from this ought to be ascribed to the great mercy of God. In the mean time, if we are not worse than stupid, we must aim with all our might at the advancement of the glory of Christ, which is connected with ours. I deem it unnecessary to explain at present in what sense he represents the glory as belonging to God and Christ in common, as I have explained this elsewhere.[1]

[1] See p. 370.

1. Now we beseech you, brethren, by the coming of our Lord Jesus Christ, and *by* our gathering together unto him,

2. That ye be not soon shaken in mind, or be troubled, neither by spirit, nor by word, nor by letter as from us, as that the day of Christ is at hand.

1. Rogo autem vos, fratres, per adventum (*vel, de adventu*) Domini nostri Iesu Christi, et nostri in ipsum aggregationem,

2. Ne cito dimoveamini a mente, neque turbemini vel per spiritum, vel per sermonem, vel per epistolam, tanquam a nobis scriptam, quasi instet dies Christi.

1. *Now I beseech you, by the coming.* It may indeed be read, as I have noted on the margin, CONCERNING *the coming*, but it suits better to view it as an earnest entreaty, taken from the subject in hand, just as in 1 Cor. xv. 31, when discoursing as to the hope of a resurrection, he makes use of an oath by that *glory* which is to be hoped for by believers. And this has much more efficacy when he adjures believers by the coming of Christ, not to imagine rashly that his day is at hand, for he at the same time admonishes us not to think of it but with reverence and sobriety. For it is customary to adjure by those things which are regarded by us with reverence. The meaning therefore is, " As you set a high value on the coming of Christ, when he will gather us to himself, and will truly perfect that unity of the body which we cherish as yet only in part through means of faith, so I earnestly beseech you by his coming not to be too credulous, should any one affirm, on whatever pretext, that his day is at hand."

As he had in his former Epistle adverted to some extent to the resurrection, it is possible that some fickle and fanatical persons took occasion from this to mark out a near and fixed day. For it is not likely that this error had taken its rise earlier among the Thessalonians. For Timothy, on returning thence, had informed Paul as to their entire condition, and as a prudent and experienced man had omitted nothing that was of importance. Now if Paul had received notice of it, he could not have been silent as to a matter of so great consequence. Thus I am of opinion, that when Paul's Epistle had been read, which contained a lively view

however, was an utterly ruinous fancy,[1] as were also other things of the same nature, which were afterwards disseminated, not without artifice on the part of Satan. For when any day is said to be *near*, if it does not quickly arrive, mankind being naturally impatient of longer delay, their spirits begin to languish, and that languishing is followed up shortly afterwards by despair.

This, therefore, was Satan's subtlety : as he could not openly overturn the hope of a resurrection with the view of secretly undermining it, as if by pits underground,[2] he promised that the day of it would be near, and would soon arrive. Afterwards, too, he did not cease to contrive various things, with the view of effacing, by little and little, the belief of a resurrection from the minds of men, as he could not openly eradicate it. It is, indeed, a plausible thing to say that the day of our redemption is definitely fixed, and on this account it meets with applause on the part of the multitude, as we see that the dreams of Lactantius and the Chiliasts[3] of old gave much delight, and yet they had no other tendency than that of overthrowing the hope of a resurrection. This was not the design of Lactantius, but Satan, in accordance with his subtlety, perverted his curiosity, and that of those like him, so as to leave nothing in religion definite or fixed, and even at the present day he does not cease to employ the same means. We now see how necessary Paul's admonition was, as but for this all religion would have been overturned among the Thessalonians under a specious pretext.

2. *That ye be not soon shaken in judgment.* He employs the term *judgment* to denote that settled faith which rests on sound doctrine. Now, by means of that fancy which he rejects, they would have been carried away as it were into ecstasy. He notices, also, three kinds of imposture, as to

---

[1] " Vne fantasie merueilleusement pernicieuse, et pour ruiner tout;"— " A fancy that was singularly destructive, and utterly ruinous."
[2] See CALVIN on the Corinthians, vol. i. p. 38.
[3] See p. 296.

phecies, and it appears that this mode of speaking was common among the pious, so that they applied the term *spirit* to prophesyings, with the view of putting honour upon them. For, in order that prophecies may have due authority, we must look to the Spirit of God rather than to men. But as the devil is wont to *transform himself into an angel of light*, (2 Cor. xi. 14,) impostors stole this title, in order that they might impose upon the simple. But although Paul could have stript them of this mask, he, nevertheless, preferred to speak in this manner, by way of concession, as though he had said, "However they may pretend to have the spirit of revelation, believe them not." John, in like manner, says: "*Try the spirits, whether they are of God.*" (1 John iv. 1.)

Speech, in my opinion, includes every kind of doctrine, while false teachers insist in the way of reasons or conjectures, or other pretexts. What he adds as to *epistle*, is an evidence that this impudence is ancient—that of feigning the names of others.[1] So much the more wonderful is the mercy of God towards us, in that while Paul's name was on false grounds made use of in spurious writings, his writings have, nevertheless, been preserved entire even to our times. This, unquestionably, could not have taken place accidentally, or as the effect of mere human industry, if God himself had not by his power restrained Satan and all his ministers.

As if the day of Christ were at hand. This may seem to be at variance with many passages of Scripture, in which the Spirit declares that that day is at hand. But the solution is easy, for it is *at hand* with regard to God, with whom *one day is as a thousand years.* (2 Peter iii. 8.) In the mean time, the Lord would have us be constantly waiting for him in such a way as not to limit him to a certain time. *Watch*, says he, *for ye know neither the day nor the hour.* (Matt. xxiv. 32.) On the other hand, those false prophets whom Paul exposes, while they ought to have kept men's minds in suspense, bid them feel assured of his speedy

[1] "Des grands personnages;"—"Of great personages."

3. Let no man deceive you by any means: for *that day shall not come*, except there come a falling away first, and that man of sin be revealed, the son of perdition;

4. Who opposeth and exalteth himself above all that is called God, or that is worshipped; so that he, as God, sitteth in the temple of God, shewing himself that he is God.

3. Ne quis vos decipiat ullo modo: quia nisi prius venerit discessio, et nisi revelatus fuerit sceleratus ille filius perditus,

4. Adversarius, et qui se extollit adversus omne, quod dicitur Deus, aut numen: ita ut ipse in templo Dei tanquam Deus sedeat, ostendens se ipsum quasi sit Deus.

3. *Let no man deceive you.* That they may not groundlessly promise themselves the arrival in so short a time of the joyful day of redemption, he presents to them a melancholy prediction as to the future scattering of the Church. This discourse entirely corresponds with that which Christ held in the presence of his disciples, when they had asked him respecting the end of the world. For he exhorts them to prepare themselves for enduring hard conflicts,[1] (Matt. xxiv. 6,) and after he has discoursed of the most grievous and previously unheard of calamities, by which the earth was to be reduced almost to a desert, he adds, that the *end is not yet*, but that *these things are the beginnings of sorrows.* In the same way, Paul declares that believers must exercise warfare for a long period, before gaining a triumph.

We have here, however, a remarkable passage, and one that is in the highest degree worthy of observation. This was a grievous and dangerous temptation, which might shake even the most confirmed, and make them loose their footing —to see the Church, which had by means of such labours been raised up gradually and with difficulty to some considerable standing, fall down suddenly, as if torn down by a tempest. Paul, accordingly, fortifies beforehand the minds, not merely of the Thessalonians, but of all the pious, that when the Church should come to be in a scattered condition, they might not be alarmed, as though it were a thing that was new and unlooked for.

As, however, interpreters have twisted this passage in

[1] " Merveilleux et durs combats;"—" Singular and hard conflicts."

not come, until the world has fallen into apostasy, and the reign of Antichrist has obtained a footing in the Church; for as to the exposition that some have given of this passage, as referring to the downfal of the Roman empire, it is too silly to require a lengthened refutation. I am also surprised, that so many writers, in other respects learned and acute, have fallen into a blunder in a matter that is so easy, were it not that when one has committed a mistake, others follow in troops without consideration. Paul, therefore, employs the term *apostasy* to mean—a treacherous departure from God, and that not on the part of one or a few individuals, but such as would spread itself far and wide among a large multitude of persons. For when *apostasy* is made mention of without anything being added, it cannot be restricted to a few. Now, none can be termed *apostates*, but such as have previously made a profession of Christ and the gospel. Paul, therefore, predicts a certain general revolt of the visible Church. "The Church must be reduced to an unsightly and dreadful state of ruin, before its full restoration be effected."

From this we may readily gather, how useful this prediction of Paul is, for it might have seemed as though that could not be a building of God, that was suddenly overthrown, and lay so long in ruins, had not Paul long before intimated that it would be so. Nay more, many in the present day, when they consider with themselves the long-continued dispersion of the Church, begin to waver, as if this had not been regulated by the purpose of God. The Romanists, also, with the view of justifying the tyranny of their idol, make use of this pretext—that it was not possible that Christ would forsake his spouse. The weak, however, have something here on which to rest, when they learn that the unseemly state of matters which they behold in the Church was long since foretold; while, on the other hand, the impudence of the Romanists is openly exposed, inasmuch as Paul declares that a revolt will come, when the world has been brought under Christ's authority. Now, we shall see presently, why it is that the Lord has permitted the Church,

Has been revealed. It was no better than an old wife's fable that was contrived respecting Nero, that he was carried up from the world, destined to return again to harass the Church[1] by his tyranny ; and yet the minds of the ancients were so bewitched, that they imagined that Nero would be Antichrist.[2] Paul, however, does not speak of one individual, but of a kingdom, that was to be taken possession of by Satan, that he might set up a seat of abomination in the midst of God's temple—which we see accomplished in Popery. The revolt, it is true, has spread more widely, for Mahomet, as he was an apostate, turned away the Turks, his followers, from Christ. All heretics have broken the unity of the Church by their sects, and thus there have been a corresponding number of revolts from Christ.

Paul, however, when he has given warning that there would be such a scattering, that the greater part would revolt from Christ, adds something more serious—that there would be such a confusion, that the vicar of Satan would hold supreme power in the Church, and would preside there in the place of God. Now he describes that reign of abomination under the name of a single person, because it is only one reign, though one succeeds another. My readers now understand, that all the sects by which the Church has been lessened from the beginning, have been so many streams of revolt which began to draw away the water from the right course, but that the sect of Mahomet was like a violent bursting forth of water, that took away about the half of the Church by its violence. It remained, also, that Antichrist should infect the remaining part with his poison. Thus,

[1] " Pour tourmenter griefuement l'Eglise ;"—" To torment the Church grievously."

[2] The strange notion here referred to by CALVIN as to NERO, is accounted for by Cornelius à Lapide in his Commentary on the Revelation, p. 212, from the circumstance that Alcazar having explained the expression which occurs in Rev. xiii. 3, " I saw one of the heads as it were killed to death," as referring to Nero killed, and soon afterwards raised up, *as it were*, and reviving in the person of DOMITIAN his successor, some of the ancients, understanding *literally* what was meant by him *figuratively*, conceived the idea that Nero would be Antichrist, and would be raised up, and appear again in the end of the world.—*Ed.*

In the exposition which I bring forward, there is nothing forced. Believers in that age dreamed that they would be transported to heaven, after having endured troubles during a short period. Paul, however, on the other hand, foretells that, after they have had foreign enemies for some time molesting them, they will have more evils to endure from enemies at home, inasmuch as many of those that have made a profession of attachment to Christ would be hurried away into base treachery, and inasmuch as the temple of God itself would be polluted by sacrilegious tyranny, so that Christ's greatest enemy would exercise dominion there. The term *revelation* is taken here to denote manifest possession of tyranny, as if Paul had said that the day of Christ would not come until this tyrant had openly manifested himself, and had, as it were, designedly overturned the whole order of the Church.

4. *An adversary, and that exalteth himself.* The two epithets—*man of sin,* and *son of perdition*—intimate, in the first place, how dreadful the confusion would be, that the unseemliness of it might not discourage weak minds; and farther, they tend to stir up the pious to a feeling of detestation, lest they should degenerate along with others. Paul, however, now draws, as if in a picture, a striking likeness of Antichrist; for it may be easily gathered from these words what is the nature of his kingdom, and in what things it consists. For, when he calls him an *adversary,* when he says that he will claim for himself those things which belong to God, so that he is worshipped in the temple as God, he places his kingdom in direct opposition to the kingdom of Christ. Hence, as the kingdom of Christ is spiritual, so this tyranny must be upon souls, that it may rival the kingdom of Christ. We shall also find him afterwards assigning to him the power of deceiving, by means of wicked doctrines and pretended miracles. If, accordingly, you would know Antichrist, you must view him as diametrically opposed to Christ.[1]

[1] " The name of the Man of Sin is not *Antitheos,* but ἀντίχριστος—not one

one that is called. It may, however, be conjectured, both from the old translation[1] and from some Greek commentaries, that Paul's words have been corrupted. The mistake, too, of a single letter was readily fallen into, especially when the shape of the letter was much similar; for, where there was written πᾶν τὸ, (*everything,*) some transcriber, or too daring reader, turned it into πάντα, (*every one.*) This difference, however, is not of so much importance as to the sense, for Paul undoubtedly means that Antichrist would take to himself those things that belonged to God alone, so that he would *exalt himself* above every divine claim, that all religion and all worship of God might lie under his feet. This expression then, *everything that is reckoned to be God,* is equivalent to *everything that is reckoned as Divinity,* and σέβασμα, that is, in which the veneration due to God consists.

Here, however, the subject treated of is not the name of God himself, but his majesty and worship, and, in general, everything that he claims for himself. "True religion is that by which the true God alone is worshipped; *that,* the *son of perdition* will transfer to himself." Now, every one that has learned from Scripture what are the things that more especially belong to God, and will, on the other hand, observe what the Pope claims for himself—though he were but a boy of ten years of age—will have no great difficulty in recognising Antichrist. Scripture declares that God is the *alone Lawgiver* (James iv. 12) *who is able to save and to destroy;* the alone King, whose office it is to govern souls by his word. It represents him as the author of all sacred rites;[2] it teaches that righteousness and salvation are

that directly invadeth the properties of the supreme God, but of God incarnate, or Christ as Mediator. . . . he usurpeth the authority due to Christ."—*Dr. Manton's* Sermons on 2d Thess. ii. p. 89.—*Ed.*

[1] The rendering of the Vulgate is as follows,—" Supra omne quod dicitur Deus aut quod colitur;"—" Above everything that is called God, or that is worshipped." *Wyclif* (1380) renders thus: " Ouer alle thing that is seid God, or that is worschipid."—*Ed.*

[2] " Que c'est a luy seul d'establir seruice diuin, et ceremonies qui en dependent;"—" That it belongs to him alone to establish divine worship, and the rites that are connected with it."

things that the Pope does not affirm to be under his authority. He boasts that it is his to bind consciences with such laws as seem good to him, and subject them to everlasting punishment. As to sacraments, he either institutes new ones, according to his own inclination,[1] or he corrupts and deforms those which had been instituted by Christ— nay, sets them aside altogether, that he may substitute in their place the sacrileges[2] which he has invented. He contrives means of attaining salvation that are altogether at variance with the doctrine of the Gospel; and, in fine, he does not hesitate to change the whole of religion at his own pleasure. What is it, I pray you, for one to lift up himself above everything that is reckoned God, if the Pope does not do so? When he thus robs God of his honour, he leaves him nothing remaining but an empty title of Deity,[3] while he transfers to himself the whole of his power. And this is what Paul adds shortly afterwards, that *the son of perdition would shew himself as God.* For, as has been said, he does not insist upon the simple term *God*, but intimates, that the pride[4] of Antichrist would be such, that, raising himself above the number and rank of servants, and mounting the judgment-seat of God,[5] would reign, not with a human, but with a divine authority. For we know that whatever is raised up into the place of God is an idol, though it should not bear the name of God.

In the temple of God. By this one term there is a sufficient refutation of the error, nay more, the stupidity of those who reckon the Pope to be Vicar of Christ, on the ground that he has his seat in the Church, in whatever manner he may conduct himself; for Paul places Antichrist nowhere else than in the very sanctuary of God. For this is not a foreign, but

---

[1] "Selon son plaisir et fantasie;"—"According to his own pleasure and fancy."
[2] "Sacrileges abominables;"—"Abominable sacrileges."
[3] "Le titre de Dieu par imagination;"—"The title of God by imagination."
[4] "L'orgüeil et arrogance;"—"The pride and arrogance."
[5] "Auec vne fierete intolerable;"—"With an intolerable presumption."

as the den of so many superstitions, while it was destined to be the *pillar of the truth?* (1 Tim. iii. 15.) I answer, that it is thus represented, not on the ground of its retaining all the qualities of the Church, but because it has something of it remaining. I accordingly acknowledge, that that is the *temple of God* in which the Pope bears rule, but at the same time profaned by innumerable sacrileges.

5. Remember ye not, that, when I was yet with you, I told you these things?	5. Annon memoria tenetis, quod, quum adhuc essem apud vos, haec vobis dicebam?
6. And now ye know what withholdeth, that he might be revealed in his time.	6. Et nunc quid detineat, scitis, donec ille reveletur suo tempore.
7. For the mystery of iniquity doth already work: only he who now letteth *will let*, until he be taken out of the way:	7. Mysterium enim iam operatur iniquitatis, solum tenens modo donec e medio tollatur.
8. And then shall that Wicked be revealed, whom the Lord shall consume with the spirit of his mouth, and shall destroy with the brightness of his coming.	8. Et tunc revelabitur iniquus ille, quem Dominus destruet spiritu oris sui, et abolebit illustratione adventus sui.

5. *Do ye not remember?* This added no small weight to the doctrine, that they had previously heard it from the mouth of Paul, that they might not think that it had been contrived by him at the instant. And as he had given them early warning as to the reign of Antichrist, and the devastation that was coming upon the Church, when no question had as yet been raised as to such things, he saw beyond all doubt that the doctrine was specially useful to be known. And, unquestionably, it is really so. Those whom he addressed were destined to see many things that would trouble them; and when posterity would see a large proportion of those who had made profession of the faith of Christ revolt from piety, maddened, as it were, by a gad-fly, or rather by a fury,[1] what could they do but waver? This,

---

[1] "Se reuolter de la vraye religion, et se precipiter en ruine comme gens forcenez, ou plustost endiablez;"—"Revolt from the true religion, and plunge themselves in ruin like persons enraged, or rather possessed."

of such vengeance. Here we may see how forgetful men are in matters affecting their everlasting salvation. We must also observe Paul's mildness; for while he might have been vehemently incensed,[4] he does but mildly reprove them; for it is a fatherly way of reproving them to say to them, that they had allowed forgetfulness of a matter so important and so useful to steal in upon their minds.

6. *And now what withholdeth.* Τὸ κατέχον means here properly an impediment or occasion of delay. Chrysostom, who thinks that this can only be understood as referring to the Spirit, or to the Roman Empire, prefers to lean to the latter opinion. He assigns a plausible reason—because Paul would not have spoken of the Spirit in enigmatical terms,[5] but in speaking of the Roman Empire wished to avoid exciting unpleasant feeling. He states also the reason why the state of the Roman Empire retards the revelation of Antichrist—that, as the monarchy of Babylon was overthrown by the Persians and Medes, and the Macedonians, having conquered the Persians, again took possession of the monarchy, and the Macedonians were at last subdued by the Romans, so Antichrist seized hold for himself of the vacant supremacy of the Roman Empire. There is not one of these things that was not afterwards confirmed by actual occurrence. Chrysostom, therefore, speaks truly in so far as concerns history. I am of opinion, however, that Paul's intention was different from this—that the doctrine of the gospel would require to be spread hither and thither, until nearly the whole world were convicted of obstinacy and deliberate malice. For there can be no doubt that the Thessalonians had heard from Paul's mouth as to this impediment,

---

[1] *Murus aheneus.* See Hor. Ep. i. 1, 60. See p. 178, *n.* 1.

[2] "Mais voici en cest endroit qui leur deuoit seruir d'vne forteresse inuincible;"—"But behold in this matter what would furnish them with an invincible fortress."

[3] "L'ingratitude execrable et vileine des hommes;"—"The execrable and base ingratitude of men."

[4] "Contre les Thessaloniciens;"—"Against the Thessalonians."

[5] "En termes couuerts ou obscurs;"—"In hidden or obscure terms."

Let my readers now consider which of the two is the more probable—either that Paul declared that the light of the gospel must be diffused through all parts of the earth before God would thus give loose reins to Satan, or that the power of the Roman Empire stood in the way of the rise of Antichrist, inasmuch as he could only break through into a vacant possession. I seem at least to hear Paul discoursing as to the universal call of the Gentiles—that the grace of God must be offered to all—that Christ must enlighten the whole world by his gospel, in order that the impiety of men might be the more fully attested and demonstrated. This, therefore, was the delay, until the career of the gospel should be completed, because a gracious invitation to salvation was first in order.[1] Hence he adds, *in his time*, because vengeance was ripe after grace had been rejected.[2]

7. *The mystery of iniquity.* This is opposed to *revelation;* for as Satan had not yet gathered so much strength, as that Antichrist could openly oppress the Church, he says that he is carrying on secretly and clandestinely[3] what he would do openly in his own time. He was therefore at that time secretly laying the foundations on which he would afterwards rear the edifice, as actually took place. And this tends to confirm more fully what I have already stated,[4] that it is not one individual that is represented under the term Antichrist, but one kingdom, which extends itself through many ages. In the same sense, John says that Antichrist will come, but that there were already many in his time. (1 John ii. 18.) For he admonishes those who were then living to be on their guard against that deadly pestilence, which was at that time shooting up in various forms. For sects were rising up which were the seeds, as it

---

[1] " D'autant que l'ordre que Dieu vouloit tenir, requeroit que le monde premierement fust d'vne liberalite gratuite conuié a salut ;"—" Inasmuch as the order that God designed to maintain, required that the world should first of all be invited to salvation by a gracious liberality."

[2] " La droite saison de la vengeance estoit apres la grace reiette ;"—" The right season of vengeance was after grace had been rejected."

[3] " Et comme par dessous terre ;"—" And as it were under ground."

[4] See p. 327.

conveys the idea of a secret manner of working, yet he has made use of the term *mystery* rather than any other, alluding to the mystery of salvation, of which he speaks elsewhere, (Col. i. 26,) for he carefully insists on the struggle of repugnancy between the Son of God and this *son of perdition*.

Only now withholding. While he makes both statements in reference to one person—that he will hold supremacy for a time, and that he will shortly be taken out of the way, I have no doubt that he refers to Antichrist; and the participle *withholding* must be explained in the future tense.² For he has, in my opinion, added this for the consolation of believers —that the reign of Antichrist will be temporary, the limits of it having been assigned to it by God; for believers might object—" Of what avail is it that the gospel is preached, if Satan is now hatching a tyranny that he is to exercise for ever ?" He accordingly exhorts to patience, because God afflicts his Church only for a time, that he may one day afford it deliverance; and, on the other hand, the perpetuity of Christ's reign must be considered, in order that believers may repose in it.

8. *And then will be revealed*—that is, when that *impediment* (τὸ κατέχον) shall be removed; for he does not point out the time of revelation as being when he, who now holds the supremacy, will be *taken out of the way*, but he has an eye to what he had said before. For he had said that there was some hinderance in the way of Antichrist's entering upon an open possession of the kingdom. He afterwards added, that he was already hatching a secret work of impiety. In the *third* place, he has interspersed consolation, on the ground that this tyranny would come to an end.³ He now again repeats, that he⁴ who was as yet hidden, would be *revealed*

¹ " Le bon blé que Dieu auoit semé en son champ;"—" The good wheat that God had sown in his field."

² " Faut resoudre ce participe *Tenant* en vn temps futur *Tiendra;"—* " We must explain this participle, *withholding*, in the future tense—*He will withhold.*"

³ " Que sa tyrannie deuoit prendre fin quelque fois;"—" That his tyranny must at some time have an end."

⁴ " Ce fils de perdition;"—" This son of perdition."

theless, fight vigorously under Christ,[1] and not allow themselves to be overwhelmed, although the deluge of impiety should thus overspread.[2]

Whom the Lord. He had foretold the destruction of Antichrist's reign; he now points out the manner of his destruction—that he will be reduced to nothing by the *word of the Lord.* It is uncertain, however, whether he speaks of the last appearance of Christ, when he will be manifested from heaven as the Judge. The words, indeed, seem to have this meaning, but Paul does not mean that Christ would accomplish this[3] in one moment. Hence we must understand it in this sense—that Antichrist would be wholly and in every respect destroyed,[4] when that final day of the restoration of all things shall arrive. Paul, however, intimates that Christ will in the mean time, by the rays which he will emit previously to his advent, put to flight the darkness in which Antichrist will reign, just as the sun, before he is seen by us, chases away the darkness of the night by the pouring forth of his rays.[5]

This victory of the word, therefore, will shew itself in this world, for the *spirit of his mouth* simply means the word, as it also does in Isaiah xi. 4, to which passage Paul seems to allude. For the Prophet there takes in the same sense the *sceptre of his mouth,* and the *breath of his lips,* and he also furnishes Christ with these very arms, that he may rout his enemies. This is a signal commendation of true and sound doctrine—that it is represented as sufficient for putting an end to all impiety, and as destined to be invariably victorious, in opposition to all the machinations of Satan; as also when, a little afterwards, the proclamation of it is spoken of as *Christ's coming* to us.

When Paul adds, the *brightness of his coming,* he inti-

[1] " Sous l'enseigne de Christ;"—" Under Christ's banner."
[2] " Si outrageusement;"—" So outrageously."
[3] " Cela tout;"—" All this."
[4] " Descomfit;"—" Defeated."
[5] " Estendant la vertu de ses rayons tout a l'enuiron;"—" Diffusing the virtue of his rays all around."

he indirectly intimates, that Antichrist will be permitted to reign for a time, when Christ has, in a manner, withdrawn, as usually happens, whenever on his presenting himself we turn our back upon him. And, undoubtedly, that is a sad departure[1] of Christ, when he has taken away his light from men, which has been improperly and unworthily received,[2] in accordance with what follows. In the mean time Paul teaches, that by his presence alone all the elect of God will be abundantly safe, in opposition to all the subtleties of Satan.

9. *Even him*, whose coming is after the working of Satan, with all power, and signs, and lying wonders,	9. Cuius adventus est secundum operationem (*vel, efficaciam*) Satanae, in omni potentia, et signis et prodigiis mendacibus,
10. And with all deceivableness of unrighteousness in them that perish; because they received not the love of the truth, that they might be saved.	10. Et in omni deceptione iniustitiae, in iis qui pereunt: pro eo quod dilectionem veritatis non sunt amplexi, ut salvi fierent.
11. And for this cause God shall send them strong delusion, that they should believe a lie;	11. Propterea mittet illis Deus operationem (*vel, efficaciam*) imposturae, ut credant mendacio:
12. That they all might be damned who believed not the truth, but had pleasure in unrighteousness.	12. Ut iudicentur omnes qui non crediderunt veritati, sed oblectati sunt iniustitia.

9. *Whose coming.* He confirms what he has said by an argument from contraries. For as Antichrist cannot stand otherwise than through the impostures of Satan, he must necessarily vanish as soon as Christ shines forth. In fine, as it is only in darkness that he reigns, the dawn of the day puts to flight and extinguishes the thick darkness of his reign. We are now in possession of Paul's design, for he meant to say, that Christ would have no difficulty in destroying the tyranny of Antichrist, which was supported by no resources but those of Satan. In the mean time, however, he points out the marks by which that *wicked one* may be

---

[1] " Vn triste et pitoyable department;"—" A sad and lamentable departure."

[2] " Laquelle ils auoyent reiettee ou receué irreueremment, et autrement qu'il n'appartenoit;"—" Which they had rejected or received irreverently, and otherwise than was befitting."

in signs and lying wonders, and in all deceivableness. And assuredly, in order that this may be opposed to the kingdom of Christ, it must consist partly in false doctrine and errors, and partly in pretended miracles. For the kingdom of Christ consists of the doctrine of truth, and the power of the Spirit. Satan, accordingly, with the view of opposing Christ in the person of his Vicar, puts on Christ's mask,[1] while he, nevertheless, at the same time chooses armour, with which he may directly oppose Christ. Christ, by the doctrine of his gospel, enlightens our minds in eternal life; Antichrist, trained up under Satan's tuition, by wicked doctrine, involves the wicked in ruin;[2] Christ puts forth the power of his Spirit for salvation, and seals his gospel by miracles; the adversary,[3] by the efficacy of Satan, alienates us from the Holy Spirit, and by his enchantments confirms miserable men[4] in error.

He gives the name of *miracles of falsehood,* not merely to such as are falsely and deceptively contrived by cunning men with a view to impose upon the simple—a kind of deception with which all Papacy abounds, for they are a part of his power which he has previously touched upon; but takes falsehood as consisting in this, that Satan draws to a contrary end works which otherwise are truly works of God, and abuses miracles so as to obscure God's glory.[5] In the mean time, however, there can be no doubt, that he deceives by means of enchantments—an example of which we have in Pharaoh's magicians. (Exod. vii. 11.)

10. *In those that perish.* He limits the power of Satan, as not being able to injure the elect of God, just as Christ, also, exempts them from this danger. (Matt. xxiv. 24.) From

---
[1] " Et s'en desguise;"—" And disguises himself with it."
[2] " En ruine et perdition eternelle;"—" In eternal ruin and perdition."
[3] Our author evidently means Antichrist, alluding to the term applied to him by Paul in the 4th verse.—*Ed.*
[4] " Les poures aveugles;"—" The poor blind."
[5] It is observed by Dr. Manton, in his Sermons on 2d Thess. ii., (pp. 175-177,) that " there are seven points in Popery that are sought to be confirmed by Miracles.—1. Pilgrimages. 2. Prayers for the Dead. 3. Purgatory. 4. The Invocation of Saints. 5. The Adoration of Images. 6. The Adoration of the Host. 7. The Primacy of the Pope."—*Ed.*

cessary. For all the pious, but for this, would of necessity be overpowered with fear, if they saw a yawning gulf pervading the whole path, along which they must pass. Hence Paul, however he may wish them to be in a state of anxiety, that they may be on their guard, lest by excessive carelessness they should fall back, nay, even throw themselves into ruin, does, nevertheless, bid them cherish good hope, inasmuch as Satan's power is bridled, that he may not be able to involve any but the wicked in ruin.

Because they received not the love. Lest the wicked should complain that they perish innocently,[1] and that they have been appointed to death rather from cruelty on the part of God, than from any fault on their part, Paul shews on what good grounds it is that so severe vengeance from God is to come upon them—because they have not received in the temper of mind with which they ought the truth which was presented to them, nay more, of their own accord refused salvation. And from this appears more clearly what I have already stated—that the gospel required to be preached to the world before God would give Satan so much permission,[2] for he would never have allowed his temple to be so basely profaned,[3] had he not been provoked by extreme ingratitude on the part of men. In short, Paul declares that Antichrist will be the minister of God's righteous vengeance against those who, being called to salvation, have rejected the gospel, and have preferred to apply their mind to impiety and errors. Hence there is no reason why Papists should now object, that it is at variance with the clemency of Christ to cast off his Church in this manner. For though the domination of Antichrist has been cruel, none have perished but those who were deserving of it, nay more, did of their own accord *choose death.* (Prov. viii. 36.) And unquestionably, while the voice of the Son of God has sounded forth every-

[1] "Sans cause et estans innocens;"— "Without cause, and being innocent."
[2] See p. 332.
[3] "Vileinement et horriblement;"—"Basely and horribly."

nevertheless, few that have truly and heartily given themselves to Christ. Hence it is not to be wondered, if similar vengeance quickly follows such a criminal[2] contempt.

It is asked whether the punishment of blindness does not fall on any but those who have on set purpose rebelled against the gospel. I answer, that this special judgment by which God has avenged open contumacy,[3] does not stand in the way of his striking down with stupidity,[4] as often as seems good to him, those that have never heard a single word respecting Christ, for Paul does not discourse in a general way as to the reasons why God has from the beginning permitted Satan to go at large with his falsehoods, but as to what a horrible vengeance impends over gross despisers of new and previously unwonted grace.[5]

He uses the expression—*receiving the love of the* truth, to mean—applying the mind to the love of it. Hence we learn that faith is always conjoined with a sweet and voluntary reverence for God, because we do not properly believe the word of God, unless it is lovely and pleasant to us.

11. *The working of delusion.* He means that errors will not merely have a place, but the wicked will be blinded, so that they will rush forward to ruin without consideration. For as God enlightens us inwardly by his Spirit, that his doctrine may be efficacious in us, and opens our eyes and hearts, that it may make its way thither, so by a righteous judgment he delivers over to a *reprobate mind* (Rom. i. 28) those whom he has appointed to destruction, that with closed eyes and a senseless mind, they may, as if bewitched, deliver themselves over to Satan and his ministers to be deceived. And assuredly we have a notable specimen of this in the Papacy. No words can express how monstrous a sink of errors[6] there is *there,* how gross and shameful an absurdity

---

[1] " Endurcies et obstinees ;"—" Hardened and obstinate."

[2] " Si execrable ;"—" So execrable."

[3] " Le mespris orgueilleux de sa Parolle ;"—" Proud contempt of his Word."

[4] " Estourdissement et stupidite ;"—" Giddiness and stupidity."

[5] " C'est ascauoir de l'Euangile ;"—" That is, of the Gospel."

[6] " Quel monstrueux et horrible retrait d'erreurs ;"—" What a monstrous and horrible nest of errors."

sound doctrine, can think of such monstrous things without the greatest horror. How, then, could the whole world be lost in astonishment at them, were it not that men have been struck with blindness by the Lord, and converted, as it were, into stumps?

12. *That all may be condemned.* That is, that they may receive the punishment due to their impiety. Thus, those that perish have no just ground to expostulate with God, inasmuch as they have obtained what they sought. For we must keep in view what is stated in Deut. xiii. 3, that the hearts of men are subjected to trial, when false doctrines come abroad, inasmuch as they have no power except among those who do not love God with a sincere heart. Let those, then, who *take pleasure in unrighteousness*, reap the fruit of it. When he says *all*, he means that contempt of God finds no excuse in the great crowd and multitude of those who refuse to obey the gospel, for God is the Judge of the whole world, so that he will inflict punishment upon a hundred thousand, no less than upon one individual.

The participle εὐδοκήσαντες (*taking pleasure*) means (so to speak) a voluntary inclination to evil, for in this way every excuse is cut off from the ungrateful, when they take so much *pleasure in unrighteousness*, as to prefer it to the righteousness of God. For by what violence will they say that they have been impelled to alienate themselves by a mad revolt[1] from God, towards whom they were led by the guidance of nature? It is at least manifest that they willingly and knowingly lent an ear to falsehoods.

13. But we are bound to give thanks alway to God for you, brethren beloved of the Lord, because God hath from the beginning chosen you to salvation through sanctification of the Spirit, and belief of the truth:

13. Nos autem debemus gratias agere Deo semper de vobis, fratres dilecti a Domino, quia elegit vos Deus ab initio in salutem, in sanctificatione Spiritus, et fide veritatis:

14. Whereunto he called you by our gospel, to the obtaining of the glory of our Lord Jesus Christ.

14. Quo vocavit vos per evangelium nostrum, in possessionem gloriae (*vel, gloriosam*) Domini nostri Iesu Christi.

[1] " En se reuoltant malicieusement ;"—" By revolting maliciously."

faith may not waver from fear of the revolt that was to take place. At the same time, he had it in view to consult, not *their* welfare only, but also that of posterity.[1] And he does not merely confirm them that they may not fall over the same precipice with the world, but by this comparison he extols the more the grace of God towards them, in that, while they see almost the whole world hurried forward to death at the same time, as if by a violent tempest, they are, by the hand of God, maintained in a quiet and secure condition of life.[2] Thus we must contemplate the judgments of God upon the reprobate in such a way that they may be, as it were, mirrors to us for considering his mercy towards us. For we must draw this conclusion, that it is owing solely to the singular grace of God that we do not miserably perish with them.

He calls them *beloved of the Lord,* for this reason, that they may the better consider that the sole reason why they are exempted from the almost universal overthrow of the world, was because God exercised towards them unmerited love. Thus Moses admonished the Jews—"God did not elevate you so magnificently because ye were more powerful than others, or were numerous, but because he loved your fathers." (Deut. vii. 7, 8.) For, when we hear the term *love,* that statement of John must immediately occur to our mind —*Not that we first loved him.* (1 John iv. 19.) In short, Paul here does two things; for he confirms faith, lest the pious should give way from being overcome with fear, and he exhorts them to gratitude, that they may value so much the higher the mercy of God towards them.

Hath chosen you. He states the reason why all are not involved and swallowed up in the same ruin—because Satan has no power over any that God has chosen, so as to prevent them from being saved, though heaven and earth were to be confounded. This passage is read in various ways.

[1] "Mais aussi pour les autres fideles, qui viendroyent apres;"—"But also for other believers, who should come after."

[2] "En vn estat ferme et paisible, qui mene a la vie;"—"In a secure and peaceable condition, which leads to life."

have ἀπ' ἀρχῆς, I have in preference followed this reading. Should any one prefer *first-fruits*, the meaning will be, that believers have been, as it were, set aside for a sacred offering, by a metaphor taken from the ancient custom of the law. Let us, however, hold by what is more generally received, that he says that the Thessalonians were *chosen from the beginning*.

Some understand the meaning to be, that they had been called among the first; but this is foreign to Paul's meaning, and does not accord with the connection of the passage. For he does not merely exempt from fear a few individuals, who had been led to Christ immediately on the commencement of the gospel, but this consolation belongs to all the elect of God, without exception. When, therefore, he says *from the beginning*, he means that there is no danger lest their salvation, which is founded on God's eternal election, should be overthrown, whatever tumultuous changes may occur. "However Satan may mix and confound all things in the world, your salvation, notwithstanding, has been placed on a footing of safety, prior to the creation of the world." Here, therefore, is the true port of safety, that God, who elected us of old,[2] will deliver us from all the evils that threaten us. For we are elected to salvation; we shall, therefore, be safe from destruction. But as it is not for us to penetrate into God's secret counsel, to seek *there* assurance of our salvation, he specifies signs or tokens of election, which should suffice us for the assurance of it.

In sanctification of the spirit, says he, *and belief of the truth.* This may be explained in two ways, WITH *sanctification*, or BY sanctification. It is not of much importance which of the two you select, as it is certain[3] that Paul

---

[1] *Primitias.* Wiclif (1380) following, as he is wont, the reading of the Vulgate, renders it "the first fruytis."

[2] "Des le commencement;"—"From the beginning."

[3] "S. Paul ne veut autre chose, sinon apres auoir parlé de l'election de Dieu, adiouster maintenant des signes plus prochains qui nous la manifestent;"—"St. Paul means simply, after having spoken of the election of God, to add now those nearer tokens which manifest it to us."

incomprehensible, and are conjoined with it by an indissoluble tie. Hence, in order that we may know that we are elected by God, there is no occasion to inquire as to what he decreed before the creation of the world, but we find in ourselves a satisfactory proof if he has sanctified us by his Spirit,—if he has enlightened us in the faith of his gospel. For the gospel is an evidence to us of our adoption, and the Spirit seals it, and those that are *led by the Spirit* are the *sons of God*, (Rom. viii. 14,) and he who by faith possesses Christ has everlasting life. (1 John v. 12.) These things must be carefully observed, lest, overlooking the revelation of God's will, with which he bids us rest satisfied, we should plunge into a profound labyrinth from a desire to take it from his secret counsel, from the investigation of which he draws us aside. Hence it becomes us to rest satisfied with the faith of the gospel, and that grace of the Spirit by which we have been regenerated. And by this means is refuted the wickedness[1] of those who make the election of God a pretext for every kind of iniquity, while Paul connects it with faith and regeneration in such a manner, that he would not have it judged of by us on any other grounds.

14. *To which he called us.* He repeats the same thing, though in somewhat different terms. For the sons of God are not called otherwise than to the belief of the truth. Paul, however, meant to shew here how competent a witness he is for confirming that thing of which he was a minister. He accordingly puts himself forward as a surety, that the Thessalonians may not doubt that the gospel, in which they had been instructed by him, is the safety-bringing voice of God, by which they are aroused from death, and are delivered from the tyranny of Satan. He calls it *his* gospel, not as though it had originated with him,[2] but inasmuch as the preaching of it had been committed to him.

What he adds, *to the acquisition or possession of the glory*

---

[1] " La meschancete horrible;"—" The horrible wickedness."
[2] " Non pas qu'il soit creu en son cerueau;"—" Not as though it had been contrived in his brain."

order that they may one day *possess* a glory in common with Christ, or that Christ *acquired* them with a view to his glory. And thus it will be a second means of confirmation, that he will defend them, as being nothing less than his own inheritance, and, in maintaining their salvation, will stand forward in defence of his own glory; which latter meaning, in my opinion, suits better.

15. Therefore, brethren, stand fast, and hold the traditions which ye have been taught, whether by word, or our epistle.	15. Itaque fratres, state, et tenete institutiones, quas didicistis vel per sermonem, vel per epistolam nostram.
16. Now our Lord Jesus Christ himself, and God, even our Father, which hath loved us, and hath given *us* everlasting consolation, and good hope through grace,	16. Ipse vero Dominus noster Iesus Christus, et Deus, ac Pater noster, qui dilexit nos, et dedit consolationem æternam, et spem bonam per gratiam,
17. Comfort your hearts, and stablish you in every good word and work.	17. Consoletur corda vestra, et stabiliat vos in omni opere et sermone bono.

He deduces this exhortation on good grounds from what goes before, inasmuch as our steadfastness and power of perseverance rest on nothing else than assurance of divine grace. When, however, God calls us to salvation, stretching forth, as it were, his hand to us; when Christ, by the doctrine of the gospel, presents himself to us to be enjoyed; when the Spirit is given us as a seal and earnest of eternal life, though the heaven should fall, we must, nevertheless, not become disheartened. Paul, accordingly, would have the Thessalonians stand, not merely when others continue to stand, but with a more settled stability; so that, on seeing almost all turning aside from the faith, and all things full of confusion, they will, nevertheless, retain their footing. And assuredly the calling of God ought to fortify us against all occasions of offence in such a manner, that not even the entire ruin of the world shall shake, much less overthrow, our stability.

15. *Hold fast the institutions.* Some restrict this to precepts of external polity; but this does not please me, for he points out the manner of standing firm. Now, to be fur-

doctrine under this term, as though he had said that they have ground on which they may stand firm, provided they persevere in sound doctrine, according as they had been instructed by him. I do not deny that the term παραδόσεις is fitly applied to the ordinances which are appointed by the Churches, with a view to the promoting of peace and the maintaining of order, and I admit that it is taken in this sense when human traditions are treated of, (Matt. xv. 6.) Paul, however, will be found in the next chapter making use of the term *tradition*, as meaning the rule that he had laid down, and the very signification of the term is general. The context, however, as I have said, requires that it be taken here to mean the whole of that doctrine in which they had been instructed. For the matter treated of is the most important of all—that their faith may remain secure in the midst of a dreadful agitation of the Church.

Papists, however, act a foolish part in gathering from this that their traditions ought to be observed. They reason, indeed, in this manner—that if it was allowable for Paul to enjoin traditions, it was allowable also for other teachers; and that, if it was a pious thing[1] to observe the former, the latter also ought not less to be observed. Granting them, however, that Paul speaks of precepts belonging to the external government of the Church, I say that they were, nevertheless, not contrived by him, but divinely communicated. For he declares elsewhere, (1 Cor. vii. 35,) that it was not his intention to ensnare consciences, as it was not lawful, either for himself, or for all the Apostles together. They act a still more ridiculous part in making it their aim to pass off, under this, the abominable sink of their own superstitions, as though they were the traditions of Paul. But farewell to these trifles, when we are in possession of Paul's true meaning. And we may judge in part from this Epistle what traditions he here recommends, for he says— whether *by word*, that is, discourse, or *by epistle*. Now, what do these Epistles contain but pure doctrine, which

[1] " Une bonne chose et saincte ;"—" A good thing and holy."

of the Gospel?

16. *Now the Lord himself.* When he ascribes to Christ a work altogether Divine, and represents him, in common with the Father, as the Author of the choicest blessings, as we have in this a clear proof of the divinity of Christ, so we are admonished, that we cannot obtain anything from God unless we seek it in Christ himself: and when he asks that God may give him those things which he had enjoined, he shews clearly enough how little influence exhortations have, unless God inwardly move and affect our hearts. Unquestionably there will be but an empty sound striking upon the ear, if doctrine does not receive efficacy from the Spirit.

What he afterwards adds, *who hath loved you, and hath given consolation,* &c., relates to confidence in asking; for he would have the Thessalonians feel persuaded that God will do what he prays for. And from what does he prove this? Because he once shewed that they were dear to him, while he has already conferred upon them distinguished favours, and in this manner has bound himself to them for the time to come. This is what he means by *everlasting consolation.* The term *hope,* also, has the same object in view—that they may confidently expect a never-failing continuance of gifts. But what does he ask? That God may sustain their hearts by his consolation; for this is his office, to keep them from giving way through anxiety or distrust; and farther, that he may give them perseverance, both in a pious and holy course of life, and in sound doctrine; for I am of opinion, that it is rather of this than of common discourse that he speaks, so that this agrees with what goes before.

CHAPTER III.

1. Finally, brethren, pray for us, that the word of the Lord may have *free* course, and be glorified, even as *it is* with you;	1. Quod reliquum est, orate fratres pro nobis: ut sermo Domini currat et glorificetur, quemadmodum et apud vos;

3. But the Lord is faithful, who shall stablish you, and keep *you* from evil.

4. And we have confidence in the Lord touching you, that ye both do and will do the things which we command you.

5. And the Lord direct your hearts into the love of God, and into the patient waiting for Christ.

3. Fidelis autem Dominus. qui confirmabit vos, et custodiet a maligno.

4. Confidimus autem in Domino de vobis, quod quae vobis praecipimus, et facitis, et facturi estis.

5. Dominus autem dirigat corda vestra in dilectionem Dei, et exspectationem Christi.

1. *Pray for us.* Though the Lord powerfully aided him, and though he surpassed all others in earnestness of prayer, he nevertheless does not despise the prayers of believers, by which the Lord would have us aided. It becomes us, after his example, eagerly to desire this aid, and to stir up our brethren to pray for us.

When, however, he adds—*that the word of God may have its course*, he shews that he has not so much concern and regard for himself personally, as for the entire Church. For why does he desire to be recommended to the prayers of the Thessalonians? That the doctrine of the gospel may *have its course*. He does not desire, therefore, so much that regard should be had to himself individually, as to the glory of God and the common welfare of the Church. *Course* means here dissemination;[1] *glory* means something farther,— that his preaching may have its power and efficacy for renewing men after the image of God. Hence, holiness of life and uprightness on the part of Christians is the glory of the gospel; as, on the other hand, those defame the gospel who make profession of it with the mouth, while in the meantime they live in wickedness and baseness. He says—*as among you;* for this should be a stimulus to the pious, to see all others like them. Hence those that have already entered into the kingdom of God are exhorted to pray daily that it may *come.* (Matt. vi. 10.)

2. *That we may be delivered.* The old interpreter has rendered it, not unhappily, in my opinion—*unreasonable.*[2]

---

[1] " Estendue et auancement;"—" Extension and advancement."
[2] *Importunos.* Wiclif (1380) renders it *noyous.*—*Ed.*

men, who lurked in the Church, under the name of Christians, or at least Jews, who with a mad zeal for the law furiously persecuted the gospel. He knew, however, how much danger impended over them from both these classes. Chrysostom, however, thinks that those only are meant who maliciously oppose the gospel by base doctrines,[1]—not by weapons of violence, as for example, Alexander, Hymeneus, and the like ; but for my part, I extend it generally to all kinds of dangers and enemies. He was at that time proceeding towards Jerusalem, and wrote in the midst of his journeyings. Now, he had already been divinely forewarned that *imprisonments and persecutions awaited him there.* (Acts xx. 23.) He means, however, *deliverance,* so that he may come off victorious, whether by life or by death.

All have not faith. This might be explained to mean, " Faith is not in all." This expression, however, were both ambiguous and more obscure. Let us therefore retain Paul's words, by which he intimates that faith is a gift of God that is too rare to be found in all. God, therefore, calls many who do not come to him by faith. Many pretend to come to him, who have their heart at the farthest distance from him. Farther, he does not speak of all indiscriminately, but merely animadverts upon those that belong to the Church: for the Thessalonians saw that very many held faith in abhorrence ;[2] nay, they saw how small was the number of believers. Hence it would have been unnecessary to say this as to strangers ; but Paul simply says that all that make a profession of faith are not such in reality. Should you take in all Jews, they appeared to have nearness to Christ, for they ought to have recognised him by means of the law and the prophets. Paul, there can be no question, specially marks out those with whom he would have to do. Now, it is probable that they were those who, while they had the appearance and honorary title of piety, were nevertheless very far from the reality. From this came the conflict.

[1] " Fausses et peruerses doctrines ;"—" False and perverse doctrines."
[2] " En horreur et disdain ;"—" In horror and disdain."

with wicked and perverse men, he says that faith is not common to all, because the wicked and reprobate are always mixed with the good, as *tares* are with the *good wheat.* (Matt. xiii. 25.) And this ought to be remembered by us whenever we have annoyance given us by wicked persons, who nevertheless desire to be reckoned as belonging to the society of Christians—that *all men have not faith.* Nay more, when we hear in some instances that the Church is disturbed by base factions, let this be a shield to us against offences of this nature; for we shall not merely inflict injury upon pious teachers, if we have doubts as to their fidelity, whenever domestic enemies do them harm, but our faith will from time to time waver, unless we keep in mind that among those who boast of the name of Christians there are many that are treacherous.[1]

3. *But God is faithful.* As it was possible that their minds, influenced by unfavourable reports, might come to entertain some doubts as to Paul's ministry, having taught them that faith is not always found in men, he now calls them back to God, and says that he is *faithful,* so as to confirm them against all contrivances of men, by which they will endeavour to shake them. "They, indeed, are treacherous, but there is in God a support that is abundantly secure, so as to keep you from giving way." He calls the Lord *faithful,* inasmuch as he adheres to his purpose to the end in maintaining the salvation of his people, seasonably aids them, and never forsakes them in dangers, as in 1 Cor. x. 13, *God is faithful, who will not suffer you to be tried above that ye are able to bear.*

These words, however, themselves shew that Paul was more anxious as to others than as to himself. Malicious men directed against him the stings of their malignity; the whole violence[2] of it fell upon him. In the mean time, he

---

[1] "Qu'il y a beaucoup d'infideles, desloyaux, et traistres;"—" That there are many that are unbelieving, disloyal, and traitorous."

[2] "Toute la violence et impetuosite;"—" The whole violence and impetuosity."

The term *evil* may refer as well to the thing, that is, malice, as to the persons of the wicked. I prefer, however, to interpret it of Satan, the head of all the wicked. For it were a small thing to be delivered from the cunning or violence of men, if the Lord did not protect us from all spiritual injury.

4. *We have confidence.* By this preface he prepares the way for proceeding to give the instruction, which we shall find him immediately afterwards subjoining. For the confidence which he says he has respecting them, made them much more ready to obey than if he had required obedience from them in a way of doubt or distrust. He says, however, that this hope, which he cherished in reference to them, was founded upon the Lord, inasmuch as it is his to bind their hearts to obedience, and to keep them in it; or by this expression, (as appears to me more probable,) he meant to testify, that it is not his intention to enjoin anything but by the commandment of the Lord. Here, accordingly, he marks out limits for himself as to enjoining, and for them as to obeying—that it should be only in the Lord.[1] All, therefore, that do not observe this limitation, do to no purpose resort to Paul's example, with the view of binding the Church and subjecting it to their laws. Perhaps he had this also in view, that the respect which was due to his Apostleship might remain unimpaired among the Thessalonians, however the wicked might attempt to deprive him of the honour that belonged to him; for the prayer which he immediately subjoins tends towards this object. For provided men's hearts continue to be directed towards *love to God, and patient waiting for Christ,* other things will be in a desirable state, and Paul declares that he desires nothing else. From this it is manifest, how very far he is from seeking dominion for himself peculiarly. For he is

[1] " Voyci donc les bournes qu'il limite, et pour soy et pour eux: pour soy, de ne commander rien que par le Seigneur : a eux, de ne rendre obeissance sinon au Seigneur;"—" Mark then the limits which he prescribes both for himself and for them : for himself, not to command anything but by the Lord : for them, not to render obedience except to the Lord."

expression of confidence,[1] he admonishes us that we must not relax in eagerness of prayer on the ground that we cherish good hope.

As, however, he states here in a summary manner the things that he knew to be most necessary for Christians, let every one make it his endeavour to make proficiency in these two things, in so far as he desires to make progress towards perfection. And, unquestionably, the love of God cannot reign in us unless brotherly love is also exercised. *Waiting for Christ*, on the other hand, teaches us to exercise contempt of the world, mortification of the flesh, and endurance of the cross. At the same time the expression might be explained as meaning, the *patience of Christ*—that which Christ's doctrine begets in us; but I prefer to understand it as referring to the hope of ultimate redemption. For this is the only thing that sustains us in the warfare of the present life, that we wait for the Redeemer; and farther, this waiting requires patient endurance amidst the continual exercises of the cross.

6. Now we command you, brethren, in the name of our Lord Jesus Christ, that ye withdraw yourselves from every brother that walketh disorderly, and not after the tradition which he received of us.	6. Praecipimus autem vobis, fratres in nomine Domini nostri Iesu Christi, ut vos subducatis ab omni fratre, qui inordinate ambulet, et non iuxta institutionem, quam accepit a nobis.
7. For yourselves know how ye ought to follow us: for we behaved not ourselves disorderly among you;	7. Ipsi enim scitis, quomodo oporteat nos imitari, quia non inordinate egimus inter vos:
8. Neither did we eat any man's bread for nought; but wrought with labour and travail night and day, that we might not be chargeable to any of you:	8. Neque gratis panem comedimus a quoquam, sed cum labore et sudore nocte dieque facientes opus, ne cui vestrum graves essemus.
9. Not because we have not power, but to make ourselves an ensample unto you to follow us.	9. Non quod non habeamus potestatem, sed ut nos ipsos exemplar proponeremus vobis ad imitandum vos.
10. For even when we were with you, this we commanded you, that	10. Etenim quum essemus apud vos, hoc vobis praecepimus, ut,

[1] " Quand apres auoir protesté de sa confiance, il ne laisse pas d'adiouster encore la priere auec la confiance;"—" When after having declared his confidence, he omits not to add besides, prayer along with confidence."

He now proceeds to the correcting of a particular fault. As there were some indolent, and at the same time curious and prattling persons, who, in order that they might scrape together a living at the expense of others, wandered about from house to house, he forbids that their indolence should be encouraged by indulgence,[1] and teaches that those live holily who procure for themselves the necessaries of life by honourable and useful labour. And in the first place, he applies the appellation of *disorderly* persons, not to those that are of a dissolute life, or to those whose characters are stained by flagrant crimes, but to indolent and worthless persons, who employ themselves in no honourable and useful occupation. For this truly is $\dot{a}\tau a\xi\acute{\iota}a$, (*disorder*,[2])—not considering for what purpose we were made, and regulating our life with a view to that end, while it is only when we live according to the rule prescribed to us by God that this life is duly regulated. Let this order be set aside, and there is nothing but confusion in human life. This, also, is worthy to be noticed, lest any one should take pleasure in exercising himself apart from a legitimate call from God : for God has distinguished in such a manner the life of men, in order that every one may lay himself out for the advantage of others. He, therefore, who lives to himself alone, so as to be profitable in no way to the human race, nay more, is a burden to others, giving help to no one, is on good grounds reckoned to be $\check{a}\tau a\kappa\tau o\varsigma$, (*disorderly.*) Hence Paul declares that such persons must be put away from the society of believers, that they may not bring dishonour upon the Church.

6. *Now we command you in the name.* Erasmus renders it—"*by* the name," as if it were an adjuration. While I do not altogether reject this rendering, I, at the same time, am rather of opinion that the particle *in* is redundant, as in very many other passages, and that in accordance with the

[1] "Il defend aux Thessaloniciens d'entretenir par leur liberalite ou dissimulation l'oisiuete de telles gens ;"—"He prohibits the Thessalonians from encouraging by their liberality or dissimulation the indolence of such persons."

[2] "Desordre et grande confusion ;"—"Disorder and great confusion."

a mortal man, but as from Christ himself; and Chrysostom explains it in this manner. This *withdrawment*,[1] however, of which he speaks, relates—not to public excommunication, but to private intercourse. For he simply forbids believers to have any familiar intercourse with drones of this sort, who have no honourable means of life, in which they may exercise themselves. He says, however, expressly—*from every brother*, because if they profess themselves to be Christians, they are above all others intolerable, inasmuch as they are, in a manner, the pests and stains of religion.

Not according to the injunction—namely, that which we shall find him shortly afterwards adding—that food should not be given to the man that refuses to labour. Before coming to this, however, he states what example he has given them in his own person. For doctrine obtains much more of credit and authority, when we impose upon others no other burden than we take upon ourselves. Now he mentions that he himself was engaged in *working with his hands night and day*, that he might not burden any one with expense. He had, also, touched somewhat on this point in the preceding Epistle—to which my readers must have recourse for a fuller explanation of this point.[2]

As to his saying, that he *had not eaten any one's bread for nought*, he assuredly would not have done this, though he had not *laboured with his hands*. For that which is due in the way of right, is not a thing that is gratuitous, and the price of the labour which teachers[3] lay out in behalf of the Church, is much greater than the food which they receive from it. But Paul had here in his eye inconsiderate persons, for all have not so much equity and judgment as to consider what remuneration is due to the ministers of the word. Nay more, such is the niggardliness of some, that, though they contribute nothing of their own, they envy them

---

[1] " Ceste separation ou retirement ;"—" This separation or withdrawment."
[2] See p. 253.
[3] " Les Docteurs et Ministres ;"—" Teachers and ministers."

he refrained from taking any remuneration, by which he intimates, that it is much less to be endured, that those, who do nothing, shall live on what belongs to others.[2] When he says, that they *know how they ought to imitate*, he does not simply mean that his example should be regarded by them as a law, but the meaning is, that they knew what they had seen in him that was worthy of imitation, nay more, that the very thing of which he is at present speaking, has been set before them for imitation.

9. *Not because we have not.* As Paul wished by his labouring to set an example, that idle persons might not like drones[3] eat the bread of others, so he was not willing that this very thing[4] should do injury to the ministers of the word, so that the Churches should defraud them of their proper livelihood. In this we may see his singular moderation and humanity, and how far removed he was from the ambition of those who abuse their powers, so as to infringe upon the rights of their brethren. There was a danger, lest the Thessalonians, having had from the beginning the preaching of the gospel from Paul's mouth gratuitously,[5] should lay it down as a law for the future as to other ministers; the disposition of mankind being so niggardly. Paul, accordingly, anticipates this danger, and teaches that he had a right to more than he had made use of, that others may retain their liberty unimpaired. He designed by this means to inflict the greater disgrace, as I have already noticed above, on those that do nothing, for it is an argument from the greater to the less.

10. *He that will not labour.* From its being written in Psalm cxxviii. 2—*Thou art blessed, eating of the labour of*

[1] " Comme s'ils viuoyent inutiles et oiseux;"—" As if they lived uselessly and idly."

[2] " Viuent du labeur et bien d'autruy;"—" Should live on the labour and substance of others."

[3] " Ainsi que les bourdons entre abeilles ne font point de miel, et neantmoins viuent de celuy des autres;"—" As drones among bees do not make any honey, and yet live on that of others."

[4] " Son exemple;"—" His example."

[5] " Gratuitement et sans luy bailler aucuns gages;"—" Gratuitously, and without giving him any remuneration."

idleness are accursed of God. Besides, we know that man was created with this view, that he might do something. Not only does Scripture testify this to us, but nature itself taught it to the heathen. Hence it is reasonable, that those, who wish to exempt themselves from the common law,[1] should also be deprived of food, the reward of labour. When, however, the Apostle commanded that such persons should not eat, he does not mean that he gave commandment to those persons, but forbade that the Thessalonians should encourage their indolence by supplying them with food.

It is also to be observed, that there are different ways of labouring. For whoever aids[2] the society of men by his industry, either by ruling his family, or by administering public or private affairs, or by counselling, or by teaching,[3] or in any other way, is not to be reckoned among the idle. For Paul censures those lazy drones who lived by the sweat of others, while they contribute no service in common for aiding the human race. Of this sort are our monks and priests who are largely pampered by doing nothing, excepting that they chant in the temples, for the sake of preventing weariness. This truly is, (as Plautus speaks,)[4] to "live musically."[5]

11. For we hear that there are some which walk among you disorderly, working not at all, but are busybodies.

12. Now them that are such we command and exhort by our Lord

11. Audimus enim quosdam versantes inter vos inordinate nihil operis agentes, sed curiose satagentes.

12. Talibus autem praecipimus, et obsecramus[6] per Dominum nos-

[1] ":De la loy et regle commune ;"—" From the common law and rule."
[2] " Aide et porte proufit ;"—" Aids and brings advantage."
[3] " En enseignant les autres ;"—" By instructing others."
[4] The passage alluded to is as follows : " Musice, Hercle, agitis aetatem" —(" By Hercules, you pass life musically.") *Plaut. Mostellariae, Act* iii. *Sc.* 2, 40.—*Ed.*
[5] " Plaute poete Latin ancien, quand il veut parler de gens qui viuent a leur aise, il dit qu'ils viuent musicalement, c'est a dire, en chantres. Mais a la verite on peut bien dire de ceux-ci, en tout sens qu'on le voudra prendre, qu'ils viuent musicalement ;"—" Plautus, the ancient Latin poet, when he has it in view to speak of persons who live at their ease, says that they live musically, that is to say, like singers. But truly it may be well said of those persons, in every sense in which one might choose to take it, that they live musically."
[6] " Prions, *ou*, exhortons ;"—" We pray, *or*, we exhort."

13. But ye, brethren, be not weary in well-doing.	13. Vos autem fratres, ne defatigemini benefaciendo.

11. *We hear that there are some among you.* It is probable that this kind of drones were, as it were, the seed of idle monkhood. For, from the very beginning, there were some who, under pretext of religion, either made free with the tables of others, or craftily drew to themselves the substance of the simple. They had also, even in the time of Augustine, come to prevail so much, that he was constrained to write a book expressly against idle monks, where he complains with good reason of their pride, because, despising the admonition of the Apostle, they not only excuse themselves on the ground of infirmity, but they wish to appear holier than all others, on the ground that they are exempt from labours. He inveighs, with good reason, against this unseemliness, that, while the senators are laborious, the workman, or person in humble life, does not merely live in idleness,[1] but would fain have his indolence pass for sanctity. Such are his views.[2] In the mean time, however, the evil has increased to such an extent, that idle bellies occupy nearly the tenth part of the world, whose only religion is to be well stuffed, and to have exemption from all annoyance[3] of labour. And this manner of life they dignify, sometimes with the name of the Order, sometimes with that of the Rule, of this or that personage.[4]

But what does the Spirit say, on the other hand, by the mouth of Paul? He pronounces them all to be irregular and *disorderly*, by whatever name of distinction they may be dignified. It is not necessary to relate here how much the idle life of monks has invariably displeased persons of sounder judgment. That is a memorable saying of an old

[1] "Les senateurs et les nobles ayent la main a la besogne, et cependant les manouuriers et mechaniques, non seulement viuront en oisiuete;"—"The senators and the nobles have their hand in the work, and in the mean time the workmen and mechanics will not only live in idleness."
[2] "Voyla que dit S. Augustin;"—"There you have what St. Augustine says."
[3] "Et solicitude;"—"And anxiety."
[4] "D'vn tel sainct, ou d'vn tel;"—"Of this saint, or that."

his hands is like a plunderer.[1] I do not mention other instances, nor is it necessary. Let this statement of the Apostle suffice us, in which he declares that they are dissolute, and in a manner lawless.

Doing nothing. In the Greek participles there is an elegant (προσωνομασία) *play upon words,* which I have attempted in some manner to imitate, by rendering it as meaning that they *do* nothing, but have *enough to do* in the way of curiosity.[2] He censures, however, a fault with which idle persons are, for the most part, chargeable, that, by unseasonably bustling about, they give trouble to themselves and to others. For we see, that those who have nothing to do are much more fatigued by doing nothing, than if they were employing themselves in some very important work; they run hither and thither; wherever they go, they have the appearance of great fatigue; they gather all sorts of reports, and they put them in a confused way into circulation. You would say that they bore the weight of a kingdom upon their shoulders. Could there be a more remarkable exemplification of this than there is in the monks? For what class of men have less repose? Where does curiosity reign more extensively? Now, as this disease has a ruinous effect upon the public, Paul admonishes that it ought not to be encouraged by idleness.

12. *Now we command such.* He corrects both of the faults of which he had made mention—a blustering restlessness, and retirement from useful employment. He accordingly exhorts them, in the first place, to cultivate repose—that is, to keep themselves *quietly* within the limits of their calling, or, as we commonly say, " *sans faire bruit,*" *(without making a noise.)* For the truth is this: those are the most peaceable of all, that exercise themselves in lawful employments;[3] while those that

[1] " Vn vagabond qui va pillant;"—" A vagabond that goes a-plundering."
[2] " Nihil eos *agere* operis, sed curiose *satagere.*"
[3] " Ceux qui s'exercent a bon escient en quelque labeur licite;"— " Those that exercise themselves in good earnest in any lawful employment."

should *labour*, that is, that they should be intent upon their calling, and devote themselves to lawful and honourable employments, without which the life of man is of a wandering nature. Hence, also, there follows this third injunction—that they should *eat their own bread ;* by which he means, that they should be satisfied with what belongs to them, that they may not be oppressive or unreasonable to others. *Drink water*, says Solomon, *from thine own fountains, and let the streams flow down to neighbours.* (Prov. v. 15.) This is the *first* law of equity, that no one make use of what belongs to another, but only use what he can properly call his own. The *second* is, that no one swallow up, like some abyss, what belongs to him, but that he be beneficent to neighbours, and that he may relieve their indigence by his abundance.[1] In the same manner, the Apostle exhorts those who had been formerly idle *to labour*, not merely that they may gain for themselves a livelihood, but that they may also be helpful to the necessities of their brethren, as he also teaches elsewhere. (Eph. iv. 28.)

13. *And you, brethren.* Ambrose is of opinion that this is added lest the rich should, in a niggardly spirit, refuse to lend their aid to the poor, because he had exhorted them to *eat every one his own bread.* And, unquestionably, we see how many are unbefittingly ingenious in catching at a pretext for inhumanity.[2] Chrysostom explains it thus—that indolent persons, however justly they may be condemned, must nevertheless be assisted when in want. I am simply of opinion, that Paul had it in view to provide against an occasion of offence, which might arise from the indolence of a few. For it usually happens, that those that are otherwise particularly ready and on the alert for beneficence, become cool on seeing that they have thrown away their favours by misdirecting them. Hence Paul admonishes us, that, although there are many that are undeserving,[3] while others

[1] See CALVIN on the Corinthians, vol. ii. p. 286.
[2] " Enuers les poures ;"—" Towards the poor."
[3] " Ne meritent point qu'on leur face du bien ;"—" Do not deserve that any should do them good."

worthy of being observed—that however ingratitude, moroseness, pride, arrogance, and other unseemly dispositions on the part of the poor, may have a tendency to annoy us, or to dispirit us, from a feeling of weariness, we must strive, nevertheless, never to leave off aiming at doing good.

14. And if any man obey not our word by this epistle, note that man, and have no company with him, that he may be ashamed.	14. Si quis autem non obedit sermoni nostro per epistolam, hunc notate: et ne commisceamini illi,[1] ut pudefiat:
15. Yet count *him* not as an enemy, but admonish *him* as a brother.	15. Et ne tanquam inimicum sentiatis, sed admonete tanquam fratrem.
16. Now the Lord of peace himself give you peace always by all means. The Lord *be* with you all.	16. Ipse autem Deus pacis det vobis pacem semper omnibus modis. Dominus sit cum omnibus vobis.
17. The salutation of Paul with mine own hand, which is the token in every epistle: so I write.	17. Salutatio, mea manu Pauli : quod est signum in omni epistola.
18. The grace of our Lord Jesus Christ *be* with you all. Amen.	18. Gratia Domini nostri Iesu Christi cum omnibus vobis. Amen.
¶ The second *epistle* to the Thessalonians was written from Athens.	Ad Thessalonicenses secunda missa fuit ex Athenis.

14. *If any one obeys not.* He has already declared previously, that he commands nothing but *from the Lord.* Hence the man, that would not obey, would not be contumacious against a mere man, but would be rebellious against God himself;[2] and accordingly he teaches that such persons ought to be severely chastised. And, in the *first* place, he desires that they be reported to him, that he may repress them by his authority; and, *secondly,* he orders them to be excommunicated, that, being touched with shame, they may repent. From this we infer, that we must not spare the reputation of those who cannot be arrested otherwise

---

[1] " N'obeit a nostre parolle, marquez-le par lettres, et ne conuersez point, *or*, ni obeit a nostre parolle par *ces* lettres, marquez-le, et ne conversez;"—" Does not obey our word, mark him by letters, and keep no company with him; *or*, does not obey our word by *these* letters, mark him and keep no company.".

[2] " Ce n'eust point contre vn homme mortel qu'il eust addresse son opiniastre et rebellion;"—" It would not have been against a mortal man that he had directed his stubbornness and rebellion."

may make it his endeavour to cure them.

Keep no company. I have no doubt that he refers to excommunication; for, besides that the (ἀταξία) *disorder* to which he had adverted deserved a severe chastisement, contumacy is an intolerable vice. He had said before, *Withdraw yourselves from them,* for they live in a *disorderly* manner, (verse 6.) And now he says, *Keep no company,* for they reject my admonition. He expresses, therefore, something more by this second manner of expression than by the former; for it is one thing to withdraw from intimate acquaintance with an individual, and quite another to keep altogether aloof from his society. In short, those that do not obey after being admonished, he excludes from the common society of believers. By this we are taught that we must employ the discipline of excommunication against all the obstinate[1] persons who will not otherwise allow themselves to be brought under subjection, and must be branded with disgrace, until, having been brought under and subdued, they learn to obey.

That he may be ashamed. There are, it is true, other ends to be served by excommunication—that contagion may spread no farther, that the personal wickedness of one individual may not tend to the common disgrace of the Church, and that the example of severity may induce others to *fear,* (1 Tim. v. 20;) but Paul touches upon this one merely— that those who have sinned may by shame be constrained to repentance. For those that please themselves in their vices become more and more obstinate: thus sin is nourished by indulgence and dissimulation. This, therefore, is the best remedy—when a feeling of shame is awakened in the mind of the offender, so that he begins to be displeased with himself. It would, indeed, be a small point gained to have individuals made ashamed; but Paul had an eye to farther progress—when the offender, confounded by a discovery of his own baseness, is led in this way to a full amendment: for shame, like sorrow, is a useful preparation for

---

[1] " Et endurcis;"—" And hardened."

should be increased in consequence of impunity.

15. *Regard him not as an enemy.* He immediately adds a softening of his rigour; for, as he elsewhere commands, we must take care that the offender be not *swallowed up with sorrow,* (2 Cor. ii. 7,) which would take place if severity were excessive. Hence we see that the use of discipline ought to be in such a way as to consult the welfare of those on whom the Church inflicts punishment. Now, it cannot but be that severity will fret,[2] when it goes beyond due bounds. Hence, if we wish to do good, gentleness and mildness are necessary, that those that are reproved may know that they are nevertheless loved. In short, excommunication does not tend to drive men from the Lord's flock, but rather to bring them back when wandering and going astray.

We must observe, however, by what sign he would have brotherly love shewn—not by allurements or flattery, but by *admonitions;* for in this way it will be, that all that will not be incurable will feel that concern is felt for their welfare. In the mean time, excommunication is distinguished from anathema: for as to those that the Church marks out by the severity of its censure, Paul admonishes that they should not be utterly cast away, as if they were cut off from all hope of salvation; but endeavours must be used, that they may be brought back to a sound mind.

16. *Now the Lord of peace.* This prayer seems to be connected with the preceding sentence, with the view of recommending endeavours after concord and mildness. He had forbidden them to treat even the contumacious[3] as *enemies,* but rather with a view to their being brought back to a sound mind[4] by brotherly admonitions. He could appropriately,

[1] "Tous ceux qui se desbordent et follastrent;"—"All those that break out and become wanton."
[2] "Face entameure et trop grande blessure;"—"Make an incision, and too great a wound."
[3] "Mesme les rebelles et obstinez;"—"Even the rebellious and obstinate."
[4] "A repentance et amendment;"—"To repentance and amendment."

himself to prayer, which, nevertheless, has also the force of a precept. At the same time, he may also have another thing in view—that God may restrain unruly persons,[1] that they may not disturb the peace of the Church.

17. *The salutation, with my own hand.* Here again he provides against the danger, of which he had previously made mention[2]—lest epistles falsely ascribed to him should find their way into the Churches. For this was an old artifice of Satan—to put forward spurious writings, that he might detract from the credit of those that are genuine; and farther, under pretended designations of the Apostles, to disseminate wicked errors with the view of corrupting sound doctrine. By a singular kindness on the part of God, it has been brought about that, his frauds being defeated, the doctrine of Christ has come down to us sound and entire through the ministry of Paul and others. The concluding prayer explains in what manner God aids his believing people—by the presence of Christ's grace.

[1] " Ceux qui sont desobeissans;"—" Those that are disobedient."
[2] See p. 324. The reader will find the same subject adverted to by CALVIN in p. 232.

END OF THE COMMENTARY ON THE SECOND EPISTLE TO
THE THESSALONIANS.

TABLES AND INDEX

TO THE

COMMENTARIES

ON

THE EPISTLES OF PAUL THE APOSTLE

TO

THE PHILIPPIANS, COLOSSIANS, AND THESSALONIANS.

TABLE I.

OF PASSAGES FROM THE HOLY SCRIPTURES, AND FROM THE APOCRYPHA, WHICH ARE QUOTED, OR INCIDENTALLY ILLUSTRATED, IN THE COMMENTARIES ON THE EPISTLES TO THE PHILIPPIANS, COLOSSIANS, AND THESSALONIANS.

GENESIS.

Chap.	Ver.	Page	Chap.	Ver.	Page	Chap.	Ver.	Page
i.	26	212, n. 1	ix.	6	138, 212	xiv.	13	91
iii.	22	187						

EXODUS.

vii.	11	387	xiv.	13	243	xxxii.	32	114

LEVITICUS.

xix.	14	225

DEUTERONOMY.

vii.	7, 8	341	x.	17	219	xiii.	3	340

I. KINGS.

xix.	18	62

JOB.

iv.	18	156

PSALMS.

Chap.	Ver.	Page	Chap.	Ver.	Page	Chap.	Ver.	Page
vii.	8	45	lxix.	29	114	cxxxvii.	6	51
xxxv.	19	70	lxxiii.	1-12	313	cxxxviii.	8	26, 305
xxxvii.	5	296	cxxviii.	2	354	cxlv.	18	118
lv.	22	119, 296						

| iii. | 6 | 203 | viii. | 56 | 358 | x. | 4 | 355 |
| v. | 15 | 358 | | | | | | |

ECCLESIASTES.

ix. 3 312

ISAIAH.

xi.	4	335	xlv.	28	61	lv.	11, 13	257
xvi.	9	304	xlviii.	11	56	lx.	2	72, 147
xxx.	15	144	l.	5	82			287
	21	178	liii.	1	169	lxiv.	8	26
xxiii.	22	202						

JEREMIAH.

| v. | 8 | 274 | xxiii. | 29 | 257 | xxxi. | 33 | 159 |
| xvii. | 9 | 71 | | | | | | |

EZEKIEL.

xi. 20 66

DANIEL.

xii. 2 288, *n.* 1

HOSEA.

i. 10, 11 162

ZECHARIAH.

xiv. 8 161

MALACHI.

iv. 2 288

MATTHEW.

v.	11	29	xiii.	25	132, 349	xxi.	44	48
	14	72		46	94	xxiii.	32	260
	15	72	xv.	6	345	xxiv.	6	325
vi.	10	347		11	201		24	337
	21	109	xvi.	17	197		32	324
vii.	13	315	xvii.	5	148		37	286
x.	20	224		6	110	xxv.	40	128
xiii.	13	318	xx.	28	58	xxviii.	20	44

LUKE.

vi.	25	117	xvii.	21	44	xxi.	28	43
xiii	24	315	xxi.	15	224	xxiv.	47	vii.
xvi.	15	96, 202		19	118			

JOHN.

i.	14	57	v.	20	154	xv.	1	33
	16	33		24	290	xvii.	1	57
	18	149	x.	5	88, 180		3	318
iv.	23	89		8	88		5	55
v.	17	63		27	88			

ACTS.

i.	8	319	iii.	20	315	xx.	23	255
ii.	37	255	xx.	28	348			

ROMANS.

i.	4	57	vi.	6	99	xi.	24	33
	13	263		13	184	xii.	7	217
	16	168		20	245		19	261
	19	158	vii.	24	81		21	296
	20	56	viii.	7	158	xiii.	14	204
	28	339		10	290, *n*. 3	xiv.	8	41
ii.	29	88		14	343		11	62
iii.	4	29		24	207, 239		17	200
	23	246		28	40	xv.	8	58
iv.	15	261		29	164		16	74
v.	4	41	ix.	3	55	xvi.	17, 18	87, *n*. 1
vi.	2	210	x.	5	98		25	168
	4	185	xi.	5	261			

I. CORINTHIANS.

i.	8	70, *n*. 4	ii.	14	143	x.	13	349
	18	175	iv.	1	167	xi.	7	149
	23	168	vi.	13	201	xii.	12	164
	30	159, 311	vii.	8	113	xiv.	3	299
	31	45, 73,		30, 31	206		14	269
		121,		35	345	xv.	13	280
		263, *n*. 1	ix.	5	114		20	153
ii.	2	174		11	127		31	322
	6	171		14	258		36	283
	8	55						

i.	4	167	v.	4	233	viii.	13	222, *n*. 2
	20	193		6	44	x.	17	78
ii.	7	361		17	107	xi.	8	254
iv.	7	170		18	216		14	324
	10	165	v.	21	155	xiii.	4	57

GALATIANS.

i.	10	250	v.	17	216	vi.	10	138, 225,
ii.	19	199		25	210			270
iv.	3	182		26	52, *n*. 2			

EPHESIANS.

ii.	6	101	iv.	28	358	vi.	14	289
	11	187	v.	16	225		16	47
iii.	9	168	vi.	1	220		18	297, *n*. 2
	17	44		8	222		19	224
iv.	1	121		12	263		20	224
	14	178, 300						

I. TIMOTHY.

i.	5	271	iii.	15	331	v.	3	204
iii.	2	301		16	57, 62		20	360

II. TIMOTHY.

i.	3	105	ii.	11	99	iii.	16	32, 217
	12	207		11, 12	165	iv.	10	230
ii.	10	167		19	115			

TITUS.

i. 11   301

PHILEMON.

1, 2   227, *n*. 1

HEBREWS.

iii.	14	94	xiii.	7	266	xiii.	9	145
vi.	4	298		8	176		16	128

JAMES.

ii.	19	63	iv.	12	329

II. PETER.

iii. 8   324

I. JOHN.

ii.	1	38	ii.	27	277	iv.	19	341
	18	333	iii.	14	148	v.	12	343
	23	174, 183	iv.	1	324			

REVELATION.

xiii.	3	327, *n.* 2	xx.	12	115

APOCRYPHA.

II. MACCABEES.

viii.   15   121, *n.* 1

TABLE II.

OF GREEK WORDS EXPLAINED.

	Page		Page
ἀγών	172	ἐν αὐτῷ	190
ἀκέφαλον	152	ἔνδειγμα	48
ἄν	55	ἔνδειξιν	48
ἀντιστρέφον	63	ἐν ἐμοί	45
ἀντίχριστος	328, n. 1	ἐνεργεῖν	66
ἀπάθειαν	82	ἐνεργῶν	66
ἀπαρχήν	342	ἐν παντί	119
ἀπ' ἀρχῆς	342	ἔπαινος	121, n. 2
ἀπρόσκοποι	32	ἐπεκτεινόμενος	103, n. 1
ἅπτεσθαι	200	ἐπί	214
ἅπτεσθον	200, n. 1	ἐπιεικές	117
ἀρχή	153	ἐπιστήμης	121, n. 2
ἄτακτος	352	ἐπιχορηγία	40
ἀταξία	352	ἔργου	238
ἀταξίαν	313	εὐδοκήσαμεν	265
αὐξανόμενον	140	εὐδοκήσαντες	340
βαρύ	251	εὐδοκία	66
βραβεύετο	215, n. 1	εὑρίσκομαι	97
γάρ	264	εὔφημα	121
γενόμενος	58	εὐφήμου	195
δέησις	119	ἐφ' ᾧ	123
δέξασθαι	228, n. 2	ηὐχόμην	55
δέξασθε	228, n. 2	ἥψαντο	200, n. 2
διανοίας	158	Θεῷ καὶ Πατρί	147, n. 1
διαπορείας	195	θυσίαν	74
δόσεως	127, n. 3	θλίψεις	164
ἐθελοθρησκεία	201	θυμός	210
εἰ γὰρ ἔγνωσαν	55	ἰσότητα	222
εἰκονικῶς	193	κανόνι	105, n. 2
εἰς	63	καθεύδωμεν	288, n. 1
ἐλάβετε	228, n. 2	καταβραβεύετο	193, n. 3
ἐμβατεύειν	196, 197	κατατομή	87, n. 1
ἐλφατικώτερον	199	κατ' ἐξοχήν	139
ἐμφατικωτέρως	56	κατέχον	332, 334
ἐν	63	κενοδοξία	52, n. 2

2 A

λειτουργίαν	74	πονηρῶν	348
λήψεως	127, *n.* 3	πρὸς	42
λογίζεσθαι	122	προσευχῇ	119
λογίζεσθε	122, *n.* 1	προσφιλῆ	121
λόγον	127, *n.* 3	προσωνομασία	87
λοιποί	288, *n.* 1	πρόφασις	251
μεγαλοπρεπής	121, *n.* 1	σέβασμα	329
μελετᾶν	122, *n.* 1	σεμνὸν	121
μεμψιμοιρία	70	σεμνός	121, *n.* 1
μέρος	192	σκύβαλον	96
μιμητικῶς	200	σπένδομαι	74
ὁμοουσία	149	σπονδὰς	74
ὁμοουσίαν	149	στάσις	146, *n.* 2
ὀργὴ	210	συλλαμβάνεσθαι	114
παθήματα	164, *n.* 3	σὺν	47
πάθος	208	συναθλοῦντες	46
παιδείας	121, *n.* 2	συνέσεως	143
πανοπλίαν	289	σωματικῶς	183, *n.* 1
πάντα	329	τὰ αὐτὰ	222
πᾶν τὸ	329	τὸ αὐτὸ	52
παραδόσεις	345	τὸ αὐτὸ φρονεῖν	105, *n.* 2
παρακλήσεως	50	τροπή	73, *n.* 1
παραμυθούμενοι	255	τρόπαια	73, *n.* 1
παρρησιάσωμαι	224	ὑμῶν	238
πάσῃ αἰσθήσει	31, *n.* 2	ὑπερβαῖνειν	274
περιποίησις	290	ὑπὲρ ἐκπερισσοῦ	269, *n.* 4
περισσεύειν	124	ὑπὸ	241
περιτομὴ	87, *n.* 1	ὑστερήματα	166, 269
πιθανολογία	176, *n.* 3	φιλοτιμεῖσθαι	277
πλεονεκτεῖν	274	χρηστότητα	213

TABLE III.

OF HEBREW WORDS EXPLAINED.

	Page		Page
רחמים	31	מתן ומשא	127, *n.* 3
פרש	91	חשך	147, *n.* 5

GENERAL INDEX.

A

ADMONITION, Christians exhorted to practise mutual, 217 ; necessary for the unruly, 294.

Adoption, the persecutions endured by Christians are in a manner seals of, 48 ; is a motive to a blameless life, 70 ; depends on an unmerited election, 147 ; the Holy Spirit is the seal of, 147 ; prepares for the heavenly inheritance, 147 ; is a pledge of the continued exercise of grace, 305.

Adoration, is due to God alone, 61 ; is to be rendered to Christ, 61 ; bowing the knee is a token of, 62.

Afflictions, of Christians, are not the *cause* of their salvation, 48 ; are, to believers, benefits from God, 48 ; are common to Christ and to the martyrs, 164 ; should be endured by Christians with cheerfulness, 165 ; are, to the wicked, tokens of a judgment to come, 314 ; the advantages afforded by them to believers, 314, 315.

Agreement, among Christians, is the best bulwark for repelling impious doctrines, 50 ; is a token of the prosperous condition of the Church, 51 ; the importance of it, 112 ; the bond of it, 113.

Almsgiving, is a sacrifice, 128.

Ambition, is an occasion of strife, 52 ; is the source of innumerable corruptions, 251.

Ambrose quoted, 302, 358.

Anathema, differs from excommunication, 361.

Angels, were created by Christ, 150 ; are in subjection to Christ, 151, 152 ; in what sense they needed a peace-maker, 156 ; the worshipping of, condemned, 194 ; the Theurgians pretended to have received communications from, 194, 195 ; the worship of, traced to the writings of Plato, 195 ; will come with Christ on the final day, 317.

Antichrist, supposed by some of the ancients to have been Nero, 327 ; represents—not one individual, but one kingdom, 327, 333 ; is diametrically opposed to Christ, 328 ; the marks by which he may be recognised, 329, 330 ; his reign will be but for a time, 334 ; his destruction foretold, 335 ; derives all his influence from Satan's impostures, 336 ; will be utterly overthrown by Christ, 336 ; is directly opposed to Christ, 337 ; his dominion is cruel, 338.

Apostasy, the great, predicted by Paul, 325, 326.

Apostles, import of the term, 81 ; Popish Bishops have no claim to be successors of, 292, 293 ; were Christ's *witnesses*, 319.

Apostles' Creed, referred to by CALVIN, 284, *n.* 1.

Apposition, a figure of speech, 140, 174, 318.

Apuleius quoted, 95, *n.* 1.

Archangel, what is meant by the *voice* of the, 283.

Archippus supposed by some to have planted the Church of Colosse, xi ; Paul's admonition to him, 281.

Arians, the, denied Christ's equality with the Father, 56 ; looked upon Christ as a mere creature, 150.

Aristotle quoted, 70, *n.* 3 ; 121, *n.* 1.

Assurance of faith, does not extend to others, 26 ; fear not necessarily opposed to, 68 ; the doctrine of Papists tends to shake, 68, 160, 174.

Augustine quoted, 105, *n.* 2 ; 162, 166, 167, 195, 198, 283, 284 ; his exposure of the indolence of the monks, 356.

B

BAPTISM, came in the place of circumcision, 89; is a sign of spiritual circumcision, 185; is a sacrament of the grace of God, 189.
Barnes quoted, ix.
Believers should always conjoin prayer with joy, 24, 25; will not attain perfection until the final day, 27; have fellowship with Christ in suffering, 29; their true attainments, 31; the Spirit of Christ is common to all, 40; their happiness is wholly derived from Christ, 42; overcome the fear of death, 43; death introduces them into the presence of Christ, 44; their glorying should be in God alone, 45; should be united in a holy agreement, 46, 47; their consolation under persecution, 48; their agreement is the best bulwark for repelling impious doctrines, 50; are intermingled with the wicked, 70; should shine as lamps, 71; are soldiers in the camp of Christ, 80; must glory in nothing, apart from Christ, 95; have a twofold participation in the death of Christ, 99; should endeavour to make progress in the divine life, 101, 102; have a race to run, 102; should be daily conversant with heaven, 109; have always ground of joy, 116; find consolation in prayer, 119; the dispositions which they ought to cultivate, 121; are honourably termed *saints*, 137; are imperfect, while here, 138; their faith is confirmed, when multitudes embrace the gospel, 140; are always, while here, exercised with the cross, 144; their happiness consists in cleaving to God, 154; their holiness is only commenced, 159; their fellowship with Christ, 164; their wisdom is wholly included in the gospel, 175; Satan accuses them before God, 190; should not be taken up with the things of earth; 206, 207; should avoid all unprofitable talk, 226; the perfection to be aimed at by them, 229; their hope is founded on Christ's resurrection, 247; need to be stimulated by exhortations, lay their account with persecution, 266; holiness is the design of their calling, 275; their glorious resurrection, 282, 283; are children of light, 287; have need of watchfulness, 288, 289; their victory is certain, 290; the sanctification needed by them, 304; their mutual fellowship, 311; death is to them an image of life, 314; the contrast between their present and future condition, 318; their warfare, 325; have need of patience, 334; are ordinarily few in number, 339.
Benson quoted, xiv; 261, *n*. 2.
Beza quoted, vi; 31, *n*. 1; 39, *n*. 2; 127, *n*. 3; 147, *n*. 1; 228, *n*. 2.
Biblical cabinet quoted, vii; 52, *n*. 2; 121, *n*. 1; 122, *n*. 1.
Bishop, and Pastor, are convertible terms, 23.
Bishops, Popish, have no claim to be regarded as successors of the Apostles, 292, 293.
Bloomfield quoted, 103, *n*. 1.
Body, the frailty of, 110; of Christ's flesh, employed to denote his human nature, 159; the term made use of by Paul to denote a *mass* of vices, 184.
Bodily, the adverb, employed by Paul to mean—*substantially*, 182, 183.
Böhmer, of Berlin, quoted, vi.
Bonds, the fruit of Paul's, 35, 36; Paul calls the Colossians to remember his, 231.
Book of life, import of the expression, 114.
Brentius, letter of CALVIN to, vi.
Brown's (Rev. Dr. John) "Expository Discourses on Peter" quoted, 166, *n*. 1; 276, *n*. 1; his "Discourses and Sayings of our Lord Illustrated," quoted, 74, *n*. 1.
Budaeus quoted, 197.
Byfield, on the Colossians, quoted, x.

C

CALLING. (See Effectual Calling.)
CALVIN wrote his Commentaries on Paul's Epistles under unfavourable circumstances, vi; is, notwithstanding, peculiarly successful in the exposition of them, vi, vii; is thought to have resembled Paul,

xvi; was a pupil of Maturinus Corderius, xvi, 234; dedicated to him his Commentary on the *First* Epistle to the Thessalonians, xvi, 284; dedicated to Benedict Textor his Commentary on the *Second* Epistle to the Thessalonians, xvi, 308; frequently animadverts upon the tenets of Popery, xvii.

"CALVIN and the Swiss Reformation" quoted, vii.

Canonical, origin of the epithet as applied to the general Epistles of the New Testament, 276, *n.* 1.

Capito, Wolfgang, quoted, 91.

Carefulness, the term employed to denote distrustful anxiety, 119.

Carolus, Peter, undesignedly promoted the spread of the truth, 39.

Ceremonies of the law, the, were abolished by the coming of Christ, 181; why called the *elements of the world*, 181, 182; had in them an acknowledgment of sin, 189; the substance of them is presented to us in Christ, 192; abrogated by the death of Christ, 202, 206.

Children, obedience to their parents enjoined, 219, 220.

Chiliasts, their errors refuted, 284.

Christ is our sole Advocate, 38; we must not be ashamed to confess him, 41; renunciation of him is inexcusable, 41; makes us happy both in life and in death, 42; his original dignity, 55; his eternal Divinity, 56; his extreme abasement, 58; presents an unrivalled pattern of humility, 59; adoration is due to him, 62; is the eternal God, 63; all Christians are soldiers in his camp, 80; the knowledge of him is transcendently desirable, 94; the fruits of his death and resurrection, 98; there is a twofold fellowship in his death, 99; will come to his people on the final day as a *Saviour*, 109; has authority and power to raise the dead, 111; is the proper object of faith, 138; Popery is founded on ignorance of him, 146; all the parts of our salvation are contained in him, 148; is the image of God, 149; angels are in subjection to him, 151; all things were created by him, 152; is the Head of the 155; is our peace-maker, 158; the name of, sometimes includes the whole body of believers, 164; nothing is wanting to those that have obtained him, 170; a striking proof of his Divinity, 175; Popery is wholly built on ignorance of him, 177; God has manifested himself to us fully and perfectly in him, 182, 183; his victory over Satan, 190; the magnificence of his triumph, 191; is the beginning and end of our salvation, 212; we must wait for his second coming, 246; the design of his resurrection, 280; his second advent will be sudden, 286; will avenge the injuries done to his people, 317; Antichrist is diametrically opposed to him, 328; will utterly overthrow Antichrist, 336; of what his kingdom consists, 337; a clear proof of his Divinity, 346.

Christianity, Popery is a grievous corruption of, 92; a brief definition of, 239.

Christians. See Believers.

Christopher, Duke of Wirtemberg, CALVIN dedicated to him his Commentaries on four of Paul's Epistles, vii, xvi.

Chrysostom, quoted, 32, 96, 141, 149, 192, 218, 240, 274, 297, 302, 332, 348, 353, 358.

Church, The, the blood of the martyrs the seed of the, 30; the Pope is not the head of the, 152, 153; the Papal, differs widely from the ancient, 162; the blood of Christ, and of the martyrs, constitutes, according to Papists, a treasure of, 165; in what its perfection consists, 177; Christ is the head of, 198; is like a city, 225; *in the house*, what is meant by, 230; the marks of a true, 237; Satan is constantly endeavouring to hinder the edification of, 268; its government is spiritual, 293; Paul predicts a grievous scattering of, 325.

Cicero quoted, 117, 214, *n.* 2; 226, *n.* 1.

Circumcision gave way to Baptism, 89; that on the eighth day was reckoned by the Jews of superior value, 90; was abolished by the coming of Christ, 184; was an

Clarke (Dr. Adam) quoted, xv, 40, *n.* 1; 130, *n.* 1; 164, *n.* 3; 173, *n.* 1; 183, *n.* 1; 215, *n.* 1; 269, *n.* 4; 294, *n.* 1.

Clement quoted, 113.

Cœlestinians, the, held the doctrine of a sinless perfection attainable in this life, 159, 160.

Colosse, was a city of Phrygia, x; was destroyed by an earthquake, x, 132; it is not certain by whom the gospel was first introduced into, x, xi, 132.

Colossian Christians, highly commended by Paul, 137, 140; Paul's intense concern for their welfare, 172; warned against false teachers, 180; admonished to guard against seductive errors, 192, 194.

Conjecture, Moral, a contrivance of the Schoolmen, 174.

Conscience, the unspeakable value of a good, 44; faith is the foundation of a good, 44; human traditions ensnare, 200; must not be bound, 201; the term *heart* employed to denote, 271.

Contention, in the Church, opens a door for the spread of impious doctrines, 50; a most dangerous pest, 52; ambition is a fruitful source of, 52; a querulous temper gives rise to, 70.

Contentment, Christian, a rare and excellent virtue, 124; Paul was an illustrious pattern of, 124.

Conversion, is necessary before we can serve God, 245; the end of genuine, 245.

Corderius, Maturinus, CALVIN was a pupil of, xvi, 234; CALVIN's Dedicatory Epistle to, 234.

Cornelius à Lapide quoted, 327, *n.* 2.

Covetousness, is idolatry, 209; is the source of innumerable corruptions, 251.

Cranmer's version of the Scriptures quoted, 238, *n.* 3.

Cross, the offence of the, 84; faith is inseparably connected with the, 49; the term employed to denote the preaching of the gospel, 107; of Christ, was like a triumphal car, 191.

Curiosity, a spirit of, ought not to be indulged, 169, 197.

the whole world is by nature in, 147; believers have been called out of, 148.

Davenant on the Colossians quoted, x, xii.

Day, of Christ, may be understood as referring either to death or to the resurrection, 27; of the Lord, will come suddenly, 286; believers are the children of the, 287.

Deacon, import of the term, 24.

Dead, the, are not to be prayed to, 223; we are not forbidden to mourn for, 279; we must moderate our grief for, 280.

Death, is not in itself desirable, 43; is not viewed by believers with excessive dread, 43; the term employed to mean *abrogation*, 199; of believers, is often compared to a sleep, 279; is the separation of the soul from the body, 283; is to believers an image of life, 314; everlasting, awaits the impenitent, 318.

Demas, honourably made mention of by Paul in writing to the Colossians, 230; Paul was afterwards deserted by him, 230.

Demosthenes quoted, 197, *n.* 2.

Devils, Christ is not their peace-maker, 157; Christ's victory over them, 190.

Diogenes, the Cynic, his imperfect views of the nature of religion, 245.

Dionysius, on the Celestial Hierarchy, quoted, 133.

Dionysius the younger, tyrant of Sicily, his profane boast, 313.

Discipline, must be strictly exercised when necessary, 360; yet not with excessive severity, 361; must be exercised with a view to the good of the offender, 361.

Disorderly, Paul's use of the term, 352; those that are such must be excluded from the society of believers, 352.

Docility, the best preparation for, 104; the Colossians commended for their, 140.

Doctrine, agreement among Christians is the best bulwark for repelling impious, 50; requires to be followed up with urgent exhortations, 111; the means of retaining, and restor-

sound, 336.
Doddridge quoted, xi.
Donatists, the, refuted by Augustine, 162.

E

EADIE'S (Dr.) Biblical Cyclopaedia, xi.
Edification, our speech ought to be such as tends to promote, 226; Christians must aim at promoting mutual, 291; that of the Church is the work of Pastors, 292.
Effectual calling, is a token of election, 26; perfection in holiness is its ultimate design, 271, 275; is an evidence of everlasting grace, 305.
Elect, the term sometimes employed to mean *set apart*, 213; Satan is restrained from injuring, 337; their salvation is secured, 342.
Election, effectual calling is a token of it, 26; adoption depends upon it, 147; the practical evidences of it, 240, 241; the only sure tokens of it, 342, 343.
Elements of the world, import of the expression, 181, 182.
Epaphras, supposed by some to have planted the Church of Colosse, x, 132, 133; highly commended by Paul, 141.
Epaphroditus, Paul's high commendation of him, 80; his anxious concern for his flock, 81; was mercifully restored from a dangerous distemper, 81, 82; his sickness was occasioned by incessant labour, 84.
Ephesus, Paul's Epistle to the Colossians bears a close resemblance to the Epistle addressed to the Church of, xi, xii; Paul wrote his First Epistle to the Corinthians from, 113.
Epicurus, his imperfect views of the nature of religion, 245.
Epistles, spurious, were in circulation in the first ages of the Church, 232, 362.
Equity, the twofold law of, 358.
Erasmus quoted, 46, 47, 56, 75, 105, 113, 139, 158, 172, 190, 196, 209, 238, 240, 258, 352.
Eusebius quoted, 113.

not *render evil for*, 295.
Excommunication, is necessary to be inflicted upon the contumacious, 359; the ends to be served by it, 360; differs from anathema, 361.
Exhortations, should accompany doctrine, 111; are necessary even for believers, 255.

F

FAITH, the Gospel is as nothing to us unless received by, 25; the fruits of righteousness spring from, 33; is the foundation of a good conscience, 44; is both our panoply and our victory, 47; is inseparably connected with the cross, 49; is an unmerited gift of God, 49; the righteousness of, 97; and love, constitute the entire sum of Christian excellence, 137; Christ is the proper object of it, 138; the increase of believers is a confirmation of it, 140; the relationship that it bears to the Gospel, 160; differs from mere opinion, 160, 174; steadfastness of, represented by three metaphors, 178; is founded upon the power of God, 186; we are justified by it alone, 215; its practical fruits, 239; its nature and essence, 245; resistance of Satan's temptation is a test of it, 258; constitutes the Christian's armour, 289; the increase of it is from God, 311; there is no holiness without it, 319; what is meant by the *work of*, 320; the perfecting of it is an arduous matter, 321; has always reverence for God conjoined with it, 339; is not to be found in all, 348, 349.
Faithfulness of God, the, is the security of the believer's life, 207; gives the fullest assurance of ultimate salvation, 305.
Fathers of the Old Testament, the, were participants in the grace of Christ, 189; their views were comparatively obscure, 189.
Fanatics, some in the times of CALVIN despised the outward ministry of the word, 299.
Fear, two kinds of, 68; not necessarily opposed to assurance, 68; the dis-

whatever is apart from Christ, 89; employed to denote corrupt nature, 184.

Fornication. Christians warned against, 208; pollutes the whole man, 273; involves infamy and disgrace, 274.

Foster's Essays quoted, viii.

Fuller, Rev. Andrew, quoted, xiv.

G

GENTILES, the, are under the Gospel placed on an entire equality with the Jews, 212; the universal call of, predicted, 333.

Glorying, it is only in the Lord that we have ground of, 45; vain, is a dangerous pest for disturbing the peace of the Church, 52; the doctrine of grace cuts off all ground of, 65.

God, faith is the gift of, 49; the right use of his gifts, 53; adoration is due to him alone, 61, 62; a right inclination of the will is from, 65, 66; ignorance of his Providence is the cause of all impatience, 118; the advantage to be derived from invocation of him, 120; is the Author of peace, 122; his will is to be sought for in his word, 142; we must study to make progress in the knowledge of him, 144; is invisible 149; is revealed to us in Christ alone, 150; our happiness consists in our cleaving to him, 154; his truth is the bond of holy unity, 173; has manifested himself to us fully and perfectly in Christ, 182, 183; his worship ought not to be regulated according to human fancies, 203; his faithfulness secures the believer's salvation, 207; his wrath is greatly to be deprecated, 209; why the gospel is called his *kingdom*, 229; is worthy of supreme love, 238; our salvation is wholly from him, 242, 271; how he stands affected towards us in Christ, 297; his faithfulness secures the believer's salvation, 305; is the righteous Judge of the world, 313; furnishes in his providence tokens of a judgment to come, 314.

Gospel, the, affords no enjoyment to us until received by faith, 25; whe-believers ought to stand forth for the defence of it, 38; the wicked are sometimes undesignedly the means of promoting it, 39; its transcendent dignity, 94; is, by way of eminence, the *word of truth*, 139; the relationship that faith bears to it, 160; why called a *secret*, 168; can be understood only by means of faith, 174; the wisdom of believers is wholly comprehended in it, 175; the simplicity of it despised by Papists, 176; is corrupted by human traditions, 181; should be familiarly known by all believers, 216; is the *mystery of Christ*, 224; why called the *kingdom of God*, 229; must be received with a joyful heart, 243; its tendency, 245; the lively preaching of it, 255; the credit due to it, 257; its doctrine is lovely, 293; unbelief is the occasion of resistance to it, 317; holiness on the part of Christians is the glory of it, 347; false professors defame it, 347.

Gregory quoted, 153.

H

HARMONY, is indispensable for the prosperity of the Church, 46; is the best bulwark for repelling impious doctrines, 50; the great desirableness of it, 51; God has reconciled us to himself with a view to the promotion of it, 216.

Head of the Church, the comprehensiveness of the expression, 152; Christ is the, 152; the Pope has no title to be regarded as the, 152, 153; the Church is entirely dependent on Christ, as the, 198.

Hebrew, the antiquity of the name, 91.

Hierapolis, a city of Phrygia, was destroyed by an earthquake, x, 132.

Holiness, is rarely found in the courts of sovereigns, 129; is nothing more than commenced in the present life, 159; that of Popery, consists in trifling observances, 201; monkhood, in the Papacy, constitutes the chief part of, 203; the Gospel tends to promote, 245; there is need of internal, no less than external, 271;

of Christ, 40; is common to all believers, 40; there is nothing right in man till he has been renewed by, 71; why called an *earnest*, 120; is the seal of adoption, 147; we are renewed by him in the image of God, 159; we are made heavenly by the renewing of, 208; his illuminating influence transforms the whole man, 211; obedience to God is the fruit of his operations, 243; how he may be *quenched*, 298; illuminates us chiefly by doctrine, 299; is a seal and earnest of eternal life, 344; his influence necessary in connection with doctrine, 346.

Homer's Odyssey quoted, 200, *n*. 1.

Hope, the goodness of God in the past ought to encourage, 25; that of the Christian will not put to shame, 41; of eternal life, will not be inactive, 138; the term employed to denote the object of hope, 139; of believers, is founded on Christ's resurrection, 247; leads to patience, 305.

Horace quoted, 178, *n*. 1; 226, *n*. 1; 262, *n*. 2; 332, *n*. 1.

Horne's Introduction quoted, 276, *n*. 1.

Howe quoted, xii, 31, *n*. 2; 212, *n*. 3; 269, *n*. 2; 287, *n*. 1; 288, *n*. 1.

Hug quoted, x.

Humility, a definition of true, 53; is a rare virtue, 53; Christ furnishes an extraordinary pattern of, 54, 59; the source of, 64; its fruits, 69; the worship of saints practised by Papists under pretext of, 194; the exercise of it in relation to God, 203; its limit towards men, 203; leads to kindness and gentleness, 213.

Husbands, their duties enjoined, 219.

Hymn, import of the term, 217.

I

IDLENESS, is fraught with danger to the Christian, 289; must be carefully guarded against, 298; censured by Paul, 352; is accursed, 355.

Idolatry, to seek God, apart from Christ, involves, 150; that of Papists, practised under the pretext of humility, 194; that of worshipping angels, traced to the writings Ignorance, of Christ, leads to a vain confidence, 93; in weak brethren, how it should be dealt with, 104; of God's providence, is the cause of all impatience, 118: that of Papists, 146; is the source of all errors, 176; of Christ, the foundation of Popery, 177; leads to arrogance, 299.

Illustrated commentary quoted, xiii, 36, *n*. 1; 147, *n*. 5.

Impatience, ignorance of God's providence is the source of, 118; the means by which it is to be guarded against, 239; prayer an antidote to, 297.

Imposture, three kinds of, mentioned by Paul, 323.

Indulgences, the corrupt system of, 165.

Ingratitude condemned, 179.

Invocation of God, the unspeakable advantage of, 120.

J

JEROME quoted, 23, 196.

Jews, The, the Gentiles are under the Gospel placed on an entire equality with them, 212; persecuted Christ and his Apostles, 259; incurred, in consequence of this, the wrath of God, 260; were not, however, finally cast off, 261.

Josephus quoted, 92.

Joy, of the world, is evanescent, 116; that of Christians, is permanent, 117; the Gospel ought to be received with, 243; was largely experienced by Paul in the midst of deep affliction, 268.

K

KINGDOM, of God, why the Gospel is called the, 229; Antichrist represents not one individual, but a, 327, 333.

Kiss, of charity, customary among the early Christians, 305.

Knowledge, of Christ, transcendently desirable, 94; of the will of God, to be sought in his word, 142; of God, we must endeavour to increase in, 144.

Koppe quoted, x.

Thessalonica by engaging in manual, 253; recommended by Paul on two accounts, 278; those should not eat who refuse to undergo, 353; there are various kinds of useful, 355.

Lactantius, his fanciful speculations as to the time of Christ's second coming, 323.

Laodicea, was destroyed by an earthquake, x, 132; there was a spurious epistle from, 230, 231.

Lardner, Dr., quoted, x.

Law, a twofold righteousness of the, 92; the ceremonial, was abolished by the coming of Christ, 188; of Moses, why called a *handwriting*, 189; our strength is not to be measured by the precepts of the Divine, 271, 303.

Leo, bishop of Rome, quoted, 167.

Libertines, the, despised the ministry of the word, 299.

Life, the *book* of, import of the expression, 114; newness of, the principal part of our salvation, 159; the rule, according to which it should be regulated, 352.

Livy quoted, 35, *n.* 5; 74, *n.* 3.

Love, to the brethren, the gift of God, 137; should extend to mankind universally, 138; brotherly, the hope of salvation tends to encourage, 139; *in the Spirit*, import of the expression, 141; is the bond of perfection, 214; we are not justified by it, 215; God is worthy of supreme, 238; in connection with faith, comprehends the entire sum of true piety, 268; its commencement and increase are from God, 271; forms part of the Christian's armour, 289; the Thessalonians highly commended for their, 311.

Lowth, on Isaiah, quoted, 144, *n.* 1.

Lucretius quoted, 103, *n.* 2.

Luke, the physician, commended by Paul, 230.

Lying, the vice of, condemned, 210.

M

MAHOMET, the injury done by him to the Church of Christ, 327.

Man, has need of a Peace-maker with God, 156; the *old*, what is meant to, 269; his strength is not to be measured by the precepts of the Divine law, 271, 303; the division of the constituent parts of, 304; is prone to forget the concerns of his salvation, 332.

Manton, Dr., his Sermons on 2 Thessalonians quoted, 328, *n.* 1; 337, *n.* 5.

Marcionites, the, denied the reality of Christ's human nature, 58.

Martyrs, The, the consolations by which they were sustained, 29; their blood is the seed of the Church, 30; their blood, along with that of Christ, conceived by Papists to be the treasure of the Church, 165.

Mason, Dr., of New York, quoted, vii.

Masters, their duties enjoined, 221, 222.

Merit, the doctrine of grace utterly excludes the idea of, 49; the contrivance of the Sophists as to that of Christ, 59, 60; the contrivance of the Sophists as to *subsequent grace*, as the reward of, 67; the righteousness of faith leaves no room for, 97; Scripture perverted by the Sophists to support their doctrine of, 139.

"Merits of CALVIN" quoted, vi.

Metonymy, a figure of speech, 139.

Ministers of the Gospel, must not seek their own interests, 77; are engaged in an incessant warfare, 80; faithful, are worthy of high esteem, 84; Satan endeavours to render them contemptible, 163; must make it their aim to please God, 250; should exercise a disinterested affection, 252; must be careful not to put any hinderance in the way of the Gospel, 254; will, if faithful, be partakers of Christ's triumph, 263; the interest they should feel in the welfare of the Church, 268; should endeavour to allure by kindness, 273; faithful, should be held in no ordinary esteem, 291, 292.

Moderation of spirit recommended, 117; prayer an important means of promoting, 296.

Monkhood, the principal holiness of Popery consists in, 203; its appalling abominations, 203; the time when it first came into use in

to a state of perfection, 104; their idleness, 356.
Moral conjecture, a contrivance of the schoolmen, 174.
Mortification, a twofold, 99, 208.
Mosheim's Ecclesiastical History quoted, 194, *n.* 2.
Mystery of iniquity, import of the expression, 334.

N

"NARRATIVE of a Mission to the Jews" quoted, x.
Nero, his palace was termed the *palatium*, 35; some members of his household were converts to Christianity, 129; Seneca was his preceptor, 130, *n.* 1; supposed by some of the ancients to be Antichrist, 327.

O

OATH, solemn forms of, made use of by Paul, 30, 306.
Obedience to God, a merely pretended, 202; the doctrine of the gospel leads to, 245.
Ode, import of the term, 217.
Onesimus, commended by Paul, 227.
Opinion, faith differs from mere, 160, 174.
Origen, his strange notions refuted, 284.
Orosius, Paulus, an ancient historian, quoted, 132.
Ovid quoted, 313.

P

PALEY's *Horæ Paulinæ* quoted, ix, xiii, 227, *n.* 1.
Papists, their doctrine of purgatory is altogether groundless, 63; their doctrine tends to shake assurance of faith, 68; their extravagant estimate of man's excellence, 69; their sacrifice of the Mass is utter sacrilege, 75; deny the right of private judgment, 88; mix up works with faith, 97; picture to themselves an imaginary Christ, 134; rob Christ of a great part of his glory, 146; their doctrine as to satisfactions is blasphemy, 149; less, 161, 162; their system of indulgences, 165; look upon the saints as redeemers, 166; despise the simplicity of the gospel, 176; do, in effect, charge Christ with imperfection, 182; their pretext for the worship of saints, 194; their worship of angels traced to the writings of Plato, 195; their specious pretexts, 203; the reading of the Scriptures is interdicted among them, 216; would have us pray to departed saints, 223; their baseness in prohibiting the Scriptures from being read, 306; their traditions are destitute of authority, 345.
Parents, their duty to their children enjoined, 220.
Pastors, the term synonymous with that of Bishops, 23; must exercise both authority and affection, 51; in what sense they are *priests*, 74; must not seek their own interests, 77; are engaged in an incessant warfare, 80; should be concerned for the welfare of their flock, 81; faithful, are worthy of high esteem, 84; must be constantly on the watch, 88; Satan endeavours to render them contemptible, 163; are *servants* of the Church, not *lords* over it, 167; the care which they ought to feel for their flock, even when at a distance from them, 229; must make it their aim to please God, 250; must avoid covetousness, 251; should manifest a disinterested affection for the welfare of the Church, 252; should be careful not to put any hinderance in the way of the gospel, 254; must bring forward nothing but the pure word of God, 257; will, if faithful, be sharers in Christ's triumph, 263; should, even in affliction, rejoice in the prosperity of the Church, 268; the titles of distinction with which Paul honours them, 292; faithful, should be not merely respected but loved, 293.
Patience, is the gift of God, 48; differs widely from Stoical apathy, 82; the contemplation of Divine Providence tends to promote it, 118; is necessary for believers, 207;

be exercised towards all, 294; degrees of it, 296; is the fruit and evidence of faith, 312.

Paul, CALVIN is thought to have resembled him, vii; the fruit of his *bonds*, 34, 36; why he desired to live, 43; rejoiced, even in affliction, in the prosperity of the Church, 51; needed to be tried with temptations, 83; gloried in Christ, 89; his illustrious descent, 91; was prepared to renounce everything for Christ, 94; needed, no less than others, to make progress in the divine life, 101; sets himself forth as an example, 105; gives evidence, by his tears, of his concern for the welfare of the Church, 106, 107; was unmarried, 113, 114; his joy amidst occasions of sorrow, 116; was joyful even under persecution, 165; in what respect he suffered *for* the Church, 166; earnestly desired the prayers of others in his behalf, 223; his singular zeal and prudence, 226, 227; his Epistles contain doctrine that is in force in all ages, 230; his admirable steadfastness, 249; his amazing zeal, 253; his irreproachable conduct, 254; his unreserved devotedness, 255; made regard for himself a secondary consideration, 268; his assiduity in prayer, 269; his exemplary humanity and modesty, 273; his prediction as to the rise of Antichrist, 328; eagerly desires the prayers of believers, 347; laboured among the Thessalonians gratuitously, 354.

Peace of God, its transcendent value, 120; God is the Author of, 122; of God restrains carnal affections, 215.

Pierce quoted, 87, *n.* 1; 95, *n.* 1; 121, *n.* 2.

Pelagians, their extravagant estimate of man's excellence, 69; conceived of a sinless perfection attainable in this life, 160.

Penn, Granville, quoted, 105, *n.* 2; 193, *n.* 3.

Perfection, the absurd pretensions of the monks to, 104; the Pelagians conceived it to be attainable in this life, 160; is to be found in Christ alone, 182.

were endured to a large extent by the early Christians from the Jews, 259, 260.

Perseverance, is a rare virtue, 25; Christians have an assured hope of final, 44; the necessity of it, 160; is the gift of God, 346.

Persians, The, the monarchy of Babylon was overthrown by, 332; were conquered by the Macedonians, 332.

Peter, there is no evidence of his having been Bishop of Rome, 78; nor is there evidence that he ever was at Rome, 229.

Pharisees, etymology of the term, 91.

Philippi, was the first place in Europe in which the gospel was preached, vii, ix; was so named from Philip, king of Macedon, viii, ix; noted for a signal victory, ix, 20, *n.* 1.

Philippian Christians, their zeal in supporting the cause of the gospel, 28; their flourishing condition, 123; their liberality in contributing to Paul's support, 126, 127.

Philosophy, in what sense the term is employed by Paul, 133, 180.

Piety, faith and love are the sum of true, 268.

Plato quoted, 176, *n.* 3; 195; the worship of angels traced to his writings, 195.

Plautus quoted, 95, *n.* 1; 355.

Pliny quoted, 20, *n.* 2.

Plutarch quoted. 200.

Poole's Annotations quoted, xii.

Poor, The, the duty of contributing to their relief, 358; are not unfrequently ungrateful for the bounty conferred upon them, 359.

Pope, The, is not the head of the Church, 152, 153; his kingdom is a confused mass, 199; his tyrannical enactments, 200; his arrogant pretensions, 329; claims to be the vicar of Christ, 330; in what sense he sits in the *temple of God*, 330, 331.

Popery is frequently animadverted upon in CALVIN'S Commentaries, xvii; is a grievous corruption of Christianity, 92; is utterly unscriptural, 104; the kind of theology of which it consists, 143; is founded on ignorance of Christ, 146, 177; the tyranny of its enactments, 200; its holiness consists in trifling ob-

Praetorium, import of the term, 35, 36.
Prayer, a powerful antidote to anxiety, 119; must be accompanied with thanksgiving, 119, 120; should be engaged in with assiduity and alacrity, 222; mutual, the duty and advantage of, 223; not to be offered for the dead, 223; there must be perseverance in it, 224; Paul's assiduity in, 269.
Pride, its extensive prevalence, 53; the source from which it springs, 65; the doctrine of grace tends to bring it down, 65; arises from ignorance of Christ, 93.
Prophesyings, Paul's use of the term, 299; danger of despising, 299, 300.
Prosperity, is often an occasion of emboldening the wicked in sin, 313.
Providence, ignorance of, leads to impatience, 118; duty of reposing in it with confidence, 296.
Psalm, import of the term, 217.
Purgatory, the doctrine of, altogether groundless, 63.

Q

QUIETNESS, Paul's use of the term 357, 358.
Quinctilian quoted, 35, *n.* 4; 38, *n.* 4.

R

RACE, the Christian life compared to a, 102.
Redemption, two things in which it mainly consists, 159.
Resurrection of Christ, the power of, 98; the hope of our resurrection is founded on it, 247; secures for his people a blessed resurrection, 280;
Resurrection, the doctrine of it is opposed to carnal perception, 111; the final, the hope of it inspires patience, 280; the certainty of it, 280; made known in the discourses of Christ himself, 282; some of the Thessalonians had but obscure views of it, 282; the prospect of it is consolatory to Christians, 284; some of the Thessalonians imagined that the time of it was near at hand, 323, 324.
Revenge, a spirit of, strictly prohibited, 295; patience an antidote to, 296.

quoted, 105, *n.* 1; 147, *n.* 1.
Riches, worldly, Christians must be prepared to part with, for Christ, 95; the term employed to set forth the glory of the gospel, 170; of the *assurance of understanding*—import of the expression, 174.
Righteousness, the fruits of, 33; of the law, a twofold, 92; of faith, the nature of, 97; of Christ, is received by faith, 98.

S

SACRAMENTS, the, are signs and tokens of Christ's presence, 193; the Pope alters them, or sets them aside, at his pleasure, 330.
Sacrifice, the nature of an evangelical, 74; that of the Mass, is utter sacrilege, 75; the exercise of beneficence is a, 128.
Sacrilege, the Popish sacrifice of the Mass is, 75.
Saints, the, their salvation will not be fully completed until the resurrection, 27; their afflictions are not the *cause* of their salvation, 48; the designation an honourable one, 187; are not redeemers, 166; the pretext of Papists for the worship of, 194; departed, no warrant to pray to, 223.
Salvation, is wholly of grace, 69; the hope of it is represented by the Sophists as depending on works, 139; surpasses the comprehension of our understanding, 139; all parts of it are contained in Christ, 148; its commencement and completion are from God, 242; God wills our, 289; in all its parts is the fruit of the pure grace of God, 320; mankind are prone to forgetfulness in matters affecting their, 332.
Sanctification, we are called by God with a view to it, 273; the large import of the term, 273; includes the renovation of the whole man, 303; God is the sole Author of it, 304.
Satan, puts many stumblingblocks in our way, 32; his subtle artifices, 34; is the enemy of all Christians, 80; is most desirous to undermine

held captive by him, 147; labours to bring the truth of the gospel into doubt, 161; endeavours to bring the servants of God into contempt, 163; successful resistance of his temptations is a test of faith, 258; is constantly endeavouring to hinder the edification of the Church, 263; the wicked fight under his banner, 263; it is his proper office to tempt, 266; is always on the alert against us, 289; endeavours to stir up quarrels between pastors and people, 293; his assaults are severe, 321; his subtlety, 323; all his machinations will be overthrown by means of the truth, 335; Antichrist derives all his influence from his impostures, 336; the deceptions practised by him, 337; his power is bridled, 338; cannot prevent the salvation of God's chosen people, 342.

Satisfactions, Popish, involve blasphemy, 149; ascribe merit to the blood of the martyrs, 165.

Scaliger, Joseph, quoted, v.

Schoolmen, the, their doctrine of human merit, 49; their system of free-will cannot be reconciled with the doctrine of grace, 65; moral conjecture a contrivance of, 174.

Scott, Rev. Thomas, quoted, xi.

Scriptures, the Holy, it is cruel to interdict the reading of them, 216; they are more refractory than devils themselves who interdict the reading of them, 306.

Seneca, supposed by some to have been among the *saints of Cesar's household*, 129; there is no evidence of his having been a convert to Christianity, 130; was the preceptor of Nero, 130, *n.* 1.

Servants, their duties enjoined, 220; special consolation for, 221.

Sleep, the death of believers is often compared to, 280.

Smith, Dr Pye, quoted, vi.

Smith's Dictionary of Greek Biography quoted, 132, *n.* 1.

Sobriety, spiritual, the nature of, 288.

Socrates (Tripartite History) quoted, 357.

Songs, spiritual, import of the expression, 217, 218.

merit, 59, 60; maintained that men are justified by works, 95; made the hope of salvation depend on works, 139; their detestable profanity, 167; their doctrine as to the intercession of saints and angels, 196; their doctrine as to subsequent merit, 320.

Soul, the, does not become unconscious at death, 44, 280; has two principal faculties, 304.

Spirit, the term employed to denote reason, 304; the term applied to prophesyings, 324; Holy, see Holy Spirit.

Steadfastness, the Colossian Christians commended for their, 177; of faith, represented under three metaphors, 178; Paul's admirable, 249.

Stoics, Christian patience differs widely from their apathy, 82; Christian resignation under bereavements differs greatly from their destitution of feeling, 280.

Storr quoted, 52, *n.* 2; 121, *n.* 1; 122, *n.* 1.

Suetonius quoted, 20, *n.* 2.

Suidas quoted, 96, *n.* 1.

T

TALKATIVENESS censured, 226.

Teissier, his abridgment of M. de Thou's history, quoted, v.

Temple of God, in what sense Antichrist reigns in the, 330, 331.

Temptation, successful resistance of, a test of faith, 258; we must always be on our guard against, 266.

Tertullian quoted, 30.

Textor, Benedict, CALVIN dedicated to him his Commentary on 2 Thessalonians, xvi; CALVIN's dedicatory epistle to, 308.

Textor, John, his "epistles," xvi.

Thanksgiving, should accompany prayer, 119; the happy effect arising from a spirit of, 120; the want of such a spirit exposes to serious loss, 179; should be offered up *through Christ*, 218; a twofold, is necessary, 223; should always be mingled with our desires, 297; should be rendered by us for the favours bestowed upon our brethren, 311.

Thessalonian Christians, Paul's *first*

the rise of Antichrist, xiv, xv; were most exemplary in their deportment, 239; Paul laboured among them free of charge, 253; Paul's ardent affection for them, 252, 262, 267; the doctrine of the resurrection seems to have been imperfectly understood by some of them, 282; Paul's *second* Epistle to them is supposed to have been written from Athens, 309; some of them imagined that the second coming of Christ was near at hand, 322.

Thessalonica, origin of the name, xii; was noted for idolatry, prior to the introduction of the gospel into it, xiii.

Theurgians, the, pretended to have received their doctrines through the ministry of angels, 194; were the followers of Ammonius Saccas, 194, n. 2.

Tholuck quoted, v, vi.

Thrones, the term employed to denote the heavenly palace of God's majesty, 150.

Time, the duty of redeeming, 225.

Timothy, Paul's high commendation of him, 76; his fidelity and modesty, 79; his extraordinary devotedness, 265.

Traditions, human, corrupt the simplicity of the gospel, 181; are a labyrinth, in which consciences are entangled, 200; are agreeable to corrupt nature, 202; three pretexts under which they allure, 202; of Papists, are utterly destitute of authority, 345.

Truth, the gospel is undoubted, 141; of God, is the bond of holy unity, 173; will overthrow all the machinations of Satan, 335.

Tychicus, highly commended by Paul, 226, 227.

Tyranny, the enactments of Popery involve, 200; the interdicting of the Scriptures is the exercise of a cruel, 216, 306; that of Antichrist is exercised upon souls, 328.

U

Unbelief, is the occasion of resistance to the gospel, 317; is always blind, 318.

Unbelievers, are in this life intermingled have regard to them, 225; two marks by which they are distinguished, 317; the punishment that awaits them, in the event of impenitence, 340.

Unity, Paul exhorts to a twofold, 46; the desirableness of it in the Church, 51; a most intimate, subsists between Christ and his members, 164; the truth of God is the bond of a holy, 173.

V

Vaughan, Robert, translated Calvin's Commentary on the Colossians, xvi; was the author of various works, xvi; his Dedicatory Epistle, xviii.

Virgil quoted, 20, *n.* 1; 27, *n.* 1; 60.

Vulgate, the, quoted, 105, *n.* 1; 121, *n.* 2; 147, *n.* 1; 238, *n.* 3; 329, *n.* 1; 342, 347.

W

Wahl's Key to the New Testament quoted, 114, *n.* 2.

Watchfulness, believers have need of constant, 266; two reasons why Christians should exercise unremitting, 288, 289.

Wetstein quoted, 121, *n.* 1.

Wicked, the, are sometimes undesignedly the means of promoting the gospel, 39; their agreement is accursed, 47; Christians are in this life intermingled with them, 70, 109; the difference between their situation and that of devils, 157; are spiritually dead, 187; why their punishment is often delayed, 260; fight under Satan's banner, 263; their presumptuous confidence, 287; become insolent in prosperity, 313; Christians have no reason to envy their temporary prosperity, 315; the appalling doom awaiting them, in the event of impenitence, 318.

Wiclif's version of the Scriptures quoted, 46, *n.* 1; 147, *n.* 1; 238, *n.* 3; 329, *n.* 1; 342, *n.* 1; 347, *n.* 2.

Will, a right inclination of it is from God, 65, 66; of God, is to be sought nowhere else than in his word, 142;

Wisdom, Christian, in what it consists, 32; the revealed will of God is the only true, 143; a definition of true, 171.

Word of God, The, the will of God is to be sought nowhere else than in, 142; Christians should endeavour to acquire an intimate acquaintance with it, 216; some fanatics in the times of CALVIN rejected the

World, the, was created by Christ, 111; is in a state of moral darkness, 147, 148; Christians should live above it, 205.

Wrath, the term employed to denote the judgment of God 261, 290.

X

Xenophon quoted, 200, n. 1.

ERRATA.

Page 29, line 18 from top, *for* there *read* this.
 „ 51, „ 13 „   „   *for* say *read* see.
 „ 56, „ 2 from foot, *for* ἰμφατικοτίρως *read* ἰμφατικωτίρως.
 „ 71, „ 4 „   „   *for* unbelievers *read* believers.
 „ 86, „ 3 from top, *for* we *read* to.
 „ 103, n. 1, . . . *for* ἰπικτινόμινος *read* ἰπικτινόμινος.
 „ 119, line 12 „   „ *for* 23 *read* 22.
 „ 138, „ 7 „   „ *for* us *read* you.
 „ 278, „ 3 „   „ *for* Colatis quietem *read* Maintain peace.

ON

IMPORTANT PRACTICAL SUBJECTS,

TOGETHER WITH A

DISSERTATION AND COMMENTARY

ON

THE EIGHTY-SEVENTH PSALM.

BY JOHN CALVIN.

TRANSLATED FROM THE ORIGINAL FRENCH
BY HENRY BEVERIDGE.

I.

ON SHUNNING EXTERNAL IDOLATRY.

II.

ON ENDURING PERSECUTION.

III.

ON ENJOYING CHURCH ORDINANCES.

IV.

ON SERVING GOD PURELY.

V.

DISSERTATION AND COMMENTARY ON PSALM LXXXVII.

TRANSLATOR'S PREFACE.

The following HOMILIES or SERMONS furnish valuable and authentic specimens of CALVIN'S PULPIT MINISTRATIONS. They cannot indeed be considered as exact transcripts of what he actually delivered, for it was not his practice to write in preparing for the pulpit; but the substance having been taken down by one or more of the hearers, he himself revised and re-arranged the whole previous to publication. We are thus assured that the SERMONS, in their present form, contain either what he said, or what he would have wished to say, on the subjects of which they treat.

The language is simple and unadorned, almost to rudeness, and illustrations of a very graphic but homely description are frequently introduced. No trains of reasoning occur, but each subject is plainly yet thoroughly discussed in the manner which seems best calculated to leave a permanent impression on a general and not very refined audience. Those who read the SERMONS expecting to find in them specimens of CALVIN'S commanding intellect, will be disappointed; but those who would like to see how, when the occasion required it, he could completely forget himself, throw aside all his metaphysics, adapt himself to the humblest capacities, and " become all things to all men so that he might win some," will be amply gratified.

The SERMONS having been spoken *in French*, have been translated from that language, as the *original;* but the *Latin* copy contained in the edition of CALVIN'S collated WORKS, printed at Amsterdam in 1667, in nine volumes folio, has also been consulted. The Latin translator, however, has

in Latin than it does in French; not by giving any additional matter, but by indulging in a kind of rhetorical amplification. In this way the characteristic features of the SERMONS have been effaced, and their spirit completely lost.

It may be interesting to the reader to be informed that there were two separate TRANSLATIONS of these SERMONS into English in the reign of Queen Elizabeth. The first of these was published, in 16mo, from the *Latin* version, the quaint title-page being as follows:—" Fovre Godlye Sermons agaynst the pollvtion of Idolatries; comforting men in persecutions, and teaching them what commodities thei shal find in Christes Church: Which were preached in French by the most famous clarke Jhone Caluyne, and translated, fyrst into Latin and afterward into English, by diuers godly learned men. Psal. 16. I wyl not take the names of the Idols in my mouth. Printed at London by Rouland Hall, dwelling in Golding lane at the sygne of the thre arrowes. 1561." It has an Epistle of R. Hall's to the Reader. The Editor has not discovered who these " diuers godly learned men" were. The second English translation was made by John Field from the *French* version; who in his Epistle states, that until he "had almost finished them," he was not aware of the publication of the previous performance. An exact *fac-simile* of the title-page and " Epistle Dedicatorie" of the latter version has been made, which immediately follows this brief Preface. The colophon of Field's translation is as follows:—" Imprinted at London, at the three Cranes, in the Vinetree, by Thomas Dawson, for Thomas Man. 1579."

H. B.

June 1851.

Foure
SERMONS OF
Maister Iohn Caluin,
Entreating of matters very
profitable for our time, as may
bee seene by the Pre-
face:

With a briefe exposition of the
LXXXVII. Psalme.

Translated out of the Frenche into
Englishe by *Iohn Fielde.*

❧ *Imprinted at London*
for Thomas Man, dwelling
in Pater Noster Rowe, at the
Signe of the Talbot.
1579.

To the right Hono-
rable and my verie good Lorde, Henry Earle of Huntington, Lord Hastings,

Hungerford, Botreaux, Mullens and Moyles, of *the most Honorable order of the Garter Knight, and Lorde* President of the Queenes Maiesties Councell establi-shed in the North partes, *Iohn Fielde* wisheth encrease of true faith and continuance in the zeale of his blessed religion for euer Amen.

IT may bee (right honourable & my very good Lord) that men will maruayle, whye I shoulde publishe these foure excellente Sermons of Maister Iohn Caluines, the Argumentes whereof bee not so fitte and agreeable (as they thinke) to these times: seeing GOD in mercy hath geuen vs peace, and set vs at libertie from that Romish yoke, suffering the beames of his glorious Gospel to spread far and wide, to the great comfort of many, and his owne euerlasting glory. These benefits, as they are acknowledged by me: so I beseech God to make vs all more thankfull then we haue beene, that the litle fruite they haue brought foorth amongest vs, the common ignorance that is yet vpon the face of the whole lande, the small preparation to the crosse and bending our backs too beare it with Iesus Christe our head, doe not prouoke him too geue vs ouer too followe our owne wayes, to haue no conscience nor care of any religion: as I feare me the worlde is too to ful of such, the more is the pitie. For who seeth not, that the common sort are so far from being in-structed, hauing plaide the Truantes in Gods Schole these twenty and odde yeeres, that they haue not yet taken out this one lesson, to bee of minde when God shall trie them, too separate them selues from the cursed fellowship of Antichriste. For they haue not yet learned too make any difference of religion, but bende them selues too serue all times: come there falshood or trueth, light or dark-nesse, religion or superstition, the Gospell or the Masse, Turcisme or Christianisme, al is one too them, so that they may liue at ease

lasting trueth, the seale of their adoption. Though Christe haue pronounced that whosoeuer denye him before men, hee wyll denie him before his father which is in heauen: though he say playnely that hee that will followe him must take vp his crosse and followe him, and that he that is ashamed too confesse him before men, he wil deny him before his heauenly father: yea although we bee commaunded too come out of Babylon, and it be plainely saide that the red Dragon will powre out his waters as a riuer to ouertake the woman with childe, and that the victorie of the lambe muste be by his own blood, & by the word of their testimonie, who loue not their liues vntoo the death: yet can not all this mooue them to seeke too be grounded and prepared, calling vpon God that they may stand resolute through his grace, to beare testimonie to his glorious name, who hath bestowed so many blessings vpon them. If they may haue Christe with ease, wealth, honour, with the peace of the worlde and fauour of men, if they may inioy him with their pleasures and proceeding on in sinne, they wil be content with Pharisees a litle to entertaine him, that they make a mock of him. But if in the entertaining of him, he shal neuer so litle touch their botch and pinch theyr pleasure: if hee shall come neare their purse and endanger theyr least commoditie, if he shal require mortification with obedience & sanctification, then either they wil come by night like Nicodemus, or else they wil pray him to be packing with the Gergesites, or too conclude they wil lay violent hands vpon him, and naile him faste to the crosse with the proude Scribes and Pharisees. As for the common sort they that yesterday receiued him as a king, with *osianna in excelsis*, they wil to morow cry out *Crucifige*, with the high Priests, that they may liue in securitie. These sermons therefore as for their worthinesse they haue been translated long agoe into other tongues, and (as I vnderstoode, when 1 had almost finished them) out of the Latine into ours also: so my labour being past, they being also by authoritie allowed: and I especially following maister Caluines owne french copie, somwhat differing from the other: I thought they coulde not but be very profitable, at the leaste too prepare vs against the time to come. For God hath geuen vs long peace, and our rest hauing bred rust, growen vp euen to the height of the contempt of his graces, must needes prouoke him to punish the wicked with wonted plagues & to correct vs with the fire of aduersitie, that we may be

Matt. 10. 33. 38.

Apoc. 18. 4. *Apoc.* 13. 3. 11.

Iohn. 3. 2. *Mat.* 8. 34. *Mat.* 26. 3. *Iohn.* 11. 47. *Mark.* 11. 10. *Mark.* 14. 64. 15. 12.

now they begin a litle to shew themselves, they loke big, & their hanging looks shew what malice lurketh in their cankred harts; But our God liueth and therefore wee will not feare; we know that all powers both in heauen and in earth are subject to him: and we nothing doubt though our sinnes haue strengthened the handes of his aduersaries, that they should be heauy vpon vs, yet our God will in our punishmentes geue them an euerlasting ouerthrow and an vnrecouerable confusion. Though there be many Newters which haue made a couenant with their owne heartes rather to be of all religions, and to serue al times, then to endure the least danger, yet there are an infinite number of true Christians, that by his grace to die for it, will neuer bow the Knee too Baall, will neuer pertake with the table of God and the table of deuilles, will neuer draw in that vnequall yoke togeather with such Infidelles. These shal neither the swoordes of Hazael, nor of Iehu, or of Elisha once touch, for they are marked of the Lorde. And if the woorde of God be sure as him selfe, and hee haue ioyned himselfe as head too vs his members, why shoulde we feare? If our head liue we shall liue, if he be ascended, we his members shalbe drawen vp vnto him. Our blood shalbe of strength too breake all their cheines. The shame, slaunder and reproche that they lay vpon vs, shalbe our greatest glory, and our innocency laide to theyr crueltie, shalbe strong enough to set the seale of true happinesse vpon vs for suffering for righteousnesse sake, and of wretched confusion vpon them, that so rage against such as haue done them no harme, and whom they ought too haue most esteemed of, as for whose sakes they haue & possesse al those temporall blessings that god in his mercy hath geuen them. We wil therefore in the name of our God, like wise Marriners, in this calme time prouide against stormes and tempestes. We are not ignorant what the order of nature setteth before vs: there is no sommer but bringeth a Winter, no day but hath a night: nor any professed trueth that bringeth not a tryall. Health is alwayes ioyned with sicknesse, and the bodily life is subiect to death: so the peace of the Church is seldome without aduersitie: & GOD forbid that we shoulde not prepare, euen to the powring foorth of our blood, to striue for the trueth of our God, yea too death it selfe, if God so appointe. If they be (as Chrysostom saith) not onely betraiers of the trueth that speake lyes in steede of the trueth, but also that doo not freely vtter the trueth: God forbid

Marginal notes: 1 Kinges. 19. / Matt. 5. 10.

for the glory of his name. And one thing I doe assure the Papistes of and all of Caynes progenie, that the more they kil and persecute the children of God, the more wil Christ & his Gospell floorish. Our blood willbe a fructifiyng & multipliyng seede, they haue seene it and knowen it true by long experience, & herein they be but the instruments of hastening vs too our happinesse. Not when they will, for we are not subiect vnto them. The Deuil him selfe their Father and all hellishe furyes are subiect too our God, and cannot touch one heare of our heades, tyll he haue geuen them leaue and that for our good and tryall. Let the sonnes therefore of seruitude in the pride of bondage ieare neuer so muche against the sonnes of libertie, yet a day shall come when their righteous- *Gal.* 4. nesse shall breake foorth and appeare more glorious then the Sunne and all the Starres: when as too them (what pleasures soeuer they shall vsurpe in this world) shall belong nothing but perpetuall shame, ioyned with an euill name too all posterities, and an euerlasting death in the ende worlde without ende. Wherefore (good my Lorde) I am bolde too offer vp these sermons vnto your honour, rudely translated by me, beseeching your honour in the behalfe of God's Church to accept of them. I will say nothing in their commendation, they are able and of sufficient age to speake for themselues. Onely I thought good to shew this humble duetie towards you, by this publique testimonie. And I beseech God the father of all mercies to strengthen you in that happy course of the Gospel, wherinto of his singuler goodnesse hee hath drawen you: that you may be as a bright starre in his Churche comfortably shining forth in constancie and maintenance of the same trueth, too the stirring vp of many: that not onely it may be geuen you (as the Apostle saieth) to beleeue in him, but also too suffer for him. For this is true honour too suffer for righteousnesse: The cause is it that must comfort all that are afflicted, and herein we haue wonderfully to reioyce, when it is for his name sake, herevnto also, wee must (as I haue said) prepare our selues. For it is impossible that Christe and his Crosse shoulde bee sundred. The worlde muste loue her owne, and in the worlde wee shalbe troubled. Christ in his members must be crucified til he come againe in his second & glorious coming to subdue all his enimies. The remainder of his afflictions must bee borne in our bodies, not because hee hath not suffered fully, but because wee muste bee made conformable vnto

all those Libertines, who count themselues the Familie of Loue, and the Atheistes of the worlde, who ouerthrowe all confession and profession of the Faith of Christe, beeing indifferent for all religions: that tread vnder their feete the blood of all Martyrs, and account them but for fooles. Nowe the God of all patience and comfort, blesse your honor togeather with my good Lady, that you may feele and possesse that comfort that none can take from you, Amen.

Your Honours most bounden
and Faythfull euer to commaunde,
IOHN FIELDE.

THE AUTHOR'S EPISTLE.

JOHN CALVIN

TO ALL CHRISTIANS WHO DESIRE THE ADVANCEMENT OF THE KINGDOM OF OUR LORD JESUS CHRIST.

WHEN you hear why and for what end I have been desirous to publish these SERMONS, and when you are made acquainted with the argument which they contain, you will know better how to profit by them and apply them to the use which I intended.

Although I have already written two Tracts of considerable length to demonstrate that it is not lawful for a Christian acquainted with the pure doctrine of the gospel, to make a show in any way whatever while he lives under the Papacy, of consenting and adhering to the Abuses, Superstitions, and Idolatries which there prevail, I am every day applied to by persons who ask my advice anew, as if I had never spoken on the subject. I understand, moreover, that there are others who cease not to urge their replies and subterfuges in opposition to what I have written. Hence, in order to cut short both those who continue inquiring about what ought to be sufficiently known and notorious to them, and those who think they can hide themselves as in a mantle from the judgment of God, I have deemed it expedient to revise and arrange a SERMON which I had preached on this subject, and of which the substance had been taken down. This first Sermon contains a Remonstrance, pointing out how cowardly it is for those to whom God has given a knowledge of his true gospel, to pollute themselves with the abominations of the Papists, which are quite contrary to the Christian Religion, seeing that in so doing they, as much as in them lies, deny the Lord that bought them.

But as it is impossible for a Christian man living under the tyranny of Antichrist to make a direct and pure confession of his Faith, without immediately incurring the danger of Persecution, I have added a SECOND SERMON, to exhort all believers to prize the honour and service of God more than their own life, and to strengthen them against all temptations. And, in fact, when many count it strange that they are not permitted to disguise themselves and play the counterfeit, it is not because they are not convinced that the duty of Christians is to worship Him alone in integrity and simplicity, withdrawing themselves from all pollutions and idolatries, but it is because they see that they cannot act the part of Christians without inflaming the rage of the malignant. Now men were not disposed to despise this frail and fading life, in order to seek the kingdom of God, and to follow Jesus Christ to the cross, in order to attain to the glory of his resurrection, have added the second Sermon, urging those who in the present day are far too feeble in the exercise of courage and constancy.

The object of the THIRD SERMON is to show how valuable a privilege it is, not only to be permitted to serve God Purely, and make Public Profession of His Faith, but also to belong to a regular and well-managed Church, where the Word of God is Preached and the Sacraments are duly administered; seeing that these are the means by which the children of God may be confirmed in the faith, and are incited to live and die in the obedience of His law. It seemed to me that the discussion of this subject was very necessary at present, because there are many imaginary Christians who make a mock of those who take the trouble of coming into a strange and distant land, in order to enjoy this privilege.

But as several persons are kept back and hindered from pursuing this good, which God estimates so highly, from the too great regard they have to their ease and convenience, or rather from the fear and doubt they have that they may be thrown destitute; while other persons are so delicate, that if everything does not turn out to a wish they complain or murmur, or even give themselves up to licentiousness, I have added a FOURTH SERMON, to remind Christians that they ought to be fortified against all offences, and patiently to bear all the troubles which may befall them, considering that God is so gracious as to entertain them in his house. Hence, the sum of the Fourth Sermon is, that when we have the privilege of Hearing the Word of God purely Preached, of calling upon His Name, and using the Sacraments, we have therein a sufficient compensation for all the cares, troubles, and annoyances which Satan may be able to stir up against us.

I have added A BRIEF EXPOSITION OF THE EIGHTY-SEVENTH PSALM, which seems to me appropriate, inasmuch as it treats of The Restoration of the Church. In the present day many give way to despondency on beholding her desolate, as if she were soon to perish altogether. Such persons, and believers in general, will here find ground of consolation in the hope which God gives that He will again build up His Church after she has been afflicted for a season, and make her prosperous and flourishing after she has appeared to the world to be very miserable.

I pray our gracious Lord that my labour may not be in vain, but that you may be edified by it according to my earnest desire.

GENEVA, 20th September 1552.

FOUR HOMILIES OR SERMONS,

TREATING OF MATTERS VERY USEFUL FOR OUR TIME.

First Homily or Sermon,

In which all Christians are exhorted to flee external Idolatry.

"I will not communicate in their sacrifices of blood, neither will their name pass my lips."—PSALM xvi. 3.

THE doctrine which we have here to discuss is very clear and easy, provided the greater part of those who call themselves believers do not search about for subtleties to conceal their error. The subject, summarily, is, that after having known the living God as our Father, and Jesus Christ as our Redeemer, we ought to dedicate body and soul to him, who, of his infinite goodness, has adopted us for his children, and be determined to do homage to the good Saviour for that which cost him so dear: Our duty therefore is, not only to renounce all Infidelity, but also to keep aloof from all superstitions, which are opposed as well to the service of God as to the honour of his Son, and which cannot accord with the pure doctrine of the Gospel and the pure Confession of Faith.

I have said that this doctrine is in itself very easy, and nothing would remain but to carry it fully into practice, were it not that many persons have recourse to a set of petty evasions, in order not to be found guilty in doing that which the mouth of God so often and so strongly condemns. This circumstance compels us to dwell on the point at greater length, in order that each may know what his duty is, and no one deceive himself by thinking he can escape by

God we have our Churches purged from the corruptions and Idolatries of the Papacy, it is proper, before proceeding farther, to shew that those who so think are very much mistaken.

For, in the first place, when we are shewn how offensive it must be to pollute ourselves with Idolaters, by making a show of consenting or adhering to their impieties, we are admonished to lament over our past faults, and ask pardon of God with all humility; thereupon recognising the inestimable blessing which he has bestowed upon us in lifting us out of the mire into which we had fallen. For we cannot too highly extol such a mercy. And as we know not what may happen to us, nor for what it is that God may reserve us, it is good to be forearmed, so that at whatever place we come, or by whatever temptations we may be assailed, we may not decline from the pure Word of God. There may be several now present who have to travel into Popish countries; these, being actually on the field of combat, behove to be armed.

Again, if God at present gives us the privilege of serving him purely, we know not for how long a time it is. Let us then regard the time in which we are at rest, not as if it were to last always, but as a truce, during which God gives us leisure to fortify ourselves, in order that when called to make a Confession of our Faith, we may not prove mere novices from not having prepared ourselves in due time. Moreover, we have also to think of our poor brethren who are under the tyranny of Antichrist, in order to feel pity for them, and pray God to furnish them with the constancy which he requires in his Word. Then, too, we have to urge them not to slumber nor flatter themselves, but rather, as they have learned their duty, to strive to glorify God. When we are instructed, it is not for ourselves only, but in order that each may, according to the measure of his faith, impart to his neighbours whatever he has learned in the school of Christ.

We see, then, that it is useful, not to say necessary, as

text which we have to expound suggests it.

In the present passage, David makes a great protestation, and, as it were, a solemn vow, never to participate in the sacrifices of Idolaters, nay, to have idols in such hatred and detestation that he will abstain from naming them, as if he could not name them without polluting his lips. This is not the particular act of an individual, but the example of David is a general rule for all the children of God. That we may perceive this more clearly, and also be more impressed by it, let us attend to the reason which he adds, and which is as it were the foundation of the aversion which he feels to mingle among idolaters. " The Lord," he says, " is my inheritance." Is not this common to all believers? at least there are none who do not glory in it. And, in fact, it is very certain that God having once given himself to us in the person of his Son, daily invites us to possess him, though few persons feel in this respect as they ought. For it is impossible for us to possess God on any other condition than that of being wholly his. With good cause then does David reason thus: Since God is my inheritance, I will abstain from all pollutions of Idols which would turn me aside and estrange me from him. This, too, is the reason why Isaiah, (Isaiah lvii. 9,) after reproaching the Jews with abandoning themselves to false gods of their own device, adds, " Let them, let them, I say, be thy portion," intimating by these words that God gives up all alliance with Idolaters, and deprives and disinherits them of the inestimable blessing which he had bestowed in giving himself to them.

Some one will reply, that Isaiah is there speaking of those who trust in Idols, and deceive themselves by unbelief. This I admit; but, on the other hand, I answer, that if those who at all ascribe the honour of God to Idols, are completely cut off from him, those also go astray, at least in part, who from fear and weakness give a feigned consent to Superstition. For we cannot in any way whatever, in heart or conduct, willingly or seemingly, approach Idols without departing equally far from God. Wherefore let us hold it as a fixed

with Idols, since between him and them there is such a repugnance, that he will have all his people to wage mortal war against them. And David specially intimates in this passage that he will not partake of their offerings, nor allow their names to pass his lips. He might have said, I will not defile myself with the foolish devotions of the heathen, I will not put my confidence in such delusions, I will not quit the truth of God to follow such lies. He does not speak thus, but says that he will not mix himself up with their ceremonies. His declaration therefore is, that in regard to the service of God, he will keep himself pure in body as in soul.

In the first place, then, we are here taught that it is Idolatry to shew by outward signs that we agree with the Superstitions by which the service of God is corrupted and perverted. Those who halt between two opinions allege, that since God wills to be worshipped in spirit, no worship is given to idols where no trust is put in them. The answer is easy. Though God wills to be worshipped in spirit, he by no means gives up all other kind of homage as if it did not belong to him. For he speaks in many other passages of bending the knees before him, and lifting the hands to heaven. (Psalm xxii. 30; Isaiah xlv. 23; Rom. xiv. 11; Phil. ii. 10; Psalm cxliii. 6; 1 Tim. ii. 8.) What then? the principal service which he demands is indeed spiritual, but a declaration in which believers profess that it is him alone they serve and honour is subjoined, and must always be taken in connection.

In regard to the expression on which they insist, a single passage will refute them. It is written in the second chapter of Daniel, that Shadrach, Meshach, and Abednego, in refusing to make a show of consenting to the Superstition which Nebuchadnezzar had set up, declare that they will not worship his gods. Had our good Sophists been there, they would have ridiculed the silliness of these three servants of God: for they would have said, Good folks, you do not worship when you do not give faith; there is no Idolatry when there is no devotion. But those holy persons followed better counsel. And, in fact, the answer they made was not

take from these words a rule and definition, holding it to be a real species of Idolatry to do any external act repugnant to the service of God, though it be only in pretence. It is in vain for these hypocrites to quibble and say, There is no Idolatry, for we have no trust. They stand condemned by the sentence which in the above passage the Great Judge pronounced.

But these people sometimes take lower ground, and merely try to palliate the fault which they cannot wholly excuse. They will indeed confess that the thing is wrong, but they would have it to be regarded as " a venial sin."

Were we to grant them the name for which they plead, they would gain little by it. Grant that such feigned worship of Idols is not to be called Idolatry, it will not cease to be disloyalty towards God—an act repugnant to the Confession of Faith, a pollution, and a sacrilege! Tell me, when the honour of God is violated—when we break the promise which we gave him—when we are so cowardly as indirectly to renounce our Christianity—when we act a double part, and pollute ourselves with the things which God has cursed—are we then to wipe our mouths and say we have committed a small fault? Away with such subterfuges! seeing they only serve to embolden us in wickedness without lessening our guilt.

There are other persons who put on a bolder front. For not only do they endeavour, by disguising the Word, to make it be believed that there is nothing so very great and enormous in the sin, but they maintain quite broadly that it is no sin at all. It is enough, they say, that God be served with the heart. All very true—provided the heart is not double. When there is real integrity the body will not belie it. What is it, I ask, that carries their feet to the church when they go to hear Mass? The limbs will never move of their own accord! They stand convicted, then, of some kind of affection for the service of Idols, inasmuch as they desire to please the enemies of the truth, and value their life more than the honour of God. But they carry

plausibility on their side. I must do it, however, seeing they shew so much self-complacency, and are as if they were intoxicated.

They think it enough, it seems, if God be worshipped in spirit! To whom, then, will the body belong? St. Paul exhorts us, (1 Cor. vi. 20,) to bear the Lord about in both, because both are his. God created the body, and will it be lawful to do homage with it to the Devil? It would be better to declare themselves out-and-out Manicheans, and deny that God is the Creator of the whole man. Had they the least relish for the gospel they would never run out into such extravagance; for they shew that they know not what it is to have been redeemed by the blood of the Son of God. On what ground do we hope for the resurrection of the body, but just because Christ has paid the ransom both of body and soul? St. Paul reminds us (1 Cor. vii. 23) that we ought not to be the slaves of man, since we have been purchased so dearly. Does not he, then, who addicts himself to the service of Idols, trample under foot the blood of Jesus Christ, the price of that immortal glory which we expect in our bodies? Is it reasonable that our bodies be defiled and profaned before Idols while a crown of life is promised them in heaven? Do we take the way of entering the heavenly kingdom of God when we roll ourselves in the mire of Satan?

Moreover, it has not been said without cause that our bodies are "temples of the Holy Spirit." Those, then, who know not that they ought to preserve them in all purity, plainly shew that they have no understanding of the gospel —shew also that they know nothing of Jesus Christ and of his grace. For when it is said, (Eph. v. 30,) that "we are bone of his bone and flesh of his flesh," it is to shew that we are joined to him body and soul. Hence it follows, that we cannot pollute our bodies by any kind of Superstition without excluding ourselves from that sacred union by which we are made members of the Son of God.

Let those subtle Doctors tell me if they received Baptism only in their souls? Did not God order that this symbol

contrary abominations? Is the Supper received only by the soul and not also by the hands and the mouth? Does God place the insignia of his Son in our bodies, and shall we defile it with vile impurities? It is not lawful to stamp two coins on one piece of gold, nor to attach two contrary seals to one public document, and shall man presume to falsify the Baptism and Holy Supper of Jesus Christ, and say there is no harm in it? Such persons would only have their desert were their servants to make them believe that they have their interest at heart while sleeping or gadding about, and not putting a finger to any kind of labour. If they allege that the cases are not the same, inasmuch as we cannot dispense with the services of those who are under us, I answer, that since God, without standing in need of our services, is pleased to employ us to his honour, it is a great shame that we should think ourselves quit in regard to him while doing the reverse; and a still greater shame that a mere worm of the earth should wish to take precedence of his Creator! But we must speak in still plainer terms.

They say that it is lawful for them to counterfeit among Papists. Who, then, is it that gives them the bread which they eat there? And who is it that causes the earth to bring forth fruit? If they cannot deny that God nourishes them there as elsewhere, why will they do homage to the Devil with their bodies? If they were Christians I would use higher reasons, and ask, Why it is we live here below? But the pity is that those who thus quibblingly sport with God so brutify themselves, that they require to be treated as if they were not in their sound minds.

It seems to them enough simply to allege that, in this matter, they act entirely from fear. But if this pretext avails them, then Joseph would have been guilty of no sin in yielding to his mistress, since it would not have been to gratify himself, but only to yield to the urgency by which she in a manner forced him. It must have been foolish in him to suffer so much, and expose himself to infamy, seeing he had the means of avoiding it! But we must rather abide

of the Papists, then he who becomes the mere tool of his master for any infamous purpose commits no offence. A man will be excusable in poisoning his neighbour, or committing any act of treachery, in order not to offend him to whom he is subject! I have insisted too long on a point as to which, as I have said, there is no difficulty or doubt; but it is good to see the confusion into which those fall who endeavour by finesse to escape the judgment of God.

There are some in the present day who have recourse to another mode of evasion. While confessing that it is a detestable thing to take part in the Idolatries of the heathen, they will not allow this to extend to the Superstitions of the Papacy! as if all the impieties of the heathen had been anything else than corruptions of the true service of God. Whence, I ask, did the heathen derive all their ceremonies, but just from the holy Patriarchs? The evil consisted in their adulterating that which had been well instituted by God. So much is this the case, that all the abominations which have ever existed in the world have covered themselves under the name of God and of Religion, but that has neither sufficed to justify them, nor made it lawful for believers to participate in them. But to proceed—

Though I should grant them that there is a difference between the Idolatries of the Papists and those of the heathen in bygone times, they cannot deny that God as strictly interdicted his people from the Idolatry of Bethel as from that of foreign countries. When the calves were set up in Dan and Bethel, (1 Kings xii. 28,) it was under colour of the name of God—the God who had brought his people out of Egypt. But because the worship there established was repugnant to the doctrine of the law, God condemned all those who should go and defile themselves with it. The Supper of Jesus Christ and the Mass are things every whit as incompatible as the sacrifices of Moses and of Jeroboam. Whence, then, is the dispensation which permits men to go to Mass under the pretext that it is the Supper of Jesus Christ in disguise? On the contrary, I hold that those who

than if it were not made so exactly its counterpart.

Let us then lay it down as a general rule, that all human inventions which are set up to corrupt the simple purity of the word of God, and overturn the service which he demands and approves, are real acts of sacrilege, in which Christians cannot take part without blaspheming God; in other words, without trampling his honour under their feet. I know how harsh and insupportable this strictness appears to those who would like to be handled according to their appetite. But what would they have me to do? Knowing them to be so delicate, I would willingly spare them, if it were possible for me to do so. But both they and I must condemn when God has pronounced sentence. They find no man, they say, more severe than I. Now I wish to shew them that hitherto I have only treated them too gently.

Be this as it may, they cannot exempt themselves from what the prophet Jeremiah requires of the Jews who were captive in Babylon. Not only does he prohibit them from going to the abominations of the Chaldeans, or making a show of consenting to them, but he lays them under an express obligation to shew their detestation. His injunction is, (Jer. x. 11,) "You will say to them, The gods which have not made heaven and earth will perish from the earth and from beneath the heavens." It is a circumstance well deserving of notice, that the Prophet, who had written his book in Hebrew, couches this sentence in the coarse *patois* of the children of Chaldea, as if he were compelling the Jews to change their language, the more clearly to shew the wide difference between them and idolaters.

Let our soft-hearted folks now go and complain of me as too rigid. Whether I speak out or hold my tongue, we all continue bound by this law which God lays upon us. And in fact it is not without cause that God, in speaking to his believing people, says to them, (Isaiah xliv. 2,) "You are my witnesses and my servants whom I have chosen." Whosoever would approve himself a member of Jesus Christ must shew that the title belongs to him in such a way that

I pray you, is the case of those who, all their lifelong, overthrow this testimony, as do those who not only hide their Christianity, in order to give no sign of it before men, but perform acts altogether contrary to it? All, then, that remains to the children of God who are in the midst of such pollution, is to afflict their souls after the example of righteous Lot, (2 Peter ii. 8;) in other words, to testify against evil according as God may give them means and opportunity.

Let us now proceed to specify the Idolatries which are in vogue. I have already touched a little on the MASS. Now, although there is blasphemy in it so gross and enormous that more cannot be, still advocates of a bad cause are found to quibble in regard to it. Still, whether they will or not, they are constrained to confess the truth of what I say, namely, that the Mass is in itself a renunciation of the death of Jesus Christ, and a sacrilege forged by Satan to annihilate the Sacrament of the Supper. In like manner, they cannot deny that the Prayers which are offered to Saints, and the Intercessions which are made for the Dead, are so many abuses by which the invocation of the name of God, which is sacred above all things, is profaned. And yet, while they mingle in such pollutions among the Papists, they think they incur no blame!

Their language is, What should we do? It is not permitted us to reform the things which we know to be bad, for we are private persons, and those who have public authority maintain them; therefore we must pass them by. I admit all they say, but it is nothing to the purpose. It is not for them to reform the common condition of the people, and this no one requires of them; but they are admonished to reform themselves individually, and this is an office which properly belongs to them. They are not told to purge the temples and the streets, but each is enjoined to keep his body and his soul in purity, and to take heed that God be honoured in his house. There is a wide difference between the two things—between abolishing the Mass in a country,

They still return to their old song, and allege that they do not renounce the death and passion of Jesus Christ, because they have no such intention. But I ask them, What is it that a Christian confesses, if it be not what he believes in his heart? That the act which they perform is altogether contrary to the Christian confession, is perfectly notorious: hence, as much as in them lies they renounce and abjure the pure faith. I will speak still more home. The Mass is a sacrifice in which the Papists wish to offer Jesus Christ for the purpose of reconciling themselves to God. Were that true, Jesus Christ could not by his death and passion have acquired for us righteousness and eternal salvation. Let them wind about as they may, they must still come to the point. All who go to the Mass, under colour of devotion, make a public profession of consenting to it. Thus, as much as in them lies, they shew that they do not hold their redemption to have been perfected by the death of Jesus Christ.

There are some who use rather more restraint. They receive only the Parochial Mass, in which they think there is more conformity with the Supper of Jesus Christ. And, in fact, it might be alleged that the Masses, which are said as well by hedge-priests as by canons and chaplains, and all those which are founded for the worship of an individual, or which are daily purchased, are like common prostitutes. The Parochial Mass is an adulteress who clothes herself with the name of a husband, to keep up the reputation of a respectable woman. This comparison, however, is not at all correct. A married adulteress will have some regard to decency, and not give a general welcome to all comers, whereas the Parochial Mass is the most common idolatry of all. So little ground is there to gloss it over as still retaining some trace of the Supper of Jesus Christ, that it is just as if a robber were less a robber when dressed up in the spoils of his victim, and mounted upon his horse.

We long, they say, for the Supper of Jesus Christ! Since we cannot have it pure, from the tyranny under which we live, we must be contented with a remnant, and wait till .

by way of supplying the want, protest that they do not hold Jesus Christ as the eternal and only Priest, and they every week search for a new sacrifice to wipe away their sins: for all this is in the Parochial Mass as in a Mass of Saint Nicholas, or a Mass for the Dead. They make a show of worshipping an Idol, and plume themselves as thereby seeking Jesus Christ. And in order that they may not fight against God without sword or buckler, they put forward the authority of this person and that person; as if the absolution of a man could save them from the condemnation of God.

I omit to say that they do not speak truly when they bring forward certain individuals as advocating their cause. Even were it so that a distinguished Saint at one time thought that there was no great evil in going to the Parochial Mass, since he has learned the true state of the case, so much the more weight ought they to give to his subsequent condemnation, seeing the agency of God has constrained him to it, and made him abandon the opinion which he previously entertained. But of what use is it to mince the matter? Can they foreclose God by the opinion or saying of a mortal man? We know that in his judgment truth alone reigns without respect of persons. Now, the fact is, that the Parochial Mass is instituted to sacrifice Jesus Christ, and compound with God as well for the living as for the dead; and that a morsel of bread is there worshipped as if it were the Son of God. I do not go over the things in detail; there are a thousand other pollutions: I mention only the grossest of them. Let those who make a show of consenting to them wash their hands as they may, they will not in the end make themselves a whit cleaner than Pilate was.

But it is strange how these good parishioners, when Easter comes round, go and seek a chapel apart where some semi-Christian Monk may prepare for them a bastard Supper. If the Parochial Mass, as they say, comes near to the Supper of Jesus Christ, why do they not keep to it? But after

it. And yet it is unnecessary too strongly to expose such inconstancy; for it is the true wages given to all those who are not founded in the truth of God, who punishes them by keeping them constantly on the move, and making them contradict themselves in what they do. In regard to such an adulterated Supper, I know well that they fancy great wrong is done them when they are reproved for using it. But what can we do, since it accords not with the rule of the Master?

I condemn it not because it is done in secret: for I know that never has the Supper been better dispensed, or more rightly received, then when the disciples have retired to eat it in secret, because of the tyranny of the enemy. But there are here two intolerable vices—the one, that those who thus ape the Supper, make a show of having their Mass in it, and wish it to be so thought; and the other is, that the good " Father" from whom they receive it, gives it to them not as a Christian Pastor, but in the character of a Papal Priest. They think it a good excuse to say that their Mass chanter has no intention to make them worship either the bread or the wine; that he leaves out the canon wherein the greatest impieties are contained, and gives the sacrament to all the company in both kinds. But when this proceeding will come before the Great Judge, they shall feel what they have gained by all their disguises; they must even feel it already. Here I refer to the stings and prickings which they must feel in their own consciences.

And it is here that the character of the whole proceeding must be determined: for, without going into a longer investigation, they know what they pretend to exhibit as well to the enemies of God as to all the common people. God must deny himself before he could approve of such an act of profession. Though all men in the world should have combined together to justify them, the ablest among them never can free himself from the charge of " halting between two opinions." God has declared by his Prophet, (1 Kings xviii. 21,) that he never can be induced to approve of such halting.

of such an office. True: but then the virtue of the Sacraments, they say, depends not on the worthiness of those who administer it. This I admit: nay, I go farther, and hold that were a devil to administer the Supper it would be none the worse; and, on the contrary, that were an angel to chant the Mass, it would be none the better. But we are now upon a different question, namely, whether the Orders of the Pope conferred upon a Monk, render him fit to do the office of a Pastor? If they reply that they do not consider that of any consequence, and they do not choose him in such a capacity, their conduct shews the contrary.

Even taking it for granted that they, in so far as they are personally concerned, attach no importance to the kind of individual employed, I must always insist on the nature of the outward profession which they make. Now it is plain that they cover themselves with the mask of a Priest. To celebrate the Supper of the Lord duly, it behoved them to separate themselves from the ranks of the idolaters, so as therein to have nothing in common with them. Instead of doing so they go as it were to matriculate themselves, and make a show of being members of the body, and yet they will have it that we in condemning them resemble the ancient heretics who condemned the use of the Sacraments because of the vices of men; as if we were looking to individual vices and not to the whole state of the case. I pass this briefly: but the little I say upon it is only too much to convict them of shameless effrontery. Still, if they are so dull as not to feel anything, the Word of God must suffice us; as when the Lord says by Jeremiah, (Jer. iv. 1,) "Israel, if thou art turned, turn unto me!" These words point out the candour and simplicity which ought to mark all our dealings with God. And hence St. Paul declares, (Acts xiv. 15,) that he was sent to turn the heathen from their vanities to the living God; as if he had said, that nothing was done by merely abandoning an accustomed evil, and supplying its place by other fictions, but that superstition must be abolished out and out, in order that the true religion may

side they ought to turn.

There is another class of persons who go the whole length of quitting the Mass, but would fain retain some other fragments of what they call " the service of God," in order, as they say, not to be thought altogether profane! And it is possible that some do this with a proper feeling, at least I am willing to believe they do; but still, whatever their desire may be, it does not follow that they either adopt the right rule, or use the proper measure. Some will say, We may well enough go to baptisms, for in them there is no manifest idolatry. As if that Sacrament were not so deformed and degraded in all sorts of ways as to make it seem as if Christ were still in the house of Pilate, to be scourged and subjected to every species of insult! When they say that their object is to shew that they are not people destitute of religion, let them consult their conscience, and it will answer, that their object is to content the Papists, and act a part which will enable them to avoid persecution.

Some persons watch the time so as not to be present when Mass is celebrated, and yet go to church to make it be thought that they were then actually present; others reserve merely Vespers for their share. But I should like to know from them, whether they count it nothing that incense is given to Idols—that solemn Prayer is founded on the intercession or merit of some Saint—that the *Salve Regina*, stuffed as it is with execrable and diabolical blasphemies, is sung? I omit to add, that the chanting, such as it is, being in an unknown tongue, is a manifest profanation of Sacred Scripture and of the praises of God, as St. Paul shews at length in the fourteenth chapter of the First Epistle to the Corinthians.

But say we forgive them this last fault. If they go to Vespers, in order to give some proof of their Christianity, it must be especially at High Festivals. There, then, solemn incense will be given to the principal Idols. This, as Scripture shews, is a species of Sacrifice, and was the common method which heathen persecutors employed to make the

would not bring perfumes and offer incense to Idols! Those then who go to regale themselves with the odour of such incense infect themselves with the pollutions there practised. This, however, they think that we ought to overlook. But I pray them, in God's name, to attend well to what is said in the text, viz., that idols ought to be held in such detestation by the believer, that the very mention of these must not pass his lips for fear of pollution. The expression certainly makes it incumbent on us to keep far aloof from everything that would entangle us in the pollutions of idolaters.

Now, to speak frankly of all those who, by wishing to divide between God and the devil, belong to the class of double-minded, I cannot find an analogous case more proper to paint them to the life than that of Esau. When he sees that his father Isaac sends Jacob into Mesopotamia to take a wife, because the women of the land of Canaan displeased him, and Rebecca his mother, who felt exceedingly annoyed on the subject, he indeed so far to satisfy his parents takes a new wife, but still he does not part with the one he already had. He thus retains the evil of which Isaac complained, but to modify it in some sort of way he forms this new marriage. In the same way those who are so wedded to the world that they cannot follow what God commands, will adopt many disguises, and cook up many mixtures, to shew some kind of conformity to the will of God; but still they cease not always to retain some corruption, so that nothing which they do is pure and straight.

I know well that there are many poor souls in perplexity who, without hypocrisy, desire to walk in the right path, and yet cannot disencumber themselves of many scruples. I am not astonished at this, considering the horrible confusion which reigns in the Papacy. Nay, I feel pity for those who seek the means of being able to serve God and maintaining themselves, if that were possible, among the enemies of the faith. But what more can I with one and all than simply shew them wherein they fail, in order that they may remedy what is wrong. If they come and question

God. This I say, because some persons are so importunate that it would be impossible ever to have done with them if all their difficulties were to be answered. Such persons might justly be compared to those who, after hearing a sermon exhorting them to dress themselves modestly without superfluity or pomp, would have the preacher to shape out their gowns and sew their shoes.

What then is to be done? We have in all this a certain end at which we must aim. Zeal for the house of God must fill our heart, and we must submit to the insults which we receive in his name. When such a zeal shall have been kindled in our hearts, not to be like a smothered fire but to burn incessantly, so far from permitting us to make a show of approving abominations by which God is dishonoured, it will make it impossible for us to be silent and to dissemble on seeing them. Observe that the thing spoken of is "*Zeal for the house of the Lord,*" to let us know that reference is made to the external order which is in the Church, as a means of exercising us in the Confession of our Faith.

I care not a rush for the mockers, who say that it is well for us thus to talk at our ease! It is not with me they have to do, for it is obvious I have introduced nothing of my own. As much do I say of all those philosophers who pronounce their decisions on the matter without knowing how. Since they will not listen to God, who speaks to them and would teach them, I remit them to his judgment-seat, where they shall hear his sentence, from which there will be no appeal. Since they deign not now to give heed to him as Master, they shall then, however reluctant they may be, experience him as Judge! The ablest and most crafty shall there find that they have miscalculated. However determined they may be to overthrow or obscure what is right, the fur caps which they put on, and in which admiring themselves, they grow blind, will not enable them to gain their cause.

I speak thus because Counsellors, Judges, and Advocates not only undertake to plead against God from having a pri-

so arrogant are these puny creatures, that after they have spoken the word they will not suffer either reason or truth to interfere. Though it be only in passing, I tell them it would be far better to reflect on the fearful vengeance prepared for all those who turn the truth into a lie. Let chamber and table Doctors not here assume an air which is too lofty for them, and chatter against the heavenly Master to whom it behoves all to give audience. Splendid titles will not here give any exemption—if there be any difference, it will only be that Abbots, Priors, Deans, and Archdeacons, will take the lead in going with the others into condemnation. Though courtiers are accustomed to satisfy men with their fair speeches, let them not attempt to do the same with God. Let all jesters and talking wits have done with their gibes and sneers, if they would not feel the strong hand of him whose word may well make them tremble. The deception is far too gross when they would make it be believed that by bringing me forward as a party, they will no longer have God for their judge! Let them erase my name from their papers in this cause, inasmuch as all I insist upon is that God be listened to and obeyed, while I make no claim to the government of their consciences, nor attempt in any way to subject them to my laws.

As to the others, who do not thus arrogantly reject the Word of God, and yet are so weak and cowardly that one cannot get them to move a single step, I exhort them to think a little better for themselves, and no longer indulge in self-flattery. Let them awake and open their eyes to see the full extent of the evil of their state. I know the difficulties by which they are beset, and I do not speak to them of serving God purely among idolaters, as if it were an easy matter. But if their conscience fails, let them have recourse to God, in order that he may strengthen them, and they may learn to prefer his glory to all other things besides.

I wish that all poor believers under the Papacy could hear what I say, just as the prophet Jeremiah, when in Jerusalem, sent a similar message to the people who were held captive

share of suffering, and yet they are commanded to spurn the Idolatry of Chaldea in the very heart of the country; for there is no reason why the tyranny of men should interrupt or lessen the right which God has to be honoured by us. Here there is no exemption or privilege for great or small, rich or poor. Let all, then, bend the neck in submission. Let the poor man be afraid that if he should say, " I know not what to do," God may answer, " Neither do I know what to do with thee." Let not the rich take their ease as if they were reposing on their bed; rather let them learn, after the example of St. Paul, to count all things as loss that would retard or turn them aside from their Christian course.

Meanwhile let us, too, on our side, not forget what I adverted to at the outset. Let us apply the subject for our own instruction, so as to be always ready in any quarter to which we may be removed, or under any circumstances which may befall us, to remain steadfast in the pure Confession of our Faith, detesting all Superstitions, Idolatries, and Abuses which contradict the truth of God, obscure his honour, and overturn his service.

Second Homily or Sermon,

Containing an Exhortation to suffer Persecution in following Jesus Christ and his Gospel.

"Let us go forth out of the tents after Christ, bearing his reproach."—
HEB. xiii. 13.

ALL the exhortations which can be given us to suffer patiently for the name of Jesus Christ, and in defence of the gospel, will have no effect, if we do not feel assured of the cause for which we fight. For when we are called to part with life, it is absolutely necessary to know on what grounds. The firmness necessary we cannot possess, unless it be founded on certainty of faith.

It is true that persons may be found who will foolishly expose themselves to death in maintaining some absurd opinions and reveries conceived by their own brain, but such impetuosity is more to be regarded as frenzy than as Christian zeal; and, in fact, there is neither firmness nor sound sense in those who thus, at a kind of hap-hazard, cast themselves away. But however this may be, it is in a good cause only that God can acknowledge us as his martyrs. Death is common to all, and the children of God are condemned to ignominy and tortures just as criminals are; but God makes the distinction between them, inasmuch as he cannot deny his truth. On our part, then, it is requisite that we have sure and infallible evidence of the doctrine which we maintain; and hence, as I have said, we cannot be rationally impressed by any exhortations which we receive to suffer persecution for the gospel, if no true certainty of faith has been imprinted in our hearts. For to hazard our life upon a peradventure is not natural, and though we were to do it,

not thoroughly persuaded that it is for him and his cause we suffer persecution, and the world is our enemy.

Now, when I speak of such persuasion, I mean not merely that we must know how to distinguish between true religion and the abuses or follies of men, but also that we must be thoroughly persuaded of the heavenly life, and the crown which is promised us above, after we shall have fought here below. Let us understand, then, that both of these requisites are necessary, and cannot be separated from each other.

The points, accordingly, with which we must commence, are these:—We must know well what our Christianity is, what the faith which we have to hold and follow—what the rule which God has given us; and we must be so well furnished with such instruction as to be able boldly to condemn all the falsehoods, errors, and superstitions, which Satan has introduced to corrupt the pure simplicity of the doctrine of God. Hence, we ought not to be surprised that, in the present day, we see so few persons disposed to suffer for the Gospel, and that the greater part of those who call themselves Christians know not what it is. For all are as it were lukewarm; and instead of making it their business to hear or read, count it enough to have had some slight taste of Christian faith. This is the reason why there is so little decision, and why those who are assailed immediately fall away. This fact should stimulate us to inquire more diligently into divine truth, in order to be well assured with regard to it.

Still, however, to be well informed and grounded is not the whole that is necessary. For we see some who seem to be thoroughly imbued with sound doctrine, and who, notwithstanding, have no more zeal or affection than if they had never known any more of God than some fleeting fancy. Why is this? Just because they have never comprehended the majesty of the Holy Scriptures. And, in fact, did we, such as we are, consider well that it is God who speaks to us, it is certain that we would listen more attentively, and with greater reverence. If we would think that in reading

propounded to us.

We now see THE TRUE METHOD OF PREPARING TO SUFFER FOR THE GOSPEL. *First,* We must have profited so far in the school of God as to be decided in regard to true religion and the doctrine which we are to hold; and we must despise all the wiles and impostures of Satan, and all human inventions, as things not only frivolous but also carnal, inasmuch as they corrupt Christian purity; therein differing, like true martyrs of Christ, from the fantastic persons who suffer for mere absurdities. *Second,* Feeling assured of the good cause, we must be inflamed, accordingly, to follow God whithersoever he may call us: his word must have such authority with us as it deserves, and, having withdrawn from this world, we must feel as it were enraptured in seeking the heavenly life.

But it is more than strange, that though the light of God is shining more brightly than it ever did before, there is a lamentable want of zeal! If the thought does not fill us with shame, so much the worse. For we must shortly come before the great Judge, where the iniquity which we endeavour to hide will be brought forward with such upbraidings, that we shall be utterly confounded. For, if we are obliged to bear testimony to God, according to the measure of the knowledge which he has given us, to what is it owing, I would ask, that we are so cold and timorous in entering into battle, seeing that God has so fully manifested himself at this time, that he may be said to have opened to us and displayed before us the great treasures of his secrets? May it not be said that we do not think we have to do with God? For had we any regard to his majesty we would not dare to turn the doctrine which proceeds from his mouth into some kind of philosophic speculation. In short, it is impossible to deny that it is to our great shame, not to say fearful condemnation, that we have so well known the truth of God, and have so little courage to maintain it!

Above all, when we look to the Martyrs of past times, well may we detest our own cowardice! The greater part of

was one God, whom they behoved to worship and serve—that they had been redeemed by the blood of Jesus Christ, in order that they might place their confidence of salvation in him and in his grace—and that all the inventions of men, being mere dross and rubbish, they ought to condemn all idolatries and superstitions. In one word, their theology was in substance this,—There is one God who created all the world, and declared his will to us by Moses and the Prophets, and finally by Jesus Christ and his Apostles; and we have one sole Redeemer, who purchased us by his blood, and by whose grace we hope to be saved: All the idols of the world are cursed, and deserve execration.

With a system embracing no other points than these, they went boldly to the flames, or to any other kind of death. They did not go in twos or threes, but in such bands, that the number of those who fell by the hands of tyrants is almost infinite! We, on our part, are such learned clerks, that none can be more so, (so at least we think,) and, in fact, so far as regards the knowledge of Scripture, God has so spread it out before us, that no former age was ever so highly favoured. Still, after all, there is scarcely a particle of zeal. When men manifest such indifference, it looks as if they were bent on provoking the vengeance of God.

What then should be done in order to inspire our breasts with true courage? We have, in the first place, to consider how precious the Confession of our Faith is in the sight of God. We little know how much God prizes it, if our life, which is nothing, is valued by us more highly. When it is so, we manifest a marvellous degree of stupidity. We cannot save our life at the expense of our confession, without acknowledging that we hold it in higher estimation than the honour of God and the salvation of our souls.

A heathen could say, that "It was a miserable thing to save life by giving up the only things which made life desirable!" And yet he and others like him never knew for what end men are placed in the world, and why they live in it. It is true they knew enough to say that men ought to

We know far better what the chief aim of life should be, namely, to glorify God, in order that he may be our glory. When this is not done, wo to us! And we cannot continue to live for a single moment upon the earth without heaping additional curses on our heads. Still we are not ashamed to purchase some few days to languish here below, renouncing the eternal kingdom by separating ourselves from him by whose energy we are sustained in life.

Were we to ask the most ignorant, not to say the most brutish persons in the world, Why they live? they would not venture to answer simply, that it is to eat, and drink, and sleep; for all know that they have been created for a higher and holier end. And what end can we find if it be not to honour God, and allow ourselves to be governed by him, like children by a good parent; so that after we have finished the journey of this corruptible life, we may be received into his eternal inheritance? Such is the principal, indeed the sole end. When we do not take it into account, and are intent on a brutish life, which is worse than a thousand deaths, what can we allege for our excuse? To live and not know why, is unnatural. To reject the causes for which we live, under the influence of a foolish longing for a respite of some few days, during which we are to live in the world, while separated from God—I know not how to name such infatuation and madness!

But as Persecution is always harsh and bitter, let us consider, HOW AND BY WHAT MEANS CHRISTIANS MAY BE ABLE TO FORTIFY THEMSELVES WITH PATIENCE, SO AS UNFLINCHINGLY TO EXPOSE THEIR LIFE FOR THE TRUTH OF GOD. The text which we have read out, when it is properly understood, is sufficient to induce us to do so. The Apostle says, " Let us go forth from the city after the Lord Jesus, bearing his reproach." In the first place, he reminds us, although the swords should not be drawn over us nor the fires kindled to burn us, that we cannot be truly united to the Son of God while we are rooted in this world. Wherefore, a Christian, even in repose, must always have one foot lifted to march to

Grant that this at first sight seems to us hard, still we must be satisfied with the words of St. Paul, (1 Thess. iii. 3,) "We are called and appointed to suffer." As if he had said, Such is our condition as Christians; this is the road by which we must go, if we would follow Christ.

Meanwhile, to solace our infirmity and mitigate the vexation and sorrow which persecution might cause us, a good reward is held forth: In suffering for the cause of God, we are walking step by step after the Son of God, and have him for our guide. Were it simply said, that to be Christians we must pass through all the insults of the world boldly, to meet death at all times and in whatever way God may be pleased to appoint, we might apparently have some pretext for replying, It is a strange road to go at a peradventure. But when we are commanded to follow the Lord Jesus, his guidance is too good and honourable to be refused. Now, in order that we may be more deeply moved, not only is it said that Jesus Christ walks before us as our Captain, but that we are made conformable to his image; as St. Paul speaks in the eighth chapter to the Romans, (Rom. viii. 29,) "God hath ordained all those whom he hath adopted for his children, to be made conformable to him who is the pattern and head of all."

Are we so delicate as to be unwilling to endure anything? Then we must renounce the grace of God by which he has called us to the hope of salvation. For there are two things which cannot be separated—to be members of Christ, and to be tried by many afflictions. We certainly ought to prize such a conformity to the Son of God much more than we do. It is true, that in the world's judgment there is disgrace in suffering for the gospel. But since we know that unbelievers are blind, ought we not to have better eyes than they? It is ignominy to suffer from those who occupy the seat of justice, but St. Paul shews us by his example that we have to glory in scourgings for Jesus Christ, as marks by which God recognises us and avows us for his own. And we know what St. Luke narrates of Peter and John, (Acts

Lord Jesus."

Ignominy and dignity are two opposites: so says the world which, being infatuated, judges against all reason, and in this way converts the glory of God into dishonour. But, on our part, let us not refuse to be vilified as concerns the world, in order to be honoured before God and his angels. We see what pains the ambitious take to receive the commands of a king, and what a boast they make of it. The Son of God presents his commands to us, and every one stands back! Tell me, pray, whether in so doing are we worthy of having anything in common with him? There is nothing here to attract our sensual nature, but such notwithstanding are the true escutcheons of nobility in the heavens. Imprisonment, exile, evil report, imply in men's imagination whatever is to be vituperated; but what hinders us from viewing things as God judges and declares them, save our unbelief? Wherefore, let the Name of the Son of God have all the weight with us which it deserves, that we may learn to count it honour when he stamps his marks upon us : If we act otherwise our ingratitude is insupportable!

Were God to deal with us according to our deserts, would he not have just cause to chastise us daily in a thousand ways? Nay more, a hundred thousand deaths would not suffice for a small portion of our misdeeds! Now, if in his infinite goodness he puts all our faults under his foot and abolishes them, and instead of punishing us according to our demerit, devises an admirable means to convert our afflictions into honour and a special privilege, inasmuch as through them we are taken into partnership with his Son, must it not be said, when we disdain such a happy state, that we have indeed made little progress in Christian doctrine?

Accordingly St. Peter, after exhorting us (1 Peter iv. 15) to walk so purely in the fear of God, as " not to suffer as thieves, adulterers, and murderers," immediately adds, " If we must suffer as Christians, let us glorify God for the blessing which he thus bestows upon us." It is not without cause? Here we are poor worms of the earth, creatures full of vanity, full of lies, and yet God employs us to defend his truth—an honour which pertains not even to the angels of heaven! May not this consideration alone well inflame us to offer ourselves to God to be employed in any way in such honourable service?

Many persons, however, cannot refrain from pleading against God, or, at least, from complaining against him for not better supporting their weakness. It is marvellously strange, they say, how God, after having chosen us for his children, allows us to be so trampled upon and tormented by the ungodly. I answer: Even were it not apparent why he does so, he might well exercise this authority over us, and fix our lot at his pleasure. But when we see that Jesus Christ is our pattern, ought we not, without inquiring farther, to esteem it great happiness that we are made like to him? God, however, makes it very apparent what the reasons are for which he is pleased that we should be persecuted. Had we nothing more than the consideration suggested by St. Peter, (1 Peter i. 7,) we were disdainful indeed not to acquiesce in it. He says, " Since gold and silver, which are only corruptible metals, are purified and tested by fire, it is but reasonable that our faith, which surpasses all the riches of the world, should be tried."

It were easy indeed for God to crown us at once without requiring us to sustain any combats; but as it is his pleasure that until the end of the world Christ shall reign in the midst of his enemies, (Psalm cx.,) so it is also his pleasure that we, being placed in the midst of them, shall suffer their oppression and violence till he deliver us. I know, indeed, that the flesh kicks when it is to be brought to this point, but still the will of God must have the mastery. If we feel some repugnance in ourselves, it need not surprise us; for it is only too natural for us to shun the cross. Still let us not fail to surmount it, knowing that God accepts our obedience, provided we bring all our feelings and wishes into captivity, and make them subject to him.

will lead thee whither thou wouldst not," said our Lord Jesus Christ to Peter. (John xxi. 18.) When such fears of death arise within us, let us gain the mastery over them, or rather let God gain it; and meanwhile, let us feel assured that we offer him a pleasing sacrifice when we resist and do violence to our inclinations for the purpose of placing ourselves entirely under his command: This is the principal war in which God would have his people to be engaged. He would have them strive to suppress every rebellious thought and feeling which would turn them aside from the path to which he points. And the consolations are so ample, that it may well be said, we are more than cowards if we give way!

In ancient times vast numbers of people, to obtain a simple crown of leaves, refused no toil, no pain, no trouble; nay, it even cost them nothing to die, and yet every one of them fought for a peradventure, not knowing whether he was to gain or lose the prize. God holds forth to us the immortal crown by which we may become partakers of his glory: He does not mean us to fight at hap-hazard, but all of us have a promise of the prize for which we strive. Have we any cause then to decline the struggle? Do we think it has been said in vain, "If we die with Jesus Christ we shall also live with him?" (2 Tim. ii. 11.) Our triumph is prepared, and yet we do all we can to shun the combat.

But it is said that all we teach on this subject is repugnant to human judgment. I confess it. And hence when our Saviour declares, "Blessed are they who are persecuted for righteousness' sake," (Matt. v. 10,) he gives utterance to a sentiment which is not easily received in the world. On the contrary, he wishes to account that as happiness which in the judgment of sense is misery. We seem to ourselves miserable when God leaves us to be trampled upon by the tyranny and cruelty of our enemies; but the error is that we look not to the promises of God, which assure us that all will turn to our good. We are cast down when we see the wicked stronger than we, and planting their foot on

disposed to amuse ourselves with present objects, God, in permitting the good to be maltreated and the wicked to have sway, shews by evident tokens that a day is coming on which all that is now in confusion will be reduced to order. If the period seems distant, let us run to the remedy, and not flatter ourselves in our sin; for it is certain that we have no faith if we cannot carry our views forward to the coming of Jesus Christ.

To leave no means which may be fitted to stimulate us unemployed, God sets before us PROMISES on the one hand, and THREATENINGS on the other. Do we feel that the promises have not sufficient influence, let us strengthen them by adding the threatenings. It is true we must be perverse in the extreme not to put more faith in the promises of God, when the Lord Jesus says that he will own us as his before his Father, provided we confess him before men. (Matt. x. 32; Luke xii. 8.) What should prevent us from making the confession which he requires? Let men do their utmost, they cannot do worse than murder us! and will not the heavenly life compensate for this? I do not here collect all the passages in Scripture which bear on this subject: they are so often reiterated that we ought to be thoroughly satisfied with them. When the struggle comes, if three or four passages do not suffice, a hundred surely ought to make us proof against all contrary temptations!

But if God cannot win us to himself by gentle means, must we not be mere blocks if his threatenings also fail? Jesus Christ summons all those who from fear of temporal death shall have denied the truth, to appear at the bar of God his Father, and says, that then both body and soul will be consigned to perdition. (Matt. x. 28; Luke xii. 5.) And in another passage he says that he will disclaim all those who shall have denied him before men. (Matt. x. 33; Luke xii. 10.) These words, if we are not altogether impervious to feeling, might well make our hair stand on end! Be this as it may, this much is certain; if these things do not move us as they ought, nothing remains for us but a

fidelity.

It is in vain for us to allege that pity should be shewn us, inasmuch as our nature is so frail; for it is said, on the contrary, that Moses having looked to God by faith was fortified so as not to yield under any temptation. Wherefore, when we are thus soft and easy to bend, it is a manifest sign, I do not say that we have no zeal, no firmness, but that we know nothing either of God or his kingdom. When we are reminded that we ought to be united to our Head, it seems to us a fine pretext for exemption to say, that we are men! But what were those who have trodden the path before us? Indeed, had we nothing more than pure doctrine, all the excuses we could make would be frivolous; but having so many examples which ought to supply us with the strongest proof, the more deserving are we of condemnation.

There are two points to be considered. The first is, that the whole body of the Church in general has always been, and to the end will be, liable to be afflicted by the wicked, as is said in the Psalms, (Psalm cxxix. 1,) "From my youth up they have tormented me, and dragged the plough over me from one end to the other." The Holy Spirit there brings in the ancient Church, in order that we, after being much acquainted with her afflictions, may not regard it as either new or vexatious, when the like is done to ourselves in the present day. St. Paul, also, in quoting from another Psalm, (Rom. viii. 36; Psalm xliv. 23,) a passage in which it is said, "We have been like sheep to the slaughter;" shews that that has not been for one age only, but is the ordinary condition of the Church, and shall be.

Therefore, on seeing how the Church of God is trampled upon in the present day by proud worldlings, how one barks and another bites, how they torture, how they plot against her, how she is assailed incessantly by mad dogs and savage beasts, let it remind us that the same thing was done in all the olden time. It is true God sometimes gives her a truce and time of refreshment, and hence in the Psalm above quoted, it is said, "He cutteth the cords of the wicked; and

But still it has pleased him that his Church should always have to battle so long as she is in this world, her repose being treasured up on high in the heavens. (Heb. iii. 9.)

Meanwhile, the issue of her afflictions has always been fortunate. At all events, God has caused that though she has been pressed by many calamities, she has never been completely crushed; as it is said, (Psalm vii. 15,) "The wicked with all their efforts have not succeeded in that at which they aimed." St. Paul glories in the fact, and shews that this is the course which God in mercy always takes. He says, (1 Cor. iv. 12,) "We endure tribulations, but we are not in agony; we are impoverished, but not left destitute; we are persecuted, but not forsaken; cast down, but we perish not; bearing everywhere in our body the mortification of the Lord Jesus, in order that his life may be manifested in our mortal bodies." Such being, as we see, the issue which God has at all times given to the persecutions of his Church, we ought to take courage, knowing that our forefathers, who were frail men like ourselves, always had the victory over their enemies, by remaining firm in endurance.

I only touch on this article briefly to come to the *second*, which is more to our purpose, viz., that WE OUGHT TO TAKE ADVANTAGE OF THE PARTICULAR EXAMPLES OF THE MARTYRS WHO HAVE GONE BEFORE US. These are not confined to two or three, but are, as the Apostle says, (Heb. xii. 1,) "a great and dense cloud." By this expression he intimates that the number is so great that it ought as it were completely to engross our sight. Not to be tedious, I will only mention the Jews, who were persecuted for the true Religion, as well under the tyranny of King Antiochus as a little after his death. We cannot allege that the number of sufferers was small, for it formed as it were a large army of martyrs. We cannot say that it consisted of Prophets whom God had set apart from common people; for women and young children formed part of the band. We cannot say that they got off at a cheap rate, for they were tortured as cruelly as it was

caring to be delivered, that they might obtain a better resurrection; others were proved by mockery and blows, or bonds and prisons; others were stoned or sawn asunder; others travelled up and down, wandering among mountains and caves."

Let us now compare their case with ours. If they so endured for the truth which was at that time so obscure, what ought we to do in the clear light which is now shining? God speaks to us with open mouth; the great gate of the kingdom of heaven has been opened, and Jesus Christ calls us to himself, after having come down to us that we might have him as it were present to our eyes. What a reproach would it be to us to have less zeal in suffering for the Gospel, than those had who only hailed the promises afar off—who had only a little wicket opened whereby to come to the kingdom of God, and who had only some memorial and type of Jesus Christ? These things cannot be expressed in word as they deserve, and therefore I leave each to ponder them for himself.

The doctrine now laid down, as it is general, ought to be carried into practice by all Christians, each applying it to his own use according as may be necessary. This I say, in order that those who do not see themselves in apparent danger may not think it superfluous as regards them. They are not at this hour in the hands of tyrants, but how do they know what God means to do with them hereafter? We ought therefore to be so forearmed, that if some Persecution which we did not expect arrives, we may not be taken unawares. But I much fear that there are many deaf ears in regard to this subject. So far are those who are sheltered and at their ease from preparing to suffer death when need shall be, that they do not even trouble themselves about serving God in their lives. It nevertheless continues true that this preparation for persecution ought to be our ordinary study, and especially in the times in which we live.

Those, again, whom God calls to suffer for the testimony of his Name, ought to shew by deeds that they have been

them in times past, and bestir themselves just as the soldier rushes to arms when the trumpet sounds. But how different is the result! The only question is how to find out subterfuges for escaping. I say this in regard to the greater part; for persecution is a true touchstone by which God ascertains who are his. And few are so faithful as to be prepared to meet death boldly.

It is a kind of monstrous thing, that persons who make a boast of having heard a little of the gospel, can venture to open their lips to give utterance to such quibbling. Some will say, What do we gain by confessing our faith to obstinate people who have deliberately resolved to fight against God? Is not this to cast pearls before swine? As if Jesus Christ had not distinctly declared, (Matt. viii. 38,) that he wishes to be confessed among the perverse and malignant. If they are not instructed thereby, they will at all events remain confounded; and hence confession is an odour of a sweet smell before God, even though it be deadly to the reprobate. There are some who say, What will our death profit? Will it not rather prove an offence? As if God had left them the choice of dying when they should see it good and find the occasion opportune. On the contrary, we approve our obedience by leaving in his hand the profit which is to accrue from our death.

In the *first* place, then, the Christian man, wherever he may be, must resolve, notwithstanding of dangers or threatenings, to walk in simplicity as God has commanded. Let him guard as much as he can against the ravening of the wolves, but let it not be with carnal craftiness. Above all, let him place his life in the hands of God. Has he done so? Then if he happens to fall into the hands of the enemy, let him think that God, having so arranged, is pleased to have him for one of the witnesses of his Son; and therefore that he has no means of drawing back without breaking faith with him to whom we have promised all duty in life and in death—him whose we are and to whom we belong, even though we should have made no promise.

they believe, even should they be required to do so. I am aware also of the measure observed by St. Paul, although no man was ever more determined boldly to maintain the cause of the gospel as he ought. And hence it is not without cause our Lord promises to give us, on such an occasion, " a mouth and wisdom;" (Luke xxi. 15;) as if he had said, that the office of the Holy Spirit is not only to strengthen us to be bold and valiant, but also to give us prudence and discretion, to guide us in the course which it will be expedient to take.

The substance of the whole is, that those who are in such distress are to ask and obtain such prudence from above, not following their own carnal wisdom, in searching out for a kind of loop-holes by which to escape. There are some who tell us that our Lord himself gave no answer to those who interrogated him. But I rejoin, *First*, That this does not abolish the rule which he has given us to make Confession of our Faith when so required. (1 Peter iii. 15.) *Secondly*, That he never used any disguise to save his life: and, *Thirdly*, That he never gave an answer so ambiguous, as not to embody a sufficient testimony to all that he had to say; and that, moreover, he had already satisfied those who came to interrogate him anew, with the view not of obtaining information, but merely of laying traps to ensnare him.

Let it be held, then, as a fixed point among all Christians, that they ought not to hold their life more precious than the testimony to the truth, inasmuch as God wishes to be glorified thereby. Is it in vain that he gives the name of WITNESSES (for this is the meaning of the word *Martyr*) to all who have to answer before the enemies of the faith? Is it not because he wishes to employ them for such a purpose? Here every one is not to look for his fellow, for God does not honour all alike with the call. And as we are inclined so to look, we must be the more on our guard against it. Peter having heard from the lips of our Lord Jesus, (John xxi. 18,) that he should be led in his old age where he would not, asked, What was to become of his companion John? There is not one amongst us who would not readily have put

contrary, Jesus Christ exhorts all of us in common, and each of us in particular, to hold ourselves "ready," in order that according as he shall call this one or that one, we may march forth in our turn.

I explained above how little prepared we shall be to suffer martyrdom, if we be not armed with the Divine PROMISES. It now remains to shew somewhat more fully WHAT THE PURPORT AND AIM OF THESE PROMISES ARE—not to specify them all in detail, but to shew the principal things which God wishes us to hope from him, to console us in our afflictions. Now these things, taken summarily, are three. The *first* is, THAT INASMUCH AS OUR LIFE AND DEATH ARE IN HIS HAND, HE WILL SO PRESERVE US BY HIS MIGHT THAT NOT A HAIR WILL BE PLUCKED OUT OF OUR HEADS WITHOUT HIS LEAVE. Believers, therefore, ought to feel assured into whatever hands they may fall, that God is not divested of the guardianship which he exercises over their persons. Were such a persuasion well imprinted on our hearts, we should be delivered from the greater part of the doubts and perplexities which torment us and obstruct us in our duty.

We see tyrants let loose: thereupon it seems to us that God no longer possesses any means of saving us, and we are tempted to provide for our own affairs as if nothing more were to be expected from him. On the contrary, his Providence, as he unfolds it, ought to be regarded by us as an impregnable fortress. Let us labour, then, to learn the full import of the expression, that our bodies are in the hands of him who created them. For this reason he has sometimes delivered his people in a miraculous manner, and beyond all human expectation, as Shedrach, Meshach, and Abednego, from the fiery furnace, Daniel from the den of lions, Peter from Herod's prison, where he was locked in, chained, and guarded so closely. By these examples he meant to testify that he holds our enemies in check, although it may not seem so, and has power to withdraw us from the midst of death when he pleases: Not that he always does it; but in reserving authority to himself to dispose of us for life and

with whatever fury they may rush against us, it belongs to him alone to order our life.

If he permits tyrants to slay us, it is not because our life is not dear to him, and in greater honour an hundred times than it deserves. Such being the case, having declared by the mouth of David, (Psalm cxvi. 13,) that the death of the saints is precious in his sight, he says also by the mouth of Isaiah, (xxvi. 21,) that the earth will discover the blood which seems to be concealed. Let the enemies of the gospel, then, be as prodigal as they will of the blood of Martyrs, they shall have to render a fearful account of it even to its last drop! In the present day, they indulge in proud derision while consigning believers to the flames; and after having bathed in their blood, they are intoxicated by it to such a degree as to count all the murders which they commit mere festive sport. But if we have patience to wait, God will shew in the end that it is not in vain he has taxed our life at so high a value. Meanwhile, let it not offend us that it seems to confirm the gospel, which in worth surpasses heaven and earth!

To be better assured that God does not leave us as it were forsaken in the hands of tyrants, let us remember the declaration of Jesus Christ, when he says (Acts ix. 4) that he himself is persecuted in his members. God had indeed said before, by Zechariah, (Zech. ii. 8,) "He who touches you touches the apple of mine eye:" But here it is said much more expressly, that if we suffer for the gospel, it is as much as if the Son of God were suffering in person. Let us know, therefore, that Jesus Christ must forget himself before he can cease to think of us when we are in prison, or in danger of death for his cause; and let us know that God will take to heart all the outrages which tyrants commit upon us, just as if they were committed on his own Son.

Let us now come to the *second* point which God declares to us in his promise for our consolation. It is, that he *will so sustain us by the energy of his Spirit that our enemies, do what they may, even with Satan at their head, will gain*

which appears in the martyrs abundantly and beautifully demonstrates that God works in them mightily. In persecution there are two things grievous to the flesh, the Vituperation and insult of men, and the Tortures which the body suffers. Now, God promises to hold out his hand to us so effectually, that we shall overcome both by patience. What he thus tells us he confirms by fact. Let us take this buckler, then, to ward off all fears by which we are assailed, and let us not confine the working of the Holy Spirit within such narrow limits as to suppose that he will not easily surmount all the cruelties of men.

Of this we have had, among other examples, one which is particularly memorable. A young man who once lived with us here, having been apprehended in the town of Tournay, was condemned to have his head cut off if he recanted, and to be burned alive if he continued steadfast to his purpose! When he was asked, What he meant to do? he replied simply, " He who will give me grace to die patiently for his Name, will surely give me grace to bear the fire!" We ought to take this expression not as that of a mortal man, but as that of the Holy Spirit, to assure us that God is not less powerful to strengthen us, and render us victorious over tortures, than to make us submit willingly to a milder death. Moreover, we oftentimes see what firmness he gives to unhappy malefactors who suffer for their crimes. I speak not of the hardened, but of those who derive consolation from the grace of Jesus Christ, and by this means, with a peaceful heart, undergo the most grievous punishment which can be inflicted. One beautiful instance is seen in the thief who was converted at the death of our Lord. Will God, who thus powerfully assists poor criminals when enduring the punishment of their misdeeds, be so wanting to his own people, while fighting for his cause, as not to give them invincible courage?

The *third* point for consideration in the promises which God gives his Martyrs is, *The fruit which they ought to hope for from their sufferings, and in the end, if need be, from*

stancy—they will be gathered together with the Lord Jesus into his immortal glory. But as we have above spoken of this at some length, it is enough here to recall it to remembrance. Let believers, then, learn to lift up their heads towards the crown of glory and immortality to which God invites them, that thus they may not feel reluctant to quit the present life for such a recompense; and, to feel well assured of this inestimable blessing, let them have always before their eyes the conformity which they thus have to our Lord Jesus Christ; beholding death in the midst of life, just as he, by the reproach of the cross, attained to THE GLORIOUS RESURRECTION, wherein consists all our felicity, joy, and triumph!

Third Homily or Sermon,

Shewing how highly Believers ought to prize the Privilege of being in the Church of God, where they are at Liberty to Worship him Purely.

> "I have asked one thing of God, and it will I seek after—to dwell in the house of the Lord all the days of my life, to see the beauty of the Lord, and behold his temple."—PSALM xxvii. 4.

WE find a strange diversity in the wishes of men; and yet there is one point in which they all agree and are alike. It is in finding their amusement here below in the world. Every one has, indeed, his own end, his own particular method; but in all quarters this vanity prevails, the vanity of seeking wellbeing and felicity only in this corruptible life. This shews that men are in a very degraded state: for we were created for a quite contrary end, namely, while living in the world, to aspire to the kingdom of God; and this is the reason why the present life is termed a passage or path. Wherefore, in the case of every one who would not of his own accord defraud himself of the eternal heritage of God, the point at which he must begin is by cutting off all foolish and fickle desires which might tend to engross him and bind him to this world, that his principal desire may be to go to God, and there may be nothing to hinder him at least from tending thither. I say *at least*, inasmuch as it were very requisite that all earthly affections, which do nothing but distract us from God, were completely plucked out of our hearts, so that we might be able to speed quickly in the journey which we have to make.

But because we are far from possessing such purity, it

that in the midst of our weaknesses we may nevertheless prefer the heavenly life to all that the world can bestow. The next thing then is, to CONSIDER WHAT THE MEANS ARE WHICH MAY ENABLE US TO SUCCEED.

Now, it does not belong to us to devise means. We must take the means which God has appointed, and of these the principal are here mentioned by David, namely, THE ORDER AND GOVERNMENT WHICH GOD HAS ESTABLISHED IN HIS CHURCH; or, to express it otherwise, that we be taught by his word—that we worship him with one accord, and call upon his name—and that we have the use of the Sacraments to assist us herein. Such is the way in which we must exercise ourselves in order to be more and more confirmed in the faith, in the fear of God, in holiness, in contempt of the world, and in the love of the heavenly life.

Accordingly, it is with a view to this David declares that he desires above all things to dwell in the temple of God. For under the term *Temple* he comprehends THE LIBERTY OF WORSHIPPING GOD PURELY WITH THE FAITHFUL, of making a Confession of Faith, Praying, and Partaking of the Sacraments. At this time God had chosen a certain place where men should offer sacrifice and pay homage to him, accompanied with the declaration, that they held him to be the only God; where they might be instructed in his Law, and behold the symbols of his presence. And, in fact, he sufficiently explains what he has in view in desiring to dwell in the temple, when he adds, that it is to see the beauty of God. Herein he shews that the temple was nothing in itself, and that his attention was fixed on the use to which it was devoted. Did we imagine that he was amused with a material building, we should do him much wrong and injury, for then his wishes might be imputed to superstition and not ascribed to virtue. We must hold it certain then, that he is declaring the high value which he sets on the external order by which the faithful are brought into the Church. In one word, he intimates, that it is an inestimable blessing and privilege to be in the Church of God, so as to

Let us observe well who it is that speaks. It is not a poor, ignorant, coarse, and illiterate individual, but a Prophet as excellent and as much illumined by the Holy Spirit as any one that has ever existed. He speaks not of what is useful and good for the common herd of men, but he declares in regard to himself, that there is nothing he more desires than to be able to attend the assembly of the people of God, to the end that he may be always more and more edified by the doctrine of salvation which is there preached, and by the sacraments. Nor does he make this protestation here only, but in many other passages, as in the preceding Psalm, (Psalm xxvi. 8,) when he says, " O Lord, I have loved the habitation of thy house, and the place where thy glory has its abode." Again, (Psalm xlii. 1, 2,) " As the hart longs to refresh itself in the water, so my soul longs after thee, O God; my soul burns with thirst in seeking God. When will it be that I shall come to appear before the face of the living God?"

It was surely enough to have said thus much, but his desire transports him still higher, for he adds, that he had fed upon tears while he was deprived of the privilege of coming to the temple. He adds, moreover, that his heart melted away when he thought of the time when he went to the temple, praising God among the body of the faithful. After groaning deeply, stating his plaint, and giving utterance to his regret, he finds no better consolation than the hope which he entertains that God will restore to him the privilege which he had lost. He exclaims, (Psalm lxxxiv. 12,) " My soul, why art thou troubled, and why art thou so tumultuous within me? I shall yet again see the face of the Lord." He repeats the same thing in Psalm xliii.; but the strength of his feelings on the subject is most forcibly declared in Psalm lxxxiv. For, after exclaiming that his heart and his body thrill with the eager desire he had to enter the courts of the Lord, he adds the reason, that " those who dwell in the house of God are happy, because they praise him;" that is, because with one accord they

Seeing that David, who was so far advanced in all holiness, and was even as an angel of heaven dwelling in the world, felt he had so great need of being aided and stimulated by the means of grace which God has given to his people, I would ask, In what case must we be—we who are so rude and so earthly, whose faith is so small, and whose devotion is so meagre and cold? We might easily conclude, that even though David, from the perfection to which he had attained, should have been able to dispense with such inferior aids, yet to us, considering our infirmity, they are more than necessary. But then, those who are the most perfect are much better acquainted with their deficiency than those who have made no progress at all. Is David richly endowed with evangelical virtues? That only makes him feel with greater force how requisite it is for him to be more inflamed by the preaching of the Law, by the Sacraments, and by other similar exercises. On the other hand, those worthless boasters, who in the present day hold all those things in no account, shew plainly that they are not imbued with one particle of Christianity.

The persons I refer to are the Closet Philosophers who live under the Papacy. It is rather odd, they say, if one cannot be a Christian without trotting to Geneva to have one's ears stuffed with sermons, and to use the ceremonies which are practised there! Cannot we read and pray to God apart by ourselves? is there any necessity for going into a Church to be taught, while each has the Scriptures in his own house? To this my answer is, that we do not lay down a law for any one to stir from the place where he is. Nay, when a man will live purely, and serve God as he ought in the midst of the Papal tyranny, I prize him a hundred times more, other things being equal, than ourselves, who are at liberty and in repose.

But here two questions are to be considered; *first*, Whether they who, feeling their infirmity, come and seek in a Christian Church such confirmation as David in his time attributed to the Temple of Jerusalem, do not do well?

destitute of the ordinary means which were to conduct them to God? Beasts which have no reason will bray for their pasture; and will those, who call themselves "children of God," feel no anxiety for that which is to nourish and maintain their faith? Nay, not contented with disdainfully trampling these precious gifts of God under their feet, they jeer at those who run into a foreign land to seek and enjoy them. In regard to their pride, which makes them imagine that Sermons, Public Prayers, and the Sacraments, are to them a kind of superfluous things, no other evidence is necessary to condemn them and banish them from the Church of God.

Accordingly, Paul does not say that the Order which our Lord has put into his Church is merely for the rude and simple, but he makes it common to all, without excepting a single individual. He says, (Eph. iv. 11,) "He has ordained Apostles, Pastors, and Teachers, for the establishment of the saints, for the edification of the body of Christ, till we all come in the unity of faith, to a perfect man, to the measure of the full age of Christ." Observe well, it is not said that God has left the Scriptures for every one to read, but has appointed a government that there may be persons to teach; under this comprehending all the rest, which in a manner depend upon it. Though an individual reads in private, that does not hinder him from listening in public. And whom does he address? Great and small indifferently. Does he say that it is for one day? On the contrary, he commands the same course to be followed until death; for now is the time of our complete preparation. Those then who deign not to rank themselves with those who are to profit in all faith and virtue by the common order of the Church, could not take a more effectual means of cutting themselves off from the company of the children of God! It is vain to cavil. The declaration of St. Paul is too manifest, (Eph. iv. 4,) that no man belongs to the body of Christ, or should be kept in it, who does not submit to the general rule. Wherefore, brethren, let us humble ourselves,

But some one will say, Possibly David was speaking with reference to the time of figures; because God then governed his people after the fashion of little children, as St. Paul says, (Gal. iv. 3,) and therefore his longings after the Temple are not applicable to us in the present day, seeing we are compared to those who have ceased to be children, and have become full-grown men. To this I answer, in the first place, that the necessity of being instructed by Sermons, confirmed by the Sacraments, and exercised by Public Prayers and Confession of Faith, is common to us with the Fathers of old. And to this effect are the numerous Promises which occur principally in the prophet Isaiah, where God says, (Isaiah lx. 4,) that his Church will have an infinite number of children, and that after she has conceived and borne she will nourish them. It cannot be denied that this is applicable to the kingdom of Jesus Christ and to our time.

God expressly sends his children into the bosom of the Church. Why so? Just because this is the order he has established whereby to gather together his children as it were by flocks. This is very well expressed by a fine similitude which the same prophet employs, saying, (Isaiah lx. 8,) that Christians will be like pigeons returning in flights to their dove-cot. And what, pray, is this dove-cot, but just every place where the Word of God is preached, where the Sacraments are administered, and the name of God is proclaimed? In fact, those who imagine themselves so robust as to have no need of this external guidance, take a very wrong view of their condition. For why has God given us the SACRAMENTS, but just because clothed with our bodies we are too dull and heavy to apprehend spiritual things, without being aided by visible signs? Angels, it is true, have the reality which the Sacraments figure, and that suffices them; but God must come lower down to us, because of our rudeness. Let imaginative Christians divest themselves of their bodies, and make themselves angels of heaven, and then they will be able to dispense with those little helps of which they make such small account.

Has he the means of plunging into all kinds of pleasures? He still remains steady to his purpose—his true happiness is in having access to the Temple, to participate in the service of the Church.

We see, therefore, that it was not without reason David declared that he had asked "one thing;" for so dear was it to him that he would at any time have given all the rest in exchange for it. Let us now consider who among us has such discretion as David. Will those who are satisfied with the good which is in their hands, prize the liberty of being able to call purely upon the Name of God, of hearing his Word preached, and of using the Sacraments more than their domestic repose? There are very few who do so: nay rather, their fat makes them sleepy, or they only think of making good cheer. In short, the fashion now-a-days is to prize a well-stocked larder more than the Temple of God!

If we speak of troublous times coming, every one will fear to be pillaged by war, to suffer damage, molestation, and annoyance; but as to losing the preaching of the doctrine of Salvation, the use of the Sacraments, and such helps as are given us to draw near to God, they make no mention of it; and, accordingly, we perceive not that those who are deprived of such privileges give themselves much concern. If their income does not last them out the whole year, and keep up such a style as their ambition longs for, if their gains and traffic are diminished, if their credit decays, they torment themselves out of all measure; and yet the ordinary nourishment of the children of God (the want of which ought to make them feel as if famished) is a mere nothing to them! God, however, plainly shews by the threatening which he denounces, that no worse evil can befall us: He says, (Amos viii. 11,) "I will send them a famine, not of bread or of water, (as if he had said, that were a small matter,) but of hearing my Word!" Wherefore, brethren, let us beware of allowing ourselves to be stupified by Satan and the world, and let us always hold this privilege in estimation above all others—the privilege of being entertained

This is still more strongly expressed by what David adds: He will "seek after" the thing which he has asked. Hereby he intimates that he has not had a sudden fit of devotion, which will by and bye cool away, but that he has been, and will be constant in the pursuit of this blessing. We see some persons whose affections for a short time are so lively, that to all appearance they are ready to quit all things to-morrow; but the constancy of which David speaks is a rare quality. Nay, the great majority, instead of stirring the fire to kindle up the good zeal with which God has inspired them, extinguish it of their own accord.

We have a similar testimony to David's zeal in another Psalm, which I have already quoted. Because it might have been alleged that though he was chased from the land of Judea, there were many other places to which he might retire, he exclaims, (Psalm lxxxiv. 4,) "Thy altars, O Lord of hosts, my God and my King!" As if he had said, he could find no place delightful, although he possessed all the palaces of the world, while he had no admission to the Temple of God. He complains that the sparrows and swallows there find a place to make their nests, and that he is worse off than they. How so? Is it because he has neither room nor kitchen? He does not allege that, but he finds no good nor proper dwelling, seeing he is kept back from the altars of God.

It is very certain that if this doctrine had gained an entrance into our heart, we would not be as we are—some irregular, and others totally abandoned in regard to the means which God has placed in our hands to forward us in the path of everlasting life. What! some from ambition cling to high estates and dignities, or are stimulated to acquire them; others are inflamed and hurried along by avarice; many have nothing at heart but their pleasures and giddy delights. All have their desires and longings, but yet none exclaims, Thy altars, O Lord! where are thy altars, my God, my King? And, in fact, worldly vanities rule too strongly over them to allow God to be obeyed.

easy to make such a fair show before men as to make it be imagined that we are all on flame. But here David shews a way by which a man will be able to say that he sincerely desires to belong to the flock, I mean, by continuing to have the longing when he has God only for witness. When we come before such a Judge all hypocrisy must cease, and there must be nothing but truth and plain dealing. Would we then follow the example of David? Let each retire into his own conscience, and laying his case before God, say, "Lord, thou knowest how I prize the privilege of being in thy house above all worldly blessings!"

Moreover, we are here admonished not to keep champing the bit by confining ourselves to groans and lamentations. We must send up our sighs directly to him who can relieve our distress. In fact, we ought to understand that the fearful confusion prevailing at present throughout the world, in that the whole service of God is corrupted, the Word of God falsified, the Sacraments bastardized, is a just punishment for our sins! To whom then shall we have recourse to enjoy pure doctrine and Sacraments, and liberty to call upon the Name of God, and make Confession of our Faith, but to him who chastises us by depriving us of these blessings?

But let not the rigour of God's chastisements have the effect of dissuading us from going to him: far less let it have the effect of making us kick against the pricks, and disdain to seek the cure at the hands of him who makes the sore. David assuredly knew very well that he was not banished from the land of Judea without the Providence of God, and yet he fails not to go to him and lay his complaints before him: not that he did not feel it to be a hard and heavy trial to see himself banished apparently by God. But the faith which he has in the promise which had been made to him, raises his thoughts upward to supplicate God that he would restore for ever what he has taken from him for a time.

Methinks I have already sufficiently applied the doctrine of the text to ourselves, and the circumstances of the present

been minced and minced again into minute fragments! Though, to say the truth, it is neither rudeness nor obscurity of doctrine that hinders them, but they twist themselves about in search of all possible and imaginary subterfuges to darken that which in itself is perfectly clear. This opposition to the doctrine obliges us to spread it out, and shew more fully how it applies to the present time.

I admit that there is no longer any material Temple to which we must go a pilgrimage to sacrifice to God; but that now we are his spiritual temples, and that we ought in every place to lift up pure hands to heaven. Still the injunction to invoke his Name in the company of the faithful remains in force for ever: for this forms no part of the figures of the Old Testament, but is the rule which our Lord Jesus has given us until the end of the world. Wherefore, although we differ from David in regard to the Temple of Zion and the sacrifices, we are like him in that we have to pray to God in common, and assemble together to make Confession of our Faith.

It is very true that we are no longer like little children kept under the tutelage of the Law of Moses, but are men, and will continue so till God shall take us away out of the world. Hence, although the shadows and figures which existed in the time of David are no longer applicable to us, it is still necessary for us to be urged and led by the preaching of the gospel and by the Sacraments. If any one maintains the contrary, experience alone is required to confute him: for the ablest make it abundantly manifest how necessary it is that God aid their weakness.

The point we are now discussing is not, Whether God can conduct his people without any inferior means, but How he is pleased to conduct them? Now, it is certain that, seeing our weakness, he has given us a kind of props or staves for support. What folly is it then, I ask, when we feel our limbs failing, to refuse to lay hold of props, as if they could not be of any use to us! Let us understand, then, that whatever difference there may be between us and the Jews,

things external as that he cannot when he pleases act without any medium, but here we treat of the perpetual order which he has established in his Church, and not of what he does extraordinarily by miracle. Those, therefore, who are deprived of the use of the Sacraments, and of the liberty of being able to call upon his name, and feel not their misfortune and misery so as to groan over them, are more stupid than the brutes!

I say, moreover, that if David in his time had just cause to say, (Psalm lxxxiv. 2, 3, 5,) " O Lord, how desirable thy Temple is! Happy those who dwell in thy house! My soul is on flame with the desire which it has to enter the courts of the Lord," we in the present day ought to be doubly moved and inflamed. For what were the blessings of the Temple which David regretted so much, as to be weary of his life when he saw himself deprived of them? No doubt, in substance they were those which we have in the present day, but we know that they were obscure shadows, in which God did not display his grace with anything like the fulness in which we have it at present.

God manifests himself to us so familiarly in the order of his Church, that the heavens, so to speak, are opened to us. The Sacraments do not shew us Jesus Christ from a distance, as under the law, but set him before our eyes. We must, therefore, be very ungrateful if we do not prefer these blessings to all that David could find of old in the Temple of Zion. We are no longer in the Court, as David terms it. There is no veil hung up to keep us at a distance from the Sanctuary. In one word, we shew very little respect to the infinite magnitude of the blessings which God bestows upon us, when at the very least our longing is not equal to that of David. This I say merely by way of doctrine. The application will come afterwards in its own place.

It remains to see more distinctly WHAT THIS LONGING WAS, that we may conform to it as our rule. " One thing," he says, " have I asked of the Lord." In speaking of one thing only, he intimates that he was so strongly attached to it,

of all his wishes, and that this was the only point in which he was deficient? On the contrary, he was a fugitive from the land of his birth, banished even from his father's house, and the society of his relations and friends; he was stript of all his goods, deprived of all his offices and honours, which had been great; he had been robbed of his wife. In short, here is a man who is desolate in everything and in every respect, and yet it is the want of one thing only that he regrets—that of access to the Temple. On the other hand, when he thanks God for all the blessings which he has bestowed upon him, (Psalm xxiii. 6,) after speaking of eating and drinking, of rest and bodily convenience, he sums up the whole with saying that he will "dwell in the Temple of God," thereby declaring that though at his ease and in possession of all luxuries, he has nothing more precious than the privilege of going with the body of the faithful, and thereby being conducted to the sovereign good.

Observe well, then, that David alike in his afflictions and in his prosperity, always displayed the same courage in endeavouring to enjoy the privilege which God had given to the children of Israel; and this is no small virtue. We see some persons who, when pressed with misfortune and in anguish, will remember God; but the moment they are delivered and find themselves at their ease, his name is no more mentioned. What is worse, they kick against him like horses too well fed. Others are so annoyed and feel so despitefully towards God in their adversity, that they cannot bear to hear him spoken of. Is David cast down into such depths of poverty that he is to all appearance the most miserable creature in the world?—so far is he from being so overpowered by distress as to be annoyed and disdainful when others speak to him of God, that it is the only subject in which he finds consolation! Even though he cannot think of God without lamenting his being banished from his Temple, and shut out from the use of the Sacraments, and the other exercises of faith, he has no greater pleasure than in expressing regret for the loss. Has he surmounted all his

are no longer tied to a particular spot. The view which David took of the matter touches us no less than it did him. It is true that the haughty and arrogant care little about assembling to hear Sermon, to engage in Public Prayer, and receive the Sacraments; but this is the fault of not examining their consciences. On our part, independent of the ordinance which God has made on the subject, let it be enough for us that he is pleased to maintain our faith by such humble means; and, moreover, as we have said, that we are sensible of the benefit which we derive from them.

Be this as it may, since St. Paul declares that the way to come to perfection is to observe the Order which Christ established in the Church when he gave some pastors, cursed be the extravagance and presumption of those who would leap into the air, and pretend to mount to heaven by their speculations, despising both Sermons and the use of the Sacraments, as if they were external things, and not very requisite! Observe, brethren, of what people I speak. I acknowledge that God guards his own people under the captivity of Antichrist, although they are destitute of the aids which are free to us here. The Word of God is not preached to them, they have no place where it is permitted them to make Confession of their Faith; the Sacraments are taken from them; but because in separating themselves from the abominations of Antichrist, they sigh and regret that they have not that which would be of so much advantage, God works in them by the energy of his Spirit, and supplies what is wanting.

But there are persons who, being for the most part in such desolate circumstances, nevertheless take pleasure in it, and though famished have no appetite. I mean the persons who counterfeit philosophers; persons who, contenting themselves with reading three or four pages on a subject, say that they know everything about it that is necessary to be known! Such persons (so it seems to them) have no need of being preached to. As to the Supper, it is all one whether they ever approach it. As to the External Order

I ask, Must not such persons be more than blind? And yet they will blame us for exhorting those to whom our Lord has manifested his truth, to use means which God ordains for the increase, preservation, and perseverance of our faith. And why so, but just because they are annoyed at being awakened to a sense of their own destitution? Assuming that they do not commit idolatry with the Papists, is it not an accursed bondage not to be able to confess the name of God and of Jesus Christ? The Holy Spirit, wishing to prick the hearts of the faithful who were captive in Babylon, puts the following words into their mouths:—(Psalm cxxxvii. 4,) " How shall we sing the praises of the Lord in a strange land?" I admit that, in the present day, the kingdom of God is everywhere, and that there is no longer any distinction between Judea and other countries: Still, however, I hold that the country in which the service of God is abolished, and religion annihilated, well deserves to be regarded as strange and profane. Those, then, who feel no regret at not daring to make profession of their faith, and celebrate the Name of God, must be devoid of feeling. Let the children of God be warned by this remonstrance, not to fall, of their own accord, into the same state.

As to the jeering prattle of those who, making a mock of us, say that " No man can get to Paradise without going the way of Geneva!" I answer, that would to God they had the courage to assemble themselves in the name of Jesus Christ, wherever they may be, and set up some form of Church, as well in their own houses as in those of their neighbours, in order to do in their own place what we do here in our Churches! But what? Not deigning to use means which God gives them, they wish to be saved. It is therefore just the same as if they were to ask, whether they may not reach the harbour by sailing in an opposite course; and whether, while tempting God, they cannot enjoy his grace? Now, let them make themselves as great and strong as they will to break their own necks, but let all believers beware of climbing up along with them, and whoever has not the means of being in the

thing but thy altars do I desire, my God and King!" Let this fire remain always kindled in all good hearts; in order that, whatever happens, they may not weary of being thus treated, nor be cooled by length of time, nor cease from always desiring to be brought into the fold. Moreover, let each be on the alert quickly to avail himself of instruction the moment our Lord may furnish the means: for this is the way to shew that we are not feigning when we request to dwell in the house of the Lord.

It remains now, in conclusion, to attend to what David adds, viz., that HE WILL SEE THE BEAUTY OF THE LORD, AND BEHOLD HIS TEMPLE; for we do not at all exercise ourselves with the faithful, in all the external Order of the Church, if we do not make it our constant aim to know God better and better. Here two things are requisite,—the one is, That we be diligent in our attendance on the Public Sermons and Prayers; and second is, That we know why; for there are many who come with a foolish devotion, imagining that they have acquitted themselves well by merely shewing their faces in the church. Let us be on our guard, then, brethren, for there is a danger that the majority may find themselves condemned in regard to both.

How many are there who shun Sermons, and would be very glad never to have mention made of them! But I pass by those who shew themselves out and out despisers of God. I speak only of the contempt or indifference which many shew who would never think of coming to Sermon, if it were not Sunday; and yet it is only by way of acquittance, as if they had a running account with God! The bell tolls every day, but it is enough for them to appear every eight days. The Sunday summons them to church four times; but they think they do well if they appear only once, as there are some who deem every second Sunday sufficient. In short, the great body verify the old proverb, "*Near the church and far from God!*" Of those, even, who have forsaken their country to come hither and serve God, there are some whose conduct is abundantly lax.

sight of THE PROPER MODE OF CONTEMPLATING. We must be enraptured with admiration of it, and transformed into its likeness, as St. Paul says. (2 Cor. iii. 18.) And to be so it behoves us to be more attentive than we are, or have been accustomed to be, in considering what God sets before us in his temple. For why is it that we derive so little benefit from Sermons and Sacraments, but just that we give no attentive heed to what is said and done? Thus our ears are beaten, but our hearts are no way touched. Moreover, there are many who do not listen to a Sermon out and out, but only to bits of it in passing here and there.

Wherefore, it is not without cause that David speaks of being attentive in visiting the Temple of the Lord. And, in fact, the great treasures of Divine wisdom which are there set before us well deserve to fix and engage our attention. Now, as I have already hinted, God does not wish us to look and then come away empty. Let us know, then, that we have profited by the doctrine when we are duly trained to serve God. This is what David means in the eighty-fourth Psalm, in the passage already quoted, "Those who dwell in the house of God will praise him." (Psalm lxxxiv. 5.) For what purpose do we assemble? Why is the gospel preached to us? Why have we Baptism and the Supper, but just that the Lord may be magnified in us? Now, this magnifying or praise does not lie merely at the tip of the tongue, but extends over the whole life; and hence it is said in another passage, (Psalm xxvi. 6,) "I will wash my hands in integrity, O Lord; then will I go to thy altar."

We now see the true use of the whole Order of the Church; it is, that we may serve God purely. In the time of the law, those who came to worship in the Temple, and the priests who entered to perform their office, washed themselves. The ceremony is abolished, but we ought to retain the reality. Inasmuch as we have the means of going in to the service of God, we ought to walk with more integrity than others; for the more the assistance which God gives us, the less is our excuse if we do not make it available. If

cient light; if we forget our duty, it is not for want of being urged to it. In short, God omits no method of advancing our salvation.

Let us, therefore, fear the reproach which God utters by his prophet Isaiah, (Isaiah lxv. 2,) "All day have I stretched out my hands to this rebellious people." If those who are wandering in the deserts of the Papacy will not be spared when they do not walk aright, what, I ask, will become of us who are brought up as it were in the house, under the eyes of our heavenly Father? Some have quitted the land of their nativity to form themselves into a Christian Church; others have been more favourably dealt with, in that God has come and visited them in their own home. Now, if those who are natives of the place do not in acknowledgment of the great privilege dedicate themselves entirely to God who has thus drawn near to them, will such ingratitude remain unpunished? Rather, let them say, "Lord, thou hast built thy Temple and dressed thy Altar in the midst of us; be graciously pleased, then, to purify us, that we may not by our defilements pollute thy holy gifts, and that we may not turn the glory of thy benefits into a reproach."

As to those who have come from distant lands, let them take heed to conduct themselves holily, as in the house of God. It had been easy for them to lead a life of dissipation elsewhere, and they had no occasion to move one foot from the Papacy if their object was to follow a dissolute course. And in fact there are some who had far better have had a millstone about their necks than have set foot in this Church to behave so ill as they do! Some connect themselves with scoffers to harden them in their wickedness; others will be gluttons and drunkards; others seditious and noisy. There are households where husbands and wives live like dogs and cats. There are some who swell out their means; and counterfeiting lords, without any ground for it, give themselves up to worldly pomp and luxury. Others become so delicate that they no longer know what work is,

to say against the angels of heaven; and while besmeared with their own vices make all their holiness consist in throwing out scandal against their neighbours. Meanwhile, they all seem to think that God is under great obligation to them, because " they have made the journey to Geneva !" as if it would not have been far better had they remained where they were, instead of coming to cause such scandal in the Church of God.

Now, in so far as there has been anything wrong before, let every one in his own particular case endeavour to amend it; and if there are some persons altogether incorrigible, let the children of God provide themselves with this doctrine, so as not to be infected by their bad lives. We cannot help feeling when we see the Church of God thus profaned. But since we must be like good grain amongst chaff, let us exercise patience till such time as God shall separate us from the counsel of the ungodly. There also can be no doubt that our Church here is a kind of touchstone by which many are to be proved. Be this as it may, let us strive, since God has been pleased to gather us into his family, to conduct ourselves with all purity, renouncing all worldly pollution, in order that the Lord Jesus may acknowledge us ON THE GREAT DAY, and count us in the number of those who have borne his Name unfeignedly.

Fourth Homily or Sermon,

Shewing what Pains we ought to take to Secure the Liberty of Serving God Purely in the Christian Church.

" My heart said of thee, Seek my face; I will seek thy face, O Lord."
PSALM xxvii. 8.

As men plunge into strange confusion by giving loose reins to their appetites and wishes, so they shew great wisdom when they inquire into what God commands them with the view of following it. Of this we have here a fine example. David was indeed a man subject to the very passions by which we are tormented and tossed about, and there is no doubt that he was urged by many temptations which were apt to lead him far astray. But to have a remedy for all occasions of backsliding and obtain sure guidance, he fixes his eye on what God shews him, and meditates and ruminates thereon.

The substance is, that GOD INVITES AND EXHORTS ALL BELIEVERS TO SEEK HIS FACE. David declares that he had made this command his study; so that there is as it were harmonious concord between God who speaks, saying, " Seek me," and him who answers, " Yes, my God, I will seek thee." We must here see, why God specially uses the term *face?* For if he had not some face in which he might manifest himself, it would be mockery to command us to seek it. I am aware that several who would be thought subtle expositors, will not allow more to be meant by this than if it were said, "Seek me:" but those who are versed in Scripture, know well that God meant to specify the method which he has observed at all times in shewing and manifesting himself privately to men. And, in fact, a very common

Because God, who is incomprehensible in his essence and his majesty, uses the means which he knows to be adapted to the infirmity and rudeness of men, in order to lead them to himself.

It is true that the world is always forging false resemblances of God; for all those which we imagine out of our own brain, are mere masks by which God is so disfigured; or, to speak more clearly, when men devise some figure or image in order to have God visible, they make nothing but an ape. But when God represents himself according to his good pleasure, and gives us signs and marks by which we may know him, he then as it were assumes a face. Thereupon he commands each of us to turn our view towards it, and be careful to keep our eye fixed upon it; for our sovereign good, and that by which we ought to be fully satisfied, is to enjoy the countenance of our God, as it is said in the sixteenth Psalm.

Now, as we cannot mount so high without a ladder, the next best blessing which he can bestow is to furnish us with the means of arriving at the first. Hence, let us observe that this passage in which God says, "Seek my face," is just as it were an opening of the door to give us an entrance into everlasting life. It was not a great thing apparently to go in the time of David to the Temple to see the many ceremonies which were there performed; but if we reflect well on the spiritual pattern which was shewn to Moses in the mount, we will not think it strange that God calls it his face. And, in fact, since Jesus Christ was there revealed, why should we not say that God was there manifested.

Let us now see WHETHER GOD HAS NOT ORDAINED SOME EXTERNAL METHOD OF BEING BEHELD BY US? It is true that he has appeared to us by his Son, who is his living image, and in whose person he wishes to be known in perfection; but St. Paul declares again and again that the gospel is the mirror in which Jesus Christ is to be beheld. (2 Cor. iv. 4.) The same thing may be affirmed of the Sacraments, and in general of the Order which God has established in his Church. Therefore let the proud boasters of this world jeer

this honour to his Word and Sacraments—to behold him there as face to face. Not that we are to be detained here below by the corruptible elements of the world, like the Papists, who make Idols of all the signs which God has given us to conduct us to Jesus Christ; but thus far, that in order one day fully to enjoy the presence of God, we must now tend towards him by these inferior means. It is true, that what I say must not be interpreted too strictly, as if believers never draw near to God except when they come to church. That were gross superstition! But I mean that we must not set God above the clouds, as some fanatics do, and there survey whatever of his high majesty we are pleased to see, casting behind the Preaching of the Gospel and all other similar means, as if we could behold his face by shutting our eyes. For, in truth, those who despise the use of the Sacraments, as well as of the whole Order of the Church, deign not to look at God when he appears to them.

Let us now consider HOW NECESSARY IT IS THAT GOD INCITE US TO COME TO HIM. We have already mentioned the great favour and honour which he confers upon us in inviting us to himself so gently, for the purpose of furthering our salvation and leading us to true and perfect felicity, from which in ourselves we are at a great distance. But we have also to observe, that it is not without real necessity God stimulates and solicits us in order to keep us from being miserable.

In the first place, It is pitiable to think how bewildered our view is; for the vanities of the world engross all our senses, and Satan employs an infinite number of illusions to deceive us. It is true that all his subtleties are mere mummeries or farcical sports, fit only to amuse fools; but experience shews how absurd and infatuated we are in yielding to their seductions. Wherefore, if we were prudent, the voice of God would always be sounding in our ears, "SEEK MY FACE." But what do I say? Just as careful as God is on his side, are we lazy and sluggish on ours. Nay, would to God we were not like restive horses which move backward when they should go on!

meditated in his heart on the doctrine that he and all believers ought to seek the face of God, shews us what we ought to study, if we would not have God to have called us to himself in vain.

Two articles worthy of notice are here conjoined. The *first* is, That when God spake, saying, SEEK MY FACE, David answered with the proper feeling in the affirmative. The *second* is, That after having so answered, he says, that he will actually employ himself in seeking the face of God. And, in fact, we have here the order in which we ought to proceed in listening and giving entrance to what God tells us, as is also shewn us in another passage in the Psalms, (Psalm xcv. 8,) " To-day, in hearing his voice, harden not your hearts." There are very few, however, who thus act. A great number, to excuse themselves, will say: Yes, it is right: It is not lawful to reply against God. But the answer which is thus given by the mouth, in few instances lodges itself in the heart.

Let us therefore learn to begin with replying, in all sincerity, that WE ARE CONSCIOUS OF THE BLESSING WHICH HE BESTOWS UPON US IN INVITING US TO SEEK HIS FACE. After this, the rest will follow as a matter of course. We will labour diligently to perform that which we know to be so justly commanded, and for our special good. For David shews that his was not a cold and lifeless meditation, which failed to move either arms or limbs. After concluding that it was necessary to seek God, he immediately commences the search, and declares that he will continue it. It is a great shame for those who call themselves Christians to fail so much in both respects.

Some will allege that *It is not lawful for them to quit their native land, although they are there destitute of the food of life, and there is nothing but desolation as regards the Order of the Church.* Why is it not lawful? Because of the duty which they owe to their natural Prince. To this I will not make a long reply. I ask, if they were unable to find either meat or drink at home, would they be detained by

die of hunger. I will put a much weaker case. Suppose that by going to a foreign land their wealth would be increased sixfold, they would have no great difficulty in determining to go and take possession! Of what use, then, is it to adduce such fallacious pretexts, since it is perfectly obvious that there is no sincerity in what they say. There is no question here about going into the land of an enemy, where they might be constrained to bear arms against their Prince, and make war upon their native country; but merely, about seeking a place to serve God peaceably, without being any way hindered from praying for their Prince and for all his subjects. In short, the retirement of which we speak is of the very same kind as that which takes place every day for the sake of worldly advantages, and is never regarded as a crime.

But let us see whether the necessity of the case does not furnish a valid excuse. On the one hand, God says, " Seek my face." On the other hand, Princes interfere and insist that men should turn their backs upon him; or, rather, they deprive poor souls of their ordinary nourishment, and instead of the face of God place before their eyes the marks of superstition! Must Princes be preferred to the living God? If they will listen to him, it were better to go a thousand leagues to see his face, when he shews it, than to hug themselves in their nest. As often, then, and in as far as Princes attempt anything to the prejudice of him who possesses sovereign authority over them, no wrong is done them in obeying him.

But apart from what I have now said, the persons so unhappily situated, abundantly shew that they have seldom thought of their condition. What is the bondage in which they are held? Were not their conscience asleep, it would be impossible for them not to be in continual distress, as if they were in the torments of Gehenna. What kind of permission have they to honour God in their households? It is not necessary to go farther. Suppose that one of them has a child born to him: his duty is to present it to God with

know that in the Papacy Baptism is so corrupted and so bedaubed with superstitions and abominations, that an infant cannot receive it without being polluted. Hence, a father cannot get his child baptized without sin. If he dispense with Baptism, the evil is as great, were it no more than the scandal which is given by rejecting the Sacrament which the Son of God has instituted. What miserable perplexity is here, where an act can neither be done nor left undone without offending God! I say no more, for this one example is one too much. Should a man have continued all his lifelong languishing thus miserably, the great assaults will take place at death, when the devil will appear with all his train. Should the poor captive have been prevented in time past from serving God from regard to his wife and family, the case is worse than ever.

Those who doubt whether it be lawful for them to quit such a slough, or rather such an abyss of hell, under pretext of the subjection which they owe to earthly Princes, completely pervert the order of nature! It is certain that the prayer which God wishes us to offer up for our Princes is conformable to the authority which he gives them over us, and to the duty which he obliges us to perform to and for them. Now St. Paul exhorts us to pray to God for kings and magistrates, in order that we may lead a peaceable life in all honesty in the fear of God. (1 Tim. ii. 2.) It follows, that the subjection due to earthly Princes is carried too far when the honour and service of the heavenly King are postponed to it.

It is true that the poor Jews were obliged to remain under the captivity of Babylon till the term which was assigned them. But let the people with whom I debate shew that we are obliged to deprive ourselves voluntarily of the spiritual blessings which God gives to his children! They feel the necessity which lies upon them—their infirmity urges them—God shews them the remedy. Is it rational to say, they must not presume to aid themselves, lest they displease those who are taking the bread out of their mouths?

abandoning the other under pretext of seeking God. Not that they are to estrange themselves from him in order to live together, but because each is bound to the utmost to labour to win over the other. Here, then, is what they ought to do. *The husband* must remonstrate with his wife, telling her how unhappy they are in being separated from the company of the faithful, in having neither Sermons nor Sacraments, which are pledges to assure us that God dwells with us. Hereupon, let him exhort her to take courage, and if he cannot gain her so soon as he could fain wish, let him not grow weary until he has gained his point. Should the wife contradict him, let him not cease to importune her until she shews herself quite obstinate. If after doing all that in him lies, he cannot longer remain, he is perfectly free: he has performed his duty, and it is not his fault that she does not follow him, as she is bound to do. Such separation is not divorce. The husband only goes before to shew his wife the way.

In regard to *the wife*, a still closer tie binds her, inasmuch as she is not the head. Hence she must endeavour by all possible means to induce her husband to set them both at liberty. After she has done everything in her power, she is not at liberty to leave him to whom she is subject, unless some persecution should arise, exposing her to manifest danger, and more especially unless the husband should, like a kind of firebrand, be pursuing her to death. In that case she does not withdraw from her husband, but flees from the evil prepared for her and the rage of her enemies, in accordance with the permission and sanction of God. In short, the violence offered her delivers her and sets her free; for it is no worldly regard that should retain either husband or wife, but solely the love which they owe each other in the Lord, binding them to attempt each other's salvation.

Let us now return and consider the high estimation in which David held the privilege of seeking the face of God in accordance with the description he also gives of it in Psalm lxxxiv., saying, that "it is better to live a single day

the life of believers cannot be too brief, provided God by his grace makes them, while living in the world, to employ themselves in serving and honouring him, in confirming themselves in his promises, and confessing his name. Should any one reply, that that may well be done in a desert, or among the enemies of the faith, I answer, that it is not without cause David makes special mention of the courts of the Temple; for he considers how necessary the Order of the Church is to all mortal men, considering their rudeness and infirmity. Were the hearts of all deeply impressed with this passage, viz., to go into a Christian Church where they might be able to die in peace, there is not one who would not readily pack up and be off. But how different is it! All desire to live here at their ease, and each according to his particular passion. This is the reason why the Temple of God is despised.

Many, moreover, are ingenious in placing disagreeable objects before their eyes to dissuade themselves from imitating the affection which David had. They say, What shall we gain by change of place? Wherever we go we shall find the fashion followed as in our own country; everything now-a-days is corrupt; everywhere are there scandals to offend, and temptations to seduce us. I admit all this; but were it a question concerning their bodies, and were they informed in what place they might find good physicians, proper remedies, and other helps, would they answer, It matters not, for one may become sick anywhere? I admit that wherever they may be they will meet with opportunities of doing wrong, and dissipation in greater or less degree. But there is a great difference between having the means which God has given to keep us right, and remedy what is wrong, and being absolutely destitute of them.

Assuming that all vices prevail equally in the world, and infect the air like a pestilence, is it not a great advantage to have the preservatives which God has ordained for his children? to have the purgatives and medicines by which he is pleased to cure us? I mean, of course, the doctrine of

which tends to stimulate and awaken us, and prevent our being poisoned by the temptations of the world. Every one knows that there is nothing of all this in the Papacy, but quite the contrary. Let us beware, then, while assistance is so necessary to us, of rejecting the assistance which God offers.

There are some persons who express their disrelish still more strongly. They say, What should we go to do in a Church where we shall see troubles and scandals that are now unknown to us? If in the places where the gospel is preached there were such a discipline as might be well fitted to edify us, and we were assured of meeting only with angels to lead us into Paradise, we would be off at once; but say we are actually arrived, we shall hear many things which will only scandalize, and see more than there is any occasion for. There will be a host of debauchees, who defame the gospel by their dissolute lives. Vanity, pomp, drunkenness, and the like, will be too much in vogue. Still worse, we shall see despisers of God so monstrous that nothing worse can be beheld in the Papacy. There will also be abuses and corruptions in the administration of justice as elsewhere. Even in Preachers themselves shall we see much that is blameworthy. Some will be indifferent, or they will be so bent on their own interest that their office will give them little concern. Still worse, there are scoffers whose only wish is to make good cheer, and who will become the accomplices of the most wicked in order to have license to live as they list.

Granting that things are ten times worse, it is still a frivolous excuse for those who bar themselves out from approaching the Church of God. Let us turn our attention to the example of David. Tell me, if in the time of Saul the administration of justice was as pure as might be wished? On the contrary, we hear the complaints which David often makes of the malice, fraud, cruelty, and pride of the king, as well as his officers. Did the Priests and Levites conduct themselves so holily that there was good cause to be satisfied? Nay, we are able to gather that a large proportion

manifest vices. Here then is the Church of God full of many corruptions, and yet David is not thereby dissuaded from entering it, nor is his longing for it cooled.

The temptation to this is marvellously strong. This I admit. For the greater the zeal which a man feels for the honour of God, the more just cause has he to feel saddened and wearied at seeing the insults which are offered to him by defiling his Church! But the remedy by which we are to get over all this is shewn us by David; and it is to "SEEK THE FACE OF GOD," and take such delight in beholding it that, in spite of all the annoyances which Satan stirs up, we can still arrive at the conclusion, that nothing is finer nor more pleasant than to dwell in the Temple where it is seen. Hence as often and to whatever extent such scandals come before us, let us remember that it is Satan who is employing his accustomed artifice to disturb our view; and thereupon let us have the wisdom not to be turned aside from looking at the face of God, which will at last be displayed to us in all its effulgence.

Poor Idolaters might put us to shame! Some one of them, after he has mispent his money, and worn his body in the toil of a foolish pilgrimage, should he on reaching the spot fall in with a landlord who fleeces him, with street bullies who offer him violence, and priests who insult him, in short, find everything in confusion, will not for that give up his devotion; for he will say that he came to see and worship the body of St. Benedict, or the Image of Our Lady, or some such relic! Shall the mere sight of some piece of carrion, or of an ape, have more power to make unbelievers adhere obstinately to their superstitions, than the face of God in inspiring us with constancy to follow what is right? We see this thing and that thing which offends us; but God recalls us to himself, and wishes that, on beholding his face, we take such pleasure in it as will enable us to bear everything else with patience.

Be it, therefore, the buckler and refuge of all true believers to keep themselves before the face of God, in spite of

no sacrifice will seem to us too great; although, to tell the truth, the great majority are impeded not so much by mental scruples, as by difficulties which only concern the body: not that the children of God have not very serious struggles in their consciences, when they find in Churches which are called Reformed, such scandals as those we have mentioned. This makes it necessary that those who are deliberating about withdrawing to the places where the gospel is preached, should be warned of the bad things which they have to meet with, that they may be prepared to resist them. Let all those who experience these strengthen themselves, and, regardless of Satan, continue to "seek the face of God."

But when all is told, it is mere distrust that retards the great majority; and as men are ingenious in inventing excuses, the rich come forward with them on the one hand, and the poor on the other. "How can it be possible for me," some wealthy worldling will say, "to divest myself of what I have? How shall I part with all my goods? I have a wife and children; we have been accustomed to be well fed without working, what shall we do in a foreign land where we have neither rent nor revenue?" On the other hand, the poor man says, "I have very little, but I have friends who are kind to me: I am accustomed to live by my labour; what shall I do in a strange land without a penny in my pocket, quite unknown, without favour or support?"

It may be that these excuses are partly true; and, at all events, without inquiring farther, I concede to all that it is a very vexatious thing to quit not merely the land of our birth, but the place to which we have become habituated. Still they are only thinking how to put obstacles in the way of their coming to God; in other words, although they do not find things so difficult as they make them, they are very glad to shelter themselves by having recourse to any kind of pretext whatever. Moreover, when they have uttered these specious complaints, they think that they have shut God's mouth, and that if he continues to urge them further, he does them great wrong, as if he were compelling them to do

in passing through parched villages and deserts on their way to the Temple of God, will dig for themselves wells or cisterns. (Psalm lxxxiv. 6.) And I believe this is sufficient answer for those who would not deliberately fight against God. Let them, then, who find themselves so beset with difficulties, that there is neither road nor path, remember that even the deserts, where not a drop of water can be found, ought not to stop their passage.

To obtain a clearer view of this matter, let us observe, *first,* That God makes his children seek him, not through verdant meadows and pleasant shady groves, but among wild and rugged paths, among dreary wastes and sandy deserts, among bleak hideous regions; and all this to exercise their faith, and prove the zeal and longing which they have to come to him. Wherefore, although we may be unable to come to God, without passing through some desert or savage tract, let us know that it is not now for the first time God deals so with his people, and let us take courage to follow those who have so long gone before us.

The *second* point to be observed is, That there ought to be such and so great ardour in the children of God, that nothing can have the effect of turning them aside when going to worship him. This is seen at present in very few; nay, almost all are so delicate that a mere straw in their way (so to speak) is sufficient all at once to bring them to a stand! "I cannot go a step farther," they will say. Why not? Because they deign not to take the trouble of surmounting the minutest obstacle. But so far from being discouraged so easily, the greatest difficulties ought not to deter us.

To make us thus bold, let us remember that God acknowledges none for his children save those who seek him in dry and barren places, and hollow out cisterns where there was not a drop of water. The meaning of this expression is, that there is scarcely any kind of annoyance which it does not behove us to endure in order to enjoy the face of God. Is there a question, then, with any as to looking out for a place where they may have the liberty to serve God and worship

they hunger and thirst by the way? still let them faint not. Let no man here jeer at me, as if I were dictating to others while sitting at my ease. It is the Spirit of God who teaches us to dig up the ground with our nails, sooner than be turned aside or kept back from coming to the Temple of God.

But if those who are in distant countries, and are, as the world would judge, shut out from all means of reaching a land where the gospel is preached, have no valid excuse, what condemnation, let me ask, must those expect who have the gospel at their door, and will not walk one step to come to Christ? Sermons are daily preached and Prayers offered, and though the gutter of a street is all that has to be passed, each one says that he has some business that keeps him at home! In short, many seem to make their happiness consist in turning away from God, for they think they have gained everything when they have discovered the most frivolous imaginable subterfuge.

Now, since we are so much inclined to remain away from God, not to say inclined to remove to a distance from him, after he has drawn near to us, let us supplicate him to strengthen us in such a manner that we may walk on boldly till we find fountains where there was nothing but drought before. And even should we fail to find this, let us hollow out cisterns, and wait for rain from heaven. If it is not the good pleasure of God to send us his aid so soon, let us still continue to pass onwards. I suppose that this will seem dark to many persons; but why so, except from want of practice? We might be preached to for a hundred thousand years, and never understand a word until we have learned by experience what is meant by a parched land, when we have to come to God! Still all believers should be familiar with this doctrine, teaching them to prepare and fortify themselves against all the trials which Satan may devise to stop them short in the path which leads to God. And, in fact, all those who employ themselves faithfully in seeking God, although they stir not from a particular spot, fail not to meet with difficult rencounters which would have the

It is pitiable, however, (as I have already observed,) that a great number of persons allow themselves to be overcome by the difficulties which they meet. They will say, indeed, that they must shew courage, and it may seem that they have deliberately resolved; but when the occasion comes their courage fails, and those who began well very often tire out at midway. The more necessary, therefore, is it for us to remember the lesson of digging wells, that is, of searching out methods, which may not be apparent, of continuing always to press onwards. Let us strive, I say, and beyond all human strength. If things do not succeed as we wish, let us not cease patiently to pursue the right path in which God has placed us. It is certain that when we invoke God with true faith, he may convert deserts into fountains of water; but still, on the other hand, it behoves us to put our own shoulders to the work; for God does not wish us to remain in a kind of stupor, without moving arms or limbs, he rather *commands* us to dig wells. Let us labour then in digging, till we have accomplished our journey.

Let us look at those poor unhappy soldiers who sell their lives at so much a month! If they are in a camp, what hardships they endure; if besieged, it is still worse: if they march through a country, neither cold, nor heat, nor wind, nor rain, impedes their progress: sometimes if they do not dig for water, they will not find a single drop. There is no toil, no privation, no mishap which they do not succeed in surmounting. And after all this is done, whether they succeed or not, they have lost their pains, inasmuch as they have only served Satan. The Son of God of his infinite goodness has elected us to be his soldiers; and we know what wages he has provided for us. How much more courageous, then, ought we to be in his service than those poor desperate men in purchasing their ruin!

Here, however, the question for consideration is not merely how many leagues each must walk from his house to a place where he may be able to worship God freely, make confession of his faith, and hear the pure doctrine of the gospel

house of God one year or more? Continuing to do so, we shall daily find new deserts; for we shall be afflicted at one time by sickness, at another by poverty; our wife or children will die; the means of serving God as formerly will be taken away; we shall be agitated by disquietudes and various troubles. Wherefore, it is requisite till our last hour that we have our hands ready to dig wells, and our nails to scratch the ground if need be.

Should any one exclaim, How then! are we not in the Temple of God? I answer, that we are to go out and in daily. We behold the face of God, but are not yet satisfied as we shall be when he shall have gathered us to himself. It is necessary, therefore, for all to apply this to their own use; and as Satan ceases not to throw obstacles in the way of all those who are tending towards God, let each obtain reinforcement to do to-morrow what he is doing to-day. For if the enemy wearies not in his endeavours to make us fall back, far less ought we to lose courage in advancing and continuing without end and without intermission to gather new strength. For this purpose, it is necessary that our heart should be deeply impressed with the same feeling which David had: "I would rather, he says, (Psalm lxxxiv. 11,) dwell in the porch of the house of God than in the tents and pavilions of the ungodly." Here he declares, that to secure the privilege of dwelling in the house of God, he cares not how much he should be humbled and abused. Consider, I pray, what his state had been. He was the king's son-in-law, and yet he is contented to be thrust back and ranked with the lowest of the people, provided he can have some little nook in the Temple. Did the same desire reign in all, they would not find so much difficulty in declaring themselves. They would not remain so long hesitating about the exchange which they have to make in leaving their home and country to come into the Church of God.

But there are very few who will and can bear to be lessened. Each would like to be carried in a sedan to worship God where it may be done freely, and would like also that

In so wishing, how do they value Christ? All they are willing to do is to employ themselves, at his request, by way of pastime, which is a very poor consideration. Although we were worth nothing, he of his infinite goodness valued us so highly, that for our salvation he spared not himself—himself, in whom the perfection of being resides! We regret to quit some corruptible good, and be made a little worse in our condition by not continuing so much at our ease as we have been. This is very far from following the course which St. Paul has pointed out to us by his own example, viz., to "count all things as loss" which hinder us from possessing Christ, (Phil. iii. 8,) and cast them away as noxious, knowing that whatever separates us from true life can only drag us to death. It is also very far from following the exhortation which Jesus Christ has given us, (Matt. xiii. 45, 46,) to sell and quit all that we have in the world for the kingdom of heaven, knowing that it is a precious jewel, more valuable than all the things which men desire and prize so much, were they a thousand times told.

Should any rejoin that it is quite possible for a man to reach the kingdom of heaven without abandoning his home; I answer, that it was not without cause Christ employed the term *"kingdom of heaven,"* to designate the preaching of the gospel. Those, then, who are altogether destitute of it, and do not make it their special business to search out all possible means of enjoying it, shew that they are far too much rivetted to the good things of this world, and are not yet disposed to exchange them for the kingdom of heaven. If they could possess both together, good and well; but if they cannot retain their possessions and hug themselves in their nest without defrauding themselves of the food of the children of God; nay, if they cannot maintain themselves in the state in which they are, their duty is to pay due regard to the necessity which God imposes on them. It is easy for them to bring forward excuses of all sorts, but what will they avail when the great Judge will thunder with dreadful voice against all those who shall have preferred the ter-

It is strange how many imagine that they close our mouths if we do not assign them some status and livelihood while they are serving God. "My circumstances," they say, "are so and so in my own country; if I leave it, what is to become of me, or how am I to be maintained?" As if God had ordained those who preach the gospel to become innkeepers, (*maitres d'hotel,*) to lodge all who come into his domains, and give each, according to his worth, board and wages! If we can help them by counsel or advice we are bound to do so, though they should not require it of us; but if it is not in our power, does it follow that we have lost the right of teaching every man what God commands? Had they learned and remembered the doctrine of David, to prefer a little corner in the porch of God's Temple to the highest and most honourable places which they might be able to choose among unbelievers, they would not find themselves in so much difficulty about taking advice. But the evil is, that they would like to keep all they have, and cannot bear to be curtailed in houses and riches, or deprived of ease and luxury: in other words, they cannot bend their necks and stoop to bear the yoke of Jesus Christ. As to this, let them plead as long as they please, in the end they must lose their cause.

As to those who have already quitted their country to come to a place where they can serve God freely, and where the truth of the gospel is faithfully preached to them, it is very necessary that they should frequently call this passage to mind, in order that they may exercise themselves in the practice of it from day to day, and become inured to it by long habit. For many things may happen in course of time, and do happen in fact, to discourage those who may have had an ardent zeal. Those who are admitted to the Churches of God are not always received as they deserve. The proper order is often reversed, so that those who are worthy of being brought farthest forward are sometimes kept farthest back. This might tempt them also to draw back from their salvation, by leaving off the good course which they have

Let all good believers, then, while they have not all that they might wish, but on the contrary feel themselves annoyed in many ways from having quitted their country, learn to console themselves by this single consideration—Still, after all, we are in the house of God!

Now, let worldlings mock as much as they please, and proudly jeer at us as a despised people, it is enough that God does us the honour of maintaining us in his Palace and Sanctuary. We see what pains ambitious fools take to be received into the court of some Prince, and count themselves happy if they can only get the length of the kitchen or the hall! Now, though we should be the merest outcasts according to the world's judgment, provided we belong to the Church of God, he introduces us to the great and admirable secrets of his wisdom, as familiarly as a father communicates with his children. We are very ungracious if this recompense does not satisfy us.

It is true that believers might be strongly tempted when their affairs are going backward, and the wicked triumphing in the height of prosperity; but when they consider, on the other hand, that God has chosen them to be of his house, and keeps them in it, this consolation must be worth very little if it suffices not to calm all the regrets and troubles by which they may be agitated. And, in fact, those who murmur and feel chagrined from not being treated by God as they desire, or repent of having begun well, shew plainly that they have not followed the advice of our Saviour, (Luke xiv. 28,) to calculate carefully in beginning a building how much it will cost, that they may not begin to be annoyed after they have expended too much, and leave off the work before it is finished.

A still worse case is that of those who in thus growing weary in the middle of their journey, break off without being able to shew any cause. In this there is great effrontery. Some who had neither houses nor lands, and to whom it was all one whether they lived in their own country or at the other end of the world, are not ashamed to reproach God

it is mere mockery to magnify its amount, and make a penny seem a pound! Yet one's ears are perpetually dunned by such murmurings. Would God that these people were very much at their ease and very far from us! Still, neither rich nor poor have any just excuse for throwing off the service of God, because of the afflictions which may in consequence befall them. But as it is difficult for us to act on this principle, the effectual remedy is pointed out to us in the eighty-fourth Psalm, where David, after exclaiming, " Blessed is the man that trusteth in the Lord," adds, " and in whose heart are his ways." (Psalm lxxxiv. 5.) As if he had said, Who has his heart disposed to walk according as God commands?

Here there are two things which must not be separated from each other—we must put our hope in God, and we must walk in the right path.

Wherefore, whenever our frailty hinders us from moving forwards, or even makes us so cowardly that we would be disposed, at every stroke, to turn our backs, let us strengthen ourselves in faith and hope, entreating our gracious God so to fix our eye upon him, that nothing may disturb us, and that we may be able to build on his promises, which assure us that he will be with us both in life and in death.

END OF THE HOMILIES OR SERMONS.

COMMENTARY

ON

THE EIGHTY-SEVENTH PSALM.

THE DISSERTATION OR ARGUMENT.

WE see how the children of the world, when matters go well with them, are pleased with their condition, and how they lift their heads, proudly despising the Church of God; and although they may even be sometimes subdued by affliction, they cannot give up the folly and extravagance of delighting in finding earthly good. Meanwhile, they care nothing for Religion or the Service of God; because, contenting themselves with their luxuries, riches, conveniences, pomp, and honours, they seem to themselves happy without any aid from God. Now, it happens oftentimes that God treats such people according to their wishes, as if he meant to fatten them up, until the fit time for punishing them be come; and that, on the other hand, he inflicts upon his Church many strokes of adversity, and treats her very harshly, or rather leaves her to languish in a poor and wretched condition, so much so that she might consider herself miserable: at least she is subjected to the derision and insults of worldlings. In order, then, that believers may not be deceived by such appearances, they require to be presented with another and a loftier view, that thus they may be fully persuaded of what is said in Psalm xxxiii. 12, "Happy is the people that has the Lord for its God."

The scope of the present PSALM is to shew that it is the Church of God alone which in dignity and excellence surpasses all the kingdoms and governments of the world, be-

the fearful tempests and troubles and changes by which the world is shaken, she remains and stands fast; and especially, being thus miraculously saved by the grace of God, continues to fight valiantly until she reach the crown of glory which is prepared for her on high.

It is certainly a singular manifestation of Divine favour, and a miracle worthy of remembrance, that among the many revolutions which take place in the governments of the world, he maintains his Church from age to age, and allows her not to be destroyed. But, as oftentimes, while unbelievers wallow in wealth, and flourish in credit and authority, the poor Church is seen tossed about by evils and dangers in endless number, nay, is seen almost overwhelmed, just like a ship on the point of foundering, her felicity consists principally in the eternal state which God has established for her in his kingdom.

The circumstance of the time at which this PSALM was composed will greatly assist us in understanding it. For although the people were then returned from Babylon, where they had so long been held captive, although the Church was gathered as it were into one body, to be no longer scattered as it had been, although the Temple was built, and the altar prepared on which sacrifices were to be offered, and the whole service of God restored; nevertheless, because the number of persons who had returned to the Holy Land was but a handful, in comparison of the great multitude that had been carried away, and those who remained were daily diminished by hostile violence and outrage, so that the people were in a humiliating condition, while, moreover, the Temple itself had not now the majesty it formerly had—all this made it exceedingly difficult for believers to hope well of the time to come; so that, even in the most favourable view, it seemed impossible that they should ever be restored to the state from which they had fallen.

There was danger, therefore, that in calling to remembrance their discomfiture and defeat, and thinking also of the many evils which ceased not to oppress them, they

against the discouragement caused by these calamities; and for this purpose God promises not only that they shall recover what they have lost, but enjoins them to hope for far better; in other words, an incomparable glory, in accordance with the promise which he had given them by his prophet Haggai, (Hag. ii. 10,) that "the majesty of the Second Temple would be greater than that of the first."

It now remains to apply the Psalm to our own use. God intended that the consolation contained in it should be of such power and importance, in regard to the believers of that time, as not only to prevent them being overwhelmed by so many evils, but as to draw them forth from the tomb, (so to speak,) and lift them up to heaven. Now, since we know that the things which were predicted of that time have been accomplished, we are more than ungrateful if the experience which the Fathers of old had, combined with the Divine promises, suffices not doubly to confirm our faith.

Words cannot express how much Jesus Christ has, by his coming, adorned and magnified his Church. Then the true Religion, previously shut up within the country of Judea, was extended over all the world; and God, who was known before only by a single race, began to be invoked in all languages and by all nations:—then the world, which had been divided, and, as it were, torn into so many sects, errors, and superstitions, was joined and united in a holy concord of faith:—then the inhabitants of all countries turned with ardent longing to the Jews, whom they had held in utter abhorrence. Kings and nations also, of their own accord, yielded themselves up to Jesus Christ to be his subjects. Wolves and lions were changed into lambs. God shed upon his faithful followers the gifts of his Spirit, surpassing all terrestrial glory.

It is indeed something great and wonderful that the body of the Church has been assembled and composed of such different members, separated from each other by the remotest countries, and yet with all this has been maintained and augmented! God must indeed have worked mightily to

dignity of the Church had never been described in the present PSALM, still the incomparable graces which God displayed on the coming of his Son shew us that the Church is truly a heavenly and not an earthly kingdom. Moreover, ever since that time, when God thus magnified his Church, and arrayed her in splendour, it has become necessary for believers, in order to form a due estimate of her dignity, to look higher than human sense can reach; for, during the period when she flourished, as we have described, there was no pomp of gold or silver or precious stones. Nay, her triumphs were in the blood of Martyrs; and in proportion as she was rich in spirit, was she poor in worldly wealth;—in proportion as she was precious and lovely in holiness, before God and angels, was she contemptible to the world. She had many declared enemies who persecuted her cruelly, or who plotted her internal ruin by underhand means. There were many traitors and wicked conspirators, just as the devil never ceases to molest her by hypocrites. In a word, her dignity was still hidden under the cross of Christ. On the other hand, it might easily be judged that all the dignity which she possesses is spiritual, and hence cannot be seen by the carnal eye.

The consolation contained in this PSALM, therefore, could not but be very proper and seasonable for that time, inasmuch as it admonished the faithful to think of a more perfect state of the Church than that which was apparent; but it is far more necessary for us in the present day. For the sins of our fathers, God for a long time permitted the noble and magnificent form in which he had arrayed his Church to be disfigured, and in its place was substituted an "Abomination of Desolation!" And even at present the poor Church is oppressed through our transgressions, and groans under the cruel tyranny of the adversaries of the Truth—under the calumnies and reproaches of her enemies—under the mockery of the devil and the ungodly; so that worldlings, who desire to be at ease, shun nothing more strongly than to be held and reputed to belong to the ranks

her without being wretched! From all this it is easy to see how useful the doctrine of this PSALM is at present, and how incumbent it is to meditate upon it without ceasing.

Eighty-seventh Psalm.

VERSE 1. *To the sons of Korah, a Psalm to be sung: His foundations are the holy mountains.*

THE name of the sons of Korah may have been inserted here, not as if they had composed the Psalm, but because they were the appointed musicians to sing it in the temple: although it may also be said that some member of that family was possibly its author. In regard to the text, when it is said that "His foundations are the holy mountains," the reference must be to God. Several have expounded it of the Church, or of the temple; but both are incongruous. Some have supposed the Psalm itself to be referred to, as if it were said, The argument or subject of the Psalm is to treat of the holy mountains, where the temple was built; but this is equally incongruous.

The intention of the Prophet is, as I have already hinted, to declare that God has selected the holy mountains, there to found his royal city Jerusalem, and his temple. For it is afterwards added in the context, "The sovereign himself will establish it." It is certain, indeed, that God is the true and principal founder of all the cities of the world, but to no other city than Jerusalem is this distinguished honour attributed—that it is the eternal resting-place of God, and that he will dwell there because he has built it. It is necessary always to keep this distinction in view, that other cities were built by the power and authority of God only for earthly policy; whereas Jerusalem was his sanctuary, and had been specially erected as the seat of his majesty. Ac-

the Lord hath founded Zion." Moreover, though the whole country of Judea was dedicated to him, it is said that, when rejecting all the rest, he reserved to himself the city of Jerusalem to reign there. This follows in the next verse.

VERSE 2. *The Lord loveth the gates of Zion above all the tabernacles of Jacob.*

To this corresponds the declaration in the seventy-eighth Psalm, (verse 60,) that God has rejected Shiloh, the lineage of Ephraim, and the tabernacle of Joseph, to dwell in Zion, which he loves. Observe also the reason specified by the Prophet why God has preferred a certain place to all others —not for the dignity of the place, but for the love which he has borne to it. Wherefore, if it is asked whence Jerusalem derives this privilege, of being the holy city of God and his royal palace? the answer is easy and brief,—Because so it has pleased God. This pleasure is as it were the source or root of his love. The end in view was, that there might be some place in which Religion might have its abode, to cherish a firm unity of faith among the Jews, till the coming of our Lord Jesus Christ, and that in the end the gospel should proceed from thence to be published over all the world. And thus the Prophet, to magnify the city of Jerusalem, says that God is its founder, and presides in it as its Governor.

But in order that men may not take occasion to plume themselves on this honour, he adds, and declares, that whatever excellence Jerusalem possesses must be attributed to the free grace and adoption of God. In putting *Zion* for the whole city, and *Gates* for the whole circuit of the walls, he employs a part to designate the whole. By the *Mountains*, spoken of in the plural, are commonly understood Zion and Moriah, which were the summits, situated near each other, like two horns. Now, though I wish not to condemn the exposition, it seems to me that the meaning of the term may be extended, so as to include the whole district: For Jerusalem stood among mountains.

Literally it is, "What is said in thee are glorious things." Now we have to look to the meaning of the Prophet, or rather the meaning of the Holy Spirit speaking here. The condition of the Jewish people was at that time very contemptible, so that no account was made of it. They had many powerful enemies on all sides, who were molesting them, and few individuals were found courageous enough to repel affronts. Every day new and unexpected changes were taking place, so that all things thus falling into decay, it seemed that the whole must finally be ruined. Hence, it was scarcely possible to hope that Jerusalem would ever be restored. Now, in order that the hearts of believers might not be overwhelmed with sadness and despair, they are here supported by the Prophet, by what God has declared in regard to the future state of his Church: For there is no doubt he here withdraws the view of believers from present things, to lead it to the promises which assured them of an incredible glory shortly to be given by God to the Church. Thus, although nothing which then appeared could furnish cause of joy to the children of God, the Prophet commands them to raise their thoughts on high, in accordance with the promise given them, in order to wait patiently until the things promised should be accomplished. By this means they were warned and exhorted to read attentively, and meditate day and night on the ancient prophecies touching the restoration of the Church, and especially on those which are contained in the book of Isaiah, from the fortieth chapter to the end; also to hearken and give credit to the Prophets sent after that time, to console them, and announce the kingdom of Jesus Christ as drawing near. From this it follows, that the only way of judging correctly of the felicity of the Church, is to estimate it according to the Word of God.

> VERSE 4. *I will make mention of Rahab and Babylon among them who know me: here are Palestine, and Tyre, with Ethiopia: this man was born there.*

The name Rahab is used in other passages of Scripture for

cent state of the Church, which was then hid. He says, then, that those who had previously been mortal enemies, or were complete strangers to her, will not only be her intimate friends, but incorporated as it were into one body, so as to be accounted citizens of Jerusalem. He says, I will take into account, or enrol Egypt and Babylon among my friends and household. Then he adds, that the Philistines, those of Tyre and Ethiopia, who had hitherto been at great variance with the people of God, will be as good friends as if they had been natives of Judea. Now, in so speaking he specifies a singular dignity in the Church, viz., that those who despised her, or would have wished to destroy her, will give in their submission, and even count it a high honour to be acknowledged among her people. For the Prophet intimates that all will of their own accord renounce the lands of their nativity, to which they previously attached all their glory. It is therefore just as if he had said, In whatever quarter men may be born, in Palestine, or Tyre, or Ethiopia, they will be very glad to be numbered with the people of God, and acknowledged as citizens of Jerusalem.

The Jewish Rabbins make a curious gloss upon this passage. It is, that in other nations few persons distinguished for intellect or virtue will arise, but that among the Jews there will be a great number: as if it had been said, that in each country it would be difficult to find one praise-worthy individual, so that all such might easily be pointed out with the finger; whereas in Zion the number would abound.

Christian expositors are unanimous in referring this to our Saviour, and hold that the reason is here given why strangers, that is, the enemies of the Church, will desire to be enrolled in it, viz., because the Son of God will be born there, whose office it is to gather men who have been widely scattered into a holy unity of faith, and collect the scattered members so as to form out of them one complete body. Now, this sentiment is very true in itself, but it is not suitable to the passage. And we must always be sedulously on our

then, to have the pure and simple exposition that every one, regarding it as a great blessing, will long to be received into the citizenship of the Church. This is still more fully confirmed by what follows.

> VERSE 5. *And it will be said of Zion, This and that man were born in it, and the Supreme will be he who will establish it.*

As I have already said, the Prophet continues his subject, meaning to intimate, that God will collect from all the countries of the world persons to be incorporated into his Church as new citizens. Although he uses a different mode of expression, his meaning is, that strangers will be accounted among the chosen people of God, as if they were descended from the lineage of Abraham. He had said in the previous context, that the Chaldeans and Egyptians would become of the household of the Church; that the Ethiopians, Philistines, and Tyrians would ask to be enrolled in the number of her children. Now he adds, in confirmation of his statement, that the band will be large, and almost numberless, to people and fill the city of Jerusalem, which for a time had been deserted, or rather, was inhabited only by a handful of people in comparison of those who were to come to it.

What is here briefly promised is declared at greater length in Isaiah, when he says, (Isaiah liv. 1,) "Rejoice, O barren, thou that didst not bear; for the widow shall have more children than she that hath an husband. Enlarge the place of thy tents, and strengthen thy cords," &c. Again, (Isaiah lxiv. 1,) "Thy children will come from all distant countries: lift up thine eyes and look around; all these will be assembled to thee." And in the forty-fourth chapter he uses the same mode of speech as that which we read here, or one very much resembling it, "This one will say, I am the Lord's; another will call himself by the name of Israel. This one will write with his hand, I am the Lord's, and another will surname himself by the name of Israel."

and the like, will be united to the fold of God. For although they were not natives of Zion and children of the soil, and it was only by adoption that they were to be incorporated with the chosen people; still, because our entrance into the Church is a kind of second birth, the similitude is very appropriate: and, in fact, Jesus Christ allies himself and intermarries with believers, on the express condition, that they will "forget their people and their father's house." (Psalm xlv. 10.) This is the reason why St. Paul says that we begin to be children of God and of the Church when we are regenerated of incorruptible seed, and formed into new creatures; and, in fact, there is no other way by which we are regenerated into the heavenly life than by the ministry and through the medium of the Church. Meanwhile, let us remember the distinction which Paul makes between the earthly Jerusalem, which, as she is in bondage, can only give birth to slaves; and the heavenly Jerusalem, which by means of the gospel conceives and gives birth to free children.

The concluding part of the verse contains a promise of lasting duration to the Church; for we often see that while cities rise to riches and splendour, their prosperity is very short-lived. In order, therefore, that we may not suppose the prosperity of the Church to be thus evanescent, the Prophet declares that it will have its power of endurance in God, and so be permanent; as if he had said, No wonder if other cities are always in movement and subject to numerous revolutions, seeing that they turn and whirl with the world, and have no eternal guardians. But the condition of this new Jerusalem will be different, for its prosperity being founded on God, will be maintained till heaven and earth pass away.

VERSE 6. *The Lord will record, writing of the people, This person was born there.*

The Prophet means that the name of Zion will be so noble and honourable, that every one will desire to be re-

sense then is, When the Lord will make a muster of the people, or enrol them, the greatest blessing and honour which he can bestow on his chosen will be to account them citizens of Zion rather than of any other city; for it will be a more splendid nobility to have some little corner among the commonalty of the Church than to be much esteemed or to have rule in another place. Meanwhile, the Prophet informs us whence such blessing proceeds, and how those who were strangers are suddenly introduced into the Church, namely, by the grace of God.

In fact, those who are slaves of Satan and of sin will never, by their own industry, acquire any right and title to be citizens of heaven. It is God alone who of his own good pleasure arranges nations in their order, and distinguishes them from each other as seems to him good, seeing that, by nature, one common condition belongs to all. The enrolment here spoken of means the call by which God declares who they are whom he has elected: for although he enrolled his children in the Book of Life before the creation of the world, he, however, inserts them formally in his register when he gives them the seal of his adoption, calling them to his truth, and renewing them by his Spirit.

VERSE 7. *And as well the singers as the players on flutes. All my fountains are in thee.*

The obscurity of this passage is caused partly by its brevity and partly by a word of doubtful meaning. All Commentators agree that the term *Fountain* is here used by way of simile; but some refer it to the affections of the heart, others to the thoughts. Some translate *veins,* or *melodies;* and I would approve of their view, if the idiom of the Hebrew tongue could admit it; but as this would be somewhat forced, I adopt that which is most appropriate and natural; and it is, that the Prophet, by this term, means *the eyes* or *look;* as if he had said, I shall always have my eye turned, or my view fixed upon thee; for even the root of the word in Hebrew means *eye.*

an elliptical sentence, but that does not hinder us from being able easily to gather its meaning, viz., That there will be such ample cause of joy in the Church after its restoration, that the praises of God will be sounded within it incessantly, as well by the voice as by instrumental music. He thus confirms what he had said of the magnificent reparation of Zion and Jerusalem, shewing that from the great felicity which will then exist, there will be cause of rejoicing, singing, and praising God for evermore. Meanwhile, he also shews to what end and with what intent God so liberally enriches his Church with gifts and graces, namely, that believers may shew by hymns, praises, and songs, that they are not ungrateful to him. On the other hand, we have to note the zeal, love, solicitude, and affection of the Prophet towards the Church. For he gives evidence of this in order to exhort us all to follow his example, according to what is said in another passage, (Psalm cxxxvii. 5,) "Let my right hand forget its cunning, if Jerusalem be not my chiefest joy." Now, then, let all our senses and affections be concentrated on the Church, seeing we find it difficult to withdraw them from the vanities of this world, by which they are distracted and led astray. This do when, despising honours, pleasures, riches, and worldly pomp, we shall learn to be satisfied with the spiritual glory of THE KINGDOM OF CHRIST.

THE END.

INDEX

TO THE

HOMILIES OR SERMONS, AND EXPOSITION OF PSALM LXXXVII.

A

ABBOTS, 414.
Adoption, 482.
Adversity, different ways in which men act under, 442; is to be expected, 467; Church of God often smitten by, 472, 473.
Antiochus Epiphanes, persecution of the Jews under, 427, 428.
Archdeacons, 414.
Ark of the Covenant designated by "the face of God," 454.

B

BABYLON, state of the Jews after their return from, 473.
Babylonians, Jews forbidden to give any countenance to the idolatries of, 405, 415; their introduction into the Church predicted, 479-481.
Backsliding, fixing the eye on what God shews us a remedy for all occasions of, 453.
Baptism, ordinance of, 402; corrupted by the Papacy, 411, 458; as administered by the Papists, not to be countenanced, 411; design of its institution, 450; duty of parents to have their children baptized, 458.
Believers, their bodies temples of the Holy Spirit, 402.
Benedict, Saint, 462.
Bethel, Idolatry of, interdicted as well as that of foreign countries, 404.
Body, The, God to be worshipped by the homage of, as well as of the Spirit, 402, 403; not to be defiled and profaned before idols, 402.
Bodies of believers temples of the Holy Spirit, 402,
Book of Life, 482.

C

CALLING, Effectual, is the enrolment of God's people in his register, 482.
Calvin, his pulpit ministrations, 387; why so few in his time were disposed to suffer for the gospel, 417; extensive knowledge of the Scriptures in his day, 419; and opposition made to the Church, 426; complains of the little value set on Church ordinances in his day, 443, 444, 449, 464, 465; reference to the state of the Church in his time, 445, 451, 452. See *Geneva.*
Chaldeans. See *Babylonians.*
Chanting in an unknown tongue, Popish, 411.
Chastisements inflicted by God, our duty under, 445.
Children, duty of parents to have their children baptized, 458.
Children, martyrdom of, under Antiochus Epiphanes, 427.
Children of God, Sacraments instituted for gathering together, 440; character of, 464; we become such by regeneration, 481.
Christ, the Mass a denial of the perfection of the redemption accomplished by his death, 407; and of his being eternal and only Priest, 408; extension and glory of the Church by the coming of, 474, 475, 479; honour of suffering persecution for, 422, 423; reward of con-

to the Jews under the law, 441; is the living image of God, 454; is to be seen in the word and sacraments, 454, 455; our reluctance to make sacrifices for, 468.

Christians acquainted with the pure gospel may not lawfully make a show of consenting to the abuses, superstitions, and idolatries of the Papacy, 395, 397-400. See *Papacy. Persecution.*

Church of God, a state of persecution the ordinary condition of, 426; has never been completely crushed by persecution, 427; her state of minority under the law, 440; instituted for gathering together the children of God, *ib.*; reference to the state of, in Calvin's time, 445, 451, 452; corruptions in her ought not to prevent us from entering into her fellowship, 461, 462; despised by the men of the world, 472; is often smitten by adversity, 472, 473; stability and permanence of, 473, 481; extension and glory of, by Christ's coming, 474, 475, 479; in what her glory consists, 475; her incomparable glory predicted, 396, 474, 478, 479; introduction of the Gentiles into, predicted, 479-481; high honour of being true members of, 482; why God so liberally enriches her with gifts and graces, 483. See *Jerusalem.*

Church, Regular and well managed, privilege of belonging to, 396, 435-441, 449, 469, 470; duty of setting up, 448; some have quitted the land of their nativity to form themselves into, 451; necessity of, 460.

Church members exhorted to conduct themselves holily, 451, 452.

Church ordinances. See *Ordinances.*

Cities, God the founder of, 476; their prosperity often short lived, 481.

Confession of the truth of God, joining in the superstitions of the Papacy inconsistent with, 400, 401, 407, 409, 410; precious in the sight of God, 419, 429; life not to be valued more highly than, 419, 420, 429, 430; reward of, 425; prudence and discretion to be observed in, 430; duty of, 436, 440, 445; bond-444.

Courage, Christian, difference between, and rashness, 417.

D

DANIEL, his miraculous deliverance from the lions' den, 431; his companions refuse to make a show of worshipping Nebuchadnezzar's golden image, 400; their miraculous deliverance from the fiery furnace, 431.

David, his abhorrence of idolatry, 399, 400; the need he felt of being aided by the means of grace, 435-438; how highly he prized the temple, 441-444, 467, 469; his exercise under God's chastisements, 445; his seeking God's face, 453, 456; estimation in which he held this privilege, 459, 460.

Dawson, Thomas, 388.

Dead, The, we are not to join in the intercessions made for, by the Papists, 406; mass for, 408.

Deans, 414.

Death, threatening against such as deny the truth of Christ from the fear of, 425.

Decision, importance of, in order to our being prepared to suffer persecution for the true religion, 418.

Dedication of body and soul to God, duty of, 397, 399, 451.

Denying the truth of Christ from the fear of death, threatening denounced against such as do so, 425.

Devotion, sudden fits of, 444.

Devotions of the heathen, 400; and of Papists, 462.

E

EGYPT, Rahab used for, 478.

Egyptians, their introduction into the Church predicted, 479-481.

Elizabeth, translations of Calvin's Sermons in the reign of, 388.

End for which man was created, 420, 435.

England, delivered from the yoke of Popery, 390.

Esau, his double-mindedness, 412.

Ethiopians, their introduction into the Church predicted, 479-481.

FACE of God, all believers invited and exhorted to seek, 453; our sluggishness in seeking, 455; high estimation in which David held the seeking of, 453, 456, 459, 460; the sanctuary and the ark of the covenant designated by, 454.
Faith, The certainty of, sustains the spirit of martyrdom, 416.
Family of love, a sect so called, 394.
Fanatics who despise the preaching of the gospel and the sacraments condemned, 455.
Felicity. See *Happiness*.
Festivals, Popish high, 411.
Field, John, 388; his dedication of his Translation of Calvin's Sermons to Henry Earl of Huntington, 390-394.
Flesh, The, suffering persecution for the sake of the gospel repugnant to, 423, 424.
Frenzy, difference between it and Christian zeal, 416.

G

GATES put for the whole circuit of the walls of Jerusalem, 477.
Geneva, 438, 448, 452.
Gentiles, their introduction into the Church predicted, 479-481.
Glorifying God should be the chief aim of our life, 420.
God, duty of dedication of soul and body to, 397, 399; gives up all alliance with idolaters, 399; external expressions of religious homage to be rendered to him alone, 400; to be worshipped by the homage of the body as well as of the spirit, 402, 403; the glorifying of him should be the chief aim of our life, 420; his grace not bound to the sacraments, 441; images of, 454; Christ the living image of, *ib.*; service of, not to be thrown off because of the afflictions which may in consequence befall us, 470, 471.
God's face. See *Face of God*.
Gospel, The, true method of preparing to suffer persecution for, 417, 418; as to the lawfulness of quitting our native land when in it we are destitute of, 456-470; reciprocal duties of husband and wife in contemplating phrase "the kingdom of heaven," 468.
Grace of God not bound to the sacraments, 441.

H

HALL, Rouland, 388.
Happiness, common for men to seek it in this world, 485.
Heathen, The, their religious ceremonies derived from the holy patriarchs, 404; idolatries of, compared with the superstitions of the Papacy, *ib.*
Heathen virtues, character of, 420.
Heathen writer, quotation from, 419.
Holy Spirit. See *Spirit*.
Homage, Religious, external expressions of, to be rendered to God alone, 400.
Human inventions in religion not to be countenanced, 405, 418.
Huntington, Henry, Earl of, dedication of John Field's translation of Calvin's Sermons to, 390-394.
Husband, duty of, as to his wife in contemplating quitting his native land, when in it he is without the gospel, 459.

I

IDOLATERS, God gives up all alliance with, 399; self-denied devotions of Popish, 455, 462.
Idolatry, all Christians exhorted to flee from, 397, 398; David's abhorrence of, 399, 400; Jews often abandoned themselves to, 399; feigned worship of idols amounts to, 401; all kinds of, forbidden, 404; the Jews forbidden to give any countenance to, 405, 415. See *Idols*.
Idolatry of the Mass, 408.
Idolatry of Bethel interdicted by God as well as that of foreign countries, 404.
Idolatries of the heathen compared with the superstitions of the Papacy, 404.
Idolatrizing to avoid the rage of Papists inexcusable, 404.
Idols, such as have God for their inheritance will have no fellowship with, 399, 400; are worshipped if reverenced by external signs, though we

412. See *Idolaters. Idolatry.*
Images of God, 454.
Intercession or merit of some saint, Popish prayer founded on, 411.
Intercession for the dead by Papists not to be joined in, 406.
Inventions in religion, human, not to be countenanced, 405, 418.

J

JERUSALEM, city of, its distinction as the eternal resting-place of God, 476; whence this distinction, 477; distinction between the earthly and heavenly Jerusalem, 481. See *Church.*
Jerusalem, second temple of, 473, 474.
Jewish Rabbins, 479.
Jews often abandoned themselves to false gods, 399; forbidden to give any countenance to idolatry, 405, 415; their persecution under Antiochus Epiphanes, 427, 428; their state after their return from Babylon, 473, 474, 478.
Joseph, his refusing to yield to his mistress, 403.

K

KINGDOM of God, man created to aspire to, 435.
"Kingdom of heaven," the phrase employed to designate the preaching of the gospel, 468.
Kingdoms of the world, the Church of God superior to, in stability, 472, 473.
Korah, sons of, 476.

L

LAW, advantages of enjoying the preaching of, 438.
Law or legal dispensation, Christ more clearly exhibited to us now than to the Jews under, 441.
Life, not to be valued more highly than the confession of the truth of God, 419, 420, 429, 430; the glorifying of God should be the chief aim of, 420; book of, 482.
Longing for Church ordinances, 441-445.

MALEFACTORS, firmness with which God enables those of them who derive consolation from the grace of Christ to suffer for their crimes, 433.
Man created to aspire to the kingdom of God, 435.
Man, Thomas, 388.
Manicheans, 402.
Martyr apprehended in Tournay and condemned to death, anecdote of, 433, 434.
Martyrdom, the spirit of, sustained by the certainty of faith, 416, 417; encouragement to suffer it from the example of the saints who have gone before us, 427, 428; and from the reward promised, 433.
Martyrs, 394, 475; suffered death because they would not offer incense to idols, 412; it is only when we suffer in a good cause that God can acknowledge us as, 416, 417; courage of the ancient, 418, 412; their persecutors shall have to render a fearful account of the blood of, 432; their invincible constancy owing to God's working mightily in them, 433; witnesses, the meaning of the term, 430.
Mary, Virgin, Popish worship of, 411, 462.
Mass, unlawful to be present at, 401, 404; profanes the Lord's Supper, 404, 406, 408-410; being present at, amounts to a public profession of consenting to, 407; denies the perfection of the redemption accomplished by the death of Christ, *ib.*; and that Christ is eternal and only priest, 408; Mass for the dead, *ib.*; idolatry of, 408, 410.
Mass, Parochial, described, 407, 408.
Merit or intercession of some saint, Popish prayer founded on, 411.
Ministry of the word, the means of regeneration, 481.
Moriah, mount, 477.
Music, vocal and instrumental, celebration of God's praises by, 483.

N

NEBUCHADNEZZAR's image, Daniel's three companions refuse to make a show of worshipping, 400.
Nicholas, Saint, 408.

OLYMPIC Games, reference to, 424.
Ordinances, Church, privilege of enjoying, 435-440, 448, 460, 469; longing for, 441-445; Calvin's complaints of the little value set upon, in his time, 443, 449, 464, 465; ardour with which we should seek the enjoyment of, 464.

P

PALESTINE, 479.

Papacy, The, Christians acquainted with the pure gospel cannot lawfully make a show of consenting and adhering to the abuses, superstitions, and idolatries of, 395, 397-415; (see *Persecution;*) evasions by which some vindicated themselves for doing this, 400-406; idolatrizing to avoid the rage of, inexcusable, 404; idolatries of the heathen compared with the superstitions of, *ib.*; baptism corrupted by, 411, 458; idolatry of, 451, 455; want of the means of grace under, 461.

Papal tyranny, the man to be commended who lives purely and serves God as he ought under, 438.

Parents, duty of, to have their children baptized, 458.

Pastors, Christian, Popish priests not, 409, 410.

People of God, should feel assured when they fall into the hands of their persecutors that their bodies are in the hands of God, 431, 432; are often miraculously delivered from their persecutors, 431; Christ suffers in them when they are persecuted, 432.

Permanence of the Church, 473, 481.

Persecution for the gospel, Christians ought to endure it rather than make a show of consenting and adhering to the abuses, superstitions, and idolatries of the Papacy, 395, 396, 416, &c.; true method of preparing for enduring, 417, 418, 420; Christians hereby conformed to Christ, 421, 423; honour of suffering, 422, 423; reasons for which God is pleased that his people should suffer, 423; is repugnant to the flesh, 423, 424; promises and threatenings employed to stimulate us to endure, 425; the suffer it from the example of the martyrs who have gone before us, 427, 428; and from the reward promised, 421, 424; 433, 434; and from God's promise to sustain us by the energy of his Spirit, 432, 433; Christians should be prepared for, 428, 431; the greater part seek subterfuges for escaping, 429; is often in the form of vituperations and tortures, 433; the people of God, on falling into the hands of their persecutors, should feel assured that their bodies are in the hands of God, 431, 432.

Persecutors are held in check by God, 431; will have to render a fearful account for the blood of the martyrs they have shed, 432.

Persecutors, Heathen, the common method they took to make the weak renounce their God, 411, 412.

Peter, his deliverance from Herod's prison, 431.

Philistines, their introduction into the Church predicted, 479-481.

Pope, The, 410, 415.

Popery, England delivered from the yoke of, 390.

Popish high festivals, 411.

Popish prayer, founded on the intercession or merit of some saint, 411.

Popish priests, 409, 410.

Popish worship of the Virgin Mary, 411.

Praise of God, the celebration of, by vocal and instrumental music, 483.

Prayers, public, duty and advantage of waiting upon, 439, 440, 443, 445, 449, 460, 461.

Prayer for princes how to be regulated, 458.

Prayer, Popish, founded on the intercession or merit of some saint, 411.

Prayers offered to saints by the Papacy not to be joined in, 406.

Preaching of the word in purity, advantage of enjoying, 396, 438, 443, 460, 469; the private reading of the Scriptures does not supersede the necessity of attendance upon, 438, 439; Calvin's complaints of the little value set upon, in his time, 443, 449, 464, 465; the loss of, a great calamity, 443, 444; fanatics who despise it condemned, 455; the means of regeneration, 481.

458.
Priors, 414.
Profession of the truth of Christ. See *Confession.*
Prophecies touching the restoration of the Church, 478, 479.
Prosperity of cities often short lived, 481.

R

RABBINS, Jewish, 479.
Rahab used for Egypt, 478.
Rashness, difference between, and Christian courage, 417.
Redemption, accomplished by Christ's death, the perfection of, denied by the Mass, 407.
Regeneration, we become the children of God by, 481; is effected by the instrumentality of the ministry of the word, *ib.*
Religious homage, external professions of, to be rendered to God alone, 400.

S

SACRAMENTS, The, privilege of enjoying, 396, 436, 438-443, 445, 460, 461; their virtue not dependent on the worthiness of those who administer them, 410; ancient heretics, who condemned their use because of the vices of men, *ib.*; grace of God not bound to, 441; virtue of the Spirit not bound to, *ib.*; Calvin's complaint of the little value set upon, in his time, 448; inattention when observing them, 450; Christ to be seen in, 454, 455; fanatics condemned who despise, 455.
Sacrifices for Christ, our reluctance to make, 468-471.
Saints, departed, prayers offered to, by the Papacy not to be joined in, 406.
Salvation, Our, no method of advancing it omitted by God, 451.
Sanctuary, designated by "the face of God," 454.
Saul, want of the pure administration of justice, and the corruption of manners in the time of, 461.
Scriptures, The Holy, we are to guard against wresting, 480; reverence due to, 417, 418; the observance of the public ordinances of the Church believers, 458.
Sermons, Public, the private reading of the Scriptures does not supersede the necessity of waiting upon, 438-440, 449; inattention when hearing them censured, 450.
Service of God, that country to be regarded as strange and profane in which it is abolished, 448; not to be thrown off because of the afflictions that may in consequence befall us, 470, 471.
Shiloh, rejected by God as his resting-place, 477.
Slanderers, 452.
Soldiers of Christ, motives to excite them to be courageous in his service, 466.
Spirit, Holy, bodies of believers temples of, 402; renewing of, 482; encouragement to suffer persecution for the gospel from God's promise to sustain us by the energy of, 432, 433; his virtue not bound to the sacraments, 441.
Stability of the Church of God, 473, 481.
Superstitions, by which the service of God is corrupted, idolatry to join in, 400; ought to be thoroughly abolished, 410; obstinacy with which Papists adhere to, 462.
Supper, Lord's, 403; the Mass profanes, 404, 406, 408-410; design of its institution, 450.

T

TEMPLE of Jerusalem, purpose of, 436; its ordinances obscure shadows of what we now have, 441; second Temple, 478.
Temple, the liberty of worshipping God in purity with the faithful comprehended under the term, 436, 437; how highly David prized it, 441-444, 460, 467, 469.
Temples of the Holy Spirit, bodies of believers are, 402.
Thief on the cross, 433.
Tortures, God promises to enable his people to overcome persecution by, 433.
Tournay, anecdote of martyr apprehended at, and condemned to death, 433.

2 I

Church predicted, 479-481.
Tyranny, Papal, the man to be commended who lives purely, and serves God as he ought under, 438.

U

UNKNOWN tongue, Popish chanting in, 411.

V

VESPERS, Popish, 411.
Virgin Mary, Popish worship of, 411, 462.
Virtues, Heathen, character of, 420.
Vituperation, God promises to enable his people patiently to bear persecution by, 433.

W

WICKED, The, the Church always liable to be afflicted by, 426.

gospel, 459.
Witnesses. See *Martyrs*.
Women, martyrdom of, under the reign of Antiochus Epiphanes, 427.
Word of God, Christ to be seen in, 455. See *Preaching of the Word*.
World, The, common for men to seek felicity from, 435.
World, children of, proudly despise the Church of God, 472; their frequent prosperity for a season, 472, 473.
Wresting Scripture to be guarded against, 480.

Z

ZEAL for the house of God, 418; difference between Christian zeal and frenzy, 416; want of zeal for God censured, 418, 419.
Zion, God's dwelling-place, 477; put for the whole city of Jerusalem, *ib.*; and for the Church, 481, 482. See *Church. Jerusalem*.

www.ingramcontent.com/pod-product-compliance
Lightning Source LLC
Chambersburg PA
CBHW071432300426
44114CB00013B/1406